Setting Up LAMP:
Getting Linux, Apache, MySQL, *and* PHP Working Together

Setting Up LAMP:
Getting Linux, Apache, MySQL,
and PHP Working Together

Eric Rosebrock
Eric Filson

SYBEX®

San Francisco · London

Associate Publisher: Joel Fugazzotto
Acquisitions Editor: Tom Cirtin
Developmental Editor: Tom Cirtin
Production Editor: Lori Newman
Technical Editor: Sean Schluntz
Copyeditor: Sharon Wilkey
Compositor: Laurie Stewart, Happenstance Type-O-Rama
Proofreaders: Nancy Riddiough, Laurie O'Connell
Indexer: Nancy Guenther
Cover Designer: Caryl Gorska, Gorska Design
Cover Photographer: Peter Samuels, Tony Stone

Library of Congress Card Number: 2004104101

ISBN: 0-7821-4337-7

SYBEX and the SYBEX logo are either registered trademarks or trademarks of SYBEX Inc. in the United States and/or other countries.

Transcend Technique is a trademark of SYBEX Inc.

TRADEMARKS: SYBEX has attempted throughout this book to distinguish proprietary trademarks from descriptive terms by following the capitalization style used by the manufacturer.

The author and publisher have made their best efforts to prepare this book, and the content is based upon final release software whenever possible. Portions of the manuscript may be based upon pre-release versions supplied by software manufacturer(s). The author and the publisher make no representation or warranties of any kind with regard to the completeness or accuracy of the contents herein and accept no liability of any kind including but not limited to performance, merchantability, fitness for any particular purpose, or any losses or damages of any kind caused or alleged to be caused directly or indirectly from this book.

Manufactured in the United States of America

10 9 8 7 6 5 4 3 2 1

SOFTWARE LICENSE AGREEMENT:
TERMS AND CONDITIONS

The media and/or any online materials accompanying this book that are available now or in the future contain programs and/or text files (the "Software") to be used in connection with the book. SYBEX hereby grants to you a license to use the Software, subject to the terms that follow. Your purchase, acceptance, or use of the Software will constitute your acceptance of such terms.

The Software compilation is the property of SYBEX unless otherwise indicated and is protected by copyright to SYBEX or other copyright owner(s) as indicated in the media files (the "Owner(s)"). You are hereby granted a single-user license to use the Software for your personal, noncommercial use only. You may not reproduce, sell, distribute, publish, circulate, or commercially exploit the Software, or any portion thereof, without the written consent of SYBEX and the specific copyright owner(s) of any component software included on this media.

In the event that the Software or components include specific license requirements or end-user agreements, statements of condition, disclaimers, limitations or warranties ("End-User License"), those End-User Licenses supersede the terms and conditions herein as to that particular Software component. Your purchase, acceptance, or use of the Software will constitute your acceptance of such End-User Licenses.

By purchase, use or acceptance of the Software you further agree to comply with all export laws and regulations of the United States as such laws and regulations may exist from time to time.

Reusable Code in This Book

The author(s) created reusable code in this publication expressly for reuse by readers. Sybex grants readers limited permission to reuse the code found in this publication, its accompanying CD-ROM or available for download from our website so long as the author(s) are attributed in any application containing the reusable code and the code itself is never distributed, posted online by electronic transmission, sold, or commercially exploited as a stand-alone product.

Software Support

Components of the supplemental Software and any offers associated with them may be supported by the specific Owner(s) of that material, but they are not supported by SYBEX. Information regarding any available support may be obtained from the Owner(s) using the information provided in the appropriate read.me files or listed elsewhere on the media.

Should the manufacturer(s) or other Owner(s) cease to offer support or decline to honor any offer, SYBEX bears no responsibility. This notice concerning support for the Software is provided for your information only. SYBEX is not the agent or principal of the Owner(s), and SYBEX is in no way responsible for providing any support for the Software, nor is it liable or responsible for any support provided, or not provided, by the Owner(s).

Warranty

SYBEX warrants the enclosed media to be free of physical defects for a period of ninety (90) days after purchase. The Software is not available from SYBEX in any other form or media than that enclosed herein or posted to www.sybex.com. If you discover a defect in the media during this warranty period, you may obtain a replacement of identical format at no charge by sending the defective media, postage prepaid, with proof of purchase to:

SYBEX Inc.
Product Support Department
1151 Marina Village Parkway
Alameda, CA 94501
Web: http://www.sybex.com

After the 90-day period, you can obtain replacement media of identical format by sending us the defective disk, proof of purchase, and a check or money order for $10, payable to SYBEX.

Disclaimer

SYBEX makes no warranty or representation, either expressed or implied, with respect to the Software or its contents, quality, performance, merchantability, or fitness for a particular purpose. In no event will SYBEX, its distributors, or dealers be liable to you or any other party for direct, indirect, special, incidental, consequential, or other damages arising out of the use of or inability to use the Software or its contents even if advised of the possibility of such damage. In the event that the Software includes an online update feature, SYBEX further disclaims any obligation to provide this feature for any specific duration other than the initial posting.

The exclusion of implied warranties is not permitted by some states. Therefore, the above exclusion may not apply to you. This warranty provides you with specific legal rights; there may be other rights that you may have that vary from state to state. The pricing of the book with the Software by SYBEX reflects the allocation of risk and limitations on liability contained in this agreement of Terms and Conditions.

Shareware Distribution

This Software may contain various programs that are distributed as shareware. Copyright laws apply to both shareware and ordinary commercial software, and the copyright Owner(s) retains all rights. If you try a shareware program and continue using it, you are expected to register it. Individual programs differ on details of trial periods, registration, and payment. Please observe the requirements stated in appropriate files.

Copy Protection

The Software in whole or in part may or may not be copy-protected or encrypted. However, in all cases, reselling or redistributing these files without authorization is expressly forbidden except as specifically provided for by the Owner(s) therein.

Acknowledgments

I would like to acknowledge some of my friends and associates who have supported me with enthusiasm, kind words, and encouragement throughout the writing of this book. Thanks to Eric Filson, Genesis Font, Dustin Whittle, Chris Kozlowski, Calvin Fraites, Richard Blundell, and Jeraimee Hughes.

I would also like to thank Sybex for their support and for believing in me as an author. The Sybex team: Tom Cirtin, Joel Fugazzotto, Lori Newman, Sean Schluntz, and the rest of the folks at Sybex who have worked on our book. Sybex is a wonderful publishing company, and I only wish our readers could truly understand what an outstanding experience it is to work with professionals of this level.

Finally, I would like to thank the open source developers, community, and end users. This community has fueled my desire to progress through the learning phases and allowed me to contribute everything I can for sharing this excellent concept. Nowhere have I ever found a group of online communities that dedicate every spare moment to helping other people with learning the ways of this masterful puzzle. This has truly been the most excellent computer experience I have ever found, and it is because of you.

—Eric Rosebrock

In addition to echoing the excellent words spoken about the outstanding team at Sybex who made this book possible and the open source community who fuels the fire of the future, I would like to add a few thanks of my own. To do so, I'll need to start at the beginning with those who have been a main inspiration in my life.

First, to Roberta and John Williams, the creator and developer, respectively, of King's Quest I (among many others). This game was released in 1984 and was my main inspiration at the age of five for dedicating my life to computers. They taught me it was possible to imbue technology with creativity, giving birth to original works that can force the world to pay attention and change the way people think. I will never forget what they unwittingly gave me.

In addition, I would like to thank key individuals who stand out in my mind as supporting my drives and teaching me the ways of the world. To Rick Kelly, who showed me the behind-the-scenes of computers in the '80s. To Kenny Whisenhunt, who helped me into the world of BBSs and furthered my knowledge of computers. To Shaun Hopkins, who taught me the mystical art of business and sales. Especially to Jeremy Thompson, who has been a friend in times of need and who has shown me the way to the fine art of higher-level programming. And most recently to Eric Rosebrock, who invited me to team with him to produce this great book. Of course my family cannot go without my thanks for their enduring push to always continue my education. And once again, many thanks to the readers who now continue their pursuit of education through this book.

A very special thanks to Kevin Anderson, his beautiful wife, Susan, and darling baby girl, Eva, for their support of my work and enduring friendship; I am forever grateful. Additional thanks to Travis Turner, Mason Ambrose, and Nathan Chase.

—Eric Filson

Contents at a Glance

Contents

Introduction

Welcome to *Setting Up LAMP: Getting Linux, Apache, MySQL, and PHP Working Together.* This book is written for those people out there who either struggle with this technology or just want a simple solution that is compiled by the experts. We have taken years of experience, problem solving, experimentation, and most importantly *implementation,* and bundled it all together as an easy-to-understand practical guide for you to utilize as you set up your LAMP web server. In this book you will find the following topics thoroughly explained:

Linux   Throughout this book you will learn about Linux. We discuss where it came from and how it developed, which flavor of Linux to use, how to install it, and, most importantly, how to use it. Each chapter is a practical guide and exercise on everyday Linux techniques. If you are new to Linux, simply following the examples in this book will definitely bring you up to a level of understanding and application through real-world techniques that will hone your skills as a Linux user or administrator.

Apache Web Server   We discuss how to download, build, install, administer, and configure the Apache Web Server. We show you the best methods of how to properly build your server, understand the configuration directives, configure virtual hosts, set up password-protected directories, and much more. You will have a firm understanding of and should feel comfortable running your own Linux-based Apache Web Server when you have completed this book.

MySQL   This book discusses how to download, build, install, administer, and configure MySQL. We show you the best methods for running your own MySQL server, protecting it from the outside world, and creating user accounts, databases, and tables. We cover MySQL 5, which is the newest version, and we cover its excellent features in depth.

PHP   This book discusses how to download, build, install, administer, and configure the PHP: Hypertext Preprocessor language for your web server. Additionally, we detail how to understand PHP. We do not show you how to develop websites with PHP, however; we focus on the server-side aspects of configuring, securing, and running it.

qmail E-mail Server   In this book, we tackle one of the most popular e-mail servers: qmail. qmail is a robust replacement for the old Sendmail application, and we show you how to download, build, install, and configure it to run efficiently with spam filters, antivirus software, IMAP, POP3, and SMTP protocols. By the time you are finished with this book, you will have a top-notch, high-quality e-mail server that can be used in any application, large or small.

Conventions Used in This Book

This book uses certain typographic styles in order to help you quickly identify important information, and to avoid confusion over the meaning of words such as onscreen prompts. In particular:

- A normal, proportionally spaced font is used for the bulk of the text in the book.

- *Italicized text* indicates technical terms that are introduced for the first time in a chapter. (Italics are also used for emphasis.)

- A `monospaced` font is used to indicate the contents of configuration files, messages displayed at a text-mode Linux shell prompt, filenames, commands, and Internet URLs.

- *`Italicized monospaced text`* indicates variables—information that differs from one system or command run to another, such as the name of a client computer or a process ID number.

- **`Bold monospaced text`** is information that you're to type into the computer, usually at a Linux shell prompt. This text can also be italicized to indicate that you should substitute an appropriate value for your system.

In addition to these text conventions, which can apply to individual words or entire paragraphs, a few conventions are used to highlight segments of text:

NOTE A Note indicates information that's useful or interesting, but that's somewhat peripheral to the main discussion. A Note might be relevant to a small number of networks, for instance, or refer to an outdated feature.

TIP A Tip provides information that can save you time or frustration, and that might not be entirely obvious. A Tip might describe how to get around a limitation or how to use a feature to perform an unusual task.

WARNING Warnings describe potential pitfalls or dangers. If you fail to heed a Warning, you could end up spending a lot of time recovering from a bug or even restoring your entire system from scratch.

Sidebars

A Sidebar is like a Note but addresses a larger topic. The information in a Sidebar is useful, but it doesn't fit into the main flow of the discussion.

Help Us Help You

In the open source world, things change rapidly. In fact, things change so rapidly that information found in this book will likely become outdated over time. We ask that you help us locate and identify these changes and report them to us as quickly as possible. However, we ask that you validate the information beforehand so that we can focus on realistic information and not a simple misunderstanding on the part of the reader. It is possible that this book might have typographical errors as well due to its size and nature. If you find an error or a change that needs to be submitted, please send an e-mail to support@sybex.com, and they will route the issue to the appropriate channels (editorial staff or the authors).

## CHAPTER 1

Introducing LAMP

- What is LAMP?

- Why LAMP?

I f you are a webmaster, a web developer, or a company that is interested in running your own web server, look no further: LAMP is here. *LAMP*, which stands for *Linux, Apache, MySQL, and PHP*, is a robust combination of applications driven on the powerful Linux operating system. This combination of technologies has a proven track record of being efficient, secure, and always on the leading edge of the ever so popular Internet.

The goal of this book is to teach you how to install and configure a web server by using the LAMP technology. You can rest assured that by the time you are finished reading this book, you will have a strong, powerful, and efficient web server to host your personal websites, powerful e-commerce or business-based websites, and anything in between.

The software used in this book is completely free to use and will not cost you any money in licensing or purchasing, unless you choose to purchase discs. Additionally, all of the software is easily downloaded through the Internet.

If you are ready to save yourself time and money by running and managing your own server, then read on!

What Is LAMP?

LAMP is a proven, efficient set of software that works well as a system. The open architecture of each of these elements allows for smooth and seamless integration with one another and results in a powerful combination. Early adopters of these technologies back in 1997 were seen as radical, but today the open source movement is on the rise, and both large and small enterprises are adopting the LAMP method of development. Steering away from the high costs of implementing licensed server and client software is becoming increasingly beneficial because the stability of each application is surpassing that of its far more expensive brethren. In recent events, some governments have decided to make the jump to open source software, touting its reliability, efficiency, and substantial cost savings over proprietary solutions.

Besides reaching this dependability level capable of being embraced by entire governments, the major advantage seen by LAMP adopters is *speed*. Each component of LAMP exhibits benchmarks that far exceed those of their competitors, and as with any equation the sum is much more than its parts. Let's take a look at just the Linux/Apache combination for a moment. This outstanding combination is capable of serving more pages to its users than any other commercial or open source solution. "What about MySQL?" you might ask. MySQL is the fastest open source database available, with speed comparable to that of Oracle's. This fact alone pushed NASA (the National Aeronautics and Space Administration) to switch to MySQL in 2000. With MySQL, the level of functionality offered to its consumers grows in leaps and bounds—most notably by offering *stored procedures*, a system found only in mature databases.

Which brings us to the power of PHP. PHP is the fastest server-side scripting program on the planet. Faster than a one-legged chicken on a downhill slope, PHP whisks by Active Server Pages (ASP), Java, .Net, and ColdFusion, allowing a greater maximum user count per server while providing the same amount of functionality—taking into account proper programming methods of course.

Now that we've touched on a few of the major advantages of choosing LAMP, let's take a brief look at each of its elements.

L—Linux Operating System

Linux is the operating system that runs the applications. It is specifically noted for its speed, minimal hardware requirements, security, and remote administration. Another great key point about Linux is that it's free! Linux is a fully featured operating system that doesn't cost you anything to use. You can download it directly from the Internet, install it, and use it without ever spending a dime (except for your own hardware of course). If you're curious about how this is possible, see the "Why LAMP Is Free" section later in this chapter.

Another major advantage of Linux is its ability to run with or without a graphical user interface (GUI), depending on your needs. (The non-GUI interface could almost be related to DOS mode for those Windows users who are not yet familiar with Linux.)

Linux is a project that began as a hobby by mastermind Linus Torvalds while he was a student at the University of Helsinki in Finland. Torvalds, originally working with Minix (a small Unix system), decided to create an operating system that would exceed the Minix standards. He began his development in 1991, and his first public release was version 0.02. Development of Linux continues even now with updates released as enough major changes are made to justify a new *version* release. Now that Torvalds has gained a much larger development team, releases are becoming more and more frequent. He is also the one who chose Tux (the penguin) to be the mascot of Linux.

Because Linux is published under the GNU (GNU stands for *GNU's Not Unix*) General Public License (GPL), many companies and individuals have taken the source code and adapted it to their needs. Some (most notably Red Hat) have turned huge profits by offering support for their releases and are now closing their source to commercialize their distributions.

A—Apache Web Server

Developed by the Apache Software Foundation (ASF), *Apache* is an open source web server solution that is packed with features, is extremely fast, and works well with the Linux operating system. With the Apache web server, you can create *virtual hosts* that enable you to run multiple websites on a single server, and it has many more awesome features. The Apache web server is available for the Windows environment as well; however, your system will suffer from decreased performance because of Microsoft's memory management (a.k.a. *leaks*) and architectural differences. Therefore it is *highly* recommended that you use Linux for all your web serving needs.

A quick overview of Apache's features would include items such as enhanced logging, bandwidth throttling, directory access protection, Common Gateway Interface (CGI) support, Secure Sockets Layer (SSL) support, and a handful of other built-in modules that enable you to do all sorts of neat things with your website.

Apache is rapidly growing in popularity and is currently the number one web server solution according to Netcraft (www.netcraft.com) surveys. It has held the number one position, with a large margin, for eight years. Taking the number one spot in 1996, Apache has grown to dominate the market with more than a 69 percent saturation. Coming in a rough second place is Microsoft, with 20 percent, which has stayed about the same since 1997. Next is Sun ONE with 3 percent.

NOTE   If you are interested in more statistics about Apache, take a look at the current Netcraft Web Server Survey located at http://news.netcraft.com/archives/web_server_survey.html.

M—MySQL Database Server

MySQL is a powerful, robust database manager that enables you to store and retrieve data with a scripting language such as PHP. You can store various types of data, such as Boolean operators, text, integers, images, binary digits, and BLOBs (binary large objects) quickly and efficiently with minimal effort. Using a database is important for creating dynamic sites. The term "dynamic site" is derived from being able to utilize a single page of code to display different information based on a user's interaction. This would be virtually impossible without the use of a database and a scripting language such as PHP to manipulate the data.

MySQL is packed full of features such as data replication, table locking, query limiting, user accounts, multiple databases, persistent connections, and—as of MySQL 5—stored procedures, triggers, and views. These features will be explained in more detail later, but for now you should be aware of some of the benefits you will enjoy from implementing such a great database manager.

MySQL, developed by MySQL AB, originated from a need for the founders to use mSQL to connect to their own fast, low-level (Indexed Sequential Access Method, or ISAM) routines. After testing these procedures and functions, they were found to be neither fast nor flexible enough and so MySQL was born: a new system from almost the same Application Protocol Interface (API) as mSQL, so that any third-party code that might be written for mSQL could easily be ported to MySQL. The mascot for MySQL is the dolphin seen in their logo. Her name is Sakila, and she was given her name from a Name the Dolphin contest held by MySQL.

P–PHP Scripting Language and Engine

PHP is a recursive acronym that stands for *PHP: Hypertext Preprocessor*. This widely used general-purpose scripting language is especially suited for Web development and can be embedded into HTML. What this means to you is that it's a simple scripting language that can greatly enhance your website. You simply learn the code, apply the logic, and create a dynamic website that can interact with your users on many levels greater than the traditional "flat file" HTML methods of the Internet.

PHP's initial inception in 1995 was a simple set of Perl scripts for tracking Rasmus Lerdorf's online résumé. As time went on, Lerdorf began to write a much larger C implementation to handle the increased amount of functionality he needed, including database connectivity. Lerdorf then decided to send out an initial release, open source style, called PHP/FI for anyone to use and to improve upon. Back in the day, this stood for Personal Home Page/Forms Interpreter. By 1997, the second release was distributed (PHP/FI 2.0) and had started to gain a following of several thousand from around the globe. Although several individuals were contributing code, it was still Lerdorf who continued the majority of all development.

Mid-1997 saw the dawn of a new age of PHP: PHP 3. This version was a complete rewrite of PHP/FI 2.0 by Andi Gutmans and Zeev Suraski, who needed more juice than was previously available for a university project they had been working on. To capitalize on PHP's growing user base, Lerdorf, Gutmans, and Suraski decided to release this new creation under the PHP name and so started what we know today as PHP. In the winter of 1998, PHP 4 development was begun by Gutmans and Suraski. They released the first official version in May of 2000. PHP 4 boasted much higher performance and pushed new technologies to its ever growing fan base with HTTP sessions, output buffering, and more secure ways of handling user input.

We believe that PHP 5 will knock the butterfly off its flower when it hits. A new object-oriented model coupled with the Zend Engine 2, stack tracing, and exception handling is expected to push a wider acceptance across the planet. At the same time, an introduction of integration with external object-oriented models, such as COM and Java, will throw a wildcard into the mix. For the first time, the ability of other communities to integrate seamlessly with PHP will be available. This means that prewritten APIs will be able to be much more easily integrated with PHP, destroying the last remaining reasons for these other communities to *not* use PHP.

NOTE   Don't worry if you do not yet have a complete understanding of the LAMP technologies from these brief descriptions. Throughout the rest of the book, we will cover in depth how to install, configure, and utilize them.

Why LAMP?

If you are wondering, "Why choose LAMP?" then the answer is something you must consider for yourself. The combination has been proven on many popular websites, and the technology is free to use. These factors are why many people and businesses have chosen this combination for launching their production-based websites.

With LAMP, you have full control over your server. Most important, you have remote access, which enables you to easily administer your Linux server from anywhere in the world. Linux enables you to run the services required without running a GUI, and therefore it uses less system resources—resources that could be used to speed up the process of delivering web pages to your audience.

Why LAMP Is Free

The core of the Linux operating system (the kernel) is under the GNU General Public License (GPL). The reason Linux is licensed under the GPL is simple: you are authorized to make modifications of the software, and in turn, release your version to the public, as long as you release the source code along with it. This keeps everything under the GPL "open source" and allows other people to modify the work that you have done, and so on.

Although it is not necessary to license any open source software under GPL, the GPL does prevent the code from becoming closed to the public. Others cannot capitalize on an open source code foundation by improving upon it and then close the source, thereby making it difficult if not impossible for the open source community to develop the same functionality. This is a "remember your roots" type license and it is how great operating systems such as Linux and most of the open source software evolve. This type of peer review is the basis for what's called the *Open Source Movement.*

The GPL is written and maintained by the Free Software Foundation. If you are interested in learning more about GPL, you can visit the Free Software Foundation's website at `www.gnu.org/copyleft/gpl.html`.

Apache, MySQL, and PHP are some of the other free software applications we will be using throughout this book. Although they are not licensed under the GPL, each of these applications is under a similar license. This enables us to not only share in the work of countless numbers of developers across the globe but also to freely use and distribute these applications as we choose. From our basic Linux installation all the way to our mail server (the application responsible for sending and receiving our e-mail on our server), we will be using free software brought to us by those who love to do one thing: write software.

NOTE Some fees might be associated with free software—for example, for tech support—but these fees can be avoided by making use of the open source community itself. There are hundreds of forums and thousands of sites devoted to helping you find answers to questions that might arise, and these sites can be accessed for free. Although these sites might not answer your questions *immediately,* they should become an invaluable resource for your newfound, or newly rekindled, love of open source.

It's a safe bet that on any given day you use at least one piece of free software, even if you don't know it. In fact, this book was written on free word processing applications that come with Linux. Now, you have the opportunity to learn more about free software that you will use by following the examples we set for you in this book to create your own LAMP solution.

LAMP versus Other Solutions

Other solutions such as Microsoft's Internet Information Server (IIS) are popular. However, the lack of security and potential higher cost of hardware and maintenance keep them out of reach of many small companies. Rather than spend millions in licenses and administrative costs for an inferior product, we choose to run a Free Software solution.

In a recent study by the Robert Frances Group of Westport, Connecticut, it was found that the cost of running Linux was roughly 40 percent of that of Microsoft Windows and 14 percent of Sun Microsystems' Solaris operating systems. This alone will make any company think twice about deploying a Web-based application on Microsoft Windows. In that same study, it was also found that the typical Windows administrator managed an average of only 10 machines each, whereas Linux administrators managed many times that number.

Speed is another significant factor to most of us. We need our Web-based applications to respond quickly and remain snappy throughout the user's experience. With proper coding techniques, PHP is many times faster than Microsoft's ASP or Sun Microsystems' Java platform.

Another great feature of PHP is the ability to create command-line scripting that can perform tasks to your system at scheduled intervals by using CRON jobs within Linux. You can have PHP clean up your MySQL database weekly, or have it create backups of your website every few days, and so on. Although many PHP versus ASP debates could be spawned from these statements, the truth stands that ASP probably will never be as robust as PHP.

In the end, it's you that makes LAMP better than other platforms. Through the use of the LAMP combination, you directly contribute to the success of the software on your server.

Who Else Is Using LAMP?

The question of "Who is using LAMP?" is often asked. Because of the size of the Internet and the number of servers out there, we do not have the ability to give you a full report; however, here's a list of some of the more popular sites using LAMP:

LinuxForum.com   A free Linux support website.

ApacheFreaks.com   A free Apache web server support website.

MySQLFreaks.com   A free MySQL database manager support website.

PHPFreaks.com   A free PHP support website.

Winamp.com   The Nullsoft Winamp site is built around PHP.

DevShed.com   The open source development site Developer Shed is completely PHP driven.

MP3.com   The single largest MP3 Web-based server is built using PHP.

SpeedTV.com   SPEED TV, the television station owned by Fox, has been completely developed in PHP with a few Flash/ColdFusion elements thrown in.

Yahoo.com   Even though Yahoo does not show the `.php` extension on their files, it has been confirmed by many sources that they are using it. Here's our source: `public .yahoo.com/~radwin/talks/yahoo-phpcon2002.htm`.

Nearly 70 percent of the websites you visit are using Linux as their operating system, and MySQL AB and Zend Technologies report that "over 10 million Web-based applications have been built using MySQL and PHP through low-cost open source software stacks such as LAMP" (see `www.mysql.com/press/release_2004_05.html`). This number continues to grow as Linux and other open source projects gain momentum within the industry. Every passing year adds more credibility, more features, and more support to the LAMP solution.

If you're curious to see how many domains are using PHP, you can check the Usage Stats for PHP at `www.php.net/usage.php`. At the time of this writing, according to SecuritySpace (`www.securityspace.com/s_survey/data/index.html`), the current usage is about 4.6 million domain names that are PHP enabled.

Understanding LAMP Checklist

The following list indicates information from this chapter that you should understand. As you read this book, be sure to check out this section in each chapter and make sure you have a firm grasp of the elements within the list. Future chapters will build upon the techniques and/or information listed at the end of each chapter.

- Describe the four LAMP technologies and how they work together as a system.

- Understand the terms *open source* and *GNU General Public License.*

- Know the major reasons for choosing LAMP over another solution.

- Understand LAMP's huge impact on web development.

Although these points are not directly related to installing and configuring Linux, Apache, MySQL, and PHP, they provide a basic understanding that you can build upon to become a professional web developer for today's marketplace. Make sure you comprehend the philosophies and hard work put into these technologies that make this combination so great.

In the next chapter, we'll talk about the different Linux distributions, hardware requirements, obtaining Linux, and most important, we'll show you how to install Fedora Linux as your base operating system.

CHAPTER 2

Installing Linux

- Which Linux to Use

- Hardware Requirements

- Obtaining Fedora Linux

- Installing Fedora Linux

- First Bootup

Now that we have the history out of the way, we're almost ready to begin your installation. This chapter, apart from showing you how to install Linux, will help you make educated decisions on what hardware and Linux distributions you will merge in order to maximize your time and money. Although the software is open source, hardware is by no means free, so we've put together a hardware requirements section that will help you make an informed decision on building or choosing your box without going overboard. The Linux operating system carries extremely low overhead, so your initial investment shouldn't break the bank.

Choosing Which Linux to Use

Over the years many distributions, or *flavors*, of Linux have been developed and made available around the world. The following list includes some of the major players in the world of the penguin; although it is not a complete list of all the flavors, it's enough to familiarize yourself with a little of what's out there. Each of these distributions is a good choice, but a few stand out from the crowd in terms of reliability, availability, functionality, and ease of use. In alphabetical order we have these distributions:

Debian   Debian was officially released by Ian Murdock on August 16, 1993. Debian is the self-proclaimed *only Linux distribution to allow any developer to develop for*. Although Debian is no newcomer to the business, it has never reached the iconic status of many of the other distributions. You can learn more about Debian at `www.debian.org`.

Fedora   Fedora Linux was originally started by Warren Togami as a means of developing high-quality Red Hat Package Management system (RPM) packages for Red Hat. A 2003 announcement of Red Hat turning commercial also declared the merging of Fedora Linux into what is now the Fedora Project. You can learn more about Fedora at `fedora.redhat.com`. We will be covering this flavor of Linux in depth throughout the rest of this book.

FreeBSD   December of 1993 saw the birth of FreeBSD 1.0. It was developed based on the 4.3BSD-Lite ("Net/2") tape from U.C. Berkeley, with many components provided by 386BSD as well. *FreeBSD* was coined by David Greenman and was originally developed by Jordan Hubbard, Nate Williams, and Rod Grimes. The FreeBSD website is `www.freebsd.org`.

NOTE   Although a popular release hailed by many as one of the greats, FreeBSD is not a release of Linux. It is mentioned here because it is a popular alternative to Linux while keeping with a Unix-based architecture.

Mandrake   Created by Gaël Duval in 1998, Mandrake was begun as hobby to make Linux easier to use. July 23 of that year saw the first release and in less than 48 hours, the public responded by sending numerous ideas, one patch, and two companies announcing the sale of Mandrake on CD. Since then, Mandrake has developed into MandrakeSoft and has begun charging a small fee for their releases. The Mandrake website is `www.mandrakesoft.com`.

Slackware   Slackware's first release came in April of 1993. Slackware aims to be the most "Unix-like" Linux distribution in the world, and so far has succeeded in doing so. Patrick Volkerding developed the first release with ease of use and stability as his top priorities. The Slackware website is `www.slackware.com`.

SuSE   SuSE Linux is the only operating system listed here apart from Red Hat and Mandrake that is not "free." SuSE has been in development since 1992 in Germany, and their dedicated work has not gone unnoticed. As a leading provider of Linux, their interface is one of the most appealing with a long list of included features to round out their distro (geek term for distribution). The SuSE website is `www.suse.com`.

Red Hat   Probably the most widely spread distribution of Linux, Red Hat has now turned commercial; however, they have continued to support the open source community and freeware by spinning off a new version of Linux. Based on the Red Hat 9 release, this new version is called Fedora. The first release of Red Hat was in October of 1994; developed by Marc Ewing, it was known as the Halloween Release. 1995 saw the unveiling of the RPM system. The Red Hat website is `www.redhat.com`.

For the purposes of this book, we have chosen to use Fedora as our distribution. While choosing Fedora over the many other flavors of Linux, careful consideration was given to providing a free operating system with good stability and a great amount of user friendliness. Fedora, while being one of the newest distributions, has a background that simply cannot be ignored. Fedora uses the RPM system, which has been heavily developed and tested for more than 10 years. The market penetration achieved by the Red Hat distribution over the years has provided the base functionality of Fedora and its package management system with a test bed larger than any other in existence. In an effort to keep new and intermediate users trouble free throughout their installations, configurations, and overall operation, we have chosen Fedora. In addition, we believe Fedora to be the new up-and-comer for the future of widespread Linux.

After you feel you have mastered the techniques in this book and have a firm grasp of the Linux operating system, you might later choose to direct your attention to one of the many other flavors that you find appealing to your palate. We hope that some of you will discover a newfound passion for Linux and that you might someday choose to give back to the Linux community by furthering its development in any form possible. It's people like you who make the difference in the open source community by sharing ideas, code, and help with the rest of the world.

Meeting Hardware Requirements

Although Linux does not have severe hardware requirements by any standards, it is important to keep in mind your end goal for the server on which you will be installing Linux. You don't want it to suffer from lack of speed, but in the same respect you don't need dual Xeon processors to run your personal development server.

If you are interested in running Fedora Linux in text-only mode, you will need to meet the following minimum hardware requirements:

- 200MHz Pentium class processor or better
- 2GB hard disk space
- 64MB RAM

For graphical mode you will need at least the following:

- 400MHz Pentium II processor or better
- 3GB hard disk space
- 192MB RAM

NOTE   These are the bare-minimum system requirements. We highly recommend purchasing or building a system with better specs than listed here, especially if you plan on using your Linux box as a file server as well as a web server or if you will be serving to multiple users simultaneously.

We have put together the following system recommendations for different numbers of simultaneous users so you can get an idea of the hardware scalability structure:

System specifications for up to 50 users:

- Intel Celeron 1GHz processor
- 20GB hard disk
- 512MB RAM

System specifications for 51–250 users:

- Intel Pentium 4 2GHz processor
- 80GB hard disk
- 1GB RAM

System specifications for 251–1000 users:

- Dual Xeon > 2 GHz

- SCSI RAID with appropriate hard disk space for your needs
- 1GB RAM PC3500 DDR or higher

In today's market, anyone can put together a basic system like the one listed for up to 50 users for around $250. That includes a smaller monitor, mouse, and keyboard. Linux supports all PS/2 and Universal Serial Bus (USB) peripherals, so your choice is limited only by what's available. With such a minimal investment, it's worthwhile to be able to separate your new testing box from any PCs you might be using as desktop computers.

It is important to note that a CD-ROM drive is also highly recommended for the installation of Linux. Although it is possible to boot from a floppy disk with minimal support and to configure the installation to install from the network, it is much easier to install from a CD. You might also need the CD-ROM drive in the future for commercial software you purchase in CD format.

There are no video cards listed in the system requirements because video plays almost no part in text-only mode. If you plan on using this station in graphical mode and wish to run your monitor at a higher resolution, almost any video card with 32MB of video RAM should be more than sufficient to power the X Window (graphical) interface.

NOTE By *higher resolution* we mean 1280 x 1024 or 1600 x 1200. (We consider 1024 x 768 the base resolution now.) Based on our experience running 1280 x 1024 on X Window, it's best to have at least a 16MB card. We recommend a 32MB card because it can be purchased for the same price or just a few dollars more and it will last you a bit longer.

After you have breached the 1000 simultaneous-user mark, you might want to consider purchasing a multiple server setup to support your users. These systems are used to spread load across multiple servers and can be set up in a number of different ways. Each solution of this type is unique because it must be designed for the specific application present. SpeedTV.com, previously mentioned in the PHP site examples in Chapter 1, "Introducing LAMP," receives hundreds of thousands of unique visits a day and is backed by three dual Xeon servers to share this tremendous amount of traffic.

WARNING Even if you are supporting only five users on your system, you will need at least *two* servers if you wish to have zero downtime. This is because the installation of some software requires that certain services be shut down. During this process, your server might stop serving files and/or pages depending on what service had to be shut down. To avoid this, you can run a second *mirror* server to direct the traffic to until your necessary changes and/or upgrades have been made. After you are sure everything is working properly, you can switch back to the original, now updated, server.

Obtaining Fedora Linux

Fedora Linux can be acquired in several ways, the two most popular being to download or to purchase. This section discusses both.

If you have access to a computer that has a CD-R or CD-RW drive, you can download the complete set of installation discs, for free, directly from the Internet in International Organization for Standardization (ISO) format from a site such as LinuxForum (`http://www.linuxforum.com`). After you've located the Fedora download section, it's time to choose a version. It's best to download the newest full-release version because a full release has been deemed *stable* and is out of its testing phases. Fedora Core 2 is the newest release, so this book will be covering that version in the most detail. If you are unable to find the distribution at LinuxForum, you can check the Fedora mirrors list at `http://fedora.redhat.com/download/mirrors.html`.

The Crucial MD5 Checksum File

Make sure that there is a Message Digest 5 (MD5) checksum file located with your ISO files. The purpose of a *checksum* file is to verify that your downloaded copy of the file is an exact duplicate of the original. This can prevent people from tampering with the distribution and possibly rebuilding it with malicious code, and it can also detect any viruses that might have attached themselves as the file traveled to you.

It is always a good idea to run a checksum on your downloaded files. Even if there is no malicious code, the file can still prevent you from burning a bad disc and having to abort your installation. Many MD5 checksum programs are available as freeware on the Internet. You can also find free C scripts that will perform the same operation.

You can check the following URLs for Windows versions of a few MD5 checksum utilities:

- `http://www.irnis.net`

- `http://www.dpaehl.de`

- `http://www.brandonstaggs.com`

- `http://www.fastsum.com`

If you would like to run an MD5 checksum, you can go to the last choice listed—FastSum—for a free version. Download, install, and launch FastSum, and you are ready to verify your ISOs. To use FastSum, you will need to use the command line, so open a command window in Windows and use the following format to run the checksum:

```
FSUM "C:\directory\filename.iso" "C:\directory\md5file.md5"
```

The program will then run, and any errors or inconsistencies will be checked. If everything is in order, you are ready to continue with the installation.

After you have successfully downloaded and checked your ISO files, use your favorite burning software that supports ISO format to create your installation discs. Some popular choices are Golden Hawk Technology's CDRWin, Ahead Software's Nero Burning Rom, and Elaborate Bytes' CloneCD. After you finish burning all three discs, you are ready to begin the installation, so you can skip to the next subsection, aptly titled "Installing Fedora Linux."

If you choose, you can opt to purchase a copy of Fedora Linux on disc from one of a variety of distributors, most of which are located on the Web. Linux Central is a reliable source with prompt shipping and can be visited at www.linuxcentral.com. Linux Central provides CD sets of most major Linux distributions for excellent prices. After your CD arrives in the mail, you are ready to begin.

Installing Fedora Linux

The time has finally arrived. After familiarizing yourself with the many flavors of Linux and learning why we have chosen Fedora, you built or purchased a new or used PC, and now you are ready to install Linux.

Pre-Installation

Before you are ready to begin that actual installation, you must first perform the following steps:

1. Insert disc 1 into the CD-ROM drive. Of course you'll need to power on in order to do so.

2. You might need to change your boot order in the BIOS settings for your motherboard to boot from the CD first. To do this, pay attention to the first screen your computer shows during the boot sequence. You should notice a line that says Press <del> to Enter Setup or maybe Press <F2> to Enter BIOS or something along those lines. Follow the instructions and you will enter the BIOS configuration settings for your motherboard. The boot order is most often located under the General Settings category. Enter the General Settings category and change the first boot device to be your CD-ROM drive. After you've made the appropriate changes, choose Exit and Save Changes and wait for your computer to boot from the CD.

3. You should be presented with a screen that looks identical to Figure 2.1. This is the Fedora Core 2 Pre-installation screen. From here, hot keys will enable you to view documentation and additional specifications you can use for more advanced installations or recoveries should you be using nonstandard hardware or suffer from a corrupted kernel. The first two options that are displayed on the screen are the ones to be concerned with now.

Pre-installation screen

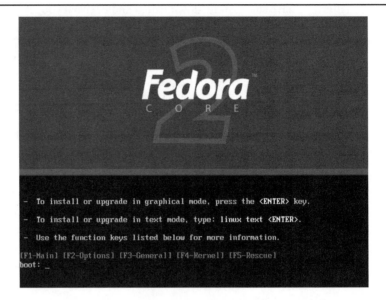

4. You will be using the second option, which provides the functionality to install or upgrade Fedora Linux by using text-only mode. This option is usually reserved for individuals who are using an older cathode ray tube, or CRT, monitor (a *green screen*), people who are experiencing difficulty displaying the VGA graphics used during the installation procedure, or those who feel the need to express their inner geek. In order to support the greatest number of users, enter the text mode by typing **linux text** and pressing Enter to continue. You'll then need to wait a brief moment while the installation detects some basic hardware and prepares the installation procedure for you.

NOTE   The first option that was listed, for those who have more up-to-date video cards, is to install Fedora by using *graphical mode*. Because this is the default option, simply pressing Enter would have begun the installation.

Installation Type Selection

You are now ready to choose your installation type, follow the steps below being sure everything is correct before proceeding on the next step:

1. The first installation screen you should see is a small text-based graphic window asking whether you would like to check the installation CDs. If you have downloaded and burned these CDs, you should run the integrity check for CD1 and CD2. It's better to wait a minimal amount of time now than to become frustrated with your installation if things head

south due to unseen problems. If you purchased the CDs, then most likely they have already been checked by the distributor. In this case you can select the Skip option and continue. If you run into problems, you can always reboot the machine and begin the installation procedure again so you can verify the CDs.

2. The next screen prompts you to select a language to use during the installation process. Simple enough, it should default to English, so selecting OK should continue you on your way. You might want to note that to switch between elements of these screens (that is, lists, check boxes, buttons, and so on) you will be using the Tab key. The spacebar will enable you to select and deselect certain options, and F12 will enable you to go directly to the next screen.

3. A few text lines appear at the bottom of the screen as the Fedora Installer tries to detect your hardware. Depending on whether your hardware is successfully identified, you will then see one or more of the following screens: Keyboard, Mouse, and Video. The Keyboard and Mouse screens are straightforward and should already have hardware settings that most closely match your hardware. If these are in error, select the proper choice and continue. If you are brought to the video card selection screen, you will need to know the type of video card you have and the resolution your monitor is capable of supporting. Make the appropriate selections and continue to the next step.

4. You are then brought to the Installation Type screen, shown in Figure 2.2. This enables you to set the overall basic packages that will be installed. The options listed here come with certain features and modules pre-installed to fit your specific application of Linux. Here's a breakdown of your options:

    Personal Desktop   This option should be selected if you wish to run your Linux box as a personal computer for desktop publishing, web browsing, e-mail, graphics, games, and so on.

    Workstation   This option provides a basic system setup with a developer's needs in mind. It focuses more heavily on libraries that might be beneficial to programmers.

    Server   Selecting the Server option installs software necessary for your Linux server to handle the routing of data to other computers on your network or the Internet.

    Custom   For the more experienced Linux user, this option affords the opportunity to select each library and package specific to your case. This is not recommended to the first-time user because it is easy to overlook something you might need.

5. Because lessons in this book are based on setting up a LAMP environment, select Server from the list by tabbing to the radio box and using the up or down arrows to highlight Server. Press Tab once more to jump down to OK and press Enter to proceed to the next screen.

FIGURE 2.2
Installation Type
Screen

Hard Disk Partitioning

The Linux operating system requires that you partition your hard disks before you can install the operating system. A *partition* is a way for the operating system to reserve a block of your hard disk space for a specific purpose. Linux will make sure these partitions do not overlap, resulting in corrupted data.

Follow these steps to partition your hard disk:

1. You should be at the Disk Partitioning Setup screen, which presents you with these options:

   Autopartition is the default, highlighted option.

   Disk Druid enables you to set up your partitions in detail by inputting the device, size, type, and mount point for each partition.

2. If you do not already have any special partitions on your drive, choose Autopartition and skip to step 3. If you do have special conditions that you need to work around, choose Disk Druid, proceed to step 2, and then skip to the rest of this section.

3. If you choose to set up your own partitions because of multiple hard drives or another reason, there are a few critical things to keep in mind. First, you must have a swap partition. A *swap partition* is used for virtual memory support. If your computer runs out of RAM for storing temporary data, this partition will be used in its place to handle any overflow. When creating your swap partition, be sure to make its size equal to twice the amount of RAM you have installed, but no greater than 2048MB (or 2GB). Next you need to create a *boot* partition. The boot partition is where your operating system kernel resides along with any files

used during the bootstrap process. A 50MB partition should be more than sufficient; if you make it too large, it could cause problems with your BIOS.

4. The last partition that is required is the *root* partition. This partition houses all the files not residing on /boot so it will make up the vast majority of your drive. A minimum of about 2.5GB is needed to install the packages required for the Server selection you made earlier.

5. If you are manually configuring your partitions, you should be aware of the partition types available:

   ext2 This filesystem is the standard Unix/Linux partition type and supports long filenames up to 255 characters.

   ext3 This filesystem is almost identical to ext2 but it allows journaling. Journaling requires less time to be spent during a system recovery because there is no need to run the fsck command, which attempts to repair the system.

   software RAID If you create two or more software RAID partitions, you can enable a RAID device. A RAID can provide faster read and/or write times as well as data redundancy should a drive fail. If you are building a system that might contain important or sensitive information, you might wish to research this further.

   swap As discussed before, this type of partition provides Linux with virtual memory support.

   vfat A vfat partition is used to create a partition compatible with a Windows 95/NT filesystem. It uses the standard FAT table format and also supports long filenames.

6. After selecting the Autopartition option and continuing to the next screen, a warning appears indicating that all the information contained on the drive will be lost. Go ahead and agree to this screen if that is okay. An Automatic Partitioning window appears in the center of the screen and prompts you for two pieces of information. The first asks how you would like to handle the existing information on your drive. Because you are installing a clean system, select Remove All Partitions on This System. Tab to the next prompt, which asks which drives you would like to use for this installation. If you have a special case and would like to keep any existing data on your computer, select the appropriate choice from the list and also tab down to the next section. From here, select all drives available on your system, and press F12 or select OK. Another warning screen is displayed, confirming that you do indeed wish to remove all the partitions on each of the drives selected. Make sure the Yes option is highlighted and press Enter to continue.

7. The Partitioning screen, shown in Figure 2.3, displays how the autopartitioner has configured your disk space. It also affords you the opportunity to make any last-minute changes to your filesystem schema before continuing with the installation. If you feel something isn't

right, refer back to step 2 for more information on specific partition options and setup, or you can press F1 for help. If everything appears okay, continue in the usual manner to bring up the next screen. At this point, if your system has only the minimum amount of RAM needed for the installation, the installer will ask whether it is okay to enable the swap partition you just enabled. This is fine, so go ahead and agree and you'll be taken to the next screen.

Selecting a Boot Loader

The next task is to select whether you would like to use the GRand Unified Bootloader (GRUB). GRUB will enable you to boot from multiple operating systems and also provide additional security from anyone who might be able to access your system locally. Follow these steps:

1. You will be using GRUB, so make sure Use GRUB Boot Loader is selected and continue.

2. The Boot Loader Configuration screen prompts you for any special options or arguments that might need to be passed to the kernel during the boot sequence. Most likely you should not need anything here, so simply pass through this page by continuing. A second page for the boot loader configuration is then displayed asking whether you would like to specify a password to access GRUB before the operating system boots. If you need tightened security, then use this option.

WARNING   Your system will be only minimally protected by the Linux login screen. This is because, unless other modifications are made (described in Chapter 6, "Linux Security"), a user located at the terminal could still gain full access. You should also note that if the hard drive is removed and installed in another computer, that user could still gain access to your files. Any sensitive information should always be encrypted on your hard disk.

FIGURE 2.3
Partitioning screen

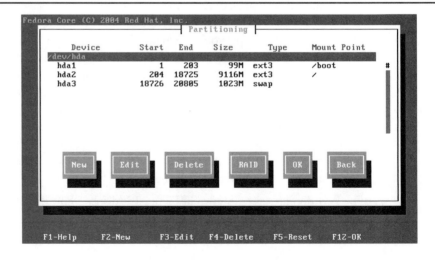

3. The next Boot Loader Configuration screen enables you to label other operating systems to boot from and to select the default option as well. You will see in Figure 2.4 that we have only one installation, and it is set to the default automatically.

4. The last Boot Loader Configuration screen asks where you would like to install the boot loader. Select the Master Boot Record (MBR) because this makes the most sense. Select OK to move on.

Configuring the Network

You have now arrived at your first bit of network configuration. Your screen now should read Network Configuration for eth0. The term *eth0* refers to your first Ethernet device readable by your computer. Those of you with multiple network cards or integrated network on your motherboard will have eth1 and eth2 successively.

When configuring eth0, Fedora's installation program will give you a short description located on the second line, as depicted in Figure 2.5. If you have multiple network adapters, note which device this is to make sure your network cable is plugged into the correct port.

The third line will ask whether you would like to configure this network device to use DHCP. *DHCP* stands for *Dynamic Host Configuration Protocol* and is used to automatically assign and provide IP addresses from a DHCP server to any computer on the network that requests one.

NOTE   You'll want to leave Activate on Boot selected for each network device that will be used on your network.

FIGURE 2.4
Boot Loader Config-
uration screen

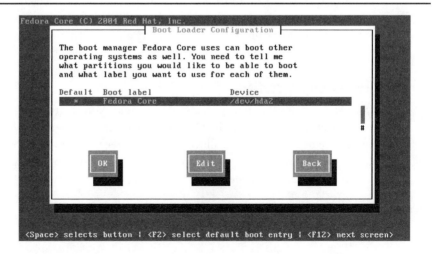

FIGURE 2.5
Network Configuration
screen

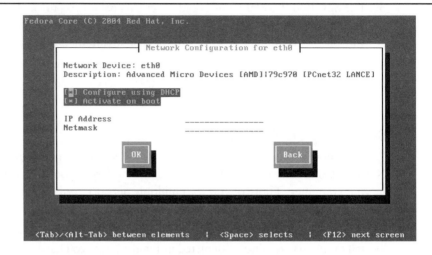

Here are the steps to configure your network:

1. If you choose to have a static IP address, deselect the Configure Using DHCP option, and the IP Address and Netmask will be available for editing. Input the static IP address now as well as the required netmask. A *netmask* is a 32-bit mask used to divide an IP address into subnets and to specify the network's available hosts. This is most commonly 255.255.255.0, which allows 2,097,150 networks and 254 hosts. After you have made the appropriate changes, continue to the next screen.

2. Now you'll do a hostname configuration. Displayed on this screen is a short description letting you know that Automatically via DHCP should be selected if your DHCP server will automatically assign you a hostname. We will assume that your network is not set up to do so, so select Manually and think of a witty and self-expressive name for your first Linux server (the name *Tux* does *not* count). Continue to the next screen.

Firewall Configuration

A *firewall* is a collection of programs and configurations that act together to examine all network packets passing through it. The firewall determines whether to forward the packets to the appropriate destination, or to allow your computer to access these ports by letting outgoing packets through the firewall. This type of control is needed to tie down your network and computer from potential outside attacks.

WARNING   We have personally witnessed systems that did not have a firewall enabled and were hacked within one hour of installation.

This process has only one step:

- Select the Enable Firewall option and continue on your way. We will discuss firewall rules and configuration in *much* greater detail in Chapter 6.

Miscellaneous Settings

In this section, you'll set language and time zone options and choose a password. But first, there are a few things you should note about selecting a password. It is far too common an occurrence for webmasters and administrators even today to use simple passwords. Words relating to themselves, birthdates, pet names, loved ones' names—*do not use these!* If you value the security of your computer, pick something random. It is not that difficult to remember a short, random sequence of numbers and letters or even special characters.

Now, with that out of the way, you're ready to set the options:

1. The next two screens, Language Support and Time Zone Selection, are self-explanatory so select the appropriate settings for you and continue.

TIP	When selecting a password, look around the room and take some random characters from things. If you have a hard time remembering a string of characters, write it down on a small scrap of paper and put it in something that you always keep with you. A wallet would suffice nicely. Don't put it under your keyboard, either! We know it's almost cliché, but people still do it.

2. The Root Password screen is displayed. Derive your password from the elements that surround you and enter it twice for confirmation. Then proceed to the next screen.

Package Selection

It's time to customize. This screen, titled Package Group Selection, permits you to select all the packages your heart desires. However, you will be installing a certain set of packages for the purposes of this book:

1. Select the X Window System option (see Figure 2.6). Then select GNOME Desktop Environment or KDE Desktop Environment, or both if you wish, and then skip down and make sure Text-based Internet is selected. Deselect any other package groups that might be on the first page and scroll down to see more options.

NOTE	Although this book will not cover X Window in depth, after you have learned the methodologies used through the Linux shell, you might wish to use the graphical interface that GNOME or KDE provides to manage your server.

2. Continue to deselect all packages on the way down to Administration Tools except for Server Configuration Tools and Development Tools. "Why am I deselecting all the servers?" you might ask. Well, good thing you asked because we were just about to tell you. When you are finished with this book, you should have a complete understanding of how to download, install, and configure each one of these servers from the latest source code. The reason being: you will need to upgrade to the latest versions of Apache, MySQL, and PHP, which might not be available on the installation discs. Leaving these off for now will afford you the opportunity to start with a clean installation of the latest stable versions of each element in the LAMP system, providing you with a well-oiled serving machine.

NOTE   You can also view and select multiple packages within a group by pressing F2 when you are over a specific group. This will enable you to tailor your installation even further to trim out any excess packages that might not pertain to you.

3. For now though, use the defaults provided and jump down to OK to proceed.

4. The next screen, Installation to Begin, tells you that a complete log of the installation will be saved to /root/install.log in case you need to access it at a later date. Continue to the next screen and you will be warned which discs you must have in order for the installation to be complete.

WARNING   Be careful here, because the default selected option is Reboot and not Continue, so pressing Enter without tabbing over will cause you to have to start over from the beginning of this chapter.

FIGURE 2.6
Package group
selection

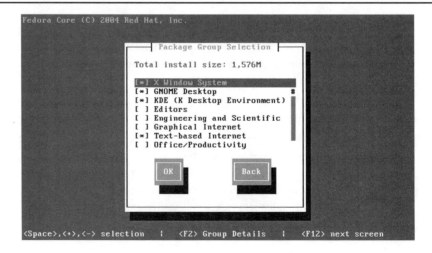

Package Installation

Ahh... the moment you've been waiting for: *break time*. Watch the installation kick off and grab yourself some refreshments (see Figure 2.7). The installation time will vary from computer to computer depending on CD-ROM and computer speed. Midway through the installation, you will be prompted to insert the second disc. Do so and continue with your break.

Boot Diskette Creation

After the package installation is complete, you will be taken to a screen asking whether you would like to make a boot diskette. If you have a floppy drive and some diskettes handy, it wouldn't be a bad idea to make a boot diskette. Should anything happen to your system, it will make the recovery process much less painful.

Installation Complete!

Your next screen will tell you the installation is complete. Congratulations—it's time to reboot your computer for the first time with a fresh installation of Fedora ready to go. Make sure to remove any media from your CD-ROM drive(s) and press Enter to reboot.

Booting Up

After you reboot, a screen for the GRUB boot loader appears (see Figure 2.8). If you opted to have the GRUB password enabled, you need to enter it here in order to continue.

FIGURE 2.7
Package installation

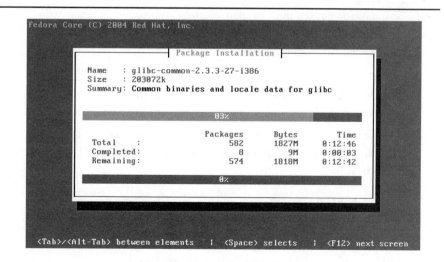

FIGURE 2.8
First GRUB screen

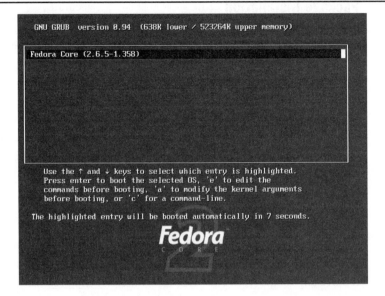

You then have about 10 seconds to choose from any of your operating system installations before GRUB will take over and start up the default installation you selected during the boot loader configuration. If you'd like, speed up the process by pressing Enter to kick off the boot sequence and you'll be brought to your first X Window interface.

NOTE   If you do not see the X Window interface and your monitor has gone dark or out of sync then you can switch to a text-only prompt by pressing Ctrl-Alt-F2. This will take you to a text prompt where you may login.

The following succession of screens will prompt you to enter the basic information to begin Fedora Linux for the first time. At this point, your mouse should be functional so click the Next button at the bottom-right corner of the screen to continue.

Next you will need to review and agree to the License Agreement for Fedora Linux. After reading the License Agreement, click Yes, I Agree to the License Agreement and continue to the next page.

Post-Installation Setup

Using the interface shown in Figure 2.9, select the appropriate date and time for your local area. If you wish, you can set up your machine to obtain its time from a network server periodically. This can be useful for setups that use more than one server as web and database servers. Having a time matched to each other will allow for more accurate recording of dates and times in the applications you develop. If you choose to Enable Network Time Protocol, select the appropriate server from the drop-down list provided and click Next to continue.

The next page prompts you to create a User Account. You need to create a new account at this time because the exercises in this book require an account other than root to be present. Enter your username, full name, and password, and click Next.

The second-to-last configuration page gives you the chance to install any additional packages from other CDs. You have all you need for now, so continue to the Finish Setup page. Nothing to do here either—simply click Next and log on to your new operating system by using the root account and your corresponding password.

Ahh, the X Window interface. See the beautiful graphics? Don't get too used to them because your final step for this chapter will be to disable X Window at startup. We'll be presenting command prompt installations for most of this book in order to familiarize you with the true power of Linux. Without a strong knowledge of the command line, you will not be able to grasp the more advanced concepts of Linux.

FIGURE 2.9
Date and Time

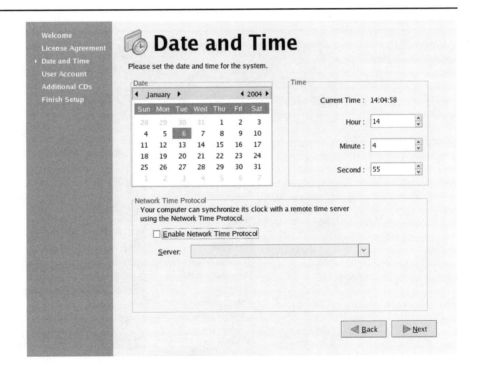

Changing the Bootup Type

In this section, we will be changing the default boot type to start in text mode only versus X Window. This is because the information contained in the book will use only the command prompt. To do so, you'll need to open a terminal window in order to modify your target file. Click the Red Hat located on the bottom left of the screen and then click System Tools ➢ Terminal, as depicted in Figure 2.10.

After you have opened a terminal window, you will be placed at a prompt similar to that in the old DOS operating system. First, change directories to the /etc directory. You can do this by using the cd command, also much like DOS. So begin with this:

```
[root@computer root]# cd /etc
```

Notice that the first section of this command is already displayed on your screen. This is referred to as the *prompt*. The prompt can be divided into three parts. The first part is the user you are currently operating as and is terminated at the @ symbol. The second section is your computer name terminated by a space. The third is your current subdirectory. The preceding command should produce another prompt with the third element of your prompt reading etc.

FIGURE 2.10
Opening a terminal window

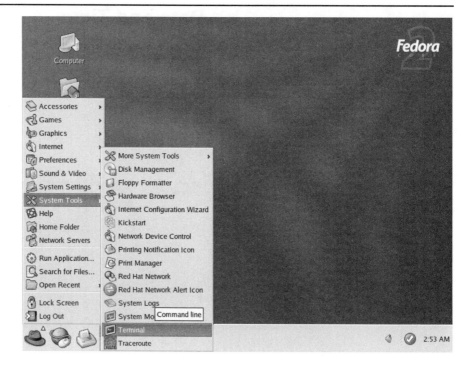

From here you will need to edit a file. For the purpose of this first exercise, you will be using vi, which stands for Visual Editor. In order to edit the target file you need, `inittab`, type the following command:

    vi inittab

The following screen brings you to the vi interface, which should look like Figure 2.11.

In Figure 2.11, you should see the *3* highlighted on the line that reads as follows:

    id:3:initdefault:

This value on your screen should be *5*, which, if you look at the text above in vi, tells your boot sequence to enter X11 mode, which is X Window. Use the arrow keys to navigate down until the 5 is highlighted. Type **x** once to remove the 5. After the 5 has been eradicated, you will need to press **i** to enter insert mode in vi. Next enter the number **3** to change the mode to Full Multiuser Support. After your 3 is in place, press Esc to exit insert mode. In order to tell vi to write the file and to quit, type a colon (**:**) and type **wq**, which stands for *write quit* and press Enter. This will drop you back to your command prompt. Now the next time you reboot your computer, you will be taken directly to a text login prompt.

FIGURE 2.11
vi inittab

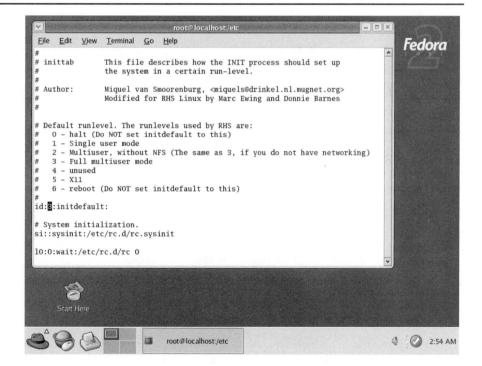

NOTE   Even though you are changing the bootup mode to text and essentially disabling the X Window interface, you can always start the X Window interface by typing **startx** from the console after you are logged in.

Take one last look at the delicious graphics of X Window and prepare to reboot! Type the following command in your terminal window to force your computer to reboot:

```
reboot
```

If the operation has gone as planned, you should have successfully surgically extracted the X Window interface on startup. Once rebooted, you should be presented with a text login prompt. Congratulations—Fedora Linux is now installed.

Linux Installation Checklist

After finishing this chapter, you should feel empowered. With your first installation of Linux, you've opened up a whole new world of possibilities. Pretty soon money will be flying at you from every direction. Okay, maybe not, but you will be learning more than ever as you begin Chapter 3, "Using Linux." Here are a few key points you should have a firm grasp of before continuing:

- Understand the major flavors of Linux and how Fedora fits into the mix.
- Determine the basic system hardware requirements for different levels of simultaneous users.
- Execute a download, checksum, and burn of your Linux ISOs.
- Be able to change your basic BIOS information, specifically the boot order of the devices on your computer.
- Start an installation and understand the differences between installation types: Personal Desktop, Workstation, Server, and Custom.
- Understand the Linux partitioning system and each filesystem type: ext2, ext3, software RAID, swap, and vfat.
- Know the functionality of the GRUB boot loader and how it affects your system.
- Have a basic knowledge of DHCP and eth0 network configuration.
- Be acquainted with packages and package groups.
- Be able to open a terminal window from the X window system, change directories, and open a file in vi.
- Know how to modify your boot sequence to change run levels.

If you haven't grasped one of these elements, take the time now to go back and review those areas. These concepts will give you a strong foundation on which to start building your knowledge base and will prepare you for the next chapter.

CHAPTER 3

Using Linux

- Booting Linux

- Introduction to the Linux Shell

- Understanding the Linux Filesytem Layout

N ow that you have your first Linux operating system installed, it's time to learn some basics. This chapter covers the boot sequence, login prompt, command-line interface (or *shell* for short), and an in-depth look into the Linux filesystem. These are the basic building blocks you need to learn before administering your server.

As with Chapter 2, "Installing Linux," if you feel you do not have a complete understanding of the principles and philosophies of this chapter, we encourage you to review any section until you understand it better. Some of you with more computer background, especially with a DOS- or Linux-based system, might grasp these concepts quicker than others. But if you feel you are having a hard time, *do not be discouraged!* After following the exercises in this chapter and practicing a little, you will be ready to begin administration in the next chapter.

Booting Linux

When your PC is initially powered up, it begins by running the Basic Input/Output System (BIOS). This system is typically located on an Erasable Programmable Read-Only Memory chip (EPROM), which tells your computer what hardware is available on which Interrupt ReQuest (IRQ) lines and channels. After your hardware has been initialized, the BIOS will then try to read the first sector of any bootable media such as a floppy disk, CD-ROM, or hard disk. As you might remember, in Chapter 2 you changed the boot sequence within the BIOS to make sure you were reading from the CD-ROM first in order to install Fedora Linux. This boot sector contains a small program that the BIOS will attempt to execute and pass control to.

During the installation process your boot loader, GRUB, was installed on the Master Boot Record (MBR). Because you don't have any media in the drive, GRUB then loads and you are taken directly to a selection screen asking you to choose which operating system to launch. If no selection is made within the 10 seconds allotted, the default operating system will attempt to run. In our case, this is Fedora Core 2. To speed up this process, simply press Enter, and Fedora will begin booting.

After Fedora begins booting, it will probe for all active devices attached to your computer. It does this by asking the BIOS what is available. As it receives this list, it begins loading the appropriate drivers and printing out the results as it goes. After the drivers have been loaded, the boot process mounts the /root partition. This partition is mounted as read-only so that it can be checked as it's mounted. If this process fails, the kernel will "panic" and immediately halt. The kernel will then start the program init, which becomes process 0 and contains the rest of the information to bring up the operating system.

Your First Package Installation

The process *init* is the master process of your system. Once ran, `init` will begin to spawn every other process that is available on your system. It will first check the `/etc/inittab` file that you changed in Chapter 2 to find the appropriate run level in which to create processes.

Next, `init` will locate the line with the action `sysinit` and execute the command file determined by that line. In our case, this is the `/etc/rc.d/rc.sysinit` file. The `rc.sysinit` file contains information that tells your system how to mount the `proc` filesystem, set the clock, start virtual memory, set the hostname, check a few key filesystems, and a few other tasks that are essential to bringing your system up. After that is complete, you will be presented with a login screen.

Because you are now at that login prompt, log in as *root* by typing **root** as your username and press Enter. The system will then ask for the password. This password is the one you chose during the installation procedure.

After you have successfully logged in, you are going to install your first package, which provides an easier editing utility than `vi`. This editor is called `pico` and it comes in the `pine` package; `pine` is a text-based e-mail program. First you will need to download `pine`. There is a specific rpm file that is made for Fedora Core 2 located on our servers via the Web at `www.linuxforum.com/lfiles/pine.i386.rpm`.

To download this package, you will be using a command called `wget`. This is a free utility for noninteractive download of files from the Web and it supports HTTP, HTTPS, and FTP protocols, as well as retrieval through HTTP proxies. To initiate the download, use this command:

```
wget http://www.linuxforum.com/lfiles/pine.i386.rpm
```

This will automatically download the newest version of `pine` compiled for Fedora Core 2 to your current directory, which is `/root`. This directory is your home directory for your *root* account. Other users' home directories will be located at `/home/username`.

Now that you have the binary distribution of `pine`, you will begin the installation process. Files with the `.rpm` extension can be installed by using the Red Hat Package Management system accessible with the command `rpm`. This command has several parameters that can be passed in order to perform different functions on packages. Parameters are passed into commands by using *flags*. A flag is usually preceded by one or two hyphens. For this command, you will be using three flags:

i designates the option to install the package.

v tells `rpm` to run in verbose mode.

h prints hash marks as the package installs.

Put together in the proper format, the command should read as follows:

```
rpm -ivh pine.i386.rpm
```

You will then be presented with a status bar of the installation, which should take only a few moments, before you are deposited at another prompt. Congratulations—you have just installed your first binary package. You will now be able to use the pico command to edit files. This command will make editing files much easier as you begin using Linux. Although it does not have some of the advanced functionality that vi does, it is a bit more user-friendly and will more closely resemble editors you are used to using.

A Closer Look at /etc/inittab

With pico now installed, you're ready to take a look at the rest of the boot process. Before the package installation, we were discussing the boot order of Linux. More specifically, we were referencing the init process launching the /etc/inittab file, which you edited in Chapter 2. Let's take another look at this file to see exactly what it does and why. Move to the /etc directory and use pico to edit the file by performing the following commands:

```
cd /etc
pico inittab
```

You will then be able to scroll through the inittab file by using the Up and Down arrow keys as well as the Ctrl+Y and Ctrl+V key combinations to move up and down pages, respectively. You will also notice a list of other hot keys located on the bottom two lines of your screen; these provide shortcuts to various other features. For now, take a closer look at the file and its parts:

```
#
# inittab    This file describes how the INIT process should
# set up the system in a certain run-level.
#
# Author:       Miquel van Smoorenburg,
# <miquels@drinkel.nl.mugnet.org>
# Modified for RHS Linux by Marc Ewing and Donnie Barnes
#

# Default runlevel. The runlevels used by RHS are:
#   0 - halt (Do NOT set initdefault to this)
#   1 - Single user mode
#   2 - Multiuser, without NFS (The same as 3, if you do
#       not have networking)
#   3 - Full multiuser mode
#   4 - unused
#   5 - X11
#   6 - reboot (Do NOT set initdefault to this)
#
id:3:initdefault:
```

The preceding lines, with the exception of the last, begin with a # symbol. This symbol "comments out" any text or code that is present for that line only. The file begins by describing the function of the file. In this case, it tells you that this file describes how the init process should be set up. It then lists the seven run levels available for this system. The first non-commented line is the line you modified in Chapter 2 in order to tell the system to boot into Full Multiuser mode instead of X11, which loads the X Window interface for Linux. Each entry within this file is set up as follows:

```
id:runlevels:action:process
```

The first line says to run initdefault at run level 3 and the ID will be set to id.

Next you will launch the /etc/rc.d/rc.sysinit script, which is responsible for, among other things, checking and mounting the /root filesystem and loading the keymap:

```
# System initialization.
si::sysinit:/etc/rc.d/rc.sysinit
```

More will be covered in the next section about the specifics of the rc.sysinit script.

Next the rc command is initialized at each run level:

```
l0:0:wait:/etc/rc.d/rc 0
l1:1:wait:/etc/rc.d/rc 1
l2:2:wait:/etc/rc.d/rc 2
l3:3:wait:/etc/rc.d/rc 3
l4:4:wait:/etc/rc.d/rc 4
l5:5:wait:/etc/rc.d/rc 5
l6:6:wait:/etc/rc.d/rc 6
```

Note that the initlevel is passed in an argument as well. For example, the script running for run level 3, as l3, is run as rc 3. In this example, the 3 is used as the argument to rc.

The next line tells the server to reboot if Ctrl+Alt+Del has been pressed. This is in case you need to halt the startup process without waiting for the entire system to finish booting.

```
# Trap CTRL-ALT-DELETE
ca::ctrlaltdel:/sbin/shutdown -t3 -r now
```

The following code line, like the preceding comment, describes setting up your system for a shutdown two minutes after a power failure notice has been registered by your system. You might wish to change the duration of time if your backup system is capable of running your computer for longer. This would afford you extra time to save any work and make a few changes before your system goes down. To change the amount of time, all you must do is modify the flag that reads +2. The 2 represents the number of minutes to wait before halting the system. Simply change this to your desired number, and your server will take care of everything else.

```
# When our UPS tells us power has failed, assume we have a
# few minutes of power left.  Schedule a shutdown for 2
```

```
# minutes from now.  This does, of course, assume you have
# power installed and your UPS connected and working
# correctly.
pf::powerfail:/sbin/shutdown -f -h +2 "Power Failure; System Shutting Down"
```

The next statement will cancel the shutdown of your system should power be restored to your battery backup:

```
# If power was restored before the shutdown kicked in,
# cancel it.
pr:12345:powerokwait:/sbin/shutdown -c "Power Restored; Shutdown Cancelled"
```

Notice the -c flag on the shutdown command. You can use this flag from the command line as well to cancel a shutdown that has been scheduled.

Whenever your computer's terminal has completely exited a shell, `init` will realize that it needs to respawn a new instance of `mingetty` and will respawn the terminal accordingly:

```
# Run gettys in standard runlevels
1:2345:respawn:/sbin/mingetty tty1
```

These lines use `mingetty` with a terminal type of tty$X$, where X is the terminal interface number. Having six terminals running means that you can log in six times as well. To switch between terminals, press Alt+FX, where X is the terminal number. By default you are using terminal 1. Try pressing Alt+F2 now and you will see another login prompt. Because you don't need to log in a second time right now, simply press Alt+F1 and you will be dropped back to your terminal that is already logged in. You can read more on shells and terminals in the "Login Process" section later in this chapter.

This last line is what was disabled when you changed your run level from 5 to 3. If the run level were still set to 5, this command would run and launch the X Window interface.

```
# Run gettys in standard runlevels
1:2345:respawn:/sbin/mingetty tty1
2:2345:respawn:/sbin/mingetty tty2
3:2345:respawn:/sbin/mingetty tty3
4:2345:respawn:/sbin/mingetty tty4
5:2345:respawn:/sbin/mingetty tty5
6:2345:respawn:/sbin/mingetty tty6

# Run xdm in runlevel 5
x:5:respawn:/etc/X11/prefdm -nodaemon
```

Linux Initialization Scripts

In the preceding section, we indicated that the second line initiated the /etc/rc.d/rc.sysinit file. Because this file contains 852 lines of code written using the Bash shell script format, we will be summarizing the actions it takes to check and mount the filesystem, load the keymap, and a few other important tasks.

The first thing the rc.sysinit file does is run itself through the initlog file for error logging. The initlog file is located in the /sbin directory and is a binary compiled to handle system logging should anything go awry.

The rc.sysinit file will then load the current hostname for your computer by consulting the /bin/hostname program. If this attempt does not return a valid hostname, it will attempt to run the /etc/sysconfig/network file, which contains important networking information and variables such as your hostname, gateway and domain name. If no file is found, networking will be disabled. If no hostname is set by this time and networking is enabled, the hostname will be set to localhost by default.

Next, the proc filesystem is mounted. This is a pseudo filesystem that acts as an interface to kernel runtime information. After it is mounted, you can list these "files," which contain variables that are constantly updated according the system's current state.

Next, the /etc/rc.d/init.d/functions file is run inline; this will provide common functions that can be accessed by the majority of scripts located in the /etc/init.d directory on your system. Residing in this file are functions such as killproc(), which will kill a process on the system, pidofproc(), which will find the process identifier (PID) of any given process, and confirm(), which will determine whether it is appropriate to run the service.

After the functions file has been run inline, some basic parameters are set up for your console, such as the system font and terminal type. A text banner is then printed to the screen with a small welcome message giving you the option to press I for an interactive startup. (You may or may not have noticed this during your initial boot sequence.) Next the graphical boot system is started, if possible.

NOTE   The graphical system will load only if the /usr partition is already mounted. If it has not been mounted, it will try again after it has run through its mounting process.

Next, your kernel's configuration parameters are set up by running the sysctl command. This command is initiated with the -e and -p parameters. The -e says to ignore errors about unknown keys, and the -p says to load the parameters based on a specified file. In this case, it is the /etc/sysctl.conf file. There are only four kernel parameters on your default system.

Next, your system clock is updated. If your system clock is controlled via a remote server, this is where the functionality resides that is responsible for setting your system time. After that has completed, the rc.sysinit file will then load your keymap. The default keymap file is /etc/sysconfig/console/default.kmap.

After your keymap is loaded, your hostname will be set, your command line will be created, and ACPI bits will be initiated. *ACPI,* or Advanced Configuration and Power Interface, is a driver controlling the voltage and power settings your motherboard receives. Next, the Universal Serial Bus (USB) devices and Human Interface Devices (HID) are initialized and mounted.

Some pre-built laptops might require a special ACPI patch or driver.

After these basic devices are mounted, your operating system will check whether there are certain switches configured for runtime and will make sure the system was shut down properly. If the system was shut down uncleanly, you will have the option to press Y to force a system integrity check or N to skip the check. If the filesystem check (which uses the command fsck) was run, your system will check for update quotas. Next, your /root filesystem will be remounted in read/write mode, and file swapping will be set up by using the command swapon. You can turn off swapping by using the swapoff command, but it is not recommended.

Next, the /etc/mtab is cleared, and the /root and /proc directories are mounted. With the /root filesystem now in read/write mode, logging can then be enabled. After this is complete, the sound modules are loaded. If the variable USEMODULES is not empty and the file /etc/modules.conf contains the text *alias sound* or *alias midi*, the modules from the subdirectories /etc/sound or /etc/midi are loaded. If the file /proc/sys/kernel/modprobe exists, and USEMODULES is enabled, the text /sbin/modprobe is written to the file /proc/sys/kernel/modprobe.

With the sound enabled, any RAID devices configured will now be initialized. First, /etc/fstab will be scanned looking for the noauto flag for the current device. If the noauto flag is found, initialization will be skipped for the device. Otherwise, Linux will attempt to use raidstart for the RAID initialization process. If raidstart fails, raidadd and raidrun will be used. If all of these fail, Linux will drop to a shell immediately.

Finally, all the other filesystems will be mounted, and the script will attempt to load the graphical boot if not previously done (as noted earlier). Once the filesystem mounts have been completed, the quotas will be checked for each of the new filesystems added, and various files within the /var directory will be removed to start fresh. Now the swap space is turned on, and if you have any USB or FireWire storage devices, they will be mounted as well.

A few other tasks will complete the /etc/rc.sysinit file and bring your system to a point where it is ready to start running the services and processes necessary for a fully operational system.

The *rc* Script and Its Kill and Startup Files

In the section covering the /etc/inittab file, you caught a glimpse of the following lines of code:

```
l0:0:wait:/etc/rc.d/rc 0
l1:1:wait:/etc/rc.d/rc 1
l2:2:wait:/etc/rc.d/rc 2
l3:3:wait:/etc/rc.d/rc 3
l4:4:wait:/etc/rc.d/rc 4
l5:5:wait:/etc/rc.d/rc 5
l6:6:wait:/etc/rc.d/rc 6
```

The rc script is responsible for initiating the kill and startup scripts that are appropriate for each run level. The first thing the rc script does is run each of the kill processes located in the /rcX.d directory, where *X* is equal to the run level (for example, rc3.d for run level 3). Each kill process is denoted by the beginning letter being a *K*. After each process has been killed, or attempted to be killed, each of the startup scripts for the appropriate run level will be run. A capital *S* is used to denote a startup script. You will notice that each of these scripts is simply a link to the actual daemon or service. This means that any of these scripts *could* potentially be run with the start or stop parameters and have the desired effect.

TIP   If you cd into the /etc/rc3.d directory and use the 11 command to retrieve a long listing of the directory, you can see that each of these files is actually a link to a script located within another directory. These links point to run level scripts.

NOTE   The /etc/rc3.d/SS99.local script points to /etc/rc.d/rc.local. This file is where most system administrators will place customizations that they wish to make to the boot process.

Run Level Scripts

The run level scripts you saw inside each /etc/rcX.d directory are soft links to the actual scripts that reside in the /etc/rc.d/init.d directory, and the directories themselves are links to the /etc/rc.d/rcX.d directories. These files represent startup and kill sequences for different daemons and processes that are needed in order for Linux to handle moving, interpolating, and processing data throughout the system. Some of these scripts might require other processes to already be running, so they must be initialized in sequence. The *kill scripts* are scripts that will end a process as gracefully as possible, releasing the system memory it uses and letting other processes know it is going offline.

A listing of the /etc/rc.d/init.d directory will reveal the many processes your system can run:

```
-rwxr-xr-x  1 root  root   1128 Oct 22 17:04 acpid
-rwxr-xr-x  1 root  root    834 Jul 10  2003 anacron
-rwxr-xr-x  1 root  root   1429 Oct 22 17:18 apmd
-rwxr-xr-x  1 root  root   1176 Sep 12 06:51 atd
-rwxr-xr-x  1 root  root   9221 Sep  8 14:11 autofs
-rwxr-xr-x  1 root  root   1316 Jun  6  2003 crond
-rwxr-xr-x  1 root  root   2312 Oct  2 12:56 cups
-rwxr-xr-x  1 root  root   1506 Oct 15 12:11 firstboot
-rwxr-xr-x  1 root  root  10198 Oct 28 17:26 functions
-rwxr-xr-x  1 root  root   1527 Aug  7 13:01 gpm
-rwxr-xr-x  1 root  root   5269 Sep 15 07:35 halt
-rwxr-xr-x  1 root  root   2601 Oct 23 06:54 httpd
-rwxr-xr-x  1 root  root   6319 Oct 23 10:18 iptables
-rwxr-xr-x  1 root  root   1414 Jul  3  2003 irda
```

```
-rwxr-xr-x   1 root   root   1744 Oct 22 10:55 irqbalance
-rwxr-xr-x   1 root   root   5838 Oct 23 14:53 isdn
-rwxr-xr-x   1 root   root   1084 Sep 25 09:22 kdcrotate
-rwxr-xr-x   1 root   root    652 Sep  3 21:33 killall
-rwxr-xr-x   1 root   root   2225 Oct 31 17:26 kudzu
-rwxr-xr-x   1 root   root   1684 Oct  2 06:03 lisa
-rwxr-xr-x   1 root   root   1746 Oct 16 15:38 messagebus
-rwxr-xr-x   1 root   root   1539 Oct 22 10:54 microcode_ctl
-rwxr-xr-x   1 root   root   2281 Oct 17 12:02 named
-rwxr-xr-x   1 root   root   5080 Jan  6  2003 netfs
-rwxr-xr-x   1 root   root   8025 Sep  9 00:47 network
-rwxr-xr-x   1 root   root   4257 Oct 22 21:17 nfs
-rwxr-xr-x   1 root   root   2833 Oct 22 21:17 nfslock
-rwxr-xr-x   1 root   root   2066 Oct 27 16:30 nscd
-rwxr-xr-x   1 root   root   3795 Oct 29 06:07 ntpd
-r-xr-xr-x   1 root   root   4590 Jan 25  2003 pcmcia
-rwxr-xr-x   1 root   root   1814 Sep 23 08:53 portmap
-rwxr-xr-x   1 root   root   1516 Jun 26  2002 random
-rwxr-xr-x   1 root   root   2246 Jan  6  2003 rawdevices
-rwxr-xr-x   1 root   root   1782 Oct 30 11:12 rhnsd
-rwxr-xr-x   1 root   root   1262 Oct 23 14:49 saslauthd
-rwxr-xr-x   1 root   root   2512 Oct 28 16:06 sendmail
-rwxr-xr-x   1 root   root   1175 Jul 10  2002 single
-rwxr-xr-x   1 root   root   3115 Oct 22 10:55 smartd
-rwxr-xr-x   1 root   root   1928 Sep 26 11:14 smb
-rwxr-xr-x   1 root   root   2647 Sep 17 12:14 sshd
-rwxr-xr-x   1 root   root   1369 Jun  6  2003 syslog
-rwxr-xr-x   1 root   root   1787 Sep 19 09:47 vncserver
-rwxr-xr-x   1 root   root   1555 Sep 26 11:14 winbind
-rwxr-xr-x   1 root   root   3428 Oct 24 18:10 xfs
-rwxr-xr-x   1 root   root   2497 Oct 12 03:41 xinetd
-rwxr-xr-x   1 root   root   2501 Sep 25 13:32 ypbind
-rwxr-xr-x   1 root   root   1036 Oct 29 09:54 yum
```

Each one of these commands can be run on the command line as well. In later exercises in this book, you will be using them quite frequently. Most of these commands can be run with the arguments start, stop, restart, and status.

Let's try checking the status of sendmail. If you are already in the /etc/rc.d/init.d/ directory, you can use this command:

```
./sendmail status
```

If not, you will need to type the full path to the command, like so:

```
/etc/rc.d/init.d/sendmail status
```

Notice that the argument for the command is passed in simply by adding a space on the end of the command and typing your argument. This is the most common method used for passing in an argument to the script you wish to run. After you have pressed Enter, you will be returned a single line of text that looks like the following:

```
sendmail (pid 1144 1135) is running...
```

This is a message from `sendmail` letting you know the process IDs it is currently running at and its status, in this case `running`. Try this with a few others if you wish. Some processes might not return anything if they are not running, and others might return a more verbose line such as the `yum` command's comment:

```
Nightly yum update is disabled.
```

After you've tested a few processes, you're ready to move on to the next section, where we will talk about the login process.

Login Process

After your system has finished booting, you are brought to a login prompt for your virtual terminal. This login prompt is displayed in this format:

```
hostname login:
```

The prompt displayed here is being created by the `mingetty` program you saw initiated within the `/etc/inittab` file. As we touched on before, this process is regenerated every time the user ends a session when at the console. If you were to log out of your system now, `mingetty` would be respawned and create a new login prompt. After you have typed in your username and pressed Enter, the login process is called, passing in your username. The login process will then prompt you to enter a password. After the password has been entered, the login process will verify that it is correct. On a successful match, it will then spawn your shell. If it fails to match the username with the password, an error message will be displayed indicating `login failure`. After you have exited your shell, `mingetty` will be respawned by `init`, and the entire process will be repeated again. This is why you saw the `respawn` command used in the `inittab` file.

NOTE   When your run level is set to 5, which is X11 or X Window, different programs are called that serve as a replacement for terminal 1. You might still have access to a normal terminal shell by switching to another terminal with the Ctrl+FX command, where *X* is the target terminal.

Exploring the Linux Shell

During the "Login Process" section, we talked about a successful login spawning a new user shell. This shell is your command-line interface that enables you to run commands locally on your system and perform any number of administration tasks. In our case, the shell used is the Bash shell.

To access the shell, however, you must pass through other programs. Most prominently, mingetty is displayed asking you for a login. The mingetty program was designed to be a minimal getty for the virtual terminals you use when accessing the system from the local keyboard and monitor; mingetty does not have all the functionality that getty does, but it requires only a fraction of the resources. If you will eventually be using the server as remote only and will not be using any local access to the system, you might wish to remove all but one of the mingetty calls in the inittab file to save approximately 8KB of memory per instance. You can still log in remotely because a remote login is usually available through the Secure Shell (SSH) connection protocols (controlled by the inetd daemon), but it is a good idea to leave one 8KB instance open in case you need to access the machine locally.

After a successful login, you are presented with a Bash shell. The *Bash shell* is a command language interpreter originally created for the GNU operating system. Bash stands for Bourne-Again SHell, which is a pun based on Stephen Bourne's name. Bourne originally created the current Unix shell /bin/sh, which first appeared in the Seventh Edition Bell Labs Research version of Unix. The Bash shell also incorporates a large amount of the /bin/csh, or C Shell, functionality to allow for a more diverse set of instructions and commands available to the user.

Although a shell is a command-line interpreter, it also acts as a programming language on its own. From this concept stems much of the power of the Linux operating system. Any shell command can be used synchronously or asynchronously. This, in effect, means that processes can be executed in order, each waiting for the previous to finish, or they can be executed in parallel (multitasking). Furthermore, there are *redirection* constructs in place that allow micro-control over the input and output of any of the commands. The shell also allows control over the commands' environments in the form of flags and other arguments.

Let's take a closer look at some fundamental principles that you should know before delving into more advanced concepts:

Tab   You can use the Tab key to finish a file or directory name for you. If you begin typing **super** for *supercalifragilisticexpialidocious*, just use Tab to auto-complete the rest of the file. If more than one word is a match for what you have typed so far, than nothing will appear to happen or auto-complete will fill in up to the fork in the matching. Pressing Tab again will give you a listing of all possible matches. After you enter a few more letters that result in only a single match for the rest of the string, pressing the Tab key again will complete the string.

Escape character   Bash uses the backslash (\) character as an escape character. An escape character preserves the literal value of the next character that follows the backslash. If you wish to have a backslash contained within an argument, then you will need to use two back-slashes (\\) in order to escape the backslash itself.

Single quotes   Single quotes are used as enclosing characters to preserve the literal value for an entire string. Use single quotes when changing to a directory that contains a space or other special character that might interfere with the command line. For instance, if you needed to move into a directory called /Special Files, you would use this command:

```
cd /'Special Files'
```

Without enclosing the directory name in quotes, you would confuse the cd command because it does not take more than one argument. You cannot use a single quote within your two enclosing single quotes.

Double quotes   Enclosing a string in double quotes will also preserve the literal value, except for the characters $, `, and \. Backslashes can be used within double quotes to escape characters as discussed previously.

ANSI-C quoting   Words that are used in the form of $'*string*' are also treated specially. Any backslashed characters contained within the string will be replaced according to the ANSI C standard. They are as follows:

```
\a   alert(bell)
\b   backspace
\e   an escape character (not ANSI C)
\f   form feed
\n   newline
\r   carriage return
\t   horizontal tab
\v   vertical tab
\\   backslash
\'   single quote
\nnn   the eight-bit character whose value is the octal value nnn (one to
three digits)
\xHH   the eight-bit character whose value is the hexadecimal value HH (one
or two hex digits)
\cx   a control-x character
```

Here is an example that substitutes a newline character and a tab:

```
echo First Line $'\n'Second Line with a $'\t'Tab
```

The result would look like:

```
First line
Second Line with a    Tab
```

Locale-specific translation   Any double-quoted string that is immediately preceded by a dollar sign will cause the string to be translated according to its current locale.

Pipelines   A *pipeline* is used to send the output of one command directly to another command. You will use the pike symbol (|) to denote a pipe. A good example is piping the result from a directory listing into the more command, which will enable you to view one page at a time in case your directory is rather large:

```
ls -al | more
```

Redirection   *Redirection* refers to a few specific characters: <, >, <<, and >>. These characters are used to redirect output information from one command or function into another or into a file. You use the command

```
ll > listing.txt
```

to push all the data retrieved from a long listing of the current directory into a file called listing.txt. You can use the opposite symbol, <, to push all of the content of a file into a command. The combination >> is used to append data to a file, and << is used to append data from a file into a command or command-line program.

> **NOTE**   You should be aware that the > is destructive, meaning that it will overwrite any content within the specified target file unless the noclobber option has been specifically set for your shell. set -C would set the noclobber option. If you still wish to overwrite a file with noclobber set then you can use >|.

Understanding the Bash Environment

After the Bash shell has been launched, a few configuration files are analyzed by the system to establish your shell's appearance. Most important, the /etc/profile file is run before your home directory, also referred to as $HOME, is scanned for one of three files. In order they are .bash_profile, .bash_login, and .profile. After one of these files is located, it is read to determine a set of environment variables for your shell. In our Fedora distribution, the .bash_profile is used, which also calls the .bashrc file. A list of the current environment variables that are set can be retrieved with the following command:

```
env
```

You will then be returned the following lines:

```
HOSTNAME=localhost.localdomain
TERM=xterm
SHELL=/bin/bash
HISTSIZE=1000
SSH_CLIENT=192.168.0.20 2200 22
SSH_TTY=/dev/pts/0
USER=efilson
LS_COLORS=no=00:fi=00:di=00;34:ln=00;36:pi=40;33:so=00;35:
bd=40;33;01:cd=40;33;01:or=01;05;37;41:mi=01;05;37;41:
```

```
ex=00;32:*.cmd=00;32:*.exe=00;32:*.com=00;32:*.btm=00;32:
*.bat=00;32:*.sh=00;32:*.csh=00;32:*.tar=00;31:*.tgz=00;31:
*.arj=00;31:*.taz=00;31:*.lzh=00;31:*.zip=00;31:*.z=00;31:
*.Z=00;31:*.gz=00;31:*.bz2=00;31:*.bz=00;31:*.tz=00;31:
*.rpm=00;31:*.cpio=00;31:*.jpg=00;35:*.gif=00;35:*.bmp=00;
35:*.xbm=00;35:*.xpm=00;35:*.png=00;35:*.tif=00;35:
MAIL=/var/spool/mail/efilson
PATH=/usr/local/bin:/bin:/usr/bin:/usr/X11R6/bin:/home/efilson/bin
INPUTRC=/etc/inputrc
PWD=/home/efilson
LANG=en_US.UTF-8
SSH_ASKPASS=/usr/libexec/openssh/gnome-ssh-askpass
SHLVL=1
HOME=/home/efilson
LOGNAME=efilson
SSH_CONNECTION=192.168.0.20 2200 192.168.0.18 22
LESSOPEN=|/usr/bin/lesspipe.sh %s
G_BROKEN_FILENAMES=1
_=/bin/env
```

Almost any program can change, unset, and create these variables. Manipulation of these variables is the key to changing the look and functionality of your shell. If you wish to create any custom variables, you can edit the .bashrc or .bash_profile files.

If you retrieve a full directory listing of your home directory (ls -al), excluding *root*'s home directory, you will also see a .bash_history file. This file is used for storing the history of commands you have typed. The number of commands stored depends on an environment variable (which by default is set to 1000). This is what enables the shortcut Up arrow and Down arrow keys to scroll through your history. Go ahead and try reviewing your previous commands by using the Up arrow. You can then use the Left and Right arrows to move through your command line and make changes before pressing Enter to run the command. This is especially useful when typing commands containing long pathnames.

There are books written on just the shell itself, so we won't spend too much time delivering all the details to you. You should know, however, that the Bash shell offers several improvements over both of its ancestors, including:

- Command-line editing
- Command history of unlimited size
- Job control
- Shell functions and aliases
- Indexed arrays of unlimited size
- Integer arithmetic in any base from 2 to 64

If you are interested in learning more about the Bash shell than is discussed here, you should visit www.linuxforum.com/bash-reference.php. There you will find a complete manual and reference guide for the Bash shell.

Navigating through Linux

If you are not used to using a command-line interface (for example, with the Bash shell or with DOS), navigating the Linux filesystem might seem complicated at first, but do not fear. We've put together a list of basic commands that will make your job much easier. The commands contained in this section are absolutely paramount, and you will need to be deeply familiar—nay, intimate—with each of them. If this is your first time using Linux, you might want to throw a bookmark in the page so that you can refer back to this section while you get adjusted to this new system architecture. The following few pages will become an invaluable resource when beginning with Linux.

You should not be intimidated by the length of the list. After you begin using Linux, these commands will become second nature. If you need any additional information on each command, simply use the man command and pass in the function name as the only argument. This will take you to the manual page for the command. You can use the arrow keys to scroll up and down, and pressing Q will exit the manual. We've provided the following functions in alphabetical order to make it a bit easier should you need to reference this section again:

cat   The cat command is used to concatenate files and print the output to the screen. Because Linux is all about text files, you can use this command to view the contents of a file without entering an editor. Simply use cat *filename* to view a file. You can also pipe the results to the less or more command to allow for interactive scrolling.

cd   The cd command stands for *change directory*. We first showed you this command in Chapter 2. The proper usage is cd *path*. This is probably the most common command you will be using for navigating your way through the Linux filesystem. You can also use the command by itself with no parameters to change to the home directory of the user who owns the shell you are currently in.

chmod   chmod is a command used to change file permissions. File permissions in Linux are displayed when retrieving a long listing of a file or files. The first block on each line will have 10 characters. The first character denotes whether the listing is a directory, file, device, link, socket, or pipe. The character d means the listing is a directory, - is for a file, b is for a buffered device, c is for an unbuffered device, l is for a link, s is for socket, and p is for pipe. The next nine characters are split into three equal sections: user : group : world. Each section of three characters represents r for read, w for write, and x for execute. For example:

```
drwxr-xr--
```

The preceding line means that the file is a directory; the user who owns the file has read, write, and execute permissions; the group who owns the file has read and execute permissions; and the *world* (meaning every other user on the system who is not the file owner and is not in the group who owns the file) has only read permissions. For the basics on file ownership, see the chown command. For now, just be familiar with the command. We will cover this in more detail in the next chapter, in the section "Managing Users and Groups."

chown   chown is used to modify the ownership of a file or directory. When retrieving a directory listing, you will find that the third and fourth blocks are username and group name, respectively. When chowning a file, simply use:

```
chown flags username:groupname
```

A common flag for this command is the -R flag, which indicates to perform this function recursively. *Recursive* means that it will repeat itself on each file contained in the directory specified and in each subdirectory of that directory, and so on. We will also be covering this command in depth in the next chapter. For now you should also be aware that you can leave off the colon and group name to change only the user who owns the file. If you wish to change just the group, you should use chgrp.

cp   The cp command is the copy command. You can use this command to create duplicates of directories or files. A common flag combination for the cp command is -rfp, which stands for *recursive force preserve*. The preserve argument will preserve the ownership and timestamp of the original file. You can also use the -l command to create a link to the file instead of actually copying it. There are soft links and hard links in Linux. A *soft link* is much like a shortcut in Windows; it merely acts as a pointer to the existing file. A *hard link* is a new name for the target file, which will update itself whenever its twin is changed, and visa versa.

exit   The exit command is used to exit a shell. If you have used the su command to log in as a different user, then typing **exit** will exit only that shell and not the entire virtual terminal.

find   The find command is your friend; this command will help you locate files in your filesystem. You might choose to use the locate command described later in this list, but it is important to note that the locate command is based on a database-type system that is updated every night at midnight. Any files created after last night at midnight will not be found. So instead, use the find command with the following syntax:

```
find path -name 'filename string'
```

You can also specify a myriad of other flags, such as time and size, to narrow your search. Use the man find command to learn more.

grep   grep is used to find file(s) that contain a string matching the argument you pass in. By default, grep will print the line in the file(s) that match your argument. Here is the proper format for the grep command:

```
grep options pattern file(s)
```

The following example will return the lines of any files inside /usr/local/apache/vdocs that match the term *PHP Freaks*:

```
grep 'PHP Freaks' /usr/local/apache/vdocs/*
```

The * tells grep to search in any files located in the given directory. The asterisk is also known as a *wildcard*.

ll   ll is just an *alias*, or shortcut, for the ls command with -al flags. The ll is short for *long listing* and is mentioned here to provide you with a shortcut for retrieving long directory listings. Check the ls command for the appropriate syntax for this command.

ls   The ls command is the directory listing command. There are a plethora of flags for this command to enable you to sort and limit your results. Running the man ls command will give you a complete listing. Some of the more popular flags are listed here:

```
-a    Do not hide directory listings that begin with .
-l    Use the long listing format
-r    Reverse the order while sorting
-t    Sort by modification time
-F    Classify: this will append indicators to the
          listing such as */=@|
```

The following example will return all of the files, including those that begin with a period, starting with the oldest file first in long listing format:

```
ls -rtal
```

This can be useful when trying to find newly added files. You can also specify a directory to list as an argument after your flags.

man   The man command is used to access your manual. One of the most useful commands in Linux, the manual can provide a wealth of information on virtually every program or command on your system. Occasionally, when using the man function, you will come across a command with multiple entries. What makes these entries unique is their locations within different sections of the manual. If this is the case, you can use the -S flag followed by a colon-separated list of sections to specify which sections to search.

mkdir   mkdir is the command used to make (create) a new directory. Just pass in the name of your directory as the only argument, and your directory will be created. If any special characters are needed, make sure you enclose the directory name string in the appropriate quotes. However, it is best to avoid using special characters in directories and filenames to avoid overcomplicating an otherwise simple command.

mv   The mv command is used to move files in your system. The optional -f flag will force the move. Both directories and files can be moved in this manner. You can also use the mv command to move a file or directory to /dev/null, which will effectively delete the file. However, it is advised that you use the rm command covered later in this list.

pico   Chapter 2 introduced you to the pico command and how to install it via an RPM distribution for Fedora Core 2. This command will be used throughout this book for its ease of use over vi for new users. A simple pico *filename* will open the file in the pico editor.

pwd   pwd stands for *print working directory*. This command will return a line indicating the directory in which you are located. This can be especially useful if you are remotely logged in and wish to copy your current location into memory to paste or print later.

rm   This command is your remove command. It is most often used with the -rf flags for *recursive* and *force*. But beware: this command will immediately remove your files. There is no *are you sure*. They are simply destroyed. Never to be seen again—by anyone. There is no undelete command to correct a mistake as in Windows. Even experienced users might slip and make a mistake with this one, so double-check your command before pressing Enter.

su   The su command stands for *switch user*. The switch user command is used to change from user to user on the system. Using the exit command will close the current user section and return you to the previous user shell you were in. When remotely logging in to a system that has multiple users, it is generally good practice to log in as your own personal username and then su to *root* by using the su - command. This will populate the appropriate log files and histories with any commands that you enter. Later, if a mistake is found, you can find which account is responsible and take the appropriate action.

tar   The tar command is another command you will use quite often. It is an archiving utility that now includes a built-in compression algorithm called gzip and another named Bzip2. You will often hear of files that contain the .tar extension as *tarballs*. This book will teach you how to download tarballs of your needed programs and install them. To untar a file, use this command:

```
tar -xvf filename
```

The optional -z flag is used if the file has a .z or .gzip extension. The -z flag when unarchiving a tar file will automatically decompress it as well. To create a tar archive, use this command:

```
tar -cvfz filename files
```

The preceding line will create a gzip tarball with a filename of *filename* and will include the files and/or directories specified for the *files* argument. For a Bzip2 file you would use the -j switch.

vi   vi stands for *visual editor*. This classic editing program for Unix houses a powerful set of functionality for finding and replacing and repeating operations to make changes and produce files very rapidly. Its abundance of functionality produces excellent results; however, it acts as a double-edged sword because it is complicated for a beginning user to grasp.

whoami   The whoami command will tell you exactly *who* you are. Not in the metaphysical sense, but which user you are in the system. Some installation commands will vary depending on whether you are *root*. Checking who you are can oftentimes bypass some frustration when programs don't seem to compile correctly.

These commands should give you an excellent foundation for navigating through the Linux filesystem. You will need to use these commands throughout your affair with Linux, so committing these to memory now is an excellent idea. If the majority of these commands are new to you, remember to place a bookmark in the beginning of this section for future reference. After you have done that, you will be ready to head into the next section.

Understanding the Linux Filesystem Layout

The Linux filesystem layout has been organized carefully so those with a basic understanding of the filesystem can find files quickly and easily. Although it might not seem so at first, after you grow accustomed to the layout, you will breeze through directories targeting the exact locations you need. Strict naming conventions and storage locations for files enable Linux to continue its open source development without anyone getting in anyone else's way. Let's take a look inside each of the root-level directories and the files they contain. Some of the more important subdirectories and their files are also included:

```
drwxr-xr-x    2 root    root     4096 Jan  9 11:37 bin
drwxr-xr-x    4 root    root     1024 Jan  8 16:41 boot
drwxr-xr-x   21 root    root   118784 Jan  9 10:19 dev
drwxr-xr-x   57 root    root     4096 Jan 13 04:02 etc
drwxr-xr-x    3 root    root     4096 Jan  9 10:15 home
drwxr-xr-x    2 root    root     4096 Oct  7 07:16 initrd
```

```
drwxr-xr-x    9 root    root    4096 Jan  9 11:33 lib
drwx------    2 root    root   16384 Jan  8 11:38 lost+found
drwxr-xr-x    2 root    root    4096 Sep  8 14:11 misc
drwxr-xr-x    3 root    root    4096 Jan  9 10:19 mnt
drwxr-xr-x    2 root    root    4096 Oct  7 07:16 opt
dr-xr-xr-x   49 root    root       0 Jan  9 05:18 proc
drwxr-x---   13 root    root    4096 Jan 13 15:09 root
drwxr-xr-x    2 root    root    8192 Jan  9 11:37 sbin
drwxrwxrwt    6 root    root    4096 Jan 13 04:02 tmp
drwxr-xr-x   15 root    root    4096 Jan  8 16:40 usr
drwxr-xr-x   19 root    root    4096 Jan  8 16:49 var
```

This is an exact representation of what you should have if you installed Fedora Core 2 from Chapter 2.

/bin

The /bin directory contains all the essential binary programs and commands needed for Linux. Go ahead and change directories into the /bin directory and retrieve a directory listing. Here you will see the majority of commands listed in the previous section, excluding commands that are built into the Bash shell. As you install software and packages on your computer, this directory will expand as new priority commands are added.

/boot

The /boot directory contains status files of the boot loader and the Linux kernel. Go ahead and cd into this directory and take a look—not really too much to see here, mostly NPTL files (Native POSIX Thread Library files) required for your boot sequence. This is also where the GRUB files are located, inside the directory /boot/grub.

/dev

The /dev directory holds the special device files. Taking a look at this directory will yield some interesting results. If you are retrieving a long listing, you will see tens of pages of results. Each one of these represents a specific device on your system, whether it is a hard (hardware) or soft (software) device. Look at where the file size is normally located; it has been split into two parts. The first part represents the *major device number*; this is a kind of parameter passed to the kernel when accessing the device and represents the device driver. The second part represents the *minor device number* and is passed to the kernel to allow further device selection.

As an example, look at the hard disk device files. These are preceded by the characters hd for IDE drives. Your first hard disk is hda. If you perform ll hda*, you will be able to see each minor device listed as well. Notice the first device number column reads 3 because it is the third device. Each listing then has a different *minor device number*, which pertains to the partition on that device, or in the case of *hda*, the 0 specifies accessing the entire drive.

> **WARNING**   Accessing the "files" in the device directory means accessing some sort of device and *not* the filesystem. Piping data to one of these devices could have a severely unexpected effect.

Some other important devices you might want to take note of include mouse, CD-ROM, CD writer, scanner, and modem. Any media devices can usually be mounted to a specific directory by using the mount command. For instance, running the command

```
mount device location
```

will mount the device specified to the location you enter. It is most commonly mounted as the device name under the /mnt directory (for example, /dev/cdrom mounted to /mnt/cdrom).

/etc

The /etc directory holds configuration files specific to your computer. Almost all major configuration files are housed here, and applications that require more than a few files will have their own subdirectories. Retrieving a listing of this directory will astound you because of the number of files located here. The sheer volume of files serves as proof to the power of Linux and its ability to be customized.

Let's look at some of the more important files located in this directory. We have sorted them by category for you for quick reference, as shown in Tables 3.1–3.3.

TABLE 3.1   Network-Related Files

File	Description
exports	Network File System (NFS) server exports
host.conf	Configuration for resolving domain names
hosts	List of hosts with IP addresses
hosts.allow	TCP wrapper allowed hosts
hosts.deny	TCP wrapper deny hosts
protocols	A list of protocols with descriptions
resolv.conf	Configuration for resolving domain names
services	Services with their ports/protocols

TABLE 3.2 Shell Profiles

File	Description
bashrc	The default for all users
csh.cshrc	The C shell profile
csh.login	C shell login functionality
profile	Bash shell profile
shells	List of all shells for your system

TABLE 3.3 Miscellaneous System Files

File	Description
passwd	User definitions
shadow	Shadow password file with MD5 passwords
group	Group definitions
gshadow	Shadow group file
aliases	System and mail aliases
aliases.db	System and mail aliases
crontab	System crontab configuration, which holds a list of commands to run on a schedule
fstab	List of filesystems and mount points
inittab	init process configuration
motd	Message off the day
mtab	List of currently mounted filesystems
printcap	Printer configuration
sysctl.conf	Kernel configuration for Fedora
syslog.conf	Configuration for logging
termcap	Terminal type descriptions

You will be using a lot of these files frequently as you customize your server to your needs. Chapters 4–7 will delve into the setup and configuration of these files for various aspects of your system. For now, just be familiar with some of the names and a general overview of what each file pertains to.

Besides the files that are located within this directory, there are also quite a few important subdirectories as well. Let's take a look at some:

/etc/cron.d   This directory houses scripts run by the crontab file. The crontab is a file parsed by the cron daemon (crond) and determines at what times a script should be run.

/etc/cron.daily   The daily cron directory will run any scripts located within it once a day. You do not need to have a crontab entry for the scripts located here.

/etc/cron.hourly   Like the /etc/cron.daily directory, this directory does not require scripts located within it to have a separate crontab entry. The only difference here is that, much like the name suggests, the scripts are run hourly.

/etc/cron.monthly   Scripts located within this directory also do not need a separate crontab entry. The only difference here is that, much like the name suggests, the scripts are run monthly.

/etc/cron.weekly   Like all of its brothers, the files here are run automatically. The weekly extension means that the files will be run weekly.

/etc/default   The /etc/default directory contains the useradd file by default (no pun intended). This file contains the following:

```
# useradd defaults file
GROUP=100
HOME=/home
INACTIVE=-1
EXPIRE=
SHELL=/bin/bash
SKEL=/etc/skel
```

Each time a new user is created, these values will be assigned to the user. When customizing your system, you might wish to change the values.

/etc/httpd   This is where your web server configuration files are located for Apache. There will be much more about this later in Chapter 8, "Apache Web Server: Installation and Configuration."

/etc/mail   This directory contains configuration files for sendmail, a program used to send mail from your system. There are various configuration files pertaining to access levels and users located here.

/etc/pcmcia   This directory contains all of the configuration and startup files necessary for Personal Computer Memory Card International Association (PCMCIA) operations. You will most likely not need these unless you are using a laptop.

/etc/ppp   Files pertaining to your Point-to-Point Protocol (PPP) are located here. PPP is used for Internet traffic. Your firewall-masq and stand-alone configuration files are also located here.

/etc/profile.d   This directory contains other profile information for the system shells. The color creation for your `ls` command is kept here as well as the alias for `ll`. Language files and `less` configuration can be found in the `lang*` and `less*` files.

/etc/rc.d   We covered the files in this directory extensively earlier in this chapter. To summarize, these files are used during the initial boot sequence in Linux to set up your filesystems and basic commands. If you would like more information on these files, see the earlier section "The `rc` Script and its Kill and Startup Files."

/etc/rpm   Earlier in this chapter, you used `rpm` to install `pine`, which includes `pico`. The configuration files for `rpm` are contained in this directory. There are relatively few files contained in this directory. The macro files contain pre-built commands that `rpm` uses internally, and the `platform` file contains a single line that states your system type.

/etc/security   The `/etc/security` directory houses files that set permissions for specified users or groups pertaining to login access and limits. We will be covering this file in more detail in Chapter 6, "Linux Security."

/etc/ssh   The `/etc/ssh` directory contains configurations and keys for the Secure Shell login procedure. A system of *keys* is used for security when you access the server remotely in order to transfer encrypted information. We will be discussing keys and `ssh` in greater detail in the next chapters. Modifying the `ssh_config` file will change settings for all users who access the system remotely through `ssh`.

/etc/sysconfig   Changing to this directory and retrieving a directory listing will present you with many of the files used in configuring your system. You can read `/usr/share/doc/initscripts-x.xx/sysconfig.txt` for the complete list with all options. The *x.xx* is the Linux kernel version. Here are some of the major configuration files contained in this directory and a few of the options available within each one:

> **/etc/sysconfig/authconfig**

```
used by authconfig to store information about the system's
user information and authentication setup; changes made to
this file have no effect until the next time authconfig is
run

    USEHESIOD=no
      Whether or not the hesiod naming service is in use.
      If not set, authconfig examines the passwd setting in
      /etc/nsswitch.conf.
    USELDAP=no
      Whether or not LDAP is used as a naming service.  If
      not set,  authconfig examines the passwd setting in
      /etc/nsswitch.conf.
```

USENIS=no
  Whether or not NIS is in use. If not set, authconfig
  examines the passwd setting in /etc/nsswitch.conf.
USEKERBEROS=no
  Whether or not Kerberos is in use. If not set,
  authconfig examines the settings in
  /etc/pam.d/system-auth.
USELDAPAUTH=no
  Whether or not LDAP is being used for authentication.
  If not set, authconfig examines the settings in
  /etc/pam.d/system-auth. Note that this option is
  separate from USELDAP, and that neither implies
  the other.
USEMD5=no
  Whether or not MD5-based hashing should be used when
  setting passwords. If not set, authconfig examines
  the settings in /etc/pam.d/system-auth. This option
  affects authentication using both local files and
  LDAP.
USESHADOW=no
  Whether or not shadow passwords are in use. If not
  set, authconfig checks for the existence of
  /etc/shadow.
USESMBAUTH=no
  Whether or not SMB authentication is in use. If not
  set, authconfig examines the settings in
  /etc/pam.d/system-auth.

/etc/sysconfig/clock

  deprecated values from earlier releases:

CLOCKMODE=GMT
  indicates that the clock is set to UTC

CLOCKMODE=ARC
    on alpha only indicates the ARC console's 42-year
    time offset is in effect currently correct values:
        UTC=true,yes
          Indicates that the hardware clock is set to
          UTC.
        UTC=no,false
          Indicates that the hardware clock is set to
          Local Time.
    Not having UTC set defaults to the last used (if
    recorded in the adjtime file), or to localtime, if
    not adjtime file exists.

ARC=true
  on alpha only indicates the ARC console's 42-year
  time offset is in effect; otherwise the normal Unix
  epoch is assumed.

SRM=true
  on alpha only indicates the SRM 1900 epoch is in
  effect; otherwise the normal Unix epoch is assumed.

ZONE="filename"
  indicates the zonefile under /usr/share/zoneinfo that
  /etc/localtime is a copy of, for example:
  ZONE="US/Eastern"

/etc/sysconfig/desktop

DESKTOP=GNOME|KDE|AnotherLevel
  This determines the default desktop for new users.
DISPLAYMANAGER=GNOME|KDE|XDM
  This determines display manager started by
  /etc/X11/prefdm, independent of the desktop.

/etc/sysconfig/init

BOOTUP=<some bootup mode>
BOOTUP=graphical
  means use X Windows graphical boot up
BOOTUP=color
  means colorized text mode boot display.
BOOTUP=verbose
  means old style display Anything else means
  simplified display, but without color or ANSI-
  formatting
LOGLEVEL=<a number>
  Sets the initial console logging level for the
  kernel. The default is 7. 8 means everything
  (including debugging); 1 means nothing except kernel
  panics. syslogd will override this once it starts.
RES_COL=<a number>
  Column of the screen to start status labels at.
  Defaults to 60
MOVE_TO_COL=<a command>
  A command to move the cursor to $RES_COL.
  Defaults to nasty ANSI sequences output by echo
  -e.

SETCOLOR_SUCCESS=<a command>
  A command to set the color to a color indicating
  success.   Defaults to nasty ANSI sequences output by
  echo -e setting the color to green.
SETCOLOR_FAILURE=<a command>
  A command to set the color to a color indicating
  failure. Defaults to nasty ANSI sequences output by
  echo -e setting the color to red.
SETCOLOR_WARNING=<a command>
  A command to set the color to a color indicating
  warning. Defaults to nasty ANSI sequences output by
  echo -e setting the color to yellow.
SETCOLOR_NORMAL=<a command>
  A command to set the color to 'normal'. Defaults to
  nasty ANSI sequences output by echo -e.
PROMPT=yes|no
  Set to 'no' to disable the key check for interactive
  mode.

/etc/sysconfig/keyboard

KEYTABLE=<keytable file>
  for example: KEYTABLE="/usr/lib/kbd/keytables/us.map"
  If you dump a keymap (using 'dumpkeys') to
  /etc/sysconfig/console/default.kmap it will be loaded
  on bootup before filesystems are mounted/checked.
  This could be useful if you need to emergency type
  the root password. This has to be a dumped keymap,
  as opposed to copying the shipped keymap files, as
  the shipped files include other maps from the
  /usr/lib/kbd/keytables directory.
KEYBOARDTYPE=sun|pc
  on SPARC only, sun means a sun keyboard is attached
  on /dev/kbd, pc means a PS/2 keyboard is on ps/2
  port.

/etc/sysconfig/mouse

MOUSETYPE=microsoft|mouseman|mousesystems|ps/2|msbm|l
ogibm|atibm|logitech|mmseries|mmhittab
XEMU3=yes|no
  (emulate three buttons with two buttons whenever
  necessary, most notably in X)
DEVICE=<a device node>
    (the device of the mouse)

/etc/sysconfig/network

```
NETWORKING=yes|no
HOSTNAME=<fully qualified domain name by default>
GATEWAY=<gateway IP>
GATEWAYDEV=<gateway device>
  (e.g. eth0)
NISDOMAIN=<nis domain name>
VLAN=yes|no
IPX=yes|no
IPXAUTOPRIMARY=on|off
  (note, that MUST be on|off, not yes|no)
IPXAUTOFRAME=on|off (again, not yes|no)
IPXINTERNALNETNUM=<netnum>
IPXINTERNALNODENUM=<nodenum>
```

All the IPX stuff is optional, and should default to off.

```
NETWORKING_IPV6=yes|no
  Enable or disable global IPv6 initialization
  Default: no
IPV6FORWARDING=yes|no
  Enable or disable global forwarding of incoming IPv6
  packes on all interfaces.  Note: Actual packet
  forwarding cannot be controlled per-device, use
  netfilter6 for such issues Default: no
IPV6INIT=yes|no
  Enable or disable IPv6 configuration for all
  interfaces Use with caution!  Default: value not set
  in this file
IPV6_AUTOCONF=yes|no
  Sets the default for device-based autoconfiguration.
  Default: yes if IPV6FORWARDING=no, no if
IPV6FORWARDING=yes
IPV6_ROUTER=yes|no
  Sets the default for device-based Host/Router
  behaviour.  Default: yes if IPV6FORWARDING=yes, no if
  IPV6FORWARDING=no
IPV6_AUTOTUNNEL=yes|no
  Controls automatic IPv6 tunneling.
  Default: no
IPV6_DEFAULTGW=<IPv6 address[%interface]>
  (optional) Add a default route through specified
  gateway An interface can be specified: required for
  link-local addresses
IPV6_DEFAULTDEV=<interface>
  (optional) Add a default route through specified
  interface without specifying next hop. Type of
```

```
     interface will be tested whether this is allowed
IPV6_RADVD_PIDFILE=<pid-file> (optional)
     Location of PID file for controlling radvd
```

/etc/sysconfig/rawdevices

This is used for setting up raw device to block device
mappings. It has the format:
```
        <rawdev> <major> <minor>
        <rawdev> <blockdev>
```
For example:
```
    /dev/raw/raw1 /dev/sda1
    /dev/raw/raw2 8 5
```

/etc/sysconfig/pcmcia

```
    PCMCIA=yes|no
    PCIC=i82365|tcic
    PCIC_OPTS=<socket driver timing parameters>
    CORE_OPTS=<pcmcia_core options>
    CARDMGR_OPTS=<cardmgr options>
```

/etc/sysconfig/saslauthd

used by the saslauthd init script (part of the cyrus-sasl
package) to control which arguments are passed to saslauthd
at startup time; changes made to this file have no effect
until saslauthd is restarted

```
    MECH=shadow
      controls which data source saslauthd will consult
      when checking user passwords; run 'saslauthd -a' to
      get a full list of available authentication
      mechanisms
    SOCKETDIR=/var/run/saslauthd
      controls in which directory saslauthd will be
      directed to create its listening socket; any change
      to this value will require a corresponding change in
      client configuration files
```

/etc/sysconfig/sendmail

```
DAEMON=yes|no
   yes implies -bd (i.e., listen on port 25 for new
   mail)
QUEUE=1h
   given to sendmail as -q$QUEUE -q option is not given
   to sendmail if /etc/sysconfig/sendmail exists and
   QUEUE is empty or undefined.
```

/etc/sysconfig/i18n

```
LANG=
   set locale for all categories, can be any two letter
   ISO language code
LC_CTYPE=
   localedata configuration for classification and
   conversion of characters
LC_COLLATE=
   localedata configuration for collation (sort order)
   of strings
LC_MESSAGES=
   localedata configuration for translation of yes and
   no messages
LC_NUMERIC=
   localedata configuration for non-monetary numeric
   data
LC_MONETARY=
   localedata configuration for monetary data
LC_TIME=
   localedata configuration for date and time
LC_ALL=
   localedata configuration overriding all of the above
LANGUAGE=
   can be a : separated list of ISO language codes
LINGUAS=
   can be a ' ' separated list of ISO language codes
```

/etc/sysconfig/harddisks

/etc/sysconfig/harddiskhd[a-h] (for specific devices) These
options are used to tune (E)IDE hard drives and other
devices - read the hdparm man page for more information

```
USE_DMA=1
   Set this to 1 to enable DMA. This might cause some
```

```
    data corruption on certain chipset / hard drive
    combinations. USE WITH CAUTION AND BACKUP.  This is
    used with the "-d" option
MULTIPLE_IO=16
    Multiple sector I/O. a feature of most modern IDE
    hard drives, permitting the transfer of multiple
    sectors per I/O interrupt, rather than the usual one
    sector per interrupt.  When this feature is enabled,
    it typically reduces operating system overhead for
    disk I/O by 30-50%.  On many systems, it also
    provides increased data throughput of anywhere from
    5% to 50%.  Some drives, however (most notably the WD
    Caviar series), seem to run slower with multiple mode
    enabled. Under rare circumstances, such failures can
    result in massive filesystem corruption. USE WITH
    CAUTION AND BACKUP.  This is the sector count for
    multiple sector I/O - the "-m" option
EIDE_32BIT=3
    (E)IDE 32-bit I/O support (to interface card). USE
    WITH CAUTION.
LOOKAHEAD=1
    Enable drive read-lookahead (safe)
EXTRA_PARAMS=<anything>
    Add any extra parameters you want to pass to hdparm
    here.
```

We have purposely left off /etc/sysconfig/network-scripts because it will be covered more in depth in Chapter 5, "Network Connectivity." For now, because we have completed the /etc directory, let's move on to the next main directory off of /root.

/home

The /home directory contains all of the users' home directories. It also contains each user's preferences for shell options and X Window interface options. Performing the ls command with the -a option in a user's home directory will show that each of the files begins with a dot (period) in order to hide the files from a normal listing. You will remember these files from the earlier discussion in the "Bash Environment" section earlier in this chapter. When a new user is added to your system, that user will have a directory listed under /home created for them automatically. We will show you how to change this configuration in the next chapter.

/lib

The /lib directory stands for *library*. The library contains the shared files needed to run the binaries in the /root filesystem. This directory also has a subdirectory called /lib/modules, which contains the dynamic loadable modules for the Linux kernel. The directory structure is set up as /lib/modules/version/. The version number will be the value of the Linux kernel you are using. In the case of Fedora Core 2, it will be 2.4.22-1.2115.nptl.

/lost+found

Your /lost+found directory is used by the filesystem should any files become corrupted. Earlier, we discussed how the system might ask you during the boot process to run a system check via the fsck command if your system was not shut down properly. If fsck then discovers any files that were damaged, they will be placed in this directory. Each mounted drive will have its own directory for just such an occasion.

If you find any files here, you should attempt to place them back where they originated and whatever you do, do not remove this directory. If the filesystem needs to recover a lost file and needs to access this directory, you could experience some unwanted results. You should also note that the files here will have most likely lost their original names. You might want to open them in an editor or cat the contents to try to determine what the file actually is.

/mnt

This directory is used as a generic mounting location for devices on your system. Chances are your CD-ROM drive has already been mounted here under /mnt/cdrom. Although mounting devices here is not necessary, it makes them easier to locate rather then having to remember or guess where a device was mounted.

/opt

The /opt directory, short for *optional*, contains software that is in addition to your server software. Examples of such software are browsers, games, or X Window editors. Not a lot of programs install their files here, only a few. The majority of your X11 applications will most likely be installed to /usr/X11R6. This directory, if you installed our recommended packages, should be empty for now. If you choose to run the X Window interface, some of your software may or may not be installed here.

/proc

This directory is your kernel and system configuration parameter directory. This directory resides in your system memory rather than on an actual drive partition. Many of the files in this directory cannot be written to, even by the *root* user. The numbered directories, or directories with an integer name, are the numerical values for each running process. The following is a list of other files and a short description of what each one does:

```
NUMBERED DIRECTORIES CONTAIN THE FOLLOWING SUBDIRECTORIES
cwd        This is a link to the current working directory
           of the process.
```

environ   This file contains the environment for the
            process.

exe   Under Linux 2.2 and 2.4 exe is a symbolic link
            containing the actual path name of the executed
            command.

fd   This is a subdirectory containing one entry for
            each file which the process has open, named by
            its file descriptor, and which is a symbolic
            link to the actual file (as the exe entry does).

maps   A file containing the currently mapped memory
            regions and their access permissions.

mem   Via the mem file one can access the pages of a
            processes memory through open(2), read(2), and
            fseek(3).

root   Unix and Linux support the idea of a per-process
            root of the filesystem, set by the chroot(2)
            system call.

stat   Status information about the process.

statm   Provides information about memory status in
            pages.

HERE ARE THE OTHER DIRECTORIES UNDER /proc

apm   Advanced power management version and battery
            information when CONFIG_APM is defined at kernel
            compilation time.

bus   Contains subdirectories for installed busses.

cmdline   Arguments passed to the Linux kernel at boot
            time.

cpuinfo   This is a collection of CPU and system
            architecture dependent items, for each supported
            architecture a different list.

devices   Text listing of major numbers and device
            groups.

dma   This is a list of the registered ISA DMA (direct
            memory access) channels in use.

driver   Empty subdirectory.

execdomains List of the execution domains (ABI
                personalities).

fb   Frame buffer information when CONFIG_FB is
            defined during kernel compilation.

Filesystems   A text listing of the filesystems which were
                compiled into the kernel.

fs   Empty subdirectory.

ide   ide exists on systems with the ide bus.

interrupts This is used to record the number of interrupts
                per each IRQ on (at least) the i386
                architechure.

iomem	I/O memory map in Linux 2.4.
ioports	This is a list of currently registered Input-Output port regions that are in use.
kcore	This file represents the physical memory of the system and is stored in the ELF core file format.
kmsg	This file can be used instead of the syslog(2) system call to read kernel messages.
ksyms	This holds the kernel exported symbol definitions used by the modules(X) tools to dynamically link and bind loadable modules.
loadavg	The load average numbers give the number of jobs in the run queue.
locks	This file shows current file locks (flock(2) and fcntl(2)) and leases (fcntl(2)).
malloc	This file is only present if CONFIGDEBUGMALLOC was defined during compilation.
meminfo	This is used by free(1) to report the amount of free and used memory (both physical and swap) on the system as well as the shared memory and buffers used by the kernel.
mounts	This is a list of all the file systems currently mounted on the system.
modules	A text list of the modules that have been loaded by the system.
mtrr	Memory Type Range Registers.
net	various net pseudo-files, all of which give the status of some part of the networking layer.
partitions	Contains major and minor numbers of each partition as well as number of blocks and partition name.
pci	This is a listing of all PCI devices found during kernel initialization and their configuration.
scsi	A directory with the scsi midlevel pseudo-file and various SCSI lowlevel driver directories, which contain a file for each SCSI host in this system, all of which give the status of some part of the SCSI IO subsystem.
self	This directory refers to the process accessing the /proc filesystem, and is identical to the /proc directory named by the process ID of the same process.
slabinfo	Information about kernel caches.
stat	kernel/system statistics.
swaps	Swap areas in use.
sys	This directory (present since 1.3.57) contains a

```
                    number of files and subdirectories corresponding
                    to kernel variables.
        sysvipc     Subdirectory containing the pseudo-files msg,
                    sem and shm.
        tty         Subdirectory containing the psuedo-files and
                    subdirectories for tty drivers and line
                    disciplines.
        uptime      This file contains two numbers: the uptime of
                    the system (seconds), and the amount of time
                    spent in idle process (seconds).
        version     This string identifies the kernel version that
                    is currently running.
```

The preceding code is a summarized version of the manual entry for proc. You can find more specifics on each one of these by reading the manual entry. Remember that when in the man command, you can press Q to exit along with Ctrl+C.

/root

This is the home directory for the *root* user. In addition to your own files, various log files will be created here for you to review should programs or processes head south.

TIP   Keep your files and directories organized. Starting a regimen of creating categorized directories and always placing the appropriate files in them will save massive amounts of time when you are searching for things.

/sbin

The /sbin directory contains binary programs required for booting the system that are not contained in /bin. Retrieve a listing of the /sbin directory and you will see that all users of the system have access to execute almost any of these commands. The /sbin directory was separated from /bin in order to create a distinction between commands that the system uses and commands that might be applicable to users of the system. Originally this separation stemmed from creating a separate directory for files that were *statically linked*, meaning they did not require any other supporting files or libraries to work. This way they could still be used in a single-user environment or when filesystems refuse to mount.

/tmp

This directory contains any temporary files currently in use by programs running on the system. Any user of the system can write to this directory, including users owned and operated by commands and programs. Fedora does not execute a cleanup of this directory on a regular basis, but you might wish to have a script run at boot or, if your system is heavily trafficked, more often by using a cron job.

/usr

The /usr directory is a *major* section of your filesystem. It contains files that are shared between users and should not be writeable by anyone but *root*. Some major software packages such as Apache will also install under their own subdirectory here. The following is a list of the subdirectories and a brief description of their content:

/usr/bin   Most user commands are stored here. All binaries that do not belong in the /bin or /sbin directories will be found here.

/usr/dict   This directory holds dictionary files for multiple language support.

/usr/etc   This directory contains configuration files for non-systemwide programs such as the programs and commands contained in /usr/bin and /usr/sbin.

/usr/games   Any default-installed games will be installed in this directory. Because this system will be used as a server, we do not cover them in this book.

/usr/include   This is the proper directory for standard include files. Different programs that you can install will deposit C and C++ files here for usage within their functionality. This allows for easy software development in Linux by using other open source include files.

/usr/kerberos   *Kerberos* is a network authentication protocol designed to provide strong key-based encryption for information transferred via secure sockets and connections.

/usr/lib   These files, much like the /lib directory's files, are for standard library files. They can be used by any programs installed, as well as by your own if you develop software for Linux.

/usr/libexec   The /usr/libexec directory holds system daemons and commands run strictly by other programs.

/usr/local   The /usr/local directory is used when an administrator account is installing software locally. Apache and MySQL will install themselves here unless otherwise directed during the installation procedures.

/usr/sbin   This directory houses programs and binaries for the system administrator that are not absolutely necessary for standard system operation. Repair files, system daemons, and administration files are kept here. Although most of them show permissions that allow any user to execute them, each one handles its own permissions whether or not the current user is allowed to run the command.

/usr/share   The /share directory contains files that are not dependent on a specific architecture. These files can be run by i386, Alpha, or any other architecture without encountering problems. The /usr/share directory is also used to store documentation and sample configuration files for applications.

/usr/src   This directory contains the kernel source code for your system. Advanced users can modify the files contained in this directory and recompile their kernel in order to create a highly customized system. This type of modification is *not* recommended for beginning users.

/usr/tmp   This is simply a link to the /var/tmp directory.

/usr/X11R6   This directory contains the X Window system and all of its related files. The host-specific information is contained in the /usr/X11R6/lib/X11 directory.

/var

The /var directory is used for files that can be shared or are in a transient state. Data that is cached, locked, spooled, and logged will be in the appropriate subdirectory under /var. If you need to find why a program is not functioning properly, you can look at its log files most likely contained here.

Using Linux Checklist

This has been your first very serious chapter. You should feel like you are well on your way to becoming a system administrator for Linux by now. With this chapter under your belt, you are fully prepared to begin learning how to administer your system. The following is a list of points you should know before continuing to the next chapter:

- Know each file called during the boot process and what processes it puts into action.
- Be able to install an RPM package.
- Understand run level scripts.
- Comprehend the login process.
- Know some of the functionality the Bash shell offers.
- Understand Bash special characters.
- Know the commands listed in the "Navigating Through Linux" section.
- Be aware of the hierarchy of the Linux filesystem and know the difference between the types of files stored in each one.

This chapter should have opened your eyes to the true power of Linux. With an understanding of the Linux filesystem and how to navigate through the Linux waters, you should begin to understand just how easily customized a system like this is. In the next chapter, you'll test these waters by performing some basic administration tasks.

CHAPTER 4

Linux Administration

- Managing Users and Groups

- Managing Services and Processes

- Managing Software

- System Backup and Recovery

With a firm understanding of the commands and functions needed to navigate through the Linux filesystem as well as an idea of where each type of file is located, you are ready to begin exploring the world of Linux administration. This chapter will teach you how to manage user accounts; how to modify certain sections of the boot process; how to stop, start, and manage processes and software; and how to run an efficient backup system for your server. Each one of these areas is extremely important to keeping a well-oiled machine and they will all be thoroughly covered in this chapter—so let's begin.

Managing Users and Groups

User accounts serve a number of purposes on any Linux system. Primarily, they give the system and other users a way to distinguish themselves and the files they own from other users and their files. When we refer to an *account*, we are talking about the user's name and all of the files and directories owned by the user.

In addition to accounts owned by people, there are also accounts owned by programs and processes that reside on your system. This level of distinction for the files a program touches or modifies is needed for multiple reasons, the first of which is security. You would not want a program that is accessible to any user on your system to have privileges allowing it to modify files and directories that only the *root* user should be allowed to access.

Most of these processes that are running in the background are referred to as *daemons*. For example, you might have a daemon running that retrieves updated files from a few servers via HTTP or FTP. This daemon might need to store its files in the /var/spool directory so that anyone can read them. This daemon user would have full access to these files, whereas each of the other users, who are owned and operated by a person, would have only read access to these files in order to prevent tampering and to prevent an inexperienced user from accidentally deleting the file(s).

As the system administrator, it is your responsibility to create each of these accounts and assign the proper levels of access to each one. This should not be taken lightly because mistakes could easily lead to your system being compromised and ultimately to you losing complete control over your system. After a malicious user gains access to your *root* account, they can completely erase all data your system has access to.

Groups, as defined by Red Hat, are "logical expressions of organization, tying users together for a common purpose." Groups help you separate types of users from each other and allow each user in a group to have the same level of access to common files and directories that they might share. When you set up your web server, you might wish to give a friend or coworker access to the web directories. Adding this person to the group that your web server user owns would allow them to access the group permissions of files that the web server group owns. We will cover this more in depth later in this section.

The */etc/passwd* File

For now, let's take a look at an account, its login information, and its files. You'll start with the /etc/passwd file. The passwd file contains one line for each user on your system. Move to your /etc directory now and pico the passwd file. You can read the information in this file by using the following format:

`login:password:UID:GID:Full Name:homedir:shell`

The login is also referred to as your *username*. Notice that the password is shown as an *x*. This is because Linux stores your password in a shadow password file. The shadow password file is used for security reasons. Your shell, which runs at your user and access level, requires access to the passwd file in order to retrieve your full name and home directory. However, allowing every user to see the passwords would open the doors for malicious users attempting to crack the password file and gain access to your system. For this reason, the actual encrypted passwords are stored elsewhere. The User ID (UID) and Group ID (GID) fields are integer values and can be modified directly in this file.

> **NOTE**   This GID is the user's *primary* GID. Others can be assigned via the group file covered later.

If you scroll to the bottom of this file, you will see the first user you created during the installation procedure at the very bottom. The UID and GID are both set to 500. This is what is referred to as User Private Groups (UPGs). UPGs are used to make default permissions for files and directories created by a user. These default permissions will ensure that no other users of the system will be able to change or delete these files. This is because the file will be owned by a user and a group that are unique.

The following default users should be installed on your system if you are running Fedora Core 2. Almost all of the default users will be at a value less than 100, with root always being 0.

```
root:x:0:0:root:/root:/bin/bash
bin:x:1:1:bin:/bin:/sbin/nologin
daemon:x:2:2:daemon:/sbin:/sbin/nologin
adm:x:3:4:adm:/var/adm:/sbin/nologin
lp:x:4:7:lp:/var/spool/lpd:/sbin/nologin
sync:x:5:0:sync:/sbin:/bin/sync
shutdown:x:6:0:shutdown:/sbin:/sbin/shutdown
halt:x:7:0:halt:/sbin:/sbin/halt
mail:x:8:12:mail:/var/spool/mail:/sbin/nologin
news:x:9:13:news:/etc/news:
uucp:x:10:14:uucp:/var/spool/uucp:/sbin/nologin
operator:x:11:0:operator:/root:/sbin/nologin
games:x:12:100:games:/usr/games:/sbin/nologin
gopher:x:13:30:gopher:/var/gopher:/sbin/nologin
ftp:x:14:50:FTP User:/var/ftp:/sbin/nologin
nobody:x:99:99:Nobody:/:/sbin/nologin
```

```
rpm:x:37:37::/var/lib/rpm:/sbin/nologin
vcsa:x:69:69:virtual console:/dev:/sbin/nologin
nscd:x:28:28:NSCD Daemon:/:/sbin/nologin
sshd:x:74:74:Priv-sep SSH:/var/empty/sshd:/sbin/nologin
rpc:x:32:32:Portmapper RPC user:/:/sbin/nologin
rpcuser:x:29:29:RPC Service User:/var/lib/nfs:/sbin/nologin
nfsnobody:x:65534:65534:Anon NFS:/var/lib/nfs:/sbin/nologin
mailnull:x:47:47::/var/spool/mqueue:/sbin/nologin
smmsp:x:51:51::/var/spool/mqueue:/sbin/nologin
pcap:x:77:77::/var/arpwatch:/sbin/nologin
apache:x:48:48:Apache:/var/www:/sbin/nologin
dbus:x:81:81:System message bus:/:/sbin/nologin
xfs:x:43:43:X Font Server:/etc/X11/fs:/sbin/nologin
named:x:25:25:Named:/var/named:/sbin/nologin
ntp:x:38:38::/etc/ntp:/sbin/nologin
desktop:x:80:80:desktop:/var/lib/menu/kde:/sbin/nologin
gdm:x:42:42::/var/gdm:/sbin/nologin
```

On line 23 is the user nfsnobody. This user has a UID and GID of 65534, which is the maximum allotted user number. No single server should ever need this many users for any reason. You can manually add lines here to add a user, but it is recommended that you use the industry standard command-line method of useradd covered later in this chapter.

The /etc/group File

This file contains virtually all of the relationships for assigning groups to users and visa versa. Exit the /etc/passwd file if it is still open and pico the /etc/group file. A list of default groups will be displayed. To read these, use this format:

```
groupname:password:GID:members
```

The groupname is much like a username for a group. This is what is displayed under a long listing of directories' contents in the group ownership column. The next field, password, is optional.

NOTE   To see all of the groups a user belongs to, you should use the id command and pass in the user you wish to query.

You might wish to add a password for a group so that users of the system can add themselves to the group, for the duration of their shell's existence, with the newgrp command. These passwords are stored in a shadow file similar to the shadow file for /etc/passwd. This can cut down on administration time if your system supports a large number of users. The GID field is the same ID that is used in the /etc/passwd file to specify a user's default group.

With a default installation, your /etc/group file should read as follows:

```
root:x:0:root
bin:x:1:root,bin,daemon
daemon:x:2:root,bin,daemon
sys:x:3:root,bin,adm
adm:x:4:root,adm,daemon
tty:x:5:
disk:x:6:root
lp:x:7:daemon,lp
mem:x:8:
kmem:x:9:
wheel:x:10:root
mail:x:12:mail
news:x:13:news
uucp:x:14:uucp
man:x:15:
games:x:20:
gopher:x:30:
dip:x:40:
ftp:x:50:
lock:x:54:
nobody:x:99:
users:x:100:
rpm:x:37:
floppy:x:19:
vcsa:x:69:
utmp:x:22:
slocate:x:21:
nscd:x:28:
sshd:x:74:
rpc:x:32:
rpcuser:x:29:
nfsnobody:x:65534:
mailnull:x:47:
smmsp:x:51:
pcap:x:77:
apache:x:48:
dbus:x:81:
xfs:x:43:
named:x:25:
ntp:x:38:
desktop:x:80:
gdm:x:42:
```

Notice that each default user has a UPG assigned to it. You should also note that the username is not required on its own UPG. For example, named, which is the UPG for named, does not need its own username listed at the end of the line. A group with more than one user assigned should list its own UPG owner. However, even if you wish a user to have root access to your system, it is best not to assign that user to the root group. It is best to have users log in as themselves and su to root. This just serves to keep security as tight as possible.

Linux Passwords

Linux passwords, as discussed earlier in this chapter, are stored in shadow files. The shadow files used by Fedora Core 2 are shadow and gshadow for users and groups, respectively, and are located with the non-shadow files in the /etc directory.

Editing these files will show an encrypted string of characters. In order to be stored, the password has been encrypted by using a one-way encryption algorithm (or hash) called Message Digest 5 (MD5). This means that the encrypted string is never translated back into its original form to be matched. Instead, the password you type when logging in is MD5 encrypted and then matched against the stored encrypted string. This ensures that if the password file is stolen, it will still be *relatively* secure. The term *relatively* is used liberally here because the password file can still be cracked.

Methods used to crack a password file of this type are commonly referred to as *brute force methods.* The cracking program must try to guess the password by encrypting its guess and matching it against the encrypted string contained in the stolen passwd file. This is why short passwords or passwords based on a single word are extremely bad. Usually the first method tried by someone trying to crack the file is to use every dictionary word.

The installed package that allows for shadowing to be enabled is accompanied by some extra functionality. This extra functionality contains the commands enabling you to add, edit, and delete users and groups as well as the commands for password aging and expiration. Password expiration enables you to specify a set amount of time until a user has to change their password. This also helps to tighten security on your server.

User Administration

Creating a new account on your system is done with the useradd command. The useradd command can also be used to update a user's information by passing in different flags. The following is the proper format for useradd:

```
useradd -flag[s] login
```

This command creates a single user with a username of login. You will then be taken to another command line with no message printed.

After initially creating the user, you will need to set a password. To set a user's password, use this command:

```
passwd username
```

If you are logged in as root when you use the passwd command, you will not need to enter the old password. If you are logged in as that user or you are a user other than root who has permission to change passwords for other users, you will need to enter the original password before you are prompted for the new one. If you make a mistake in typing the username, simply press Ctrl+C and you will be dropped back to a prompt. If you enter a new password, you will then need to retype the password for verification. After you finish, you should see this message:

```
passwd: all authentication tokens updated successfully
```

This means that the password change was successful, and you are ready to continue with your next task.

When you are adding a user, you might wish to use some of the flags listed here for customizing your user layout and structure:

-c *comment*   This adds a comment to the password file comment field, which is where the user's full name is stored.

-d *directory*   The directory argument enables you to specify the user's home directory. The default is to append the user's login to the default home directory setup on your server.

-e *expire_date*   The date must be specified in the format *YYYY-MM-DD* in order to cause a user's account to be disabled on this date. This does not remove the user or the user's files from the system.

-f *inactive_days*   Specifying a value here causes an account to be disabled x days after their password has expired. The default value is -1, which disables this feature.

-g *initial_group*   This specifies the initial group a user belongs to, in the GID field in the /etc/passwd file.

-G *group,[...]*   You can list as many groups as you wish here that the user should belong to other than his initial group.

-m   This specifies that a directory will be created, if it does not exist, to serve as the user's home directory. The default files for the user will be copied into this directory unless the -k option is specified. If -k is given, then you can specify what directory you would like the default files to be copied from. The -k option is valid only when -m is used.

-M   This option tells Linux not to create a home directory at all.

-n   This flag turns off the UPG option, in effect not creating a default group for the user with their own name. This is beneficial to setups that will be assigning all users to a users group.

-o   This turns on the ability to create a new user with a duplicate UID.

-p *password*   This specifies the password on the command line. Note that the useradd function expects this to be in an encrypted form—*not* clear text.

-r   This flag enables you to create a system account with a UID lower than 100.

-s *shell*   This lets you specify the default shell that a user is assigned.

-u *uid*   Pass in your desired UID for the user, and it shall be so.

These options provide you greater control over your user system. Mentioned in the -m flag is the directory of files used to set up a user's home directory. By default, this is the /etc/skel directory. Placing a file in this directory or modifying a file's contents will affect each user created from that point forward. You might wish to place an .htaccess file here if the account will have Web access, or perhaps a system rules and regulations document to make sure the user reads it. Creating your desired setup for new users in this directory will ensure that your modifications do not have undesired effects for users who might have already changed certain files in their home directories to modify their own environments.

To delete or remove a user, you can user the userdel command. This command takes one argument, the username, and removes a user from the system. Specifying the -r option removes that user's home directory as well. If you wish to remove all the files and directories owned by that user, it's a good idea to use the

```
find / -user username -ls
```

command to locate any files or directories owned by the user. Then you can remove whichever files you need and change the permissions and ownership for the rest.

Group Administration

If you were to retrieve a long listing of directory that contained

```
-wrxrw-r-- 1 joe       jingle     36521  Jan 9 11:37 bebop
```

you would see that the file is owned by the user joe. This does not necessarily mean that joe is in the group that owns the file: jingle. In fact, we see by the permissions in the first block that joe has execute permissions to the file, whereas users of the jingle group do not. When a user owns a file and is in the group assigned to the file as well, the user privileges will supersede the group privileges. For instance, if the user has only read permissions and the group has write and execute, the user will still have only read permissions. Make sure to keep these rules in mind as you set up your user/group system.

To create a new group, use the groupadd command. You can use the -g *gid* flag to specify a GID for the new group or you can leave it blank to select the next one available after 500. Much like the delete user command, you can use groupdel to remove a group from the list.

To administer the /etc/group file with more than adding and deleting, you can use the gpasswd command. This command has several flags you can specify to set up your system. Here we have compiled a short list to help you out:

-a *user group*   This assigns a user to the specified group.

-d *user group*   This deletes a user from the targeted group.

-R *group*   This flag disables access to a group.

-r *group*   This option removes a group password.

-M *user,[…] group*   This enables you to assign multiple users to a group.

-A *user,[…] group*   This enables you to assign a single or multiple administrators to a group at once.

Passing in no arguments will enable you to define the password to a group. Simply passing in the single argument of the group name will prompt you to enter a password.

Any user on the system can attempt to use the newgrp command to add themselves to a group. If this group has a password assigned to it, the user will be prompted to enter the correct password. If the group does not have a password, the user will not be allowed to join the group.

Modifying Users or Groups

There are a few other commonly used administrative functions for changing users and groups. We've listed them here as a resource for you to use. As for the other commands in this book, refer to the manual for each program for more information. Here are the commands:

chfn   This command is used to change a user's finger information; finger is a command that enables remote users to get basic information about users on your system.

chsh   This lets you change the default shell for a user. Simply pass in the username and then the location of your target shell.

groupmod   This enables you to modify a GID or name for a group.

id   This echoes the GID or UID values for a user.

newusers If you need to create a large number of users at once, you can use this command. This command accepts a text file as an argument that contains usernames and passwords in plain text. It will then parse the entire file and create the user accounts. See the manual for more information on the actual format.

su We discussed the su command in Chapter 2, "Installing Linux." This command is used for any user on the system to change to another user. All users except root must enter the correct password for the user they wish to change to.

Managing Services and Processes

Being able to administer the services and processes that your system runs is paramount to keeping your server running at peak performance. You must be able to identify that your system is distressed or running low on resources so you can perform preventative maintenance before it's too late. This section will teach you how to monitor your system and check for signals that your server sends out about each process. You will also learn how to perform actions on these services and processes in order to stop, start, restart, and kill them.

Gathering System Information

While using the Linux shell, you can access a wide array of commands to provide valuable system information such as file lists, running processes, system resource usage, and more. Let's cover the most important commands for your everyday use of Linux.

ps

The first command you need to be familiar with is the ps command—*ps* stands for *process status*. You can use this command to report the current status of each process currently running on the system by passing in different flags and arguments. This is a static list and does not get updated until the command is run again. If you are listing all processes, you might wish to pipe the output to the more or less command to make things a little easier to digest.

Let's take a look at some of the more common combinations passed into the ps command and the effects they have:

```
ps ax | less
```

This command reports all processes currently running for all users. If you wish to view only processes running with the appropriate users listed, you can use this command:

```
ps aux | less
```

However, viewing every process running is not usually what you will be looking for. Chances are you will probably be looking for a specific process. In this case, you can use the grep command to search for only the processes that contain the given string. The following example searches for any processes with a name that contains *foo*:

```
ps aux | grep foo
```

In addition to the basic a, u, and x flags, there are other various options and parameters you can specify to change process selection, output formatting, output modification, and other information. The www option enables you to display the entire command that launched the process. You should read the manual entry for ps for more information.

top

The next command you should be familiar with is the top command. This command provides a real-time look at your processor activity. It displays a list of the most resource-intensive tasks that are currently running. You can sort by memory and CPU usage as well as by runtime. As with almost all commands in Linux, you can also specify various options. Here are a few:

d   This flag enables you to specify the delay between each screen refresh.

P   You can use this flag up to 20 times followed by a PID to display only the given processes.

q   Use this flag sparingly. Sending this flag to top enables it to run at the highest priority if you are the super user and will not have any delay between screen refreshes.

s   This tells top to run in secure mode, which disables some of the hot keys you can use to change top while it is running.

i   This ignores idle and zombie processes.

H   This shows all threads.

b   This specifies batch mode. *Batch mode* outputs data as plain text, which is useful for piping the results to other programs or files.

After the top process is running, you will be presented with an abundance of information, much of which is abbreviations. We've put together a list compiled from the manual entry for top to help you decipher the information presented:

Processes   This is the total number of processes currently running on your system.

CPU states   This shows the percentage of CPU time in multiple modes.

Mem   This shows the memory usage statistics.

Swap   This indicates statistics on swap space.

PID   The Process ID of each task.

PPID   The Parent Process ID of each task.

UID   The User ID of each task.

USER   The username of the task's owner.

PRI   The priority of the task.

NI   The nice value of each task.

SIZE   The size of the task's code, plus data, plus stack space.

TSIZE   The code size of the task.

DSIZE   Data plus stack size.

TRS   Text resident size.

SWAP   Size of the swapped-out part of the task.

D   Size of pages marked as dirty.

STAT   The state of the task is shown here:

  S   Sleeping

  D   Uninterruptible sleep

  R   Running

  Z   Zombie

  T   Stopped or traced

  N   Process with positive nice value

  W   Swapped out process

WCMAN   This displays the address or the name of the kernel function in which the processes are currently residing.

TIME   Total CPU time the task has used since it started.

%CPU   The task's share of the total CPU time.

%MEM   The task's share of the physical memory it is currently using.

COMMAND   This is the task's command name.

In addition, while top is running, there are also interactive commands as well. You should check the manual for more information on the top command and its real-time modifications.

free

This command displays information about physical memory and swap usage and totals. Running the `free` command displays your total, used, free, shared, buffered, and cached physical memory as well as total used and free swap space. If you find this format difficult to use, you can pass in the -k, -m, and -g flags to change the formatting to kilobytes, megabytes, and gigabytes, respectively.

df

The `df` command is used to display the system's disk space usage. Without any flags, the `df` command will print something similar to the following:

```
Filesystem  1k-blocks      Used Available Use% Mounted on
/dev/hda2   10325716    2902060   6899140  30% /
/dev/hda1      15554       8656      6095  59% /boot
/dev/hda3   20722644    2664256  17005732  14% /home
none          256796          0    256796   0% /dev/shm
```

Here you can see that the partition location is displayed as well as the total, used, and available blocks. After the block listing, you are presented with the percentage of the physical disk the partition uses as well as the location where it is mounted.

The same filesystem can also be viewed in *human readable* format by using the -h flag. The result is something similar to this:

```
Filesystem       Size  Used Avail Use% Mounted on
/dev/hda2        9.8G  2.8G  6.5G  30% /
/dev/hda1         15M  8.5M  5.9M  59% /boot
/dev/hda3         20G  2.6G   16G  14% /home
none             251M     0  250M   0% /dev/shm
```

This makes formatting significantly easier to read should you be displaying the values only for reading. The last line in both of these examples reads none for the filesystem name. Reading the mount location will show that this is an entry for SysV shared memory because the mount point is /dev/shm, which stands for *shared memory*.

du

This command displays the disk usage for a specified directory. It returns a list of subdirectories as well with a subtotal for each one and a grand total for the entire directory. The du command has several useful flags. Here are some select flags that we have found the most useful:

-a   This flag displays the totals for all files, not just the directory and subdirectories. This flag can make the listing a bit long, so you will probably want to pipe the results to `less` or `more`.

-k   This translates all size values to kilobytes.

-s   This displays only a total for each argument passed in.

-x   This parameter skips any files located on a different filesystem than the one originally specified on the command line.

-h   This converts bytes to megabytes or gigabytes, which symbolizes human readable format.

If you are running a web server that houses multiple virtual domains for many users, the du command will be invaluable to you. You can also set up disk quotas, which will be covered in the next section, "Creating Disk Quotas."

diskcheck

The diskcheck command is not installed by default. However, if you require real-time background monitoring of disk usage, you should download the binary rpm from Red Hat and install it. The diskcheck command runs as an hourly cron job by default and will send mail to you if certain specified criteria are met. This ensures that if you are running out of disk space, you will be notified before it is too late. To change the notification options, you should edit the /etc/diskcheck.conf file. In this file, you can change your e-mail address for receiving notifications as well as the following variables:

defaultCutoff   This tells diskcheck to send a notification e-mail if the defaultCutoff percentage of total disk usage is met. For instance, if this value is set to 85, you will receive an e-mail after 85 percent of the disk space is used.

cutoff [/dev/partition]   Just like defaultCutoff, this value represents a percentage value, but this one relates to a specific partition on a disk. This value overrides the defaultCutoff for a disk.

cutoff [/mount/point]   You can pass in a particular mount point for this argument. You can use an integer representing the percentage reached that you would like to receive the notification at. You should note that these values do not contain the actual percentage symbol.

exclude   This is your exclusion value. Anything specified with this directive will cause a notification *not* to be sent should the partition reach its default cutoff limit. You will want to add an exclusion for your swap space because this space can be filled quite often depending on the size of your physical memory.

ignore   The ignore value will tell diskcheck to disregard an entire filesystem type. For instance, if iso9660 is specified, any filesystem in iso9660 format will not be reported to you via e-mail.

mailTo   This is the e-mail address that the mail is sent to. This is a string, so do not forget to enclose it in quotes.

`mailFrom`   This is the e-mail address that the e-mail comes "from." You can specify a name here that you could later set up filtering on within your e-mail client.

`mailProg`   This specifies the e-mail program you would like to use to send the mail. By default this is Sendmail.

lspci

The last command you should be aware of for gathering system information is the `lspci` command. This command gives you a report on all Peripheral Component Interconnect (PCI) devices contained in your system. Running this command with the -v flag specifies *verbose*, and -vv specifies *very verbose*. The result will present you with video card, peripheral, and even network card types and models. This command is useful if you are trying to locate updated drivers for your system and are unsure about your computer's hardware.

Creating Disk Quotas

In addition to monitoring the disk usage and receiving notifications from `diskcheck`, you can also monitor users' and groups' individual usage as well. This type of monitoring is especially useful for limiting other users' file size and file count on your system. This is the method that most hosting companies use to limit people to a specific amount of space they are paying for.

If you would like to add this functionality, you need to make sure that the `quota` package is installed. If it is not, you need to locate the binary package and install it. For more information on this, see the "Managing Software" section later in this chapter.

There are four main steps to creating a quota system on your server:

1. Edit the `/etc/fstab` file and enable quotas for each filesystem you need them on.

2. Remount those filesystems.

3. Create the actual quota files and generate a disk usage table.

4. Assign the quota to the users and groups.

Let's take a look at each step in more detail.

Editing the */etc/fstab* file

As the `root` user, you must first edit the `/etc/fstab` file. After you have this file open in your choice of editors, you can add the `usrquota` and `grpquota` directives to the column that contains the word *defaults*. You need to separate each directive with a comma, like so:

```
LABEL=/home /home ext3  defaults,usrquota,grpquota 1 2
```

The preceding line specifies that both user and group quotas will be turned on for this file system. After you have added the directives to each filesystem you would like to enable quota on, continue to the next step.

Remounting the Filesystems

Make sure you take note of the filesystems you will be adding quotas to because now you will need to remount each one. To do so, you should use the umount and mount commands. However, if the filesystem is currently in use, it might be easier to just reboot your computer. After that is complete, you will be ready for the next step.

Creating Quota Files

Although the system is now quota enabled, it is not yet ready to use quotas. To be able to specify the quotas for users and groups, you need to create the quota files for each filesystem. The managing of quota files is done by using the quotacheck command. This command is used to create a file when the -c flag is specified and to view verbose information as the check is running by using the -v option.

You first need to create the quota files for each filesystem by using this command:

```
quotacheck -acug
```

The -a option creates both a user and group quota file in the root of each filesystem marked with a quota in /etc/fstab. If you wish to create the quota files for just one filesystem, you can leave off the -a and pass in a specific filesystem after the flags. The -u flag specifies to create a user quota file, and the -g flag tells diskquota to create a group file. You should use these flags as needed for each filesystem.

> **NOTE**   If you are attempting to enable a quota on a filesystem that is already in use, you need to specify the -m option. This tells quotacheck to *not* attempt to remount the filesystem(s) in read-only mode.

After you are finished creating quota files for each filesystem, you need to run this command:

```
quotacheck -avug
```

This generates a table of each disk usage for each filesystem with quotas enabled. After this has finished running, you can continue to the next step.

Assigning Quotas

To edit a quota for a user, you use the edquota command. For example, if you want to edit the quota for the user foo, you use the following:

```
edquota foo
```

This then launches your default editor and displays each filesystem that quotas are enabled on. Each line represents a different filesystem, and you will be able to see the current amount of disk space used, under blocks, as well as being able to set the user's limits. You will notice that there are hard and soft columns after the blocks used as well as after the inodes column. Inodes is used to specify the *number* of files as opposed to the *size* of files. The hard values for each filesystem represent the maximum limit a user or group can reach, whereas the soft values represent the maximum limit for a set period of time. This enables a user to realize they have gone over their limit and to remove needed files rather than canceling their upload to the system immediately. You should specify these limits in blocks. After you are finished, exit and save, and the user's limits will be set.

After the quota has been saved, you can use the quota command to check. Simply pass in the username as the only argument and you will be presented with the applicable information.

After you are satisfied with your individual user quotas, you can also specify group quotas. To do so, use the following:

```
edquota -g group
```

The layout is exactly the same as editing a quota for a user, so change the settings as you see fit and save and exit once again. You can also check the quota for a group by using the -g flag to the quota command.

To assign the grace periods for soft limits, you should use the -t option for the edquota command. You will be able to edit each filesystem and the grace period for both blocks and inodes. After you are finished, save and exit and you will be ready to enable the quotas for each filesystem. You can turn on quotas by running the quotaon command. You also have the option of remounting each filesystem, as in step 2.

After you have assigned all your quotas, you will still need to perform some regular maintenance on the system. You need to keep up with the most current values to determine whether a user or group is exceeding their maximum allotted space. If they are, it is your job to notify the user and let them know what is going on. They might be inexperienced and not understand how to find out how much space they are using. To obtain a report of the current disk usage, use the repquota command and pass in the name of the filesystem you wish to have a report on. Using the -a flag and not specifying a filesystem will report on all filesystems that have quotas enabled.

If your filesystems are not unmounted cleanly—for example, during a power failure or crash—you need to rerun the quotacheck command with the -avug flags. Because there is no easy way to detect if your system has crashed after booting, you might wish to add the quotacheck -avug command to your crontab to run weekly or monthly.

If you would like to turn quotas off without losing your configuration, you can use the following to turn off all quotas

```
quotaoff -avug
```

Or you can turn off an individual quota by using this command:

```
quotaoff -vug filesystem
```

If you need to turn quotas back on, you can specify the same flags as used in the preceding examples, but instead use the quotaon command. If the filesystem has only user or only group quotas, you can adjust the -u and -g flags accordingly.

Starting and Stopping the System and Services

During administration, it might become necessary to reboot the system or shut it down entirely. To do so, you can use the shutdown command. This command has several options that enable you to specify whether you would like to reboot or to shut down and how long you would like to wait before doing so.

To shut down immediately and without warning, use the following:

```
shutdown -h now
```

The h specified here tells the system to halt. The now parameter specifies the time.

If you would like to reboot the system rather than shutting down, you could use this:

```
shutdown -r +10
```

This tells the system to reboot after 10 minutes. Specifying a time sends a message to all users with an open shell telling them that the system will be going down in the specified number of minutes. This enables users to prepare for the reboot or shutdown and save anything they might be working on.

Starting and stopping services is just as easy. The service command, which is located in the /sbin directory, is your all-in-one command that can control virtually any service on your system.

To start a service that is not already running, use this command:

```
service serviceName start
```

This attempts to bring up the specified service. If the service is not started, you will receive an error message. Some messages are more verbose than others. If the message does not give enough information for troubleshooting the problem, you should check the appropriate log files for that service.

You might also wish to stop a service from running, or if a service is not running properly, you might wish to restart it. To do so, you can use these commands, respectively:

```
service serviceName stop
service serviceName restart
```

In addition to these commands, you can also simply reload a configuration file without stopping or restarting the service. This will not work for all services but if you wish to try it, simply use `service serviceName reload`. You should notice that the only thing that changes for these commands is the last argument, which is the function you wish to perform on the service.

The last commonly used function is the `graceful` parameter. This attempts to stop and start a service with the least amount of downtime possible. This is especially useful if you are running a live server and you do not want invalid requests being sent to your users. There is another major benefit to using `graceful`: If the service cannot be restarted successfully with the new configuration file, it will not restart. Instead, the current instance of the service will continue to run in the state that it is currently in.

You can also start and stop services by using the actual service in the command line. For example you can use

```
/etc/init.d/httpd start
```

to start your web server as opposed to using the service command. There are no important features or advantages that one contains over the other; it is merely a matter of preference. It might be easier not to have to remember where the service daemon is located, however, so you wouldn't have to type the full path to the command if it is not located in a directory that is automatically registered as containing default commands.

Controlling Access to Services

Maintaining security on your Linux system is top priority. One way you can help lock down your system is by turning off or on certain services. You can restrict access to specified services as well. Because all software is prone to user error and might contain bugs, it is best not to have services running that are not used. This also helps minimize the usage of system resources.

> **NOTE** In Chapter 6, "Linux Security," we will cover iptables. *Iptables* enable you to restrict or grant access to specific services by IP addresses, IP blocks, and a number of other important distinctions.

In this section, we will focus on showing you how services are configured to run for each run level and how to change these. You might remember that in both Chapters 2 and 3 you looked at changing the `inittab` file to change your default run level. You changed this value to read 3 for Full Multiuser mode. This run level determines what scripts and services are run during the boot phase. If you ever wish to change the run level immediately, you can use

```
telinit runLevel
```

where *runlevel* is equal to the run level you wish to switch to. This will run the kill scripts located in the `/etc/rc.d/rcX.d` directory and then run the startup scripts located in the new run level's `rcX.d` directory. In both examples, the *X* denotes the run-level value.

In addition to iptables, you can also specify limited control over services controlled by xinetd by using TCP wrappers. *TCP wrappers* are a method of controlling access to servers by using the /etc/hosts.allow and /etc/hosts.deny files. These files, as the name implies, contain information and directives on how to control access from specified hosts to specified services. It is important to note that the hosts.allow file supersedes the hosts.deny file. This is because although you might need to block out the entire world, you will want to allow a few hosts. This is much better than having to specify the entire world's computers individually.

The xinetd service is a secure replacement for inetd. This service runs and listens on all ports for services that it controls in order to maintain control over the traffic being sent. If it receives traffic on a port, it will then start the appropriate server and pass on the information *if* the host requesting the server or service has access. The xinetd daemon also contains functionality that enables it to conserve system resources, create log files, and limit the rate of data coming across ports. You can edit the configuration for xinetd by editing the /etc/xinted.conf and other files located in the /etc/xinted.d directory. The /etc/xinted.d directory contains a list of services the daemon controls and whether to enable that service or not.

In addition to manually editing the config files, there are a few commands you can use that will present the information to you in an easier-to-understand manner. The first is a small text-based interface that enables you to activate and deactivate services. It is called ntsysv. Running this command will take you to a system similar to the text installation of Fedora Core 2 that you performed. You can use the arrow keys to navigate and the spacebar to stop and start services.

> **WARNING** Services controlled by xinted will be immediately affected by the ntsysv interface. Others will need to be manually stopped or started. Unfortunately, the ntsysv program will not differentiate between the two.

> **TIP** You can set up the default services for other run levels by using the --level *x* flag, where *x* is equal to the run level.

The other command used to control services for a specific run level is the chkconfig command. This command enables you by default to check the status of a service by using the following:

```
chkconfig --list serviceName
```

You will be returned a line indicating the service name(s) that match your query along with the status of that service (on or off). If you have specified a service that is in the /etc/rc.d directory, you will be returned a line containing the default status of that service for each run level.

To use this command to enable or disable a service for a particular run level or run levels, you can use the `chkconfig` command in the following format:

```
chkconfig --level runLevels serviceName [on|off]
```

You can specify any number of run levels together in one value because there are no run levels that are more than one character. For example, if you wanted to turn on the `finger` service for run levels 2, 3, and 4, you could use this command:

```
chkconfig --level 234 finger on
```

This sets up the finger service to start automatically next time the computer is booted, and because it is controlled by `xinetd`, it will be started immediately if it is not already running.

WARNING Just like the `ntsysv` command, `chkconfig` abides by the same rules of services being stopped and started.

Managing Software

Similar to most other operating systems, Linux has predefined ways in which software must be installed and handled on the system. You caught a glimpse of this when you took a look at the directory structure of the Linux filesystem. You saw separate directories for different types of software that allow for different user privileges. This section will teach you how to install these software packages on your system through a variety of different methods. These methods include the traditional source package, rpm binaries, and rpm source packages.

It is important to note that different distributions of Linux come with different package types that may or may not be specific to that system. For instance, Debian uses a file format called `.deb` to distribute its software. Debian also comes with its own set of commands to manage and acquire its packages. Because we have installed Fedora Core 2 on our server, we will be covering the Red Hat Package Management System in depth. If you have chosen to run a different flavor of Linux, then you should refer to your documentation and/or manual for more information on binary distribution files. However, the subsection covered next, "Traditional Source Tarballs," will still apply to you because the methods used are not platform dependent.

Traditional Source Tarballs

A *source tarball* is the traditional way of installing software on a Unix or Linux system. The major problem with source files is that they offer no reasonable way to remove or upgrade the installed software. If you are installing software from source, you will often need to record exactly where this software has been installed and what additional requirements it installed so you will know how to remove it if it becomes necessary to do so.

You can find source distributions in tarball format from virtually any software developer site on the Web. In fact, some developers post only source tarballs for their software, requiring you to perform a manual installation. Tarballs have either the `.tar` or `.gz` file extension, the latter meaning it is compressed by using gzip. The gzip functionality is built into the `tar` command, so you will not need anything more to use this package than is already installed on your system.

To start, first create a subdirectory within your home directory called /newapps, or something similar, in order to keep things organized. You can use the following command:

```
mkdir newapps
```

After you have created your new directory, locate the tar file of the software you would like to install via the Web, your e-mail, or other source. Whatever your source, make sure to copy it to your /root/newapps/ directory for organizational purposes. After your file is there, you will use the `tar` command to uncompress and archive the files contained within the tarball. To do this, use this command:

```
tar -xvfpz tarballname
```

This should create a new subdirectory within the /root/newapps/ directory with the appropriate name for the software.

WARNING   Some tarballs might have been created without a subdirectory prefix for the files. This will cause all the files to be untarred into your /newapps directory. You would then need to remove the files and directories the untarring created and manually create a subdirectory for the source files. To avoid this problem, you should check the files within the tarball by using the `tar` command with the `-t` flag in place of the `-x` in order to list the contents of the archive.

With the new software successfully unarchived into its own subdirectory, `cd` into the directory and retrieve a directory listing. You should see two important files that are standard practice with every tar release: `configure` and `Makefile`. These are the actual installation files for your software. They tell your system how to compile the binaries needed to run the software with your specific system specifications and architecture in mind. In addition to these two main files, you should also have an `INSTALL` or `README` file as well. These files tell you options that you can specify during your setup to customize your installation. Later in this book when we show you how to install Apache, MySQL, and PHP, you will see there are a myriad of different options you can set. In fact the sheer number of these options can be overwhelming.

Before you install any software on Linux, it is generally a good idea to take a look at recommended configuration settings for a system similar to yours. Others might have already found that certain settings will help to increase the performance of the software for your particular setup. This is especially recommended for beginners who might not know the specific effects that certain switches can have on the server.

After you have determined your specific setup, you need to move into the subdirectory containing your software to be installed and run the `configure` command, which is located in the directory.

NOTE   When running commands that are not located in a default command directory such as /bin or /usr/sbin, you need to use the full path to that directory unless your current working directory is the same as the command's directory. In that case, you can precede the command with a period and a slash (./).

Run the `./configure` command and specify any options you wish and you will most likely see a huge amount of status printing run up the screen. This is the configuration program searching for the proper libraries and any dependencies it might have on other programs. Do not be alarmed if you see a few messages saying it can't find something; chances are it will then attempt to locate an alternative for that library or command.

If the `configure` is successful, you will not receive any fatal error messages. If you *do* receive a message stating that the configuration could not continue or that the software could not be installed, you will then be told what went wrong. This is usually caused by certain modules, libraries, or processes required by the software being missing. You will need to locate these and install them before you can install the original software.

After your `configure` command has been successfully run, it is time to use the `make` command. The `make` command is a binary utility that manages the compilation process. It contains the functionality that runs the GNU C Compiler (GCC) compiler to actually turn the program into binary format for your system. This is basically taking C or C++ code and turning it into an executable file, much like what is used on an MS Windows machine. Do not be surprised if your system has its resources suddenly *very* preoccupied. The compiler is hard at work crunching a massive amount of data.

Now that your system has compiled the binary, it is time to perform the installation. You should be aware that this is the only process that actually requires *root* access. The other commands used to configure and build the binary wrote files only to the directory you were currently in. This command will then copy the required files to points throughout the filesystem, including the /bin and /sbin directories. The `root` user is the only one who should have access to some of these directories and also the ability to create new system accounts if the software requires them. To actually install your compiled binaries and the complete software package, type `make install`.

Congratulations—if you have not received any error messages, you have just completed your first source installation via a source tarball. By the end of this installation, if the software required a large amount of dependencies, you might wish you would have installed the software via a binary package. Let's take a look at the differences between the two.

Source Code versus Binary Packages

The advantages that binary packages offer come mostly from the software that manages the packages. RPM, the Red Hat Package Manager, that we have discussed before comes with functionality that enables you to have greater control of where things are installed as well as upgrading, downgrading, and removing. Think of a *package* in much the same way you would a package in real life. It's a system of combining files or objects with a related purpose for easy shipping, distribution, and storage. Our virtual packages might come in forms other than .rpm files as well. Debian uses .deb files and the Debian GNU/Linux Package Manager. However, because RPM has been widely adopted and is already an integral part of the Fedora system, we will be concentrating solely on its operation.

The biggest advantage of using a package is that the package contains information about itself. It contains all of its dependency information, versioning information, and installation locations for each file. This information is then read by the package management system; when a package is installed, the information is stored in a database that the manager uses to keep track of your packages. Now, rather than having to keep track of the installed files (and locating them yourself if they require replacement, modification, or deletion), you can use the functionality provided by your package management system to make changes automatically. This provides huge time savings on your part as an administrator, in both managing and organizing packages and files. In addition, you can save space by not having to decompress and unarchive the files located within the package to their own directory as you would with a tarball.

Another major advantage touched on previously is the ability to *upgrade* installed software. This is not nearly as easy when using standard tarballs. RPM stores information on the precise configuration you specify during the installation procedure. This means that during an update you do not have to remember the exact parameters you passed months or possibly years ago to initially install the software. In addition to upgrading, you can also *downgrade* your software. If a certain version of the software does not work well on your system, you can use a simple command to revert to an older version of the software. RPM will even notify you if any of the other installed software packages (installed through RPM) will have problems with your downgrade. You can then make an informed decision on which packages should go and which packages should stay. This type of information is priceless in the rapidly growing software market. The speed at which new versions of open source software are being released is always increasing as more and more developers join the battle.

Yes, another major bonus to using the RPM system is the ability to *verify* packages. Verification enables you to confirm whether a package has been installed as well as to determine exactly which version of that package is installed. You can even determine what file a package belongs to and where it came from!

Pay close attention to the commands used within the next section for installing and using rpms. You will be using these files for the rest of your installations in order to provide you with the most organized system possible.

RPM and RPM Source Packages

RPM has five modes, as we discussed in the preceding section: installing, uninstalling, upgrading, querying, and verifying. Each of these modes is accessed by passing different flags and parameters to the rpm command. Before you install a package, you will of course need to download the proper package. Pay close attention to the name because it holds all the clues necessary to making the correct selection for your specific system. A typical package name looks like this:

```
foo-1.1-2.i386.rpm
```

You can read this name by using the following format:

```
name-version-release.platform.rpm
```

In this format, you would be working with a package named Foo version 1.1, release 2, for the i386 architecture. For the remainder of this section, we will refer to this example as our target package. With the proper package downloaded, let's take a closer look at each mode.

Installing

To install a package, you can use the following command:

```
rpm -ivh foo-1.1-2.i386.rpm
```

You will then be presented with the name of the package being installed. Take note of this name because it might not necessarily be the name of the file. You might have downloaded a rebuilt release from a site other than the original source, and this release could have a filename not related to the package (for example, fedoratest.rpm). After the name of the packaging currently installing is printed to the screen, you should see hash marks begin to appear that act as a progress bar. Although the command for installing a package is very simple, you might receive a few errors.

Package Is Already Installed

```
Foo         package foo-1.1-2 is already installed
error: foo-1.1-2.i386.rpm cannot be installed
```

This means exactly what it tells you, *the package is already installed.* If you feel you have reached this message in error or you would like to install the package anyway, you can use the following command:

```
rpm -ivh --replacepkgs foo-1.1-2.i386.rpm
```

This automatically overwrites the current packages that reside on your system.

Conflicting Files

```
foo  /usr/bin/bar conflicts with file from apple-2.3-1
error: foo-1.1-2.i386.rpm cannot be installed
```

If you receive this message, then another package has already installed the file contained in your Foo package. To ignore this error and install the package anyway, use the following command:

```
rpm -ivh --replacefiles foo-1.1-2.i386.rpm
```

This overwrites any files that are interfering with the installation. Note that any of these optional flags can be combined.

Unresolved Dependencies

```
failed dependencies:
        pear is needed by foo-1.1-2
```

Unresolved dependencies occur when your target package requires another package to be installed. In this case, the Pear package is needed. You need to find and install the correct packages before you can continue your installation. If you feel that you've reached the message in error, you can choose to force the installation by using the following:

```
rpm -ivh --nodeps foo-1.1-2.i386.rpm
```

This installs the package, but most likely it will not function properly or will fail to work at all. It is highly recommended that you gather all of your dependencies first. There are commands that will attempt to gather and install each of the dependencies automatically through the Internet (see Chapter 6). The main command is up2date, but more on this later.

Upgrading

When attempting to upgrade a package, use the following command:

```
rpm -Uvh foo-1.1-2.i386.rpm
```

The Red Hat Package Manager then checks for a previous installation of the software you are attempting to install and makes sure the appropriate package is removed first. During this process, you might see a message that looks similar to this one:

```
saving /etc/foo.conf as /etc/foo.conf.rpmsave
```

This means that the changes you might have made to the configuration file on the version already installed might not be forward compatible with the version you are now installing. In this case, RPM automatically saves a backup version of the configuration file in case anything should go wrong. This will enable you to roll back changes made to installed packages. It is recommended that you take a look at both of these configuration files so that you can resolve any differences in configuration. You will most likely want the same setup for your software as was previously installed. Some background processes that might not be immediately evident might require the old configuration, in which case you would not know something is not functioning properly until it you have *gone live*, or put the test server into production.

NOTE   You can use the upgrade command line for *installation* of packages as well. Red Hat recommends using upgrade because it provides the same functionality that the installation does if there is no previously existing package of an older version on the system.

NOTE   *Upgrading* a package is actually a combination of *uninstalling* and *installing*. Therefore, you might receive error messages from either of these commands.

The only error message attached to the actual upgrade command is as follows:

```
foo package foo-1.2-2 (which is newer) is already installed
error: foo-1.1-2.i386.rpm cannot be installed
```

This tells you that you are trying to install a version that is older than the currently installed version. If you would like to *downgrade* the package and install the older version, you can use this command:

```
rpm -Uvh --oldpackage foo-1.1-2.i386.rpm
```

This installs the older version just as it would a newer package.

Freshening

Freshening a package is similar to upgrading a package except that it will not install a package that does not have a previously existing older copy already installed. You can use the freshening command by typing the following:

```
rpm -Fvh foo-1.1-2.i386.rpm
```

If the package Foo already exists and is older, the new version will be installed, If not, no changes will be made.

A good use for the freshening flag is when you wish to install a group of rpm files only if they already exist on the system. If you downloaded a large number of the latest distributions of multiple programs, you might not wish to delete all the packages you do not want installed. Instead, you could choose to leave them all in one directory and type the following:

```
rpm -Fvh *.rpm
```

Now RPM will install only the packages that already exist on your system—very handy if you receive a distribution CD that contains a large number of packages, many of which you do not need on your system.

Uninstalling

Uninstalling a package is simple. You do not even need to know the full version and release of a particular package. Simply use the following:

```
rpm -e foo
```

This command removes the package Foo unless there is another package that is dependent on Foo, in which case you will receive an error message:

```
removing these packages would break dependencies:
foo is needed by bar-2.0-2
```

If you are aware of this problem and you wish to remove the package anyway, use the

```
rpm -e --nodeps foo
```

command to force the removal. This flag is the same flag used when installing a package that is dependent on packages not yet residing on your system.

Querying

Querying is used to determine what packages are currently installed as well as detailed information on each one of these packages. To find the basic information on a package use the following:

```
rpm -q foo
```

This returns a single line of text that states, much like the rpm file itself, the version and release numbers. Similar to:

```
Foo-1.1-2
```

There are also *package specification options*, which can be declared on the command line in case you wish to query by something other than the package name. They are as follows:

-a   This queries all installed packages.

-f <file>   This queries the package that was installed from the file specified.

-p <package file>   This queries the package file specified.

If you wish to specify information other than the name, version, and release, you need to use *information selection options.* They are as follows:

-i   This displays package information including name, description, release, size, build date, install date, vendor, and more.

-l   This displays a list of files that the package contains.

-s   This displays the state of all files in the package.

-d   This shows a list of all files marked as documentation files.

-c   This displays any files within the package that are marked as configuration files. These are the files that will require your attention after installation.

-v   If you have specified the -l option, you can use this flag as well. This gives you a long listing format of the files within the package, much like using the ll command or the ls command with the -l flag.

Verifying

This option is used to compare various information about files installed with a package to the original package installation information. You can use any of the parameters and flags listed in the package specification options for querying. For instance:

```
rpm -Va
```

would verify *all* the packages installed, and

```
rpm -Vf /bin/vi
```

would verify the package that contains the /bin/vi file. You could also use

```
rpm -Vp foo-1.1-2.i386.rpm
```

to verify a package file against the currently installed version. This can be especially useful if you suspect that your RPM Data Base (DB) has been damaged somehow and wish to verify its contents against a known good package. If the test passes and there are no errors, you will not receive any output to the screen. If the test does not pass, you will get a string of eight characters, a possible c denoting that the file is a configuration file, and then the filename. If you receive a period, then it means that everything is okay.

Table 4.1 shows the list of error codes that could be thrown to you.

TABLE 4.1 Verifying Error Codes

Code	Error
5	MD5 checksum
S	File size
L	Symbolic link
T	File modification time
D	Device
U	User
G	Group
M	Mode
?	Unreadable file

If you receive any output, you will need to determine whether it is RPM that is damaged or the installation of that particular package that is bad. After you make the determination, take the appropriate action.

Performing System Backup and Recovery

Having a backup system in place is imperative. It cannot be stressed enough the amount of time that can be lost from having a hard disk go bad. Without a solid backup system in place, you should not feel at ease with your system. After your server is used to host web pages or server files or whatever the use, people will come to rely on your system. Millions of dollars' worth of time, energy, and resources might be housed on your system, and we're sure you do not want to explain to your users why their data is completely lost and cannot be recovered. You should instead be explaining that their data will be restored in a matter of hours.

There are many methods for data recovery on any system. You have a choice of what information you would like to back up as well as what you would like it backed up to. If you have multiple servers storing very large amounts of data on your network, you might want to look into a commercial system for backing up all of them to a central backup server. If you are housing only a limited amount of information on a bare-bones system, you might wish to back up only users' files.

However, for most systems, you will want to back up the entire system to do a full bare-metal restoration. A *bare-metal restoration* is a restoration that will start from nothing and bring your system to exactly where it was before your *incident*.

Critical Data

Your first step is to determine what information is mission critical and must be backed up. If you have already created a setup script to install everything you need on a system, you might wish to back up only the user data on your system in order to save system resources and conserve file space during a nightly backup. If you determine that your entire system needs to be backed up, you will need to pick a larger media source for backing up your files.

Only you can determine the values of the individual directories on your system. You might have a system that caters to other users, so that your most important directory would be the /home directory and all its subdirectories. You might have a system used only as a web server, with no other users but you. If so, you will want to make sure you back up the appropriate directory. You will also want to make sure that all the configuration files for your software are backed up as well. The majority of your time running a web server will be spent modifying all the configuration files, so losing these would be catastrophic.

Backup Media

There is a wide array of choices for your backup media. You should make your choice while keeping in mind the amount of data you need to back up and the speed at which you need to make your backups. Let's take a closer look at the more popular choices:

Hard disks   Hard disks make an excellent choice for rapid backup of a large amount of data. Keep in mind that you should never back up to the same hard disk on which the data is currently stored. Doing so would negate your backup if the hard disk fails. Instead you should have a separate hard disk or hard disks for your backup. There are exceptions to this rule, however, such as having hourly snapshots of your database so that you can roll back if any non-hardware-related problem occurs.

Servers   It is recommended that if you wish to perform a backup to hard disk that you use a separate server. This provides protection from power surges and complete equipment failures that could damage or possibly destroy all the hard disks contained in one server. Having a central backup server also enables you to back up all your other servers to a single location.

Tapes   Tapes are capable of storing around 40GB–80GB of files. Tapes can be useful because of their portability. A tape can be removed and stored in a fireproof vault in case of natural disaster. There are a couple hindrances, however. If you forget to remove a tape before the next backup is performed, you will lose the older backup. If the new backup is faulty, you will have lost your previous day's or week's backup.

CD-R   You can get up to 700MB (currently) on a CD. CDs are removable media as well, so you can store them in a protected area. Like tapes, they have to be changed between backups. However, because CD-RW drives can be purchased for under $50 and CD-Rs themselves can be bought for less than $0.40 apiece, this is an excellent choice for the frugal minded.

DVD-R   DVD-RW drives continue to drop in price. If your filesystem contains more than a CD can hold, you might wish to look into using a DVD-R drive for backing up your files. A single DVD can hold approximately 4GB of files and provides the same benefits as other removable media.

Backing Up Your System

There are literally hundreds of methods for backing up your filesystem. You can find many of them located on the Web, including free backup scripts for you to download and use that will provide an abundance of choices for your system. Each method will use different libraries that you might be required to download and install. You can even find complete GUI backup systems and schedulers for the X Window interface as well.

This section will cover the actual creation of the backup files in a tarball. From there you can choose to copy that tarball onto your choice of media. Multiple books have been written on backup systems for Linux, and if you require an extensive recovery system, we recommend that you purchase a book to provide you with an extended knowledge of backup systems. This section is intended to give you only a basic understanding of why you need a solid backup system in place and how to set up a simple program.

Remember that however you choose to back up your data, you need to test, test, and retest your methodologies before applying them. You should use a test system to run your scripts and scheduled jobs and then check the media to make sure all the intended files have been successfully backed up. Without testing, you might *think* you have the security of redundancy but in reality you could be left empty-handed if disaster strikes, which of course will be when you are least prepared and least expect it.

It is a good idea to automate your backup systems with a series of complete backups and incremental backups. A *complete backup* stores all the system information for a complete recovery, whereas an *incremental backup* stores only the information that has changed since the last backup. It is highly recommended that your incremental backup store all changes since your last complete backup so that you do not need to restore by using four or five backups. Instead you would restore by using only your last good complete backup—and if it has been more than 24 hours since the complete backup, you would use the most recent incremental backup.

To automate your backup system, you can choose to use the `crontab` file located in the `/etc` directory. This file contains information on scripts, processes, and commands that are run on a schedule. You system will automatically parse this file looking for any entries that need to be run and will fire off the appropriate command. It is usually standard practice to create (or download) your own backup script and have `cron` fire off that one script. This will prevent your `crontab` file from becoming messy with too many lines of code. Your command line for backing up files can become rather large before you know it. For now, let's `cd` into your home directory and deposit the scripts you are about to create there. First, create a repository for your backup files as temporary storage. Move to the root directory and type the following:

```
mkdir backups
```

You will now have a new directory named `backups`. With that done, let's look at the `tar` command you'll use for backing up your system. Go ahead and use the command:

```
pico full_backup
```

You will then be brought to a new black file. In this file you will place your `tar` command, which will look like this:

```
tar -zcvpf /backups/full_backup-`date '+%Y%m%d'`.tar.gz \
    --directory / \
    --exclude=*.iso \
    --exclude=proc \
```

```
--exclude=tmp \
--exclude=/backups \
--exclude=bufferdir \
--exclude=/dev \
.
```

An analysis of the command will show that you will be creating a backup of the / directory with a name that starts with backup- and then contains the current date in a *YYMMDD* format and finishes off the filename with the appropriate .tar.gz extension, denoting it as a gzipped tarball. You will also notice the --exclude options. These enable you to specify files (for example, the .iso files) and directories that you do not wish to include in your backup. Finally, you will notice the last line contains a single dot. This tells tar to include all other files and directories not expressly listed in your exclude arguments.

Now, if you were to keep executing this script every week, you would end up with a lot of backup files that could be taking up a ton of space. So you are going to add another line into your script that will delete any files older than 30 days. To do that, type the following:

```
find /backups/full_backup-* -mtime +30 -exec rm -rf {} \;
```

This tells the find command to run the rm -rf command for each file it finds in the /backups directory—in effect, wiping out your old backups. After this line, you might wish to add your commands for sending the completed file to a specific device such as a tape or CD-RW drive. If you would like to send this file to another computer on your network as a backup server, you should create a script for the crontab on your backup server to reach each of your other servers that are being backed up. This is done for security reasons so that a malicious user who gains access to your web server would not have access to your backup server as well. Barring that, everything is set up properly.

After you have added your line to move your file to the appropriate device/location, go ahead and save and exit the file. Then open another new file with pico that will be responsible for creating the incremental backups. Let's call it incremental_backup. With that file open, let's use the following for your script:

```
theString = "`date +%u` days ago"
sunday = `date -d "$theString"`

tar -zcvpf --newer $sunday /backups/incremental_backup- \
    `date '+%Y%m%d'`.tar.gz \
    --directory / \
    --exclude=*.iso \
    --exclude=proc \
    --exclude=tmp \
    --exclude=bufferdir \
    --exclude=/dev \
    --exclude=/backups \
    .
```

This will create a tarball that contains only files that are newer than the last full backup (on Sunday) as your incremental backup. Next you'll use the same command as the full backup script to delete any older files, but this time you want to delete only incremental files that are older than one week. So use the following command:

```
find /backups/incremental_backup-* -mtime +14 -exec rm -rf {} \;
```

Here you see that the -mtime flag now has a +14 argument for the number of days and that you are now finding files that begin with incremental. These are the two areas that have changed for your new script. After that has been added, add the same command you used in your full backup script to transfer the directory or single file to your device or location of choice. With that finished, you will be ready to add your cron job into the system to automatically run these scripts when required.

To run your newly created scripts automatically, you'll be using the /etc/crontab file. You can edit the crontab file and have your changes automatically take effect by using the crontab -e command. If you are logged in as *root*, then you will be taken to the crontab file in vi. Once you exit and write the changes, the crontab will automatically make its changes. Try that now and take a look at the format. Here you have six parameters per line:

minute   This is an integer value from 0 to 59 representing the time at which to run this script.

hour   This is also an integer representing the hour at which to run this script or command. It should be a value from 0 to 23.

dayOfMonth   The dayOfMonth value should be from 1–31 for the day of the month the script or command specified should be run.

monthOfYear   This is a value from 1–12 representing the month of the year.

dayOfWeek   dayOfWeek should be a value from 0–7, which represents Sunday through Monday, with the 7 representing Sunday once again.

shellCommand   At last, this indicates the full path to the script or command that should be run when the preceding requirements are met.

Using the preceding format, you can determine that the line for your full_backup script should read as follows:

```
0 2 * * 0 /root/full_backup
```

This will cause your full backup script to run weekly at 2:00 A.M. every Sunday. Notice that the asterisks denote a null value for that argument. For the incremental script, you will add a line to run the backup every night at 2:00 A.M. except for Sunday. To do this, let's use the following:

```
0 2 * * 1-6 /root/incremental_backup
```

Now your `crontab` is ready to be saved. After it is saved, you can exit. Congratulations—you have successfully set up a basic backup system for your Linux server.

System Restoration

Restoring your system is significantly easier than setting up an entire backup system. When restoring your system, you should take care, however. When running the command

```
tar -zxvpf full_backupX.tar.gz --directory /
```

you will automatically copy over any files that are still on the system. If you are worried about the system not restoring correctly or if any of the files in the tarball might not be the correct ones, you might wish to change the `--directory` to read `/root/test` or some other testing directory you have created. This way, you can parse through each file individually and make sure it is the correct one. This will allow for selective restores as well. A selective restore is usually used when a particular user might experience corrupted files.

If only a few files are needed out of the tarball, you can specify the filenames (including path) as the last parameter in the `tar` command. This extracts only the wanted files and maintains the rest of your filesystem the way it is.

Linux Administration Checklist

After reading this chapter, you should feel comfortable moving around the Linux filesystem and you should have a basic understanding of some of the more common administration tasks. Since finishing this chapter, you should be able to do the following:

- Add, modify, and delete users.
- Add, modify, and delete groups.
- Change passwords.
- Gather system information on memory and disk usage.
- Enable filesystem quotas for users and groups.
- Start and stop processes.
- Use limited control over processes.
- Install a program or software from a source tarball.
- Install, uninstall, and query rpm binary packages.
- Be able to build your own binary package from source.
- Determine what backup method is best for distinct server and network configurations.

- Add and remove cron jobs.

- Restore your system from a backup.

We have covered quite a few administrative tasks over the course of this chapter, and you should start to feel confident with your newfound skills in Linux. With your skill set beginning to grow, it is time to move on to the next chapter and discover how to set up some more of the advanced configuration for your network.

CHAPTER 5

Network Connectivity

- TCP/IP

- Configuring Your Address

- Hardware

- Understanding a Firewall

- DNS

Networking, as defined by Merriam-Webster online is "the exchange of information or services among individuals, groups, or institutions." In this strict definition of the word, we can see that forms of networking have been around for far longer than the age of computers.

A good example of networking is smoke signals sent by Native Americans to others located too far away for verbal communication. If one American Indian needed to warn another on the other side of a plain, they might use smoke signals to communicate without having to travel far distances. If that message needed to be passed on, the receiver of the first message would resend or broadcast the message to whomever was next on the way to its intended destination. This is networking. When information is passed on through multiple points before arriving at its intended destination, a network is established that makes that possible. The example of smoke signals is referred to as an *ad hoc network*—a network fashioned from what is immediately available. It does not run through a planned system that contains a router to centralize the distribution of data. In the plains of early North America, the signals were seen and interpreted by the nearest individuals who could then resend the message as they saw fit toward the final destination.

Hundreds of years later, in the present day and age, we have computers sending information across wires, fiber optics, and satellites to millions of users across the world. Anyone on a computer can reach anyone else on a computer throughout the world, assuming they are both connected to the same network. In the vast majority of cases, of course, that network is the Internet.

The Internet is a massive network, not simply a few friends sending smoke signals to people they already know. Procedures and standards have to be in place in order for networking equipment to know where the information is from and where it's going. The network must also have a universal language so that each machine can communicate with the whole; this is often referred to as a *protocol*.

There are a few major protocols that have been developed over the years. The first, and most popular, is TCP/IP, which stands for Transmission Control Protocol/Internet Protocol. We will be covering this protocol extensively later in this chapter. The other two main network protocols are UUCP and IPX. UUCP, or Unix to Unix Copy Protocol, was originally developed for sending and receiving news and mail messages across dial-up telephone connections. Because this has become a mostly outdated practice for server-level applications, UUCP has been pushed to the background. This is not to say, however, that UUCP is not suited for specific applications. The last protocol, IPX (Internetwork Packet Exchange), is used most commonly to connect to Novell NetWare environments. Because this book is a guide to setting up and administering a web server, we will be focusing primarily on TCP/IP.

Using TCP/IP

TCP/IP originated from a research project funded by the United States Defense Advanced Research Projects Agency (DARPA). Research began in 1969 on a system called ARPANET, which stands for Advanced Research Projects Agency Network. This network system was the beginning of what is now the Internet. Research continued on ARPANET as an experiment until 1975, when it was deemed operational and moved into service. After another eight years had passed, the protocol suite TCP/IP was released and adopted by all machines on the network as a mandatory standard. By 1990 ARPANET was no more because it had morphed into what is now the Internet. This was the beginning of TCP/IP and the reason why it is so largely used throughout the world. Many companies have adopted the same protocol to use on internal local area networks (LANs) as well.

In relation to our smoke signal example, TCP/IP would indicate where the people look for the smoke signals and how they send them. The problem this poses for our natives is distinguishing whom the message is for. Back then a series of signals would probably determine its destination. In the twenty-first century, this is accomplished by using host names, IP addresses, and hardware addresses. The most verbose and expressive form of addressing is the host names. The natives in our example had names themselves, which were translated into smoke signals, whereas our computers are given names by us and the message is sent via packets. Addressing is crucial if we want our intended receiver to eventually get our information.

Internet Protocol

Let's take a closer look at the Internet Protocol (IP). The *Internet Protocol* is the governing protocol in charge of the exchange of datagrams to a remote host. You will also hear the term *packets* used instead of *datagrams;* these terms are almost completely interchangeable except that *datagram* implies a packet that is being *routed* and not just a packet of information by itself.

It is important to note that IP is completely independent of hardware used, which means it needs its own addressing scheme in order to transmit data. This is where IP addresses come in. We'll speak more on this later in this section—for now just understand why IP addresses are used.

You also need to understand that Internet Protocol (by design) is not reliable. Say you access a website and begin downloading a large file that generates enough traffic to flood your gateway. Maybe your gateway is an older machine and is tight on resources. Because your machine happens to be out of buffer space at the current moment, it is unable to accept the incoming datagram in order to forward it. Therefore, IP just drops that packet—it will never resurface and is lost forever. Instead, it is the communicating hosts' responsibility to check the integrity and completeness of the file being transferred and re-ask for the packets should they be missing in action. This brings us to TCP.

Transmission Control Protocol

It is TCP's job to control this interaction between hosts. TCP works by creating an interpreter for commands and programs to write to, thereby making the transmission of data transparent to programs wanting to interact with it. TCP does this by establishing a connection between one or more ports on each of the hosts. It then breaks your information into packets and sends those packets to the receiving host. The receiving host puts the packets back together and verifies the integrity to make sure the file is okay. Again, this process is, in the majority of cases, completely invisible to the programs that use it.

The downside of TCP becomes apparent when attempting to transfer multiple instances of small bits of information. Let's say you wish to retrieve a small amount of data from your database. Through TCP you would need to send at least three datagrams to establish a connection, then another three datagrams to send and verify the data, and yet another three to close out the connection. In other words, you would have to present nine packets for only one packet of actual information. To combat this, the User Datagram Protocol (UDP) was created.

User Datagram Protocol

The UDP protocol does not require a connection with another host in order to send its data. Instead, UDP will send its packet of information with the correct address attached to it and hope that it is received by the proper computer. After the packet is received on the other end, the server will perform the requested operation or procedure and then place the return information in another packet to send back to the original host.

There is also an optional feature of UDP that we touched on in Chapter 2, "Installing Linux": the ability to run a *checksum*. This means that all of the checksum information must be stored within that one packet but on the same note, it gives that single packet the ability to know if it is correct or not.

The disadvantage of UDP is a large packet size and the fact that UDP was not built with packet loss in mind. Because UDP will not handle resending a packet, the originator of the request must resend the original packet and have the server reprocess the request for the return packet. As you can imagine, not too many programs are able to fit their information into a single packet and so the use of UDP is limited. Many applications and programs will use the speed benefit over TCP to their advantage, however; online games and most streaming multimedia are excellent examples of such applications.

Ports

Ports are like different radio frequencies on a single radio. If your radio had the capability to monitor every frequency at the same time with a different daemon or process, each separate frequency would be considered a port. Ports, however, are not measured by the frequency of a radio wave but are instead numbered from 0–65,000. You might already know that the default port for connecting to a web server is port 80 or that FTP's default port is 21. You will see ports expressed many times as the IP address followed by a colon and then the port number. For instance, if you have a router that enables you to SSH into it, it might come with an SSH daemon that listens on port 1100. To SSH into that router, you would use a command similar to the following:

```
ssh 192.168.1.2:1100
```

Ports are split into two groups. Anything numbered under 1024 is considered a *privileged* port, and its configuration cannot be changed by anyone but the system administrator. Ports 1024 and above are open for any users to access and use as they see fit. File-sharing programs, Internet Relay Chat (IRC), and other programs can be set up to use these ports.

The reason for having privileged ports is security. If any user were able to access any port, they would be able to view all the information passed through that port. If this information is in clear text and not encrypted, as on most mail servers, then sensitive information could fall into the wrong hands. Because ports below 1024 can be administered only by the *root* user, they also are labeled as *trusted* ports. If you were to access a web server or FTP server running on a port number above 1024, you could not be sure that the system administrator would even be aware of these services being run. Any user on the system could have started these services unless their access had otherwise been restricted.

Addressing

As we discussed earlier in this section, IP networking uses IP addresses. *IP addresses* are composed of four hexadecimal couplets, which are usually converted to decimal form for ease of use. Each set is separated by periods and contains a value from 0 to 255. This is sometimes referred to as *dotted quad notation.*

Each machine on your network must have an IP address for your network if it wishes to use TCP/IP. You must *also* have one or more IP addresses that represent you on the Internet as well. There are predefined ranges reserved for private networks to use depending on the type of naming scheme they are using. The naming scheme used is dependent on the size of the network and the number of subnets and hosts that are required. Each of the addresses within the proper range is then routed on the Internet. The ranges are as follows:

Class A   `10.0.0.0` through `10.255.255.255`

Class B   `172.16.0.0` through `172.31.255.255`

Class C   `192.168.0.0` through `192.168.255.255`

NOTE   Each of these ranges contains multiple subnets within the given network. For instance, in the Class B range 172.16.1.0, 172.16.2.0 and 172.16.3.0 are all subnets within the network. All 0s in the host portion of an address specifies the entire network.

When you apply to your Internet Service Provider (ISP) for IP addresses, you will be given a few IP addresses (depending on how large your network is) to assign to your network. You can then set up your network so that each computer will have its own outside IP address. Alternately, you could assign a single outside IP address to a set of computers by using a router. The router will then forward the packets to the appropriate destination within your network.

Each class type allows for a certain number of subnets and a certain number of hosts on each subnet:

Class A   Class A uses the first couplet to specify the network address. The next three couplets are available for you to divide into subnets and hosts as you see fit.

Class B   In a Class B network, the first *two* couplets are used to specify the network while the third and fourth are available for local subnets and hosts.

Class C   Finally, Class C uses the first three couplets to determine the network address, with the last being used for subnets and hosts. This last octet can be broken down even further by segmenting the 254 available hosts into their own subnets.

Class A, the rarest of the classes, will allow for 128 networks of about 1.6 million hosts per network. Class B will allow 16,320 networks to each contain 65,024 hosts, and Class C will allow for 2 million networks to have 254 hosts each.

There are also two other classes, which are reserved for special purposes: classes D and E, which fall into a range of 224.0.0.0 through 255.255.255.255. IP multicasting, which allows for packets to be sent to multiple hosts at the same time, uses these addresses. If you were to perform the math on each of the network to host numbers in the examples, you would find that only 254 numbers per octet are used to calculate the final numbers. This is because a value of 0 in an octet would refer to that particular network, and a value of 255 would refer to all hosts on that network.

NOTE   An address that specifies all hosts on a network is called the *broadcast address*.

For instance, if you were running a Class B network, 149.74.0.0 would specify the network, and 149.74.255.255 would specify all hosts on that network.

As we mentioned before, it is also possible to subnet a Class C network. To do this, you divide your 254 addresses into subnets by using a *subnet mask*. A subnet mask is used to define what subnet a host belongs to. For instance, if you were to use a submask of 255.255.255.240, you would allow for 16 subnets. This is because 240 in binary is 4 bits (11110000), and 2 to the power of 4 is 16. Now to determine how many hosts you are allowed to have for each subnet, you must look at how many bits off you have in 240 (11110000). In this case it is 16 as well. However, you must lose two because the first must be your subnet address and the last must be the broadcast address. This gives you 14 hosts per subnet.

In addition, specific IP addresses are reserved for special purposes. Two examples are 0.0.0.0 and 127.0.0.0. The first specifies the *default route* used for IP, and the second is the *loopback address*. If datagrams are sent to the loopback address, the machine will treat the packet as if it came from a different network. This enables you to develop and test applications and programs that use networking without having to set up an entire network or more than one computer to send and receive from. All development can be performed isolated on a single machine.

After you choose which class is right for your application, you must then decide whether to assign each host a static IP address individually or to use the Dynamic Host Configuration Protocol (DHCP). We touched on this briefly during Chapter 2. Running one of your machines, usually the gateway, as a DHCP server will enable any machine that attaches to your local network to be automatically assigned an IP address. The next section will help you decide which method is best suited to your purpose and will detail how to set up each type of environment.

Configuring Your Address

Now that you know the basics of IP addressing, you can begin to look objectively at which solution is best suited for your situation. Static IPs will give you definite IP addresses for each machine on your network and will never change if the machine becomes disconnected or needs to reboot. Even if you are running a DHCP server, however, you can still use static IP addresses that fit in the range of your network configuration. For our examples within this chapter, we will be using Class C IP addresses because it is unlikely you will need to create subnets for your first Linux server.

First decide whether this machine is going to be connecting to a gateway or connecting directly to the Internet. If it will be connecting directly to the Internet, you need to specify only your Internet IP address as a static IP. If you are connecting through a gateway, you need to specify your internal address either by entering a static IP or by configuring your server to connect to your network's DHCP server. After this is completed, you need to tell your firewall, if you are using one, to allow traffic for the ports you want available to your server's IP address. This will allow outside users who are directed to your server's IP address access to the specified ports.

There is one other solution you might be implementing, and that is configuring your server on a network, although it does not need to serve pages to the outside world. This would be the case if you are using this server as a development platform and only people involved in the project need to access this machine from your local network. This setup gives you the opportunity to either give your machine a static IP address or use the DHCP server on your network to automatically obtain one.

In this section, you'll learn how to change the proper settings on your server to fit your needs.

Static IP

IP addresses must be assigned to an individual Ethernet device. The configuration file for each device is located, on Fedora Core 2, under the following directory:

```
/etc/sysconfig/network-scripts/
```

Each file will be named ifcfg-eth*X*, where *X* is the number of the device. If multiple addresses need to be assigned to a single device, you can also configure virtual devices. They use the same filename with a colon and virtual device number following the device file. The following shows eth0 configured with its main configuration file and three virtual devices:

```
-rw-r--r--  1 root    root    108 Feb 26 11:51 ifcfg-eth0
-rw-r--r--  1 root    root    108 Feb 26 11:51 ifcfg-eth0:1
-rw-r--r--  1 root    root    108 Feb 26 11:51 ifcfg-eth0:2
-rw-r--r--  1 root    root    108 Feb 26 11:51 ifcfg-eth0:3
```

If you need to create another device or virtual device, you can simply copy one of the existing files and edit it to change its configuration. Go ahead and pico your ifcfg-eth0 file and take a look at its contents. You should get something similar to the following:

```
DEVICE=eth0
ONBOOT=yes
BOOTPROTO=static
IPADDR=192.168.0.13
NETMASK=255.255.255.0
GATEWAY=192.168.0.1
```

This configuration says that the network device eth0 will be active ONBOOT and uses a static IP address that is given on the IPADDR line. It also shows the netmask and gateway for this device as well, because our test box needs to use a gateway. You should note that in a virtual device, your device line needs to read just as your filename does, with a colon and the virtual device number.

After you have edited the required information, you can save and exit. Repeat this process for each device and virtual device and you will be ready to bring the network interfaces down and then back up again. To do this, you need to use the commands ifup and ifdown. The only argument you need to pass in is the device. You do not need to bring each virtual device up separately. Bringing up the device itself will automatically bring the others up. Go ahead and run the following:

```
ifdown eth0
```

If the command is successful, you will not receive any message. Now run its counterpart, using this command:

```
ifup eth0
```

If you do not receive any error messages, everything has been successful.

You can try to test your connection by using `ping domainName` to ping a known server You should be returned lines of information telling you how long each ping took. If you are not returned this information, you need to do some basic troubleshooting.

First, see if the ping is even initiating. You might receive an error message that states the domain is an `unknown host`. If this is the case, and you know that your domain name is correct, you should try pinging your gateway. If you are unable to ping your gateway, you know you need to troubleshoot your networking device. If you are able to ping your gateway, you know that your internal network is configured properly and you need to troubleshoot your DNS configuration. You can further check this by specifying an IP address instead of a domain name. Use a known good IP address that accepts pings and try again. If it works, then you just need to reconfigure your DNS. See the section "Using DNS" later in this chapter for more information.

If your domain name *is* resolving and your pings are timing out, you have a problem with your network configuration. This means that your machine can access your DNS but not the rest of the world. You then need to double-check your configuration files that you just edited for any errors. After you have located your problem, remember to bring your interfaces down and then back up again in order for the changes to take effect. Then use the `ping` command to test your connection again.

DHCP

To configure DHCP on your machine, we will assume you are using a separate machine for your DHCP server. Just like the static IP address configuration, you will be editing the `ifcfg-ethX` files located in the `/etc/sysconfig/network-scripts/` directory. There are only a few differences in the file configuration between static and dynamic assignments: the `IPADDR` line, which will not exist, and the `BOOTPROTO`, which should read `dhcp`. Here is an example:

```
DEVICE=eth0
ONBOOT=yes
BOOTPROTO=dhcp
NETMASK=255.255.255.0
GATEWAY=192.168.0.1
```

You can also choose to leave the NETMASK and GATEWAY lines off, and Linux will attempt to retrieve the proper netmask and gateway for your system from the DHCP server. In this case, because your DHCP server will be assigning your machine an IP address in the range of 192.168.0.50–150, it will also assign Class C network values and will use 255.255.255.0 for your netmask. Your gateway will most likely be 192.168.0.1, unless it has been set up differently on your DHCP server.

TIP	For both static and dynamic IP addresses, you can also use the netconfig command. This will launch an ANSI graphic program that will enable you to configure your network interfaces. Anything changed this way will be written to the proper configuration files and will be activated immediately.

Remember that if you are using this server as a web server for the outside world, your machine must have a static IP address associated with its domain name. If this is the case and you are using DHCP, you need to configure your router to associate the outside static IP address with your internal static or dynamic IP address. If you are directly connected to the Internet and use the static IP address, which your domain name(s) resolve to, you do not need to perform any additional setup. If you are setting up an advanced network or will be connecting to the Internet via an advanced network, you need to contact your network in order to coordinate your configuration; we recommend that you purchase a book devoted to this topic if you will be designing and implementing the network yourself.

Setting Up Hardware

Until now, we have discussed operations that happen on the *Network layer*. This term is used to describe the layer of logic that deals with the software of networking, using IP addresses to identify local and remote computers. Now we'll show you the hardware aspect of addressing computers and how the software places the information on the wire and receives it for processing as well.

To do this, we must first present the difference in addressing. Your hardware will use *Media Access Control (MAC) addresses* to identify the devices on your network. As you might recall, when we configured our IP addresses we talked about *virtual* interfaces on a single device: eth0. This device is the only hardware device and the only one that has a MAC address.

MAC addresses are, for the most part, permanently affixed to the device by the manufacturer. This enables the addresses to be unique and allows specific addressing to a single computer on your network without having to interpolate the IP address for each packet. In the "Internet Protocol" section, we talked about how TCP sends traffic to other computers by using the IP address. Let's take a look at what part hardware and MAC addressing plays in establishing a connection with a remote computer.

Let's assume that your machine has an IP address of 192.168.1.2 and you wish to establish an SSH connection with 192.168.1.3. Because your subnet mask is 255.255.255.0, your computer knows that you are on the same network as the remote computer you wish to contact. Therefore, you send out an ARP broadcast. *ARP*, which stands for *Address Resolution Protocol*, is in charge of determining the correct MAC address for the IP address you wish to contact. Now the ARP request will carry the MAC address of your local computer as well as the IP address for the computer you wish to contact. Every machine on your network will receive this request and process it to determine whether that computer is the proper computer. Only the computer with the IP address matching the request will answer. The packet sent back by that computer will include that computer's own MAC address and will be addressed to your MAC address. If a packet is addressed to a specific MAC address, every other computer on your network will completely ignore the packet and will not waste resources reading it.

If your destination address were to be somewhere outside your subnet, the router used to access this other network would reply with its MAC address. This enables the packet handling and forwarding to remain invisible to the networking layer specific to your machine. The major plus is that you will probably never have to deal with a device's actual MAC address. You might hear the term *Data-Link layer* used to describe this hardware routing logic.

In this section, we'll introduce you to the types of hardware available that are the backbone of the Data-Link layer. We will discuss the purpose of the devices and some of the benefits and downsides to each as well.

Network Cards

The *network card* is the device, usually installed in a computer, that connects you to a network. Network cards can have two types of connections: *coaxial*, which is similar to a cable TV wire, or *unshielded twisted pair (UTP)*, which contains pairs of copper wires. Category 5 (CAT5) is the most common twisted pair and uses an RJ-45 connector on both ends. The coaxial is used for 10Base2 connections, whereas a CAT5 cable is used for 10/100/1000Base-T connections. Your network card is most likely installed internally on your computer in a Peripheral Component Interconnect slot (PCI), or in the case of older computers it might be plugged into an Industry Standard Architecture slot. Newer motherboards now come with network devices built in and might have one or two ports already available.

In addition to internal cards, there are external as well. Some of them might use a USB connection, and others might use FireWire or a different technology.

Regardless of the type of card, they all perform the same function of connecting you to one or more networks. You will also hear these cards referred to as *NICs*, or *network interface cards*. The bottom line is, any computer that needs to connect to a network must have one of these cards unless it will be accessing a network only via model or serial connection.

NICs are available in different speeds. A 10Base-T connection is capable of transferring 10 megabits per second (Mbps). This is relatively low by today's standards. Most cards available today and those that are built in to motherboards are 10/100Base-T. This means they can operate on 10Base-T and 100Base-T networks. You can now find, however, 10/100/1000Base-T technology; if everything on your network is capable, you can hit speeds of up to 1 gigabit per second (Gbps). Not many networks have this implemented yet, and hardware that implements gigabit technology is still a little pricey. In the future, even cable modem and DSL access will be available in gigabit speeds. Limited systems are already being tested in limited communities.

Hubs

Hubs are passive network devices that share all packets transferred in the network with all other connected devices. Hubs come in different sizes and types for different applications:

Stand-alone hubs   Stand-alone hubs are usually for networks with fewer than 12 devices. These are the cheapest solutions and are usually found in home networks or small offices.

Stackable hubs   Stackable hubs are almost identical to stand-alone hubs, except you can stack (or connect) them to expand the total number of allotted devices. When these hubs are connected, they act as one modular hub.

Modular hubs   A modular hub is usually a specialized case that allows for multiple hub cards to be added as need be. This offers a slight performance increase over a stackable hub because each hub card is connected via a backplane-type application (similar to a motherboard) and allows higher transfer speeds. A modular hub system comes with a management option as well so that different cards can be linked together while remaining separate from other hubs that are linked together.

Hubs definitely have their advantages. You can find an eight-port hub for under $50, and there is no configuration necessary at all. Simply plug everything in and you are ready to go.

The problem with using hubs is, you have every device on your network sending traffic to everyone else all at once. If two machines try to send data at the same time, a *collision* will occur. A collision results in both packets being dropped. This is when, from our earlier examples, TCP would take over and ask for the packets to be re-sent. Although this is not a problem when it occurs infrequently, collisions can cause larger networks to suffer from serious degradation of services and to fail to operate anywhere near optimal levels. If this is the case, switches and routers need to be considered.

Switches

A *switch*, unlike a hub, is an *active* network appliance. It separates each of the devices that are connected to it into separate collision domains, or *nodes*, in order to drastically reduce the number of collisions. Each packet when received is analyzed, and the destination is determined by the

MAC address. A switch also stops bad or misaligned packets from being transferred throughout the network. Because the packets are regenerated from the switch, it also allows for greater traveling length to its next hop within the network without using bridges. (We'll discuss bridges in more detail later in this section.)

Switches are also capable of linking to each other in order to provide higher amounts of bandwidth to more important or higher-trafficked servers. When a network uses multiple switches linked together, it is often referred to as a *collapsed backbone network.*

It is also possible for some switches to run in *full duplex* mode. This will, if the client machines also have full duplex enabled, double the connection speed by allowing data to flow in both directions at maximum speed. This would bring a Fast Ethernet network (100Base-T) up to a combined 200Mbps.

Switches vary on ease of use depending on type and manufacturer. Almost all switches today have the capability to "learn" your network. After it is installed, the switch learns the location of each network device, depending on its connection and by building a table that it saves internally. As packets come in, the switch uses this table to determine where to send the packet. While they are, for the most part, easy to set up, switches can require a significant amount of customization and configuration for more advanced networks.

A switch is generally three to five times the cost of a hub and has the same number of ports, which is one of the reasons it is not generally used in small networks. However, the main reason they are not used is because the packet processing time is greater than that of a hub. A hub does not take any time to analyze a packet before sending it on; it simply duplicates the packet on all connected ports. A switch reduces the number of collisions on a network but increases the amount of time each packet takes to be processed. The performance gain versus cost comparison does not match up, so if you have a small network, a hub is most likely your best solution.

Routers

A *router* works in a similar manner to a switch but defines separate networks logically instead of physically. It uses IP addresses instead of MAC addresses to determine what packets go where. Because it uses IP addresses, a router falls into the Network layer rather than the Data-Link layer. Routers do not need to be a stand-alone network appliance either; they can be a computer set up with at least two network cards. Your Linux machine is capable of acting like a router.

Most routers also have the capability to use filtering. *Filtering* is, at its base level, a firewall action. Filtering allows packets of information, based on their IP and destination port, to be forwarded or dropped. This prevents unwanted or mischievous packets from entering one network from another. A router's efficiency is measured by its latency, or lack thereof. The less time it takes to process a packet, the faster your network will be. You might sometimes hear the term *PPS*, which stands for packets per second.

There aren't necessarily any advantages or disadvantages to a router. Simply stated, if you need one, you need one.

Routing Switches

A *routing switch* is a new technology that is still largely experimental. A routing switch, or *layer 3 switch*, combines the packet handling of a router and the speed of switching. These routing switches operate on both the Data-Link and Network layers (levels 2 and 3, respectively).

These advanced machines are aimed mostly at large-scale businesses and networks that require complicated switching and routing. A multilayer switch has the capability to analyze the flow of data between each port and make "intelligent" decisions on how to connect these ports for optimum performance. It runs its own internal and updatable set of functions, which are complicated and can require massive amounts of diagnosis and tweaking to run at peak levels. As technology progresses and becomes cheaper, we are likely to see more of multilayer switches.

Bridges

A *bridge* is used to connect separate networks. A bridge is also called a *store-and-forward device* because, much like a switch, it uses a buffer to temporarily store the packets as it analyzes them to determine whether they should be forwarded through the network. If the packet's destination and source network locations match, the bridge will drop the packet and not retransmit it. If they are different, the packet will be forwarded across the bridge. This enables both networks to be split into separate collision domains, just like in a switch.

Problems arise, however, when too many bridges are connected. Because bridges have the capability to "learn," and because of the nature of the self-learning, network loops can occur. A *network loop* occurs when two separate bridges have different "ideas" on where a device is on a network. They could end up passing a packet back and forth, hence the *loop*. To combat this, a software standard, now found in the IEEE 802.1d specification, called the Spanning Tree Algorithm was created. This standard describes how switches and bridges communicate to avoid such problems. Switches and hubs can also become victims of the same situation.

Repeaters

A *repeater* is a simple device that does not require any configuration. Aptly named, it is used to duplicate a signal, exactly as it was received, onto the other end of the connection. Repeaters are used at locations where network cables must run long distances. They essentially boost a signal, much the same way an amplifier would do, to try to maintain data integrity across the lengthened media. A repeater does not analyze a packet and then reconstruct it as a switch or bridge would; it instead amplifies the exact signal. This is done for the sake of speed but comes at a cost: any line noise is amplified along with the data and can cause signal corruption, leading to packet loss due to bad or misaligned packets.

Understanding Firewalls

A *firewall* is a computer or appliance that connects two or more networks and has the ability to filter out packets by consulting predetermined tables that the system administrator must specify. A firewall can be as simple as allowing only one computer inside one network to access the second network at all, or it could be complex enough to allow only information from a specific IP address to reach a specific destination for a specific port. Although firewalls can vary in complexity, they always aim to accomplish two goals: keeping outsiders from getting in and keeping insiders from getting out. There are different methods of going about this, but all of them fall into the filtering or proxy categories.

The first type, *filtering*, works on a network level. This is the same type that is built into the Linux kernel and blocks selected network packets based on preset rules. Each incoming and outgoing packet is analyzed for its type, source and destination addresses, and port. Because so little data is read in and logged, these types of firewalls use few system resources and offer low latency times. A filtering firewall does not allow users to be able to identify themselves, however. You cannot and do not need to log in to a filtering firewall and ask for different privileges. Instead, your privileges to and from the outside world are based on your IP address. This can present problems if different users travel from computer to computer and need different levels of access from their peers, which brings us to our next type of firewall: the proxy firewall.

The *proxy* firewall is meant more for monitoring traffic coming from within your network than it is for keeping traffic out. It leaves hard evidence of exactly who transferred what kind of data. Proxies can be divided into two categories: application and SOCKS.

An *application proxy* allows users from the inside network to log on to it and then the proxy will access whatever service the user requests instead of the user directly connecting to the service. The proxy transfers the proper information to the user and becomes invisible to the user. Because every bit of information is taken in by a proxy, it is capable of storing or modifying any information. Whether it's a word from a web page or a file from an FTP server, an application proxy can log it and change it.

A *SOCKS server* is much like an old switchboard. It simply cross-wires your computer to another outside the network. This type of firewall does not allow the user to log in; however, it does allow you to record the users' destinations.

There are many ways to configure a firewall. You might wish to have a stand-alone firewall system for a larger network and could configure your switch to connect directly to the firewall, or you could simply use a Linux machine to be both your firewall and router. Regardless of your type of firewall, it needs to be located between your LAN and the outside world. If your LAN has more than one connection to the Internet, you need to have both of these ISPs run through your firewall. Any deviance from this will leave your network wide open for attack.

If you are setting up a filtering firewall, you will not need much of a system at all. A filtering firewall will not be running any applications outside of the required functions to make it act like a firewall, whereas a proxy will need to be as powerful as possible because it must spawn a different program for each user connected through it. When you have 50 or more users all trying to use the same resources, your firewall can become painfully slow.

In this section, we'll detail the configuration of a basic Linux firewall for your local machine only. Setting up an entire firewall scheme for a large network can become complicated and due to its lengthy nature is beyond the realm of this book. If you want a more in-depth look into firewalls, we recommend purchasing a book dedicated to the subject.

The Linux Kernel as a Firewall

Different versions of the Linux kernel have been developed with different firewall techniques in place. Version 2.2 used IP chains, which many felt were overly complicated, and so a hybrid was created for 2.4 and above that uses a chaining-type structure but separated into comprehensive tables. When a packet is received via one of its networks, it is analyzed for its specific data and follows the rules set forth, in order, in the tables created by the administrator. We will not be delving into the specifics here because the next chapter covers them in greater detail. For now, you should understand the possibility of using Linux as a firewall and the speed benefit that is attributed to the data handling being done at such a rudimentary level.

IP tables offer the ability to load-balance across multiple ISPs for your network, or to segment your network to use different ISPs to communicate through. The possibilities are endless when using IP tables, but care should be taken so as not to overcomplicate your statements. Returning months down the line to a configuration file that looks like some sort of encrypted file can become frustrating very quickly.

Why Close Ports

Blocking ports on your server reduces the possibility of a malicious user exploiting your system. Different daemons on your system run at different levels of access because they need to be able to modify certain files throughout your system. A malicious user who has no business accessing some of these ports might develop an exploit in order to "trick" one of the daemons into letting him run commands at his level of access.

To prevent situations like this from happening, we close ports on our system to the outside world unless certain criteria are met. These criteria can be based on a destination or source IP address, domain name, block of IPs, packet type, or other factor. You will want to block every possible port on your system that is not necessary. This is why it is easier to begin your rules with *block everything* and then list ports you would like to leave open.

There are also rules that can be set in place to prevent denial of service attacks, by blocking an IP address that attempts to send too many requests as once. We'll cover this more in depth in the next chapter as we continue to discuss firewall configuration and security.

How a Firewall Can Increase Security

A firewall can increase security only if it is absolute. As you begin to create more and more exceptions, holes can open up in your defenses. You might even have a few holes caused from insecure pre-installed components such as Open DataBase Connection's (ODBC) ability to accept connections directly from HTTP. As well, your firewall cannot protect you against inexperienced users on the inside of your network who might open a Trojan horse or worm, which could open up a port within your network.

Other holes might become evident as well. For instance, if you have a Data Management Zone (DMZ) set up and one of the computers in the DMZ has access to the rest of your network without passing through the firewall, or the firewall has rules to allow a greater amount of access to a computer on your network that is logically situated in the DMZ, then you will also have holes in your security scheme. There is a myriad of types of data-driven network attacks as well. These can stem from customized scripts on web pages to viruses to buffer overruns.

> **WARNING**   Just because you have a firewall installed and running does not mean your network is secure.

You should pay close attention to your network topography and logical and physical network separations. You can never be too safe where security is concerned. This is another reason why it is so important to always keep your software up-to-date. After security holes are discovered within a program, it is usually only a matter of days before a patch is released to fix the problem. Staying on top of current releases is part of your responsibility as a system administrator.

Using DNS

The Domain Name System is best explained by first giving you some background on how it began. In 1984, Paul Mockapetris developed DNS to combat the problem of the current system. The system at the time was constructed of a single table containing an entry for each of the registered domain names and their IP addresses. It was maintained by the Stanford Research Institute's Network Information Center (SRI-NIC). Periodically, system administrators would download the newest table and update their server.

As the Internet grew, however, the table became completely unmanageable. Although it worked well for simple lookups, there were no procedures in place to pass out the new information automatically and efficiently. That is where Mockapetris came into play. He developed a system whereby the data is not stored on any one server. This type of database is called a *distributed* database because its contents are indeed distributed throughout the network. This type of database allows for almost unlimited growth. He named this system the Domain Name System.

The Domain Name Space

To completely understand how this system works, you need to have a firm understanding of the domain name space. A domain name space can be represented as an inverted tree.

At the top we have simply a period that represents the root level. The next level contains your *top-level* domains. These are the .com, .net, .tv, and so on, *extensions* on your domain name. The next level down from the top-level domains contains the base domain name, such as *linuxforum* in www.linuxforum.com. Beyond that can be an infinite number of levels, each consisting of a subdomain within the domain or subdomain it belongs to. In our previous example, www would be a subdomain of linuxforum.com. Think of subdomains as subfolders within folders. Each of these subdomains must be specified in the DNS zone file as well as the web server configuration files. The subdomains do not necessarily need to be names of services such as www or ftp, either. You can have any name you wish as long as there is an entry for it on the proper server that will be responsible for handling the request.

DNS Operation

The Domain Name System is responsible for translating a domain name into an IP address. Domain names are used for virtually every web service, including HTTP, mail, FTP, and so on. Domain names are registered through an issuing authority, or *domain registrar*, such as netsol.com or directnic.com. The personal information you provide your registrar with for that domain is then stored in a *root DNS server*. This root DNS server is responsible for distributing this information to any DNS servers across the world when it is requested. This is called *propagation*. DNS propagation usually takes between 24 and 48 hours to take effect globally but can be much shorter for your own zone depending on the administrator's configuration settings.

When you type a domain name into your or FTP client, your computer asks its primary name server for the proper IP address. If your name server has ever fielded a request for that domain, the server will locate the domain within its own cache and reply with the proper IP address, as long as the time to live (TTL) has not expired. If your name server has never fielded a request for the domain, the DNS server will attempt to locate the proper address by using a set of functions referred to as a *resolver*. It does this by asking the next server up the tree what the proper IP address is for the given domain. If that server fails to come up with an answer, the DNS server will keep trying a different server until it reaches an answer. If no answer comes back within a reasonable amount of time, the client application making the request will most likely display a message saying that it has timed out. If this happens and you know the domain exists, you could choose to keep trying until your DNS finds a match on a remote server. If the domain is not valid, however, you are out of luck and your attempts are futile.

A domain name resolution request to a server contains five basic parts:

Header section   The header section contains errors, flags, and other miscellaneous settings.

Question section   The question section carries the domain name that is being queried.

Answer section   This section contains the answer to the question.

Authority section   The authority section contains a list of name servers that might be able to answer the question at hand.

Additional information section   This section holds other records that are not the requested domain but might be similar or relevant to the question.

Here we see the breakdown of how DNS processes its requests. When you type in a domain to be resolved, a message is sent to your name server. If that name server does not know the answer, it in turn queries another name server. This second name server sends back one of two responses: either your answer (the actual IP address the domain resolved to) or entries in the authority section of the response (a list of other name servers). If your original DNS server does not receive an answer, it tries to contact each one of those servers and find out the proper answer. If no answer is forthcoming, it will dig down deeper by using the referrals from each of the new recommendations by those servers. Most likely, however, your DNS will receive an actual answer back during the first round of queries.

If an answer that is received back comes with an *authoritative source* flag, your DNS will update itself automatically and cache the address so that DNS will not have to go through this same process again. If another request is made for the same domain, it will not reply with the authoritative source flag because it is not coming from such a source.

There are a variety of tools available for finding out information about a specific domain. One of the most popular on Linux is the `dig` command. This command is used to query a DNS name server for a specific domain. It is a powerful and versatile command for your administration arsenal and should not be overlooked.

Go ahead and perform a `dig linuxforum.com` and you'll be greeted with the following output:

```
; <<>> DiG 9.2.2-P3 <<>> linuxforum.com
;; global options:  printcmd
;; Got answer:
;; ->>HEADER<<- opcode: QUERY, status: NOERROR, id: 62984
;; flags: qr rd ra; QUERY: 1, ANSWER: 1, AUTHORITY: 3, ADDITIONAL: 0

;; QUESTION SECTION:
;linuxforum.com.                        IN      A
```

```
;; ANSWER SECTION:
linuxforum.com.    38400    IN    A      66.98.196.36

;; AUTHORITY SECTION:
linuxforum.com.    38400    IN    NS     NS4.W3FREAKS.com.
linuxforum.com.    38400    IN    NS     NS1.W3FREAKS.com.
linuxforum.com.    38400    IN    NS     NS2.W3FREAKS.com.

;; Query time: 337 msec
;; SERVER: 192.168.0.1#53(192.168.0.1)
;; WHEN: Tue Feb  3 04:41:03 2004
;; MSG SIZE  rcvd: 111
```

The previous query was performed without specifying a **type**. By default, type A was specified. The actual syntax for **dig** is as follows:

```
dig @server name type
```

Our previous query also left off server, which is reserved for an IP address or hostname, but we specified the name and the default type. Other types are MX, SIG, MB, CNAME, ANY, and so forth.

You can also perform a reverse DNS lookup through **dig**. Try using the command **dig -x** **dig -x** *ipAddress* and you will be returned an answer as to what primary domain that IP resolved to.

You can see the upcoming "Record Types" subsection for a complete list and short description. In addition to types of queries, there are almost 40 options you can specify to retrieve specific information about a server or domain name. Listed here are a few that we feel are most important. Try experimenting with the options and learning the different results:

-b *source*   This option sets the source IP address to be the given IP. This IP address must be bound to a local network device.

-f *filename*   Specifying this option enables **dig** to operate in batch mode, retrieving its list of queries from the file specified. Each query should be constructed as it would on the command line and should be one per line.

-p *port*   If you plan on querying a nonstandard port, you can simply specify this option followed by the port number.

-x *ipAddress*   This enables you to perform a reverse DNS lookup, which means that the specified IP address will be resolved into a domain name. When this occurs, you do not need to specify the *name* or *type*.

Performing a man on dig will also display an extended list of options. These options are specified by using a + followed by an optional no to state whether to include or not include the value for the following option. Here are some of the more important items you might use:

+[no]tcp   Use [do not use] TCP when querying a name server. The default is UDP unless the type is set to AXFR or IXFR.

+domain=*domainName*   This option enables you to set the search list to contain only the domain provided as if it were specified in a domain directive in the /etc/resolv.conf file. It also enables search list processing, much like the +search option.

+[no]search   Use [do not use] the search list as specified by the resolv.conf file.

+[no]cdflag   This sets the Checking Disabled bit in your query. The server will *not* perform the Domain Name System SECurity (DNSSEC) lookup and will return all other information specified.

+[no]recursive   This set [unsets] the capability of your name server to perform recursive queries on other name servers. This is automatically enabled unless you are specifying the nssearch or trace options.

+[no]nssearch   This useful specification enables you to tell your server to look for an authoritative name server for the specified domain. This ensures that the IP address is cached to your name server as well.

+[no]trace   Although trace is disabled by default, it has an interesting behavior. Much like the name suggests, it traces each of the queries made to each name server in order to resolve a domain name. Each of the answers from each of the queries will be printed to the screen.

+[no]cmd   You can use this option to toggle the comment field, which is initially printed when the command is run. This is the one that includes the options specified and the versioning info. This can be especially useful if you are running dig in batch mode.

+[no]comments   This flag toggles the display of the actual comment field in a name server answer.

+[no]qr   The qr option turns on [off] the printing of the query used to query the name server. By default, this option is off.

+[no]question   Show [do not show] the question portion of the response.

+[no]answer   Show [do not show] the answer portion of the response.

+[no]authority   Show [do not show] the authority portion of the response.

+[no]additional   Show [do not show] the additional portion of the response.

+tries=*number*   This sets the maximum number of tries before failing.

+[no]besteffort   This attempts to display the answer received even if it has been marked as invalid or corrupted.

These options should provide you with enough functionality to find any answer you could ever want to name-server-related questions. Learning to use the `dig` tool can provide huge benefits for you when tracking down DNS and resolution problems.

The */etc/resolv.conf* File

This file houses the name server addresses for your server to use, in order, so that it can resolve any given domain name. This is the only file you need to configure in order to run a DNS client. Although your file most likely contains only one line specifying the DNS server you provided during the installation, a number of other lines can be added, each with slightly different functionality.

For instance, you might have a file that looks like the following:

```
;
;        Sample /etc/resolv.conf
;
domain          somewhere.COM
search          search.COM
nameserver      192.168.0.1
nameserver      192.168.0.2
sortlist        192.168.0.0
hostresorder    bind local
options         ndots:2
```

Let's take a closer look at each of the sections:

domain   This specifies the current zone. This domain is automatically appended to any domain specified that does not contain a period. For instance, if you were to specify `foo` for your domain name, it would automatically be translated into `foo.somewhere.com`.

search   This specifies a list of possible zones to query. This list, if present, will override the local domain.

nameserver   This option specifies the name server to use in order to resolve domains. You can have up to three name servers listed in this file, and they will be queried in order from top to bottom.

sortlist   IP address and netmask pairs can be listed here. When a query is returned, all those that match the network given will be returned before any others.

hostresorder   This determines the order in which different resolution techniques are tried. You can use `bind`, `nis`, and `local` for your ordering, where `local` refers to the /etc/hosts file.

options   This contains any additional features you would like disabled or enabled. You can specify `ndots`, `timeout`, `attempts`, `rotate`, `no-check-names`, and `inet6`.

The /etc/hosts File

The /etc/hosts file contains a list of hosts and their IP addresses. This file is used for local machines on your network or custom pointers to a specific IP address. A standard default hosts file should look like this:

```
# Do not remove the following line, or various programs
# that require network functionality will fail.
127.0.0.1              localhost.localdomain localhost
```

This file simply shows that using `localhost` will point to the loopback interface, `127.0.0.1`. This line is required by the Linux operating system and cannot be removed. You should also add the IP addresses of any local machines on your network. This will help when SSHing into your server from within your network. During most connection processes, the server will attempt to perform a reverse DNS lookup on the IP address you are connecting from. If no domain name can be found, you will be left waiting quite a while until it times out.

TIP   To resolve the above issue, you can add your computer name or host name to a line beginning with its local IP address. This will make quick work of the reverse lookup.

You can also add any number of hosts that might be specific to your setup. Remember that if your hosts file contains a duplicate host that might resolve to a different IP address via a BIND query, you must have the `hostresorder` value set in your /etc/resolv.conf file to look up using `local` first.

Record Types

Listed here are the record types that can be used with the `dig` command and that any BIND9 utility should be capable of handling:

A   Address

AAAA   IPv6 address

AFSDB   Andrew File System DataBase location

CNAME   Canonical name

HINFO   Host information

ISDN   Integrated Services Digital Network

KEY   Public key

KX   Key exchanger

LOC   Location

MB   Mailbox

MX   Mail exchanger

NS   Name server

NSAP   Network service access point address

NXT   Next

PTR   Pointer

PX   Pointer to X.400 / RFC 822 information

RP   Responsible person

RT   Route through

SIG   Cryptographic signature

SOA   Start of authority

SRV   Server

TXT   Text

WKS   Well-known service

X25   X25

Network Connectivity Checklist

After reading this chapter, you should have a good idea of the philosophies behind a network and the travel and flow of information across the many aspects of it. Although this chapter did not delve into specific setups for any given case, it did cover the philosophy and methods of the techniques used to create a smooth-running network. You should have a firm grasp of the following areas before continuing:

- Understand TCP/IP.
- Know the difference between TCP and UDP.

- Understand the functionality of ports and how they operate.
- Be familiar with the purpose and type of addressing on both the Network and Data-Link layers.
- Understand the setup of a static or dynamic IP address for your server.
- Know the differences between a hub, switch, bridge, router, and repeater.
- Understand the functionality of a firewall and how it works.
- Be familiar with the Domain Name System and how it propagates itself.
- Know how to use the `dig` command.

After you are comfortable with the information covered in this chapter, it is time to secure you server from the outside world by taking a closer look at security. Chapter 6, "Linux Security," will help you establish a firewall setup for your machine so you will be ready to begin the installation and configuration of your services for your user base.

CHAPTER 6

Linux Security

- Disabling Unwanted Services

- Staying Up-to-Date

- Controlling Root Access

- Configuring the Firewall

- Network Monitoring and Testing Applications

The time has come when you must face one of the most difficult aspects of maintaining your Linux system: security. Security is something that should not be taken lightly on a system such as the one you are building. Your system is going to be connected to the Internet and it's going to be under the microscope of people trying to break into your vault.

Linux security is any system administrator's nightmare. It doesn't have to be, but it is. The problem is that you are running open source software that is potentially vulnerable—until the patches and updates become available.

In this chapter, we're going to cover what needs to be done to secure your Linux system and to reduce the worries that you might have while your system is online.

Disabling Unwanted Services

The best way to get a strong handle on your system is to figure out what services are running during startup and to disable them if they are not needed. Linux is built for a multi-role purpose, so some services will be running, such as print services, Telnet, Samba, and more.

In this section, you will learn about two utilities—chkconfig and ntsysv—that can be used to manage services. You'll also learn how to determine the purpose of a service that's running and you'll see examples of how we disable them on startup.

> **WARNING**   For compatibility purposes, determine which utility you are going to use for enabling and disabling services and stick with that utility. It is best if you do not use both chkconfig and ntsysv.

Utilizing *chkconfig*

The chkconfig utility is a simple command-line tool that maintains startup services by altering the /etc/rc0-6.d files. This is the primary way to disable and enable startup services from the command line. In Chapter 4, "Linux Administration," we talked about chkconfig extensively, however this chapter will go in depth with hands-on examples. Here are the important commands for the chkconfig program:

chkconfig --list   This option lists the current configured services and the run levels they are set to utilize.

chkconfig --add *name*   This option enables you to add a new service from a startup script that you might have placed in your /etc/init.d directory.

chkconfig --del *name*   This option deletes a service from the /rc directories.

chkconfig --level *level name*   This option configures a service for a particular run level.

chkconfig *name* on|off|reset   This option turns on, turns off, or resets a service.

Let's run through an exercise of using chkconfig to add, enable, and disable a service. First, you should take a look at which services are currently handled through chkconfig. Run the following command:

```
chkconfig --list
```

You should see output similar to the following. Note that we have truncated the output for the purposes of this book:

```
gpm      0:off  1:off  2:on   3:on   4:on   5:on   6:off
kudzu    0:off  1:off  2:off  3:on   4:on   5:on   6:off
syslog   0:off  1:off  2:on   3:on   4:on   5:on   6:off
xinetd based services:
         chargen-udp:    off
         rsync:          off
         chargen:        off
         daytime-udp:    off
         daytime:        off
         echo-udp:       off
         echo:           off
         services:       off
         ktalk:          off
         sgi_fam:        on
         time:           off
         time-udp:       off
         cups-lpd:       off
```

Let's take the gpm service as an example of what is happening when you list your output. The gpm service is set to operate in run levels 2, 3, 4, and 5 and not in run levels 0, 1 and 6.

WARNING Before you go wild and start disabling services, please review the section "Determining the Purpose of a Service" later in this chapter.

Adding a Service with *chkconfig*

Let's pretend that you have a service named foo in your /etc/init.d directory and you want to add it to your system startup. Simply run this command:

```
chkconfig --add foo
```

You should see the foo service listed when you use the --list option now.

When you use chkconfig, there is a requirement for your scripts in the /etc/init.d directory: you must have a line that defines the run levels your script will start up, the run levels your script will stop, and the priorities it will use. This line looks similar to this:

```
# chkconfig: 345 96 96
```

Enabling or Disabling a Service with *chkconfig*

Even though you added the service named foo to chkconfig, this does not mean that it will start at boot or during a run level. You can enable a service by running the following command:

```
chkconfig foo on
```

Or you can disable it:

```
chkconfig foo off
```

If you turn on the service, it will automatically be available for the run levels configured by the script. If you turn it off, it will be completely disabled on all run levels.

Setting Service Run Levels with *chkconfig*

If you want to set a run level for a service, you can do so by running the following command:

```
chkconfig --level level name on | off
```

Let's view a more practical usage of this command for foo. If you were to turn off run level 3 for foo, you would use this command:

```
chkconfig --level 3 foo off
```

If you wanted to turn run level 3 back on for foo, you would run the following command:

```
chkconfig --level 3 foo on
```

Deleting a Service with *chkconfig*

In the previous example, "Adding a Service with chkconfig," you enabled foo. Now let's delete this service:

```
chkconfig --del foo
```

Now the foo service is deleted.

You should run chkconfig --list to determine which services are not required by your system to run, and disable them.

NOTE Simply deleting the service from chkconfig will not delete the scripts located in /etc/ init.d.

Utilizing *ntsysv*

Let's take a look at what's set to start up on your Fedora box. Most Linux distributions have the command ntsysv, which enables you to configure run-level services. Simply running this command will show you something similar to Figure 6.1.

To enable services, you simply scroll the list by using your Down or Up arrows and press your spacebar to enable or disable an item. If there is a star (*) indicated, that means the service will run at boot. After you are finished, tab down to the OK section and press Enter.

FIGURE 6.1
The ntsysv screen

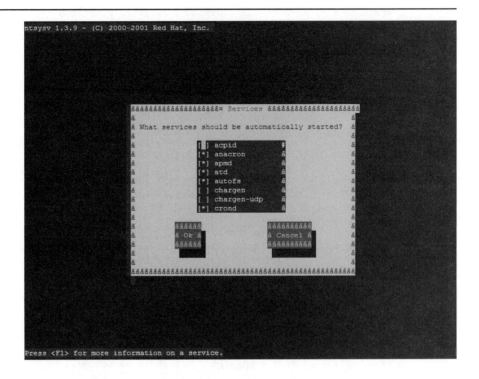

Determining the Purpose of a Service

If you are unsure of what a service is used for, you can open your /etc/init.d directory and look at each of the files. We prefer to use the more command in this particular case because it simply shows you the file and will prevent you from editing it. Listing 6.1 shows you the contents of our Fedora /etc/init.d directory.

Listing 6.1   **The /etc/init.d Directory**

```
[root@test init.d]# ls -al
total 240
drwxr-xr-x    2 root root   4096 Jan 22 10:20 .
drwxr-xr-x   10 root root   4096 Jan 22 09:58 ..
-rwxr-xr-x    1 root root   1128 Oct 22 17:04 acpid
-rwxr-xr-x    1 root root    834 Jul 10  2003 anacron
-rwxr-xr-x    1 root root   1429 Oct 22 17:18 apmd
-rwxr-xr-x    1 root root   1176 Sep 12 06:51 atd
-rwxr-xr-x    1 root root   9221 Sep  8 14:11 autofs
-rwxr-xr-x    1 root root   1316 Jun  6  2003 crond
-rwxr-xr-x    1 root root   2312 Oct  2 12:56 cups
-rwxr-xr-x    1 root root   1506 Oct 15 12:11 firstboot
```

```
-rwxr-xr-x   1 root root  10198 Oct 28 17:26 functions
-rwxr-xr-x   1 root root   1527 Aug  7 13:01 gpm
-rwxr-xr-x   1 root root   5269 Sep 15 07:35 halt
-rwxr-xr-x   1 root root   2601 Oct 23 06:54 httpd
-rwxr-xr-x   1 root root   6319 Oct 23 10:18 iptables
-rwxr-xr-x   1 root root   1414 Jul  3  2003 irda
-rwxr-xr-x   1 root root   1744 Oct 22 10:55 irqbalance
-rwxr-xr-x   1 root root   5838 Oct 23 14:53 isdn
-rwxr-xr-x   1 root root   1084 Sep 25 09:22 kdcrotate
-rwxr-xr-x   1 root root    652 Sep  3 21:33 killall
-rwxr-xr-x   1 root root   2225 Oct 31 17:26 kudzu
-rwxr-xr-x   1 root root   1684 Oct  2 06:03 lisa
-rwxr-xr-x   1 root root   1746 Oct 16 15:38 messagebus
-rwxr-xr-x   1 root root   1539 Oct 22 10:54 microcode_ctl
-rwxr-xr-x   1 root root   2281 Oct 17 12:02 named
-rwxr-xr-x   1 root root   5080 Jan  6  2003 netfs
-rwxr-xr-x   1 root root   8025 Sep  9 00:47 network
-rwxr-xr-x   1 root root   4257 Oct 22 21:17 nfs
-rwxr-xr-x   1 root root   2833 Oct 22 21:17 nfslock
-rwxr-xr-x   1 root root   2066 Oct 27 16:30 nscd
-rwxr-xr-x   1 root root   3795 Oct 29 06:07 ntpd
-r-xr-xr-x   1 root root   4590 Jan 25  2003 pcmcia
-rwxr-xr-x   1 root root   1814 Sep 23 08:53 portmap
-rwxr-xr-x   1 root root   1516 Jun 26  2002 random
-rwxr-xr-x   1 root root   2246 Jan  6  2003 rawdevices
-rwxr-xr-x   1 root root   1782 Oct 30 11:12 rhnsd
-rwxr-xr-x   1 root root   1262 Oct 23 14:49 saslauthd
-rwxr-xr-x   1 root root   2512 Oct 28 16:06 sendmail
-rwxr-xr-x   1 root root   1175 Jul 10  2002 single
-rwxr-xr-x   1 root root   3115 Oct 22 10:55 smartd
-rwxr-xr-x   1 root root   1928 Sep 26 11:14 smb
-rwxr-xr-x   1 root root   2647 Sep 17 12:14 sshd
-rwxr-xr-x   1 root root   1369 Jun  6  2003 syslog
-rwxr-xr-x   1 root root   1787 Sep 19 09:47 vncserver
-rwxr-xr-x   1 root root   1555 Sep 26 11:14 winbind
-rwxr-xr-x   1 root root   3428 Oct 24 18:10 xfs
-rwxr-xr-x   1 root root   2497 Oct 12 03:41 xinetd
-rwxr-xr-x   1 root root   2501 Sep 25 13:32 ypbind
-rwxr-xr-x   1 root root   1036 Oct 29 09:54 yum
```

As you can see, quite a few services are in the /etc/init.d directory.

Let's take a look at the isdn service. Simply run the command more isdn and you should see output much like Listing 6.2. Take note that we truncated the results of the more command for this book because it was not necessary to show you the startup script code.

Listing 6.2   `isdn`

```
[root@test init.d]# more isdn
#! /bin/bash
#
# chkconfig: 2345 9 91
# description: start and stop ISDN services
```

The most important information you'll need at this moment is the description. This script clearly is used to start and stop ISDN services. If your Linux box does not have ISDN, you should ensure that this item is disabled.

Disabling Services

Earlier we mentioned `chkconfig` and `ntsysv` as methods to disable and enable startup services. Depending on which method you wish to use, run `chkconfig` or `ntsysv` (we prefer `chkconfig`) and choose which services you wish to disable.

On our server, we disabled the following services:

acpid   `acpid` is a daemon for delivering ACPI events. It listens on the file `/proc/acpi/event` and when an event occurs, it executes the required program to handle it. If your system does not use ACPI, then you can disable this service.

chargen   `chargen` is handled by `xinetd` and it returns pseudo-random characters to the requestor. This service can be vulnerable to DOS attacks and should be disabled unless you find a use for it.

chargen-udp   This is the same as `chargen`, except it utilizes UDP. This service can be vulnerable to DOS attacks and should be disabled unless you find a use for it.

cups-lpd   This is the Common UNIX Printing System (CUPS) Line Print Daemon (LPD) mini-server that supports legacy client systems using the LPD protocol. If your system does not have a printer installed, this service should be disabled.

daytime   This simple protocol enables clients to retrieve the current date and time from a remote server. While useful at a basic level, the `daytime` protocol is most often used for debugging purposes rather than actually acquiring the current date and time. This service is handled by `xinetd` and should be disabled.

daytime-udp   This is the UDP layer for `daytime`. This should be disabled if you are not using `daytime`.

echo This service is used for testing purposes. It simply returns text to your console that is sent to it. It is handled by xinetd and should be disabled.

echo-udp This service is the UDP layer for echo and should be disabled if you are not using echo.

gpm This is the General Purpose Mouse daemon, which provides mouse support for the console. If you are running a remote system, you can disable this service.

httpd This is the default Apache web server runtime script. For now, disable this service because you are going to uninstall the default version of Apache in Chapter 8, "Apache Web Server: Installation and Configuration."

ktalk This is a graphical talk client for K Desktop Environment (KDE). If you are running in console mode for your web server, this service should be disabled.

xinetd This is a service wrapper and a replacement for inetd. This wrapper handles a handful of services that we have listed in this section. You can disable xinetd and decide which of the services it handles that you might want to manually enable.

WARNING If you have Telnet in your services we recommend that you disable it. Telnet is the old remote text-based management terminal for Linux, which was replaced by the more secure SSH. Some Linux distributions still install Telnet and enable it by default. Due to the lack of updated security protocols, Telnet has proven to be a security hole for any server on the Internet that is not specifically blocking Telnet ports through firewalls.

Staying Up-to-Date

Staying up-to-date is probably one of the best ways to keep your system secure. There are new patches and fixes for Linux almost every day. The open source community is constantly trying to find exploits and bugs in its software so that they can release patches and make the environment as secure as possible. In this section, we are going to cover how to use the more popular update applications to ensure your system is as safe as possible.

Using up2date

Red Hat and Fedora have an integrated system of keeping Linux updated with the latest software and security patches. This is called up2date and it's an excellent program that will connect to the Red Hat network, download a list of the available updates, compare the updates to your system, and then download and apply the updates as necessary. If you're a Windows user, this is similar to the Windows Update program.

To run your up2date program, simply type **up2date** into the command line. You'll be prompted with a screen that has a list of configuration options. This screen enables you to skip certain downloads such as kernel, kernel modules, and so on. This screen might be handy if you are compiling a custom kernel or want to stay on the version of any particular software you are currently using.

For now, you will accept the default options and simply press Enter to continue. Next, you're prompted to import the RPM-GPG key. Simply type the following into your command line:

```
rpm --import /usr/share/rhn/RPM-GPG-KEY
```

Now you are all set to run the up2date program and get your system updated! All you have to do is run the following command:

```
up2date --update
```

You will see your system begin updating itself.

Using APT Package Management

Debian and other flavors of Linux use a system called Advanced Package Tool (APT). APT enables you to retrieve files from a remote server for your system and then update your system accordingly. This is similar in concept to the Red Hat up2date system.

To obtain APT for Fedora, you can go to yarrow.freshrpms.net and then click apt in the left column. Grab the RPM and install it. Here's how we performed the installation:

```
cd /usr/local/src
wget http://ftp.freshrpms.net/pub/freshrpms/fedora/linux/1/apt/apt-
➡0.5.15cnc3-0.1.fr.i386.rpm
rpm -ivh apt-0.5.15cnc3-0.1.fr.i386.rpm
```

You should see the installation progress on your screen. After it is installed, you can run the apt-get command to compare your system against the updates available and then download the updates and install them. To upgrade with APT, type the following:

```
apt-get -u upgrade
```

After you run this command, you will see a list of packages that were found to upgrade. You will be prompted to enter Yes or No to proceed. If you select Yes, the updates will begin to download and install.

Using Yum Package Management

Yum (which stands for *Yellowdog Updater, Modified*) is another package update management utility for Linux. It is similar in design and concept to up2date and APT. The great thing is that Yum comes installed on Fedora, so you do not have to go out and find the installation files.

To run Yum, you simply type the following:

```
yum update
```

A connection will be made to a remote server, and the RPM file headers will be compared, downloaded, and updated if your versions are out-of-date.

If you would like to learn more about Yum, visit the `linux.duke.edu/projects/yum` website.

Regardless of which update utility you use, you should always make a conscious effort to log in to your system periodically and run the respective update commands. Some people prefer to run these update utilities on a `cron` job, but we feel that is a bad idea because if something goes wrong or your system stops working, you might not have any idea of what updates were installed. If you manually update your system, you at least have a chance to monitor the output and take corrective action on the spot.

Controlling Root Access

Root access is great, but it could also be defined as the *root of all evil*—no pun intended. With root access, you have no limits to what can be done to your system. Therefore, it is imperative that you control it to the best of your ability. You can do this by creating a user account for yourself with limited privileges and simply switching over to root as you need to run specific commands and perform certain operations. Let's begin by creating your user account.

Creating a Standard User Account

From this point forward, you are going to log in under your own user account and get out of the bad habit of logging in as `root`. Naturally, you're going to need to create your own user account—if you did not do this during the installation process.

Before you add a user, it is a good idea to create a group for the user to belong to. This will allow greater control over what groups you assign users to and avoid creating a new group for each and every user on your system. Many groups are already configured on your system, but to be safe, you'll create your own so that you do not inherit any permission that could be dangerous to the system. To do this, you simply run the `groupadd` command. For this example, you are going to create the group `testuser`:

```
groupadd testuser
```

Next, you need to understand the `useradd` command. This command has some arguments that you can pass to it during runtime. These arguments enable you to define the user's home directory, group, comments, the number of days to expire the account, and more. The output of `useradd --help` is as follows:

```
usage: useradd  [-u uid [-o]] [-g group] [-G group,...]
                [-d home] [-s shell] [-c comment] [-m [-k template]]
                [-f inactive] [-e expire ] [-p passwd] [-M] [-n] [-r] name
        useradd  -D [-g group] [-b base] [-s shell]
                [-f inactive] [-e expire ]
```

From there, you're going to build a command line with the information you need. Here's the command you are going to use:

```
useradd -d /home/testuser -g testuser -s /bin/bash testuser
```

Let's break this command down for better understanding:

useradd followed by additional arguments and then the last argument is the username you wish to add.

-d /home/testuser is the user's home directory, where their files will be stored.

-g testuser is the group that the user belongs to.

-s /bin/bash is the default shell the user will have. There are many variations, but you can take a look at /etc/shells to see which ones are available. We recommend using /bin/bash as it is a more fulfilled shell environment.

After you add your user, you will need to set a password for the user. Simply run the passwd testuser command and you'll be prompted twice for a password.

Now that you have a standard user on your system, you can log in as that user and begin to use your nonprivileged access. Don't worry—you'll be able to switch to super user mode when you need to.

Disabling Remote Root Login

Now that you can log in remotely as a standard user, let's disable remote root login access. This prevents those hackers out there from potentially gaining root access through the means of SSH.

You need to switch to super user mode to perform this operation. Let's do that now. Simply issue the su - command at the console. You'll be prompted for your root user password. After you have been authenticated, you are now acting on behalf of root and you have inherited the permissions temporarily.

Let's edit the /etc/ssh/sshd_config file to prevent root from logging in. Scroll down to a line that appears like this:

```
# PermitRootLogin yes
```

Change it to the following:

```
PermitRootLogin no
```

Next, you'll enable the SSH2 protocol and disable the SSH1 protocol because most security holes found in SSH are from the SSH1 protocol version. Find this line:

```
#Protocol 2,1
```

And change it to this:

```
Protocol 2
```

Now you need to restart the SSH daemon. Issue the command `/etc/init.d/sshd restart` and then attempt to log in as `root` from another remote console. You should notice that you get `access denied` errors each time you type the correct password. You've successfully harnessed root's remote privileges!

Your system is really starting to shape up! Your next step is to create a firewall that prevents any additional unwanted access.

Configuring the Firewall

The Linux kernel comes with a special built-in firewall protection called `iptables`. This protection is also known as `netfilter/iptables`. An `iptables` firewall works by filtering packets, network translation and port translation through the kernel. Here are some of the main features of `iptables`:

- Stateless packet filtering (IPv4 and IPv6)

- Stateful packet filtering (IPv4)

- Various means of Network Address Translation and Network Address Port Translation (NAT/NAPT)

- Flexible and extensible infrastructure

- Multiple layers of API for third-party extensions

- Large number of patches, plug-ins, and modules available in a *patch-o-matic* repository

Some of the things you can do with `iptables` include building Internet firewalls, using NAT, implementing transparent proxies, and more.

To fully explain `iptables` is beyond the scope of this book. However, we are going to cover the firewall implementation needed to secure your web server. As we progress through the next chapters, you'll add additional rules and open ports as needed for your operations. For now, you just need to secure your server and do everything you can to prevent intruders.

NOTE   For detailed information on Linux security, pick up another book on that topic. Try *Linux Security* by Ramón J. Hontañón (Sybex, 2001) and *Firewalls 24Seven*, second edition, by Matthew Strebe and Charles Perkins (Sybex, 2002).

Creating the Firewall Rules Script

Most Linux distributions install their own set of firewall scripts by default. This is a nice gesture, and they do work; however, when it comes to security, we feel that you should manually configure your own version of the firewall. If you are interested in reviewing these pre-installed scripts, check the following files: `/etc/rc.d/init.d/iptables`, `/etc/sysconfig/iptables`, and `/etc/sysconfig/iptables-config`. However, we will not utilize these scripts.

Your first step is to create a script that will contain all of the rules needed to run your firewall. This script will define which ports you want open on your server and restrict unwanted access from penetrating into your ports.

We prefer to save our firewall script somewhere like `/usr/local/etc`, so let's move into that directory and begin working.

We use `pico` as our command-line editor of choice, so let's get started. Run `pico /usr/local/etc/firewall`. Now you can begin coding the script.

In Listing 6.3, you will see the full script. After the listing, we will explain each element for you.

Listing 6.3   Firewall Rules Script

```
#!/bin/sh
# Change the part after the = to the where you
# IPTABLES is on your system

IPTABLES=/sbin/iptables

# Flush existing rules

$IPTABLES -F INPUT

# Allow connections going outbound
# from this machine to reply back

$IPTABLES -A INPUT -j ACCEPT -m state --state \
    ESTABLISHED -i eth0 -p icmp

$IPTABLES -A INPUT -j ACCEPT -m state --state \
    ESTABLISHED -i eth0 -p tcp

$IPTABLES -A INPUT -j ACCEPT -m state --state \
    ESTABLISHED -i eth0 -p udp

#Allow incoming SSH requests

$IPTABLES -A INPUT -p tcp --dport 22 -j ACCEPT

#Allow incoming DNS

$IPTABLES -A INPUT -p udp --dport 53 -j ACCEPT
$IPTABLES -A INPUT -p tcp --dport 53 -j ACCEPT

#Allow incoming HTTP requests (to Web server)
```

```
$IPTABLES -A INPUT -p tcp --dport 80 -j ACCEPT
$IPTABLES -A INPUT -p tcp --dport 443 -j ACCEPT


#Allow Ping echo

$IPTABLES -A INPUT -p icmp -j ACCEPT

# Load Modules
        insmod ip_conntrack_ftp
        insmod ipt_LOG
        insmod ipt_REJECT
        insmod ipt_limit
        insmod ipt_state

# The logging is set so if more than 5 packets are dropped
# in three seconds they will be ignored. This
# helps to prevent a DOS attack
# crashing the computer the firewall is running on

$IPTABLES -A INPUT -m limit --limit 3/second \
--limit-burst 5 -i ! lo -j LOG

# Drop and log all other data

$IPTABLES -A INPUT -i ! lo -j DROP
```

Let's begin to understand the firewall script in Listing 6.3. The first line is our bash shell line. It's called the *shebang* and might be required by some systems to run properly:

```
#!/bin/sh
```

Next, you will see some comments throughout the script. This helps keep track of what you're doing and is a simple way to take notes. Sometimes in scripting, you will have so much code that keeping notes helps you refresh your memory later. Simply put a comment symbol (#) in front of each line on a comment to prevent the script from attempting to execute your comments when it is run:

```
# Change the part after the = to the where you
# IPTABLES is on your system
```

Now you are going to create a *variable*, or a *shortcut*, to your iptables executable. This variable prevents you from having to type the full command each time you need it. In this case, you are going to create $IPTABLES with the value of /sbin/iptables:

```
IPTABLES=/sbin/iptables
```

Your next task is to flush out any existing rules from your INPUT chain. This enables you to clear out any old information before you attempt to set up your rules. The -F option is really useful when you make a change to this script and delete a rule, so next time all you have to do is run this script again, and all of the old rules will be removed and any new rules will be entered:

```
# Flush existing rules

$IPTABLES -F INPUT
```

Your firewall will be set up to block anything coming in on a port that you have not defined as open. This could cause some problems because now if you send a response by using a particular program and that response comes back into your machine, it could be blocked by the firewall. This is where the ESTABLISHED state option comes in.

Using the ESTABLISHED state option basically says, "If I send a response out on port 99, allow the response to come back into my machine on port 99 even though I have not specifically opened that port for public access." So based on this, you are going to include the next three rules to allow Transmission Control Protocol (TCP), User Datagram Protocol (UDP), and Internet Control Message Protocol (ICMP) responses to come back to you:

```
# Allow connections going outbound
# from this machine to reply back

$IPTABLES -A INPUT -j ACCEPT -m state --state \
    ESTABLISHED -i eth0 -p icmp

$IPTABLES -A INPUT -j ACCEPT -m state --state \
    ESTABLISHED -i eth0 -p tcp

$IPTABLES -A INPUT -j ACCEPT -m state --state \
    ESTABLISHED -i eth0 -p udp
```

The next rule allows SSH access via the TCP protocol through port 22. To better describe this, you call the $IPTABLES executable and then append to the INPUT chain by using -A INPUT. You describe the type of request as TCP by using the -p tcp option, and then indicate that the destination port is 22 by using the --dport 22 option. The last option is -j, which indicates "what to do with it," and here you are saying ACCEPT the request. Opposite of the ACCEPT option is DROP, which would disallow that port specifically.

```
#Allow incoming SSH requests

$IPTABLES -A INPUT -p tcp --dport 22 -j ACCEPT
```

Next you are going to allow DNS requests to be handled by this machine. Note that there are two rules: one is for TCP, and the other is for UDP because DNS uses UDP in some cases:

```
#Allow incoming DNS

$IPTABLES -A INPUT -p udp --dport 53 -j ACCEPT
$IPTABLES -A INPUT -p tcp --dport 53 -j ACCEPT
```

The last set of rules is for your web server access. This is really not important at this moment, but we're going to go ahead and include it now because you'll be setting up HTTP access shortly. Notice the two rules: one is for normal HTTP responses on port 80, and the other is for secure web server HTTPS responses on port 443:

```
#Allow incoming HTTP requests (to Web server)

$IPTABLES -A INPUT -p tcp --dport 80 -j ACCEPT
$IPTABLES -A INPUT -p tcp --dport 443 -j ACCEPT
```

One of the simplest diagnostic tools is the `ping` command. However, when your firewall is set up, you must allow your system to respond to your `ping` commands. The next rule takes care of that:

```
#Allow Ping echo

$IPTABLES -A INPUT -p icmp -j ACCEPT
```

The next section is important. It allows built-in kernel modules to be loaded and executed by `iptables`. In this case, you are loading the FTP, logging, reject, limit, and state modules into your firewall configuration. If you decide to install an FTP server later on, you will need this module loaded to allow FTP connectivity through the firewall. So for now, we will go ahead and load the FTP module along with the other modules we need:

```
# Load Modules
        insmod ip_conntrack_ftp
        insmod ipt_LOG
        insmod ipt_REJECT
        insmod ipt_limit
        insmod ipt_state
```

A valuable rule to have is one that will log any traffic that is getting bounced off of your firewall. The logging helps you figure out whether you need other ports open when trying to connect to your system.

This next rule takes care of the logging for you. However, it's limited to five packets every three seconds to prevent your system from crashing in the event of a DOS attack in which packets are getting bounced off and the logging is going crazy:

```
# The logging is set so if more than 5 packets are dropped
# in three seconds they will be ignored. This
# helps to prevent a DOS attack
# crashing the computer the firewall is running on

$IPTABLES -A INPUT -m limit --limit 3/second \
   --limit-burst 5 -i ! lo -j LOG
```

WARNING After your firewall has been configured, tested, and it works properly, you may comment the previous logging line out to prevent logging to your system log. If you need to troubleshoot your firewall, you can enable it again and then disable it after everything is working properly.

The next line is extremely important because you want to close any other ports that you have not defined to be open in this script:

```
# Drop and log all other data
$IPTABLES -A INPUT -i ! lo -j DROP
```

Now that you understand what this script is doing, save the file and then give it executable permissions. Simply chmod the script to read/write/execute permissions for only root:

```
chmod 700 /usr/local/etc/firewall
```

Before you run the script, take a look at the current firewall settings. You can do this by running the list option in iptables:

```
iptables -L
```

You should see something like this:

```
Chain INPUT (policy ACCEPT)
target     prot opt source               destination

Chain FORWARD (policy ACCEPT)
target     prot opt source               destination

Chain OUTPUT (policy ACCEPT)
target     prot opt source               destination

Chain RH-Firewall-1-INPUT (0 references)
target     prot opt source               destination
```

The preceding listing means that there are no current firewall rules configured and your system is wide open at the moment. If this is the case, you're ready to start your firewall. Otherwise, you should run the following to clean out the firewall settings that were set up during the installation of Linux:

```
/etc/init.d/iptables stop
```

You might also want to disable the iptables in the ntsysv because you are going to run your own startup script.

Now you can run your new firewall settings for the first time. Simply execute the script you created:

```
/usr/local/etc/firewall
```

You should see your system run through the modules as they are loaded. If you have already loaded your firewall since you have rebooted, iptables might output something about modules already being loaded. This is not an error and it is not a problem; it's simply a notification, and the firewall will run properly. Next, run the iptables -L command again and see what's happening with your firewall. See Listing 6.4 for the output.

Listing 6.4   Firewall Output

```
Chain INPUT (policy ACCEPT)
target prot opt source    destination
ACCEPT icmp --   anywhere anywhere    state ESTABLISHED
ACCEPT tcp  --   anywhere anywhere    state ESTABLISHED
ACCEPT udp  --   anywhere anywhere    state ESTABLISHED
ACCEPT tcp  --   anywhere anywhere    tcp dpt:ssh
ACCEPT udp  --   anywhere anywhere    udp dpt:domain
ACCEPT tcp  --   anywhere anywhere    tcp dpt:domain
ACCEPT tcp  --   anywhere anywhere    tcp dpt:http
ACCEPT tcp  --   anywhere anywhere    tcp dpt:https
ACCEPT icmp --   anywhere anywhere
LOG    all  --   anywhere anywhere    limit: avg 3/sec burst
                                            5 LOG level warning
DROP   all  --   anywhere             anywhere

Chain FORWARD (policy ACCEPT)
target prot opt source    destination

Chain OUTPUT (policy ACCEPT)
target prot opt source    destination

Chain RH-Firewall-1-INPUT (0 references)
target prot opt source    destination
```

If your firewall output matches this one, then congratulations, you have a firewall running!

Configuring the Firewall to Run at Startup

Your last task is to create a script that will handle the startup, shutdown, status display, as well as a panic mode for your firewall. Create a script at /etc/init.d/firewall with the information in Listing 6.5.

Listing 6.5   Firewall Control Script

```
#!/bin/sh
#
# This script is responsible for loading the custom
# IPTables Firewall settings.
#
```

```
# chkconfig: 345 96 96
#
# processname: /usr/local/etc/firewall
#
# description: Controls the custom built firewall rules
#
# Source function library:
. /etc/init.d/functions

RETVAL=0
start () {
    echo "Loading Firewall Rules: "
    /usr/local/etc/firewall > /dev/null
    touch /var/lock/subsys/firewall
    RETVAL=$?
    [ $RETVAL -eq 0 ] && success || failure
    echo -n "Status:"
    echo
    return $RETVAL
}

flush () {
    echo -n "Turning Firewall Off"
    iptables -F
    rm -rf /var/lock/subsys/firewall
    RETVAL=$?
    [ $RETVAL -eq 0 ] && success || failure
    echo
    return $RETVAL
}

status () {
    echo "Current Firewall Configuration:"
    RETVAL=$?
    iptables -L
    return $RETVAL
}

panic () {
    echo "Enabling Panic Mode. Only SSH access allowed!!"
    echo -n "You must run '$0 start' to allow other ports "
    echo " through the firewall again."
    echo -n "Panic Mode Status:"
    /sbin/iptables -F
    /sbin/iptables -A INPUT -p tcp --dport 22 -j ACCEPT
    /sbin/iptables -A INPUT -j DROP
    [ $RETVAL -eq 0 ] && success || failure
    echo
    return $RETVAL

}
```

```
case "$1" in
  start)
    start
    ;;
  restart)
    start
    ;;
  flush)
    flush
    ;;
  stop)
    flush
    ;;
  status)
    status
    ;;
  list)
    status
    ;;
  panic)
    panic
    ;;
  *)

    echo "Usage:$0 {start|stop|restart|flush|status|list|panic}"
    exit 1
esac

exit $RETVAL
```

After you create the script, chmod it to 700:

```
chmod 700 /etc/init.d/firewall
```

Next, you need to add the script to chkconfig by running the following command:

```
chkconfig --add firewall
```

Now your firewall will be loaded at startup. Here is a list of options for this script, so if you wish to execute /etc/init.d/firewall *command*, you can perform these actions:

start   This option starts the firewall and loads the rules from /usr/local/etc/firewall.

stop   This option flushes all of the rules from the iptables and disables the firewall.

restart   This option is an alias for start. Because your firewall rules script is designed to flush any existing rules before it loads the new rules, it is the equivalent of a firewall restart.

status   This option will perform the iptables -L command to show you how the firewall is currently configured.

list   This option is the same as the status option.

panic This option should be used only if you think you are under an attack or someone is hacking into your server. This mode will flush all existing `iptables` rules, open port 22 for SSH access, and drop any other ports. This is used to lock out anyone from coming in and allows you to maintain your SSH session. It is not 100 percent bulletproof, but it could help you in a panic mode.

Your firewall is all set now. It will prevent unwanted access to the ports that you did not specifically open and it will start up on boot. You might additionally want to link this startup script to your path so you can simply run `firewall` *option* from anywhere within your system.

```
ln -s /etc/init.d/firewall /usr/bin/firewall
```

Your system is now under the protection of a firewall. You can take a deep breath and relax a little now because you do not have to worry about intruders easily getting into your system without pulling their hair out.

Monitoring the *iptables* Log

The firewall you have created is set up to log any rejected packets to your system log located at `/var/log/messages`. If you need to monitor what is happening when you are trying to troubleshoot a connection problem, this is a good place to look. Simply type in `tail -f /var/log/messages` and you'll see the firewall logging take place as your connection fails to a desired port.

NOTE   We strongly urge you to turn off the `iptables` logging if you do not need it enabled for a troubleshooting problem. Simply disable the logging by adding a comment mark (#) to the front of the rule and then run the firewall script again.

Don't Panic, Just Drop It!

If someone is attacking your server, and you know what IP address or hostname they are coming from, you can run a simple `iptables` rule and disable any access to your server from them. You have a choice of either running the command at the command line or adding it to your firewall script and then running your firewall script again.

The rule from the command line looks like the following:

```
/sbin/iptables -I INPUT -s [IP ADDRESS] -j DROP
```

Or in your firewall script, it looks like this:

```
$IPTABLES -A INPUT -s [IP ADDRESS] -j DROP
```

NOTE   If you are manually adding a specific drop rule to your firewall script, you should add it at the beginning directly below the $IPTABLES -F (flush) lines.

This should clear up any unwanted traffic from that particular IP address. Be sure to replace *IP ADDRESS* with the real IP of the offending user.

Using Network Monitoring and Testing Applications

There are many applications out there that will enable you to test your system to ensure that it's secure. Some of these applications will require you to use a remote server to get accurate information, so it might be useful to have a second system handy. In this section, we will discuss some tools such as Nmap, Snort, traceroute and ping.

Nmap

Nmap, an abbreviation for *Network Mapper*, is a utility that enables system administrators and other curious people to scan large-scale networks to determine which services are accessible through a firewall.

Nmap can support many scanning techniques, such as UDP, TCP `connect()`, TCP SYN (half open), FTP proxy bounce attack, reverse-ident, ICMP (ping sweep), FIN, ACK sweep, XMAS Tree, SYN sweep, IP protocol, and Null scan. As you can see, this is a valuable tool for seeing how open your network is!

Nmap can be found at `www.insecure.org/nmap`, and you can compile or install it yourself. Some systems come with Nmap installed by default, so you might already have it handy. Don't worry if you do not have another Linux box around. Nmap comes with Windows binaries as well. Browse to the download section of the website and obtain a copy for the operating system you are using.

> **WARNING**   Be careful when using Nmap and do not go overboard with your scanning. If you are caught scanning networks other than your own, your activities might reflect that of a hacker, and you could face criminal charges for doing so. The bottom line: if the network is not yours, do not scan it!

Let's take a look at how to run Nmap on your system. Let's say your server's IP address is 192.168.0.15. On a different computer, run the following command:

```
nmap 192.168.0.15
```

> **NOTE**   If Nmap takes an extremely long time to run, that is a good indicator that your firewall is working well. Alternatively you can use the −F option for fast scan mode.

You should see something similar to the output in Listing 6.6. Keep in mind that you currently have the firewall running on this server.

Listing 6.6   nmap **Output with Firewall Protection**

```
[root@central root]# nmap -F 192.168.0.15

Starting nmap V. 3.00 ( www.insecure.org/nmap/ )
Interesting ports on  (192.168.0.15):
(The 1146 ports scanned but not shown below are in state: filtered)
Port       State      Service
22/tcp     open       ssh
53/tcp     closed     domain
80/tcp     closed     http
443/tcp    closed     https

Nmap run completed -- 1 IP address (1 host up) scanned in 129 seconds
```

Notice how port 22 is open for the SSH service. This means that the port was allowed to be opened on the firewall and the service is running. The other ports are closed for their respective services because the port is allowed open on your firewall but the service is not running. Either way, this is a safe system as far as port scanning goes.

Listing 6.7 depicts what the Nmap output would look like if you were not running a firewall on the machine you are scanning.

Listing 6.7   nmap **Output without Firewall Protection**

```
[root@central root]# nmap -F 192.168.0.15

Starting nmap V. 3.00 ( www.insecure.org/nmap/ )
Interesting ports on  (192.168.0.15):
(The 1147 ports scanned but not shown below are in state: closed)
Port       State      Service
22/tcp     open       ssh
111/tcp    open       sunrpc
1026/tcp   open       LSA-or-nterm

Nmap run completed -- 1 IP address (1 host up) scanned in 4 seconds
```

As you can see in the previous scan, there are a few ports open along with the services. Your firewall, when enabled, does not allow port 111 or port 1026 to be accessed, so these ports are now visible when your firewall is turned off.

If you want to learn more about Nmap, you can read the manual online at www.linuxforum .com/man/nmap.1.php or visit the www.insecure.org/nmap website.

Snort

Snort is an excellent program that can report to you in real time what packets are flowing through your Ethernet devices. Basically, it's a glorified *packet sniffer* with reporting options, a command-line interface, Web-based interfaces, and more.

Snort can be obtained from www.snort.org, and the documentation can be found on the website as well. We recommend that you grab it, read the documentation, and install it. Listing 6.8 shows an example of some output from Snort on one of our routers.

Listing 6.8   snort **Output**

```
[root@central root]# snort -v -i eth1
Running in packet dump mode
Log directory = /var/log/snort

Initializing Network Interface eth1

        --== Initializing Snort ==--
Initializing Output Plugins!
Decoding Ethernet on interface eth1

        --== Initialization Complete ==--

-*> Snort! <*-
Version 2.0.4 (Build 96)
By Martin Roesch (roesch@sourcefire.com, www.snort.org)
02/04-14:01:53.910324 99.999.99.99:445 -> 99.999.99.99:3514
TCP TTL:64 TOS:0x0 ID:0 IpLen:20 DgmLen:40 DF
***A*R** Seq: 0x0  Ack: 0xED1F9F76  Win: 0x0  TcpLen: 20
=+=+=+=+=+=+=+=+=+=+=+=+=+=+=+=+=+=+=+=+=+=+=+=+=+=+=+=+=+=+=+=+


02/04-14:01:53.913537 99.999.99.99 -> 99.999.99.99:3515
TCP TTL:64 TOS:0x10 ID:0 IpLen:20 DgmLen:48 DF
***A**S* Seq: 0x6E6A222  Ack: 0xED203090  Win: 0x400  TcpLen: 28
TCP Options (4) => MSS: 256 NOP NOP SackOK
=+=+=+=+=+=+=+=+=+=+=+=+=+=+=+=+=+=+=+=+=+=+=+=+=+=+=+=+=+=+=+=+


02/04-14:01:53.993511 99.999.99.99 -> 99.999.99.99:3515
TCP TTL:64 TOS:0x10 ID:641 IpLen:20 DgmLen:40 DF
***A**** Seq: 0x6E6A223  Ack: 0xED2030D8  Win: 0x400  TcpLen: 20
=+=+=+=+=+=+=+=+=+=+=+=+=+=+=+=+=+=+=+=+=+=+=+=+=+=+=+=+=+=+=+=+


===============================================================================
Snort analyzed 7 out of 7 packets, dropping 0(0.000%) packets

Breakdown by protocol:               Action Stats:
     TCP: 6          (85.714%)       ALERTS: 0
     UDP: 0          (0.000%)        LOGGED: 0
    ICMP: 1          (14.286%)       PASSED: 0
```

```
      ARP: 0              (0.000%)
    EAPOL: 0              (0.000%)
     IPv6: 0              (0.000%)
      IPX: 0              (0.000%)
    OTHER: 0              (0.000%)
  DISCARD: 0              (0.000%)
===============================================================================
Wireless Stats:
Breakdown by type:
    Management Packets: 0            (0.000%)
    Control Packets:    0            (0.000%)
    Data Packets:       0            (0.000%)
===============================================================================
Fragmentation Stats:
Fragmented IP Packets: 0             (0.000%)
    Fragment Trackers: 0
    Rebuilt IP Packets: 0
    Frag elements used: 0
Discarded(incomplete): 0
  Discarded(timeout): 0
  Frag2 memory faults: 0
===============================================================================
TCP Stream Reassembly Stats:
      TCP Packets Used: 0            (0.000%)
       Stream Trackers: 0
        Stream flushes: 0
         Segments used: 0
  Stream4 Memory Faults: 0
===============================================================================
Snort exiting
```

This listing illustrates how Snort will provide a large amount of information about what packets are coming in and going out, and what ports they are trafficking on.

If you would like to learn more configuring and running Snort, check out the online documentation located at: www.snort.org/docs.

Ping

The almighty Ping utility is the simplest and sometimes the most effective utility to use. It can indicate whether the server is up or responsive and can provide the general state of the connection. However, keep in mind that ping requests can be blocked by firewalls, so it might not always be as handy as it was intended.

Simply run `ping linuxforum.com` and check the output. It should be similar to Listing 6.9.

Listing 6.9   `ping` **output**

```
[root@central root]# ping linuxforum.com
PING linuxforum.com (66.98.196.36) 56(84) bytes of data.
```

```
64 bytes from smeagol.thewebfreaks.com (66.98.196.36): icmp_seq=1
➥ttl=54 time=29.4 ms
64 bytes from smeagol.thewebfreaks.com (66.98.196.36): icmp_seq=2
➥ttl=54 time=27.0 ms
64 bytes from smeagol.thewebfreaks.com (66.98.196.36): icmp_seq=3
➥ttl=54 time=33.4 ms

--- linuxforum.com ping statistics ---
3 packets transmitted, 3 received, 0% packet loss, time 2023ms
rtt min/avg/max/mdev = 27.062/29.972/33.408/2.617 ms
```

This tells you that the server is responding to your requests and that the average ping time for each of the responses is about 29 milliseconds.

We have seen times when a server is not responding to HTTP, SSH, or any other requests, but the ping time is good. This could mean that your server is under serious load and it cannot process much more than a ping. In this case, it would be a good idea to reboot it or hope that the load lifts and lets you back in within a few minutes.

Traceroute

The Traceroute utility is a lifesaver when trying to figure out routing problems. Sometimes you might have problems with your Internet connection and your ISP tells you that the problem is not on their end. The best way to tell who is not telling the truth is to pull up Traceroute and analyze the results. If you have five-millisecond route times to the first four routers, chances are your trusty ISP was telling you the truth. Let's test this out. Listing 6.10 shows a `traceroute` to yahoo.com.

Listing 6.10   `traceroute` to yahoo.com

```
[root@lightning root]# traceroute yahoo.com
traceroute to yahoo.com (66.218.71.198), 30 hops max,
➥38 byte packets
 1  207.44.240.1 (207.44.240.1)  0.465 ms  0.433 ms  0.320 ms
 2  ivhou-207-218-245-48.ev1.net (207.218.245.48)  0.480 ms
➥0.622 ms  0.487 ms
 3  ge-1-0-0.r00.hstntx01.us.bb.verio.net (129.250.10.145)  1.316
➥ ms  1.131 ms  1.153 ms
 4  p16-1-1.r21.dllstx09.us.bb.verio.net (129.250.5.42)  11.646
➥ms  11.712 ms  11.641 ms
 5  p16-7-0-0.r01.dllstx09.us.bb.verio.net (129.250.2.195)  9.309
➥ms  9.212 ms  9.140 ms
```

```
 6  so-2-3-1.edge1.Dallas1.Level3.net (4.68.127.45)  8.978 ms so-
➡ 2-3-0.edge1.Dallas1.Level3.net (4.68.127.41)  9.302 ms  9.221
➡ms
 7  so-1-2-0.bbr1.Dallas1.Level3.net (209.244.15.161)  9.092 ms
➡so-1-2-0.bbr2.Dallas1.Level3.net (209.244.15.165)  9.451 ms
➡so-1-2-0.bbr1.Dallas1.Level3.net (209.244.15.161)  9.075 ms
 8  unknown.Level3.net (209.247.9.182)  48.479 msunknown.Level3.net
(209.247.9.114)  48.293 ms unknown.Level3.net (209.247.9.182)  48.497 ms
 9  ge-9-2.ipcolo3.SanJose1.Level3.net (64.159.2.137)  48.289 ms
➡48.322 ms ge-10-2.ipcolo3.SanJose1.Level3.net (64.159.2.169)
➡48.495 ms
10  unknown.Level3.net (64.152.69.30)  50.271 ms  50.491 ms
➡50.297 ms
11  UNKNOWN-66-218-82-226.yahoo.com (66.218.82.226)  54.013 msUNKNOWN-66-218-82-
230.yahoo.com (66.218.82.230)  53.375 ms UNKNOWN-66-218-82-226.yahoo.com
(66.218.82.226)  50.326 ms
12  alteon4.68.scd.yahoo.com (66.218.68.13)  51.349 ms  50.804 ms
➡51.771 ms
```

Each hop through the Internet is recorded here with the host or router name, IP address, and time it took for the response. If you see that a particular hop is taking 999 milliseconds for a response time, you can probably bet that your problem is there.

NOTE   Some hosts/nodes are designed to not respond to `traceroute`. These hosts/nodes usually return a * in the Traceroute output.

Linux Security Checklist

This chapter has covered, in brief, some important information regarding your system. The wonderful thing is that Linux comes as a secure platform out of the box, but you need to make sure that you take the correct steps to ensure that all loose ends are tied up. After reading this chapter you should feel comfortable with the following tasks:

- Know how to disable startup services.

- Keep your system updated with the latest security patches.

- Control root access.

- Create standard user accounts with limited access.

- Configure, manage, and monitor your firewall.

- Test network connections, open ports, and troubleshoot connection problems.

Because this chapter was an accelerated preview of the process required to secure your server, you should always try to expand your knowledge with some additional reading of Linux security books. Take a look at the titles noted earlier in this chapter.

In the next chapter, we're going to cover the basics of a Mail Transfer Agent (MTA), or mail server, to take care of your electronic communications.

CHAPTER 7

Electronic Mail

- How E-mail Works

- Installing the qmail MTA

- Managing Your qmail Server

E-mail is undoubtedly the primary means of communication with any Internet-based business or hobby. Therefore, you must ensure that your e-mail operations are conducted in a manner that will accommodate your needs with minimal risks or downtime.

Determining your e-mail requirements might not be so easy. You have to figure out what you need and plan accordingly when setting up your server. The biggest mistake you can make is to start an operation without determining the requirements up front, especially when planning your e-mail server requirements.

The solution to this problem is simple. Do you plan to use this server as an e-mail server? If so, you should install a higher-grade MTA, such as qmail, and you should read "Installing the qmail MTA" later in this chapter. On the other hand, if you are not going to use this server as an e-mail server, and you want only the web server to send e-mail, you can simply close port 25 on your firewall and leave Sendmail running.

TIP   You will want port 25 closed to prevent anyone connecting to your Simple Mail Transfer Protocol (SMTP) server and attempting to relay e-mails through it. Remember, in Chapter 6, "Linux Security," you set up some firewall rules that allow established connections to utilize the ports needed to complete their transactions. Based on these rules, if your web server utilizes Sendmail to send e-mails, the port will be available because you are establishing an outward connection first.

In this chapter, we are going to discuss how e-mail works and the differences between e-mail servers. We will look at your needs for an e-mail server and provide solutions for your requirements. We will show you how to download, install, and configure the qmail e-mail server—the Sendmail replacement—with virtual domain support and more. By the end of this chapter, you will have a strong understanding of qmail and how to manage it.

Understanding How E-Mail Works

If you have lived in the virtual hosting world and never maintained your own e-mail server, you might be surprised to learn that the elements involved are easy to manage and maintain. When I first started out on the Internet, I had no desire to learn what happened on an e-mail server. However, as my Internet career progressed and I started moving into the dedicated server scene, I no longer had someone to manage my e-mail accounts for me. I was soon forced to plunge into the life of an e-mail administrator and found that it was not as hard as some technicians make it sound.

The E-Mail Message

In 1971, the first e-mail message in history was sent by an engineer named Ray Tomlinson. Until then, it was possible to send messages only to someone who was accessing the same machine as you. Tomlinson invented the use of the *at* (@) symbol to designate a user *at* another computer, or in our case now, another domain (for example, *username@someplace.com*).

An e-mail message is composed of three parts:

The header contains information indicating the type of e-mail, whom it's to, whom it's from, and even where it's been.

The body of the e-mail is the message you receive when you read the e-mail.

The attachments are typically base-64 encoded by your client before they are sent in order to make them easily readable by the e-mail servers that send, receive, and forward the email. Other e-mail attachments might be of multipart MIME format, HTML, RTF, or ASCII attachments as part of the original message.

Without delving too deep into the specifics of an e-mail header, let's take a look at a few of the header sections that contain key information enabling the e-mail to travel to its intended destination:

X-Originating-IP This designates the IP address from which the e-mail originated. It is important to note that this could be forged, or *spoofed*, so it might not always be accurate. However, the `Received` field, covered later in this list, cannot be forged.

X-Originating-Email As its title suggests, this is the e-mail address from which the message originated. Like the originating IP address, this can also be forged.

From This is the "from" address, which can also contain the user's real name. When using a mail client this is the address that is shown, you will typically see a person's name and e-mail address written as *Real Name <e-mail@server>* or *<e-mail@domain.foo>*. The less-than and greater-than symbols are used as *tags* for the e-mail address. This e-mail address can be set by the user through any client so it is also not to be trusted.

To The To directive is much the same as `From` except it states the e-mail's intended destination. It might also use the real name with the e-mail address tagged.

Received An e-mail message, after it is received, will usually have multiple `Received` entries. Every time an e-mail is forwarded by a server on its way to its destination, the server name it was received from, the server name it was received by, the time it was processed, and a unique identifier is tacked onto the header. This helps e-mail servers filter spam and enables you to track what has happened with your e-mail along its route.

Mime-Version and Content-Type These are used to specify the e-mail's contents, for example, whether it is a plain-text e-mail or is formatted in HTML. Your e-mail client will use this information to display the message to you in the correct format.

Electronic Mail Protocols

Let's take a look at some of the protocols used to run e-mail servers. The basics are SMTP, POP3, and IMAP.

SMTP

Simple Mail Transport Protocol (SMTP) is used for sending, relaying, and receiving e-mails to the appropriate servers. SMTP servers are usually run in the form of a daemon process and will accept connections on port 25. After the connection is made, the e-mail client will send its information to the daemon, and then the daemon will perform a lookup of the domain name the e-mail address belongs to. After the lookup is performed, the e-mail is relayed to the appropriate SMTP server for retrieval.

On the receiving end, depending on your configuration, the SMTP server/daemon might deliver the mail itself, or it might deliver the mail to another program to process and route to the appropriate locations.

If the appropriate destination server is not found, then the e-mail will be placed in a queue. This queue is periodically processed by the sendmail binary according to its configuration, and the server will attempt to resend the e-mail. If it fails once again, it will usually send a message to the sender letting them know that the e-mail did not reach its intended destination.

POP3

Post Office Protocol 3 (POP3) is the most popular client protocol. An e-mail client uses this protocol to receive e-mail on port 110. This protocol enables users to download their e-mail to the local computer. POP3 might also allow the e-mail to be stored locally on the user's computer and save a copy of the e-mail on the server itself.

A POP3 server requires each user to have a username and password and usually stores each of the messages in one text file. When a new message that the user has not seen before is sent to the server, it simply appends the new message to the user's file. A POP3 server understands a limited number of commands, including user, pass, quit, list, retr, dele, and top.

IMAP

Internet Mail Access Protocol (IMAP) is by far our favorite protocol when it comes to client-side e-mail. IMAP is another protocol used by a client to connect to the server and retrieve their e-mail. IMAP uses port 143 and stores the e-mail directly on the server.

There are multiple reasons you would want to store your e-mail on the server. For instance, if you format your computer, you don't have to pull your hair out trying to back up and restore your e-mail from two years ago. Additionally, you can access your mail via the web browser using webmail anywhere you go and can also have the same e-mail at home or at the office. It doesn't matter where you access your mail from; the e-mail inbox will always contain the same contents because the e-mail is stored on the server, and not downloaded to your local computer as with most POP3 protocols. An IMAP server is also capable of searching its own contents locally rather than having the user do the work on their client machine. An IMAP server enables you to create folders for storing your messages; these folders will always be there no matter where you log in from.

The setback to this is, of course, you cannot read your e-mails unless you are connected to the Internet. With the age of broadband or high-speed Interent upon us, this is usually not a factor. In fact, many clients nowadays will cache the content of the e-mails if you enable that option, and you can still read the contents. If you are not online, your e-mail client might cache any new e-mails you create and send them when it knows it has a valid connection to the Internet and can reach the IMAP server.

Electronic Mail Transport Agents

The e-mail protocols are usually bundled together within an electronic *Message Transfer Agent (MTA)*. An easy way to grasp this is to think of it as a software application that handles your e-mail server requirements.

There are quite a few MTAs out there, and some of them even come on Linux by default. For example, Fedora will install Sendmail if you select a package group that requires an e-mail server. The other MTAs we will discuss in this section are Exim, Postfix, and qmail.

Sendmail

Sendmail is the most popular Linux MTA right now. According to Dan Shearer—Computing Consultant for Adelaide in South Australia—at `http://shearer.org/en/writing/mtacomparison .html`, Sendmail accounted for delivery of slightly less than half of all Internet-related e-mail by June 2001. This equates to billions of e-mails per day.

Sendmail is installed by default on most distributions of Linux and it has a fairly low overhead. Some of the features of Sendmail include anti-spam, virtual domain support, and multiple user support.

To learn more about Sendmail, check out the official website at `www.sendmail.org`.

Exim

Exim is another MTA that has been the spawn of Sendmail problems. It was developed at the University of Cambridge in England. Exim is similar to Sendmail, but its facilities are more general. One of the great enhancements is more-flexible mail routing.

For more information about Exim, visit the official website at `www.exim.org`.

Postfix

Postfix is a freeware MTA developed by Wietse Venema. Many consider Postfix to fit somewhere between Exim and qmail in the realm of features and security. Its purpose is to enhance Sendmail's features and security and to provide an alternative to that MTA, as well as to provide direct competition to qmail.

Some of the features of Postfix include multiple transports, virtual domains, and easy-to-use configuration files.

To learn more about Postfix, visit the official website at `www.postfix.org`.

qmail

qmail is a rapidly growing MTA written by Dan Bernstein. The qmail team claims that it will make Sendmail obsolete and boasts about qmail being a *modern* SMTP server and a secure package.

qmail has quite a following; from our experience, most of the web hosting companies we have used in the past used qmail by default due to its wide support for add-ons and third-party enhancements. The features of qmail are outstanding and they include virtual domain support, awesome speed and flexibility, support for multiple third-party add-ons, Realtime Black List (RBL) support, and much more.

If you would like to learn more about qmail, you can view the official website at `www.qmail.org`. Later in this chapter, we are going to cover how to install qmail and some of the excellent third-party add-ons to build a powerful mainstream mail server.

Now that you have an understanding of the most popular MTAs out there, let's get started with installing qmail.

Installing the qmail MTA

Installing qmail is a long and tedious process during which you must take extreme consideration. Failure to perform a step properly could result in a long and strenuous troubleshooting process. One of the most important aspects about the installation is learning the location of files that make qmail run.

In this installation, you are going to install qmail with the applications required to run it, as well as some third-party applications that will ease the virtual host configurations. Additionally, you are going to configure RBL (which rejects known offending servers of spam), a server-side antivirus program called Clam AntiVirus (ClamAV), and SpamAssassin spam filter.

This chapter closely follows the standard qmail installation procedure; however, we have altered the process to include quite a few third-party add-ons for qmail. To learn more about the software you are using and to troubleshoot any problems you might have, see *Life with qmail* by Dan Bernstein, located at www.lifewithqmail.org/lwq.html.

Obtaining the Source Files

You'll start by creating a new directory to download your source files. We believe in putting your downloaded source distributions in /usr/local/src/*xxx*, where the *xxx* is the purpose of the source files. For this scenario, call this mailserver. Create your /usr/local/src/ mailserver directory as follows:

```
mkdir -p /usr/local/src/mailserver
```

Now, cd into /usr/local/src/mailserver and let's grab those files!

WARNING   Before you proceed with downloading the source files in this chapter, check for the latest versions at www.qmail.org. Look in two sections: the introduction and the "Author's Enhancement Software for qmail" section. Failure to download the current versions could leave your system with a security hole resulting in serious risks.

Download qmail Source Files

The first file you need to obtain is the actual qmail MTA. To download this, you can use wget:

```
wget http://www.qmail.org/netqmail-1.05.tar.gz
```

Download *ucspi-tcp*

The next file you need is the package that will create and receive TCP connections for qmail. This is called ucspi-tcp:

```
wget ftp://cr.yp.to/ucspi-tcp/ucspi-tcp-0.88.tar.gz
```

Download daemontools

The daemontools application enables you to manage Unix services; in this case it will be qmail:

```
wget ftp://cr.yp.to/daemontools/daemontools-0.76.tar.gz
```

Download Vpopmail

Vpopmail is a program written by Inter7 that manages virtual domains for qmail. It alters the way qmail handles mail and it enables qmail to route e-mail to the proper domain and user based on the configuration:

```
wget http://www.inter7.com/vpopmail/vpopmail-5.2.2.tar.gz
```

You can download the latest stable version at www.inter7.com.

Download Courier-IMAP

Courier-IMAP is an IMAP server that integrates well with your installation:

```
wget http://www.courier-mta.org/beta/imap/courier-imap-2.2.2.20040207.tar.bz2
```

You can download the latest stable version of Courier-IMAP, not Courier, at `www.courier-mta.org/download.php#imap`.

Download Clam AntiVirus

Clam AntiVirus is a fast, command-line, multithreaded antivirus scanner for Linux. It has the ability to scan and reject e-mails filtered through qmail and Vpopmail:

```
wget http://osdn.dl.sourceforge.net/sourceforge/clamav/clamav-0.67-1.tar.gz
```

You can download the latest stable version at `www.clamav.net`.

Download SpamAssassin

SpamAssassin is a set of Perl scripts that analyzes content and detects spam based on a set of instructions. It has worked well for our e-mail servers and we recommend that you give it a shot:

```
wget http://eu.spamassassin.org/released/Mail-SpamAssassin-2.63.tar.gz
```

You can download the latest version at `www.spamassassin.org`.

Download Qmail-Scanner

Qmail-Scanner is the application that sends e-mails through Clam AntiVirus and SpamAssassin before the e-mails are delivered to the inbox:

```
wget http://unc.dl.sourceforge.net/sourceforge/qmail-scanner/qmail-scanner-
1.20.tgz
```

You can download the latest version at `qmail-scanner.sourceforge.net`.

Download TNEF

TNEF, which stands for Transport Neutral Encapsulation Format, is an application that will decode Microsoft TNEF MIME-type attachments. It is required by Qmail-Scanner:

```
wget http://unc.dl.sourceforge.net/sourceforge/tnef/tnef-1.2.3.1.tar.gz
```

You can download the latest version at `www.sourceforge.net/projects/tnef`.

Download maildrop

The maildrop application is required by Qmail-Scanner:

```
wget http://unc.dl.sourceforge.net/sourceforge/courier/maildrop-1.6.3.tar.bz2
```

You can download the latest version at `www.flounder.net/~mrsam/maildrop`.

Preparing for Installation

Now that you have downloaded your source files, it's time to prepare for installation. You will begin by unpacking the files and creating the directories, users, and groups.

Unpack the Files

To unpack the files, you simply need to uncompress them. Use these commands:

```
cd /usr/local/src/mailserver
tar zxpf clamav*.tar.gz
tar jxpf courier-imap*.tar.bz2
tar zxpf daemontools*.tar.gz
tar jxpf maildrop*.tar.bz2
tar zxpf Mail-SpamAssassin*.tar.gz
tar zxpf netqmail*.tar.gz
tar zxpf qmail-scanner*.tgz
tar zxpf tnef*.tar.gz
tar zxpf ucspi-tcp*.tar.gz
tar zxpf vpopmail*.tar.gz
```

Now, you should have a group of directories containing the source code for all of your downloaded files. Let's move on to installing some Perl modules for supporting the applications you need to install.

Install Required Perl Modules

Qmail-Scanner is going to require a couple of support modules to be installed for Perl. You can install these easily through a system called CPAN, which stands for Comprehensive Perl Archive Network. Follow these steps:

1. Run the following:

   ```
   perl -MCPAN -e shell
   ```

2. If you have never run CPAN before, you might be prompted for some configuration defaults. Simply press Enter for each of the prompts and you should be okay with the default settings.

3. After you run the setup for CPAN, you will see a prompt that looks similar to this: cpan>

   At this point, you can simply type the module name and issue the `install` command. Install the modules for Qmail-Scanner and SpamAssassin:

   ```
   cpan> install Bundle::CPAN
   cpan> install ExUtils::MakeMaker
   cpan> install Time::HiRes
   cpan> install DB_File
   cpan> install HTML::Parser
   cpan> install Net::DNS
   quit
   ```

As you type each of these commands, you will see the files download and configure automatically for you.

At this point, you can elect to install SpamAssassin from CPAN because SpamAssassin is essentially a set of Perl scripts and is available through CPAN. If you decide to do this now, open CPAN and use `install Mail::SpamAssassin`; then skip the "Install SpamAssassin" step later in this chapter.

Installing qmail

Before installing qmail, you need to set up the directories and files that are going to be used to run and configure your e-mail server. Do so now:

```
cd /usr/local/src/mailserver
mkdir /package
mv admin /package
mkdir /var/qmail
mkdir /var/log/qmail
mkdir -p /var/qmail/supervise/qmail-send/log
mkdir -p /var/qmail/supervise/qmail-smtpd/log
mkdir -p /var/log/qmail/smtpd
```

Create Users and Groups

Your setup will require special users and groups to be installed before you configure and run the applications. You want these applications to have limited access to the system, so you will create limited-access users and groups.

Configure the users and groups for qmail:

```
groupadd nofiles
useradd -g nofiles -d /var/qmail/alias alias
useradd -g nofiles -d /var/qmail qmaild
useradd -g nofiles -d /var/qmail qmaill
useradd -g nofiles -d /var/qmail qmailp
groupadd qmail
useradd -g qmail -d /var/qmail qmailq
useradd -g qmail -d /var/qmail qmailr
useradd -g qmail -d /var/qmail -s /nonexistent qmails
```

Prepare and Build qmail

Let's get started on preparing and building qmail. Follow these steps:

1. Run the following commands:

```
cd /usr/local/src/mailserver/netqmail*
./collate.sh
```

```
cd netqmail-1.05
make setup check
```

2. You need to determine the hostname of your machine. You can do this by simply typing the `hostname` command. The output indicates your machine's hostname. If you want to temporarily change it, simply type `hostname` *new_name*, where *new_name* is the hostname of your machine.

NOTE   If your hostname is not set properly, you will need to run the `hostname` command, and then edit the applicable lines in the `/etc/hosts` and `/etc/sysconfig/network` files. If you do not edit these files, the hostname may not be set properly the next time you reboot.

3. Type the following to configure the build files:

```
./config-fast host_name
```

Be sure to substitute *host_name* with your fully qualified host name (foo.*yourdomain*.com).

Build and Install *ucspi-tcp*

This process has two steps:

1. Change to the /ucspi-tcp directory that you unpacked earlier:

```
cd /usr/local/src/mailserver/ucspi-tcp*
```

2. Perform the build:

```
patch < /usr/local/src/mailserver/netqmail-
➡1.05/other-patches/ucspi-tcp-0.88.errno.patch
make
make setup check
```

Build and Install daemontools

You again have two steps to follow:

1. Change to the location where you moved the /daemontools directory:

```
cd /package/admin/daemontools*/src
```

2. Perform the build:

```
patch < /usr/local/src/mailserver/netqmail-
➡1.05/other-patches/daemontools-0.76.errno.patch
cd ..
package/install
```

Configure qmail Startup Scripts

The qmail application requires some startup scripts to run. You will create them now:

1. Create a file named /var/qmail/rc with the following contents:

```
#!/bin/sh

exec env - PATH="/var/qmail/bin:$PATH" \
qmail-start "`cat /var/qmail/control/defaultdelivery`"
```

NOTE The preceding script uses backticks (`` ` ``) and not single quotes.

2. Change the permissions on the startup script:

```
chmod 755 /var/qmail/rc
```

Perform Mailbox Configuration

qmail accepts multiple types of mailbox delivery. For this configuration, use the Maildir configuration method. To enable this, run the following command:

```
echo ./Maildir >/var/qmail/control/defaultdelivery
```

Create qmail System Startup Scripts

The next file you are going to create is the qmail system startup script. This script is pretty long to type, so you can download it from the *Life with qmail* website (www.lifewithqmail.org) . To download the script, run the following commands:

```
cd /var/qmail/bin
wget http://www.lifewithqmail.org/qmailctl-script-dt70
mv qmailctl-script-dt70 qmailctl
chmod 755 /var/qmail/bin/qmailctl
ln -s /var/qmail/bin/qmailctl /usr/bin
```

NOTE After you run the preceding commands, you will have the qmailctl script in your /usr/bin path. This allows you to run qmailctl from anywhere within the filesystem.

For your reference, Listing 7.1 shows the script you have just downloaded.

Listing 7.1 **qmail System Startup Script**

```
#!/bin/sh

# description: the qmail MTA

PATH=/var/qmail/bin:/bin:/usr/bin:/usr/local/bin:/usr/local/sbin
export PATH
```

```
QMAILDUID=`id -u qmaild`
NOFILESGID=`id -g qmaild`

case "$1" in
  start)
    echo "Starting qmail"
    if svok /service/qmail-send ; then
      svc -u /service/qmail-send /service/qmail-send/log
    else
      echo "qmail-send supervise not running"
    fi
    if svok /service/qmail-smtpd ; then
      svc -u /service/qmail-smtpd /service/qmail-smtpd/log
    else
      echo "qmail-smtpd supervise not running"
    fi
    if [ -d /var/lock/subsys ]; then
      touch /var/lock/subsys/qmail
    fi
    ;;
  stop)
    echo "Stopping qmail..."
    echo "  qmail-smtpd"
    svc -d /service/qmail-smtpd /service/qmail-smtpd/log
    echo "  qmail-send"
    svc -d /service/qmail-send /service/qmail-send/log
    if [ -f /var/lock/subsys/qmail ]; then
      rm /var/lock/subsys/qmail
    fi
    ;;
  stat)
    svstat /service/qmail-send
    svstat /service/qmail-send/log
    svstat /service/qmail-smtpd
    svstat /service/qmail-smtpd/log
    qmail-qstat
    ;;
  doqueue|alrm|flush)
    echo "Flushing timeout table and sending ALRM signal to qmail-send."
    /var/qmail/bin/qmail-tcpok
    svc -a /service/qmail-send
    ;;
  queue)
    qmail-qstat
    qmail-qread
    ;;
  reload|hup)
    echo "Sending HUP signal to qmail-send."
    svc -h /service/qmail-send
    ;;
  pause)
    echo "Pausing qmail-send"
```

```
      svc -p /service/qmail-send
      echo "Pausing qmail-smtpd"
      svc -p /service/qmail-smtpd
      ;;
  cont)
      echo "Continuing qmail-send"
      svc -c /service/qmail-send
      echo "Continuing qmail-smtpd"
      svc -c /service/qmail-smtpd
      ;;
  restart)
      echo "Restarting qmail:"
      echo "* Stopping qmail-smtpd."
      svc -d /service/qmail-smtpd /service/qmail-smtpd/log
      echo "* Sending qmail-send SIGTERM and restarting."
      svc -t /service/qmail-send /service/qmail-send/log
      echo "* Restarting qmail-smtpd."
      svc -u /service/qmail-smtpd /service/qmail-smtpd/log
      ;;
  cdb)
      tcprules /etc/tcp.smtp.cdb /etc/tcp.smtp.tmp < /etc/tcp.smtp
      chmod 644 /etc/tcp.smtp.cdb
      echo "Reloaded /etc/tcp.smtp."
      ;;
  help)
      cat <<HELP
   stop -- stops mail service (smtp connections refused, nothing goes out)
  start -- starts mail service (smtp connection accepted, mail can go out)
  pause -- temporarily stops mail service (connections accepted, nothing leaves)
   cont -- continues paused mail service
   stat -- displays status of mail service
    cdb -- rebuild the tcpserver cdb file for smtp
restart -- stops and restarts smtp, sends qmail-send a TERM & restarts it
doqueue -- schedules queued messages for immediate delivery
 reload -- sends qmail-send HUP, rereading locals and virtualdomains
  queue -- shows status of queue
   alrm -- same as doqueue
  flush -- same as doqueue
    hup -- same as reload
HELP
      ;;
  *)
      echo "Usage: $0 {start|stop|restart|doqueue|flush|reload|stat|pause|cont
➥|cdb|queue|help}"
      exit 1
      ;;
esac

exit 0
```

Create the Supervise Scripts

To create the supervise scripts, follow these steps:

1. Create a script named

   ```
   /var/qmail/supervise/qmail-send/run
   ```

   and add the following to it:
   ```
   #!/bin/sh
   exec /var/qmail/rc
   ```

2. Make this script executable:

   ```
   chmod 755 /var/qmail/supervise/qmail-send/run
   ```

3. Create a script named

   ```
   /var/qmail/supervise/qmail-send/log/run
   ```

   and add the following to this script:
   ```
   #!/bin/sh
   exec /usr/local/bin/setuidgid \
   qmaill /usr/local/bin/multilog t /var/log/qmail
   ```

4. Make this script executable:

   ```
   chmod 755 /var/qmail/supervise/qmail-send/log/run
   ```

5. The next script is located at

   ```
   /var/qmail/supervise/qmail-smtpd/run
   ```

   Add the following to this script:
   ```
   #!/bin/sh

   QMAILDUID=`id -u qmaild`
   NOFILESGID=`id -g qmaild`
   MAXSMTPD=`cat /var/qmail/control/concurrencyincoming`
   LOCAL=`head -1 /var/qmail/control/me`

   if [ -z "$QMAILDUID" -o -z "$NOFILESGID" -o -z "$MAXSMTPD" -o -z "$LOCAL"
   ➥]; then
       echo QMAILDUID, NOFILESGID, MAXSMTPD, or LOCAL is unset in
       echo /var/qmail/supervise/qmail-smtpd/run
       exit 1
   fi

   if [ ! -f /var/qmail/control/rcpthosts ]; then
       echo "No /var/qmail/control/rcpthosts!"
       echo "Refusing to start SMTP listener because it'll create an open
   ➥relay"
   ```

```
    exit 1
fi

exec /usr/local/bin/softlimit -m 20000000 \
    /usr/local/bin/tcpserver -v -R -l "$LOCAL" -x /etc/tcp.smtp.cdb -c
➥"$MAXSMTPD" \
        -u "$QMAILDUID" -g "$NOFILESGID" 0 smtp /var/qmail/bin/qmail-smtpd
➥2>&1
```

6. Make this script executable:

```
chmod 755 /var/qmail/supervise/qmail-smtpd/run
```

7. The next file is

```
/var/qmail/supervise/qmail-smtpd/log/run
```

Add the following to this script:

```
#!/bin/sh
exec /usr/local/bin/setuidgid \
 qmaill /usr/local/bin/multilog t /var/log/qmail/smtpd
```

8. Make this script executable:

```
chmod 755 /var/qmail/supervise/qmail-smtpd/log/run
```

9. Link the /supervise directories to /service, which is where daemontools is installed:

```
ln -s /var/qmail/supervise/qmail-send /var/qmail/supervise/qmail-smtpd
➥/service
```

10. Go ahead and stop qmail from running while you perform the next few steps:

```
qmailctl stop
```

Create the *concurrencyincoming* Script

The concurrencyincoming script specifies the number of e-mails that can be processed during any one time. Create this script by running the following commands:

```
echo 20 > /var/qmail/control/concurrencyincoming
chmod 644 /var/qmail/control/concurrencyincoming
```

Control SMTP Access

qmail uses a database that enables you to control which hosts have relay permissions through your SMTP server. This is handy when trying to prevent unauthorized access by those spam mailers that are out there circulating the Net. You do not want to be a victim here, so ensure that this is done correctly! Run the following commands:

```
echo '127.:allow,RELAYCLIENT=""' >>/etc/tcp.smtp
qmailctl cdb
```

If you wish to add other servers to allow relaying through your primary e-mail server, just run the command again with the server's IP address.

Run Permissions Cleanup

You are going to ensure that the permissions have been set correctly for all the files and directories you have already created. Some of these steps might be redundant or already performed; however, it is better to be safe than sorry so you are not scratching your head later when things do not work correctly.

Run the following commands:

```
chmod 755 /var/qmail/rc
chmod 755 /var/qmail/bin/qmailctl
chmod 755 /var/qmail/supervise/qmail-send/run
chmod 755 /var/qmail/supervise/qmail-send/log/run
chmod 755 /var/qmail/supervise/qmail-smtpd/run
chmod 755 /var/qmail/supervise/qmail-smtpd/log/run
chown qmaill /var/log/qmail /var/log/qmail/smtpd
chmod 644 /var/qmail/control/concurrencyincoming
chmod 644 /etc/tcp.smtp*
```

Out with the Old: Remove Existing E-Mail Servers

It's time to clean up your old e-mail servers and get them off of your system. Due to the high dependency of Sendmail with various other applications that might be running on your system, you'll have to use qmail's binary sendmail replacement file as well.

Follow these steps:

1. Stop Sendmail, Postfix, and any other mail servers running:

WARNING The following commands could produce errors on your server if the applicable software is not installed. Disregard any error output from these.

```
/etc/init.d/sendmail stop
/etc/init.d/postfix stop
```

2. Check whether any of the other servers are installed. You'll do this by running the following commands:

```
rpm -q sendmail
rpm -q exim
rpm -q postfix
```

If any of these commands displays a package and a version, that particular server is installed.

3. On your test system, you have Sendmail and Postfix installed, so you will remove them now. With Sendmail, you have dependencies, so you can remove those dependencies as well:

```
rpm -e mutt
rpm -e fetchmail
rpm -e squirrelmail
rpm -e --nodeps sendmail
rpm -e postfix
```

4. Move the old Sendmail files that were left behind and then link the qmail Sendmail binaries to the proper paths:

WARNING   The following commands could produce errors on your server if the Sendmail files do not exist. If this happens, disregard the errors and continue.

```
mv /usr/lib/sendmail /usr/lib/sendmail.old
chmod 0 /usr/lib/sendmail.old
ln -s /var/qmail/bin/sendmail /usr/lib
mv /usr/sbin/sendmail /usr/sbin/sendmail.old
chmod 0 /usr/sbin/sendmail.old
ln -s /var/qmail/bin/sendmail /usr/sbin
```

Create qmail Alias Files

qmail requires you to set up some alias files that will forward all e-mail for the default users: root, postmaster, and mailer-daemon.

Run these commands to direct them all to root for now:

```
echo root > /var/qmail/alias/.qmail-root
echo root > /var/qmail/alias/.qmail-postmaster
ln -s .qmail-postmaster /var/qmail/alias/.qmail-mailer-daemon
chmod 644 /var/qmail/alias/.qmail-root /var/qmail/alias/.qmail-postmaster
```

Test the qmail Installation

Now, you should be finished with the basic qmail installation. Let's test tour installation out to make sure it works, and test for any permission errors:

1. Stop and then start qmail, just to make sure it's running properly:

```
qmailctl stop
qmailctl start
```

2. After you start qmail, wait a few seconds and then run this command:

```
qmailctl stat
```

You will see output such as the following:

```
/service/qmail-send: up (pid 18823) 11 seconds
/service/qmail-send/log: up (pid 18825) 11 seconds
```

```
/service/qmail-smtpd: up (pid 18828) 11 seconds
/service/qmail-smtpd/log: up (pid 18833) 11 seconds
messages in queue: 0
messages in queue but not yet preprocessed: 0
```

The important thing to notice here is the number of seconds each program is running. If the seconds is set to zero or substantially lower than any other processes, something is wrong.

3. Next, cd to the /var/qmail directory and download the excellent test script that Dan Bernstein's *Life with qmail* guide provides for testing the installation:

```
cd /var/qmail
wget http://lifewithqmail.org/inst_check
chmod 755 inst_check
./inst_check
```

If you see a message such as Congratulations, your LWQ installation looks good! Then your installation is good to go! Otherwise, if you see errors such as

```
! /var/log/qmail has wrong owner, should be qmaill
...try: chown qmaill /var/log/qmail
! /var/log/qmail/smtpd has wrong owner, should be qmaill
...try: chown qmaill /var/log/qmail/smtpd
! /etc/tcp.smtp is missing
...try: echo '127.:allow,RELAYCLIENT=""' >>/etc/tcp.smtp
! /etc/tcp.smtp.cdb is missing
...try: /var/qmail/bin/qmailctl cdb
! Sendmail is still running
...try: /init.d/sendmail stop
```

then you have not followed the directions and you need to correct whatever the script is telling you. In this example, the permissions were not set correctly on multiple directories, and the tcp.smtp database was not configured properly. Fix the errors found in the script and then run it again until you see the success message.

Installing qmail Add-Ons

Now that your basic qmail installation is complete, you need to enhance it with Vpopmail, Qmail-Scanner, ClamAV, and SpamAssassin to bring it up to your fully featured production-level server. Let's get started!

Install Vpopmail

The Vpopmail installation is pretty straightforward, so you can take care of this now:

1. Run the following commands:

```
cd /usr/local/src/mailserver/vpopmail*
groupadd -g 109 vchkpw
```

```
useradd -g vchkpw -u 109 -d /home/vpopmail vpopmail
./configure --enable-roaming-users=y
make
make install
crontab -e
```

2. Add the following cron job crontab:

```
40 * * * * /home/vpopmail/bin/clearopensmtp 2>&1 > /dev/null
```

Add a Domain and E-Mail Account to Vpopmail

Vpopmail makes it fairly easy to create a domain and e-mail accounts through the command line:

1. Create a domain for yourdomain.com and an e-mail account for admin@yourdomain.com:

```
cd /home/vpopmail/bin
./vadddomain yourdomain.com
```

2. Enter the postmaster password:

```
./vadduser admin@yourdomain.com
```

3. Enter the user password.

Now, the user admin@yourdomain.com has been configured. To set up an e-mail client for this e-mail address, you would use your server's IP address or hostname as the incoming/outgoing mail servers, and then the user would enter their full e-mail address as the username and their password as the password. Currently, you have only POP3 enabled, so let's install Courier-IMAP next.

Install Courier-IMAP

Earlier, you extracted the Courier-IMAP package. Courier-IMAP is a straightforward installation. However, you cannot preconfigure Courier-IMAP as a root user.

Follow these steps to install Courier-IMAP:

1. Change ownership of the directory created and switch to a different user:

```
cd /usr/local/src/mailserver/
chown -R someuser.someuser courier-imap*
su someuser
cd /usr/local/src/mailserver/courier-imap*
./configure --with-redhat
```

WARNING You might receive an error when the make command tries to compile the authvchkpw. Disregard this error and continue.

```
exit
cd /usr/local/src/mailserver/courier-imap*
make
make install
make install-configure
```

WARNING   Once again, disregard any errors you might receive.

2. To set up Courier-IMAP to run at startup, copy the startup script to your /etc/init.d directory:

```
cp courier-imap.sysvinit /etc/init.d/imapd
```

3. Add this to chkconfig:

```
chkconfig --add imapd
```

4. Start the Courier-IMAP:

```
/etc/init.d/imapd start
```

If you want to stop the IMAP server, simply run the following:

```
/etc/init.d/imapd stop
```

Configure qmail POP3

qmail includes a POP3 server by default; however, it requires some configuration on your part to get it started.

Follow these steps to start the qmail POP3 server:

1. Create the directories required:

```
mkdir -p /var/qmail/supervise/qmail-pop3d
mkdir -p /var/qmail/supervise/qmail-pop3d/log/
mkdir -p /var/log/qmail/pop3d
```

2. Create the run script located at /var/qmail/supervise/qmail-pop3d/run by using the following:

```
#!/bin/sh
exec /usr/local/bin/softlimit -m 20000000 \
    /usr/local/bin/tcpserver -v -R -H -l 0 0 110 \
    /var/qmail/bin/qmail-popup \
    your.domain.com  /home/vpopmail/bin/vchkpw \
    /var/qmail/bin/qmail-pop3d Maildir 2>&1
```

NOTE   Substitute your.domain.com for your hostname in the previous script.

3. Create the qmail-pop3d logging script located at /var/qmail/supervise/qmail-pop3d/log/run by using the following:

```
#!/bin/sh
exec /usr/local/bin/setuidgid qmaill \
    /usr/local/bin/multilog t \
    /var/log/qmail/pop3d
```

4. Set the appropriate permissions and link the /supervise directories as follows:

```
chown qmaill /var/log/qmail/pop3d
chmod 755 /var/qmail/supervise/qmail-pop3d/run
chmod 755 /var/qmail/supervise/qmail-pop3d/log/run
ln -s /var/qmail/supervise/qmail-pop3d /service
```

5. You are almost there! Next, you need to edit the /var/qmail/bin/qmailctl script and add the qmail-pop3d information.

- In the start section, add the following directly above the two semicolons (; ;):

```
if svok /service/qmail-pop3d ; then
    svc -u /service/qmail-pop3d /service/qmail-pop3d/log
else
    echo qmail-pop3d supervise not running
fi
```

- In the stop section, add the following directly above the two semicolons (; ;):

```
echo "  qmail-pop3d"
svc -d /service/qmail-pop3d /service/qmail-pop3d/log
```

- In the stat section, add the following directly above the qmail-qstat section:

```
svstat /service/qmail-pop3d
svstat /service/qmail-pop3d/log
```

- In the pause section, add the following directly above the two semicolons (; ;):

```
echo "Pausing qmail-pop3d"
svc -p /service/qmail-pop3d
```

- In the cont section, add the following directly above the two semicolons (; ;):

```
echo "Continuing qmail-pop3d"
svc -c /service/qmail-pop3d
```

- In the restart section, add the following directly above the two semicolons (; ;):

```
echo "* Restarting qmail-pop3d."
svc -t /service/qmail-pop3d /service/qmail-pop3d/log
```

6. Save this file and then restart qmail:

   ```
   qmailctl stop
   qmailctl start
   ```

7. To verify that qmail-pop3d is running correctly, run this:

   ```
   qmailctl stat
   ```

   You should see something like the following:

   ```
   /service/qmail-send: up (pid 30188) 9 seconds
   /service/qmail-send/log: up (pid 30206) 8 seconds
   /service/qmail-smtpd: up (pid 30194) 9 seconds
   /service/qmail-smtpd/log: up (pid 30197) 9 seconds
   /service/qmail-pop3d: up (pid 30201) 9 seconds
   /service/qmail-pop3d/log: up (pid 30205) 8 seconds
   messages in queue: 0
   messages in queue but not yet preprocessed: 0
   ```

Install ClamAV

To install ClamAV, you'll cd into the source directory to run the commands required. Use these steps for the installation:

1. Create a group and user for the ClamAV to run as:

   ```
   cd /usr/local/src/mailserver/clamav*
   groupadd clamav
   useradd -g clamav -s /bin/false -c "Clam AntiVirus" clamav
   ```

2. Run the commands required to make and install the ClamAV files:

   ```
   ./configure
   make
   make install
   ```

3. Add the log files and directories for ClamAV:

   ```
   touch /var/log/clam-update.log
   chmod 600 /var/log/clam-update.log
   chown clamav /var/log/clam-update.log
   freshclam -d -c 2 -l /var/log/clam-update.log
   ```

4. Create a cronjob for ClamAV to download the latest virus definitions every morning at 8 A.M. To add a cronjob, you will edit the cron tables and insert a new line as follows:

   ```
   crontab - e
   ```

5. Now add the following:

   ```
   0 8 * * * /usr/local/bin/freshclam --quiet -l /var/log/clam-update.log
   ```

6. Run the `freshclam` command one time to ensure that you are using the current virus definitions:

```
/usr/local/bin/freshclam -l /var/log/clam-update.log
```

And that's it! You are all set with ClamAV.

Install SpamAssassin from Source

As we stated earlier in the "Install Required Perl Modules" section, you could install SpamAssassin from CPAN, or you could install it from source. If you elected to install from source, follow these steps:

1. Run these commands:

```
cd /usr/local/src/mailserver/Mail-SpamAssassin*
perl Makefile.PL
```

2. Follow the onscreen directions when you are prompted.

3. Run `make` followed by `make install`:

```
make
make install
```

Configure SpamAssassin

SpamAssassin comes with pretty large configuration files that you can tweak to your desire. The files are located in /etc/mail/spamassassin, and you can start with the `local.cf` file.

Here is how our default `local.cf` file looks. Yours might be slightly different, depending on the version.

```
# These values can be overridden by editing ~/.spamassassin/user_prefs.cf
# (see spamassassin(1) for details)

# These should be safe assumptions and allow for simple visual sifting
# without risking lost e-mails.

required_hits 5
rewrite_subject 1
subject_tag [SPAM]
report_safe 0
```

Because the default is very basic, you'll want to modify your configuration from the previous default example. This configuration file is set up so that if SpamAssassin scores a file as a 5 or higher, it will rewrite the subject of the mail with a tag such as [SPAM] or whatever you desire. However, the body of the e-mail will still be presented to you. You will fix this by enabling the report_safe option in your configuration file. On our production server, we configured the following rules in our `local.cf`:

```
# Allow SpamAssassin to rewrite the subject line of any
```

```
# messages it classifies as spam
rewrite_subject 1

# This is the value that will prepended to the subject line
# of messages classified as spam
subject_tag [SPAM]

# Put the spam report into the headers of the message,
# rather than in the body
report_header 1

# Use condensed wording for the spam report
use_terse_report 1
```

Notice this next directive: report_safe 1 is changed from the default of 0 to a 1. The body of the e-mail will be saved as an attachment, and a score breakdown will be provided in place of the original body. This prevents spam from being opened by your users and prevents verifying to the spam senders that you've read their spam (such verification would further encourage more spam in the future).

```
# As of SpamAssassin 2.50, if SPAM is detected, by default
# a new report
# email will be created and the spam message will be
# attached as a MIME part.
# We don't like this behavior so we turn it off
report_safe 1

# Don't modify the content-type: mime header of suspect
# mail..
# Usually you would be running a virus checker from qmail
# Scanner which will block out
# any such nasty attachments
defang_mime 0

# Enable SpamAssassin's RBL checking features :
# Although we have already done some RBL filtering earier
# in qmail's rblsmtpd program,
# it is still recommended to turn on RBL checking in
# SpamAssassin, as it will run
# checks against a variety of different RBL sources, and
# the results will help
# tag spam more accurately
skip_rbl_checks 0

# If we haven't received a response from the RBL server in
# X seconds, then skip that test
rbl_timeout 3
```

```
# Examine the headers of the message for the last 3 mail
# servers that the message
# passed through. Run all of these IPs through the RBL
# checking systems
num_check_received 3


# Now we want to alter some of the default scores for RBL
# hits
#
# By default the bl.spamcop.net RBL score is 0 (disabled).
# We will override this and give any hits a score of 3
# Info about this RBL is available from
# http://spamcop.net/fom-serve/cache/290.html
score RCVD_IN_BL_SPAMCOP_NET 3
```

Setting Up *spamd* and *spamc* from Source Installation

If you did not perform the CPAN installation, your next step is to copy the spamd (daemon) and spamc (client) binaries to the proper directory and create the startup scripts required for the SpamAssassin daemon to run on your system during bootup:

```
cd /usr/local/src/mailserver/Mail-SpamAssassin*
cd spamd
cp spamd /usr/bin
cp spamc /usr/bin
cp redhat-rc-script.sh /etc/init.d/spamd
service spamd start
```

Setting Up *spamd* and *spamc* from CPAN Installation

If you installed SpamAssassin earlier by using CPAN, you need to copy the following files to start the spam daemon. Run the following commands:

```
cp /root/.cpan/build/Mail-SpamAssassin-2.63/spamd/redhat-
➥rc-script.sh /etc/init.d/spamd
cd /root/.cpan/build/Mail-SpamAssassin-2.63/spamd
cp spamd /usr /bin
cp spamc /usr /bin
service spamd start
```

Running *spamd*

Now, SpamAssassin should be running. Let's see:

```
ps aux | grep spam
```

The output should look something like the following:

```
root     13368 10.1  2.1 25780 21172 ?       S    17:09
➥0:00 /usr/bin/spamd -d -c -a -m5 -H
```

```
root     13383  0.0  0.0  4144  584 pts/2    S    17:09
➥0:00 grep spam
```

Congratulations—you have set up SpamAssassin. Let's move on to the next step, Qmail-Scanner.

Install Qmail-Scanner

Follow these steps for the Qmail-Scanner installation:

1. Qmail-Scanner requires `tnef` to be installed, so go ahead and get that taken care of:

   ```
   cd /usr/local/src/mailserver/tnef*
   ./configure
   make
   make install
   ```

2. Install `maildrop` for Qmail-Scanner to utilize:

   ```
   cd /usr/local/src/mailserver/maildrop*
   ./configure
   make
   make install
   ```

> **NOTE** Before you begin the Qmail-Scanner installation, you need to make sure you have `perl-suidperl` installed. You can find an `.rpm` version of this by querying your RPM database first with `rpm -q perl-suidperl`, and if the package is installed you can continue. If not, check `rpm.pbone.net` for a Fedora Core 2 package.

3. Install Qmail-Scanner:

   ```
   cd /usr/local/src/mailserver/qmail-scanner*
   groupadd qscand
   useradd -c "qmail-Scanner Account" -g qscand -s /bin/false qscand
   ./configure --scanners
   ➥"clamscan,verbose_spamassassin" --admin "you"
   ➥--domain "yourdomain.com" --install
   ```

4. Follow the onscreen prompts.

5. After you are finished, run the following command:

   ```
   setuidgid qmaild /var/qmail/bin/qmail-scanner-queue.pl -g
   ```

   If you see output such as

   ```
   perlscanner: generate new DB file from
   ➥/var/spool/qmailscan/quarantine-attachments.txt
   perlscanner: total of 9 entries.
   ```

   then you are all set with Qmail-Scanner.

Configure Qmail-Scanner

Qmail-Scanner is a Perl script located in `/var/qmail/bin` and it is named `qmail-scanner-queue.pl`. If you edit with your text editor, you will see a large array of options that you can configure for your server. Most of the configuration options are well documented, so we will not cover them here.

Here are the steps to configure Qmail-Scanner:

1. Your first next task is to modify the qmail run files to include the Qmail-Scanner files when mail is delivered. Edit the `/var/qmail/supervise/qmail-smtpd/run` file and add the following line directly below `LOCAL=`head -1 /var/qmail/control/me``:

    ```
    QMAILQUEUE="/var/qmail/bin/qmail-scanner-queue.pl"
    export QMAILQUEUE
    ```

2. Modify your `/etc/tcp.smtp` file to add the Qmail-Scanner by changing the first line to the following:

    ```
    127.:allow,RELAYCLIENT="",QMAILQUEUE="/var/qmail/bin/qmail-scanner-
    ➥queue.pl"
    ```

3. Restart qmail and give it a test:

    ```
    qmailctl stop
    qmailctl start
    ```

Opening Firewall Ports for the E-Mail Server

In Chapter 6, you configured a firewall to close unused ports on your server. Now, you need to add a few ports for the e-mail server to allow access to your SMTP, POP3, and IMAP protocols:

1. Edit your `/usr/local/etc/firewall` script and add the following lines directly below the port 22 SSH rule:

    ```
    $IPTABLES -A INPUT -p tcp --dport 25 -j ACCEPT
    $IPTABLES -A INPUT -p tcp --dport 110 -j ACCEPT
    $IPTABLES -A INPUT -p tcp --dport 143 -j ACCEPT
    ```

2. Run your firewall script:

    ```
    /usr/local/etc/firewall
    ```

You should now be able to access these protocols remotely.

Managing Your qmail Server

qmail management is fairly easy to handle, especially with Vpopmail enabled. This section will cover the basics involved in managing your qmail server.

Monitoring Logs

The log files for qmail are located in `/var/log/qmail` under their appropriate sections. Any time you wish to monitor a log file, you can use the `cat`, `more`, or `tail -f` commands to see what is happening.

Here's an example of real-time log monitoring of the SMTP server:

```
tail -f /var/log/qmail/smtpd/current
```

Understanding qmail Actions

The following commands are available for the `qmailctl` file that you created earlier in this chapter:

start starts the qmail server.

stop stops the qmail server.

restart restarts the qmail server.

reload sends `qmail-send` HUP, rereading locals, and virtual domains.

stat shows the status of the services.

pause pauses the server.

cont continues the server.

cdb rebuilds the `tcp.smtp` relay file.

doqueue attempts to send the queued messages immediately.

queue shows the status of the queue.

help displays the list of options for the `qmailctl` command.

Examples of using two of these commands are as follows:

```
qmailctl stop
qmailctl start
```

Managing Virtual Domains and E-Mail Accounts

Because you have Vpopmail enabled, you will utilize its features to manage the virtual domains and e-mail accounts. Take a look at the commands Vpopmail utilizes for these operations located in `/home/vpopmail/bin`:

vadddomain This command enables you to add virtual domains. Simply run it by using the following:

```
/home/vpopmail/bin/vadddomain domain.name
```

vaddaliasdomain   This command enables you to alias two domains together. For example, if you owned yourdomain.com and wanted the e-mail accounts to be aliased to yourdomain.org, you would use this command.

vdeldomain   This command deletes a virtual domain:

```
/home/vpopmail/bin/vdeldomain yourdomain.com
```

vdominfo   This command displays a virtual domain's information:

```
/home/vpopmail/bin/vdominfo yourdomain.com
```

vadduser   This command enables you to create an e-mail account for a user. To create an e-mail account, run the following:

```
/home/vpopmail/bin/vadduser you@yourdomain.com
```

valias   This command enables you to add an alias such as foo@yourdomain.com to bar@yourdomain.com. Any e-mail sent to foo will be automatically delivered to bar. Here is the command syntax:

```
/home/vpopmail/bin/valias [Local Account] [Alias Address]
```

vdeluser   This command deletes an e-mail user:

```
/home/vpopmail/bin/vdeluser you@yourdomain.com
```

vuserinfo   This command enables you to view user settings such as password, features, and others.

```
/home/Vpopmail/bin/vuserinfo you@yourdomain.com
```

There are other commands available for Vpopmail. If you are interested in learning more about them, go to the /home/vpopmail/bin directory and run each command to see what they can do.

Electronic Mail Checklist

This chapter has been a big one! If you have never had the luxury of configuring applications such as qmail on a Linux server, then pat yourself on the back. As we stated earlier, qmail is probably the most complex setup we have found to perform on a Linux server. If you ask us, we think it's worth every effort because of the number of features, stability, and security included with qmail, and the add-ons you've installed in this chapter.

After reading this chapter, you should feel comfortable with performing the following tasks:

- Use wget to download remote files.

- Unpack various compression type packages.

- Use the `configure`, `make`, and `make install` commands.

- Manage your qmail server.

- Add and remove virtual domains and e-mail accounts.

- Open new ports on your firewall.

   In the next chapter, you are going to start working on Apache Web Server. Take a break if you need it and when you are ready, let's dive into Apache Web Server. We can assure you, though, it will be much simpler than qmail.

Expanding qmail

There are many features and add-ons for qmail that make life easier. If you are interested in learning more about them, visit the following websites:

qmail.org This is the official website for qmail. Many user-contributed add-ons are available, as well as support mailing lists, frequently asked questions, and more.

Inter7.com Inter7 is a company that is driven toward enhancing qmail. They offer many great applications (including some you have already used, such as Vpopmail and Courier-IMAP). After you complete this book and have your web server set up, check out the qmailAdmin and VQAdmin programs that Inter7 offers for a Web-based administration for Vpopmail.

CHAPTER 8

Apache Web Server: Installation and Configuration

- Choosing a Version: Apache 1.3 vs. Apache 2.0

- Understanding Apache 1.3

- Preparing to Install Apache Web Sever

- Installing Apache Web Server 1.3

- Understanding the `httpd.conf` File

- Using Apache Virtual Hosts

- A Lesson in Testing Configuration File Changes

- Performing Other Apache Configurations

Apache Web Server is the most versatile web server on the Internet today. It has an endless supply of features that were drafted by the most experienced web server experts around the world—features that include name-based and IP-based virtual hosting, user authentication, URL rewriting, Server Side Include (SSI), advanced logging, environment variable handlers, content negotiation, Common Gateway Interface (CGI) handlers, Secure Sockets Layer (SSL), and much more.

Apache maintains a presence of over 65 percent of all web servers on the Internet, according to Netcraft (www.netcraft.com). This growth has shown a steady trend over the past nine years.

NOTE   If you are interested in viewing the Netcraft Web Server Surveys, please visit `http:// news.netcraft.com/archives/web_server_survey.html`.

Apache as it is known today was released on December 1, 1995. It was originally born from the Public Domain HTTPS Daemon developed by Rob McCool at the National Center for Supercomputing Applications (NCSA), University of Illinois, Urbana-Champaign. McCool left the NCSA in mid-1994, and the project was temporarily stalled. During this time, many web developers had compiled extensions and bug fixes of their own that needed a common release to the public. Out of this necessity, a small group of webmasters collaborated to form a common information space and mailing list and began work on a new release. This became Apache 0.6.2 in April of 1995. At the same time, the NCSA also began further development on their own web server and were added as honorary members to the Apache project so that they could pool their ideas and code to further the realm of web serving.

The early Apache web server was a hit, but the code base required a massive overhaul and redesign. In the next few months, Rob Hartill and the rest of the development group began developing new features while Robert Thau designed a new server architecture that provided more stability and extensibility. This gave birth to Apache 0.8 in August 1995, and with further beta testing and ports to many platforms, we were given Apache 1.0 in December of that year. In less than a year after the group was formed, Apache server took the lead as the number one web server and has stayed there ever since.

Now that you are aware of some of the features and the presence of Apache Web Server, let's get started with learning more in-depth about the current versions and what you can do with the product.

Choosing a Version: Apache 1.3 vs. Apache 2.0

Apache 1.3 is the well-established version, and Apache 2.0 is the new kid on the block. Many people believe that the Apache 1.3 series is old and no longer supported; however, this is not true. The Apache 1.3 series holds a more stable, tested, and proven code base, whereas the Apache 2.0 series is constantly going through upgrades, patches, and modifications.

New Features in Apache 2.0

Apache 2.0 was designed to update many of the core features of Apache 1.3. Let's take a look at some of the new features in Apache 2.0:

Unix threading   If your Unix system supports Portable Operating System Interface (POSIX), you can run Apache 2.0 in hybrid multiprocess, multithreaded mode and improve the scalability for some configurations.

New build system   The Apache 2.0 developers have rewritten the build system from scratch by using `autoconf` and `libtool`, which enable Apache's configuration system to be more similar to other packages you might be familiar with.

Multiprotocol support   The new infrastructure now has support for serving multiple protocols. This feature is not completed yet, so you might want to stay tuned to the Apache Web Server project website for more information.

Non-Unix platform support enhancements   Apache 2.0 now runs faster on non-Unix platforms such as Windows, BeOS, and OS/2 because of the new platform-specific multiprocessing modules (MPM) and the new Apache Portable Runtime (APR). These new enhancements eliminate the requirement for POSIX emulation layers, which caused bottlenecks in Apache 1.3.

IPv6 support   If your system supports IPv6, the APR uses IPv6 listening sockets by default.

Filtering   You now have the ability to write modules as filters that can utilize the stream of content as it is delivered to or from the server.

Multilanguage error responses   Apache now supports the ability to include, through SSI documents, error response messages that can be customized by the administrator for more consistency.

Simplified configuration   The Apache 2.0 development team has recognized the long-disputed overusage of confusing configuration directives and they have attempted to fix this problem.

Native Windows NT Unicode support   When Apache 2.0 is running on Windows NT systems, UTF-8 is now used for all filename encoding. This translates the underlying Unicode filesystem and provides multilanguage support for Windows NT/2000 and XP systems. This feature is not available on Windows 95/98 or Me systems.

Regular expression library update   Apache 2.0 now includes the Perl Compatible Regular Expressions (PCRE) library, and the regular expression evaluation uses the Perl 5 syntax.

Module Enhancements in Apache 2.0

Apache 2.0 offers a wide range of module enhancements over Apache 1.3. Let's take a look at the documented enhancements now.

mod_ssl (new SSL module)   If you wanted to use mod_ssl in Apache 1.3, it had to be compiled and installed separately. Now, Apache 2.0 has built-in mod_ssl support.

mod_dav (versioning module)   This *new* module implements the HTTP Distributed Authoring and Versioning (DAV) specification and is used for posting and maintaining web content.

mod_deflate (compression module)   This *new* module enables supported web browsers to request compressed content before delivery, which in turn saves network bandwidth. This is similar to the Apache 1.3 mod_gzip module, which was required to be installed separately.

mod_auth_digest (session-caching module)   This *new* module includes support for session caching across processes that use shared memory.

mod_charset_lite (character set translation module)   This *new* module is experimental and allows for character set translation or recoding.

mod_file_cache (file-caching module)   This module allows caching of frequently requested files that change very infrequently. The purpose of this module is to reduce the load of the server.

mod_headers (HTTP headers alteration module)   This module enables HTTP headers to be merged, replaced, or removed.

mod_proxy (proxy module)   This module has multiple features and is designed to implement a proxy or gateway for the Apache Web Server.

mod_negotiation (content negotiation module)   This module allows for selection of the document that best matches the client capability—if several documents are available. In Apache 2.0, the new directive ForceLanguagePriority now exists.

mod_autoindex (directory listing module)   This module has been updated from Apache 1.3 and now supports HTML formatting for auto-indexed directories. Additionally, the filters now allow control of sorting, version sorting, and wildcard filtering of the directory listing.

mod_include (Server Side Include, or SSI, module)   Enhancements to the Apache 1.3 mod_include module have been made for Apache 2.0, such as the use of Perl Compatible Regular Expression (PCRE) syntax and more.

mod_auth_dbm (database authentication module)   Support for multiple types of Database Management (DBM)-type databases are now available by using the AuthDBMType directive.

Which Version of Apache to Use

Choosing your Apache version is something that should be taken from the correct perspective. Apache 1.3 is proven to be stable and, most importantly, compatible with PHP. Apache 2.0 is stable; however, there have been multiple problems with PHP compatibility. Making Apache 2.0 and PHP work together is as predictable as flipping a coin. You will never know for sure whether the configuration will work properly and you might be faced with in-depth troubleshooting and problem solving trying to find out why they will not cooperate.

From our standpoint, we really hope that Apache 2.0 and PHP cooperate sooner rather than later because the features of Apache 2.0 look very promising.

For this book, we will be going with the *tried and true* concept and use the Apache 1.3 series to avoid any heartache you might have due to different configurations and *luck of the draw*.

Understanding Apache 1.3

Apache 1.3 added many useful features to Apache not previously available in older versions. A major addition that won't affect the purposes of this book is the ability to support Windows NT, Windows 95, Cygwin, and NetWare 5.*x*. Apache 1.3 also saw the addition of Dynamic Shared Object (DSO) support. This means that modules can be loaded into the server process space at runtime so that they will be available only when needed, thus cutting back on memory usage. They reorganized the source files as well, changing the `Module` lines in the configuration with `AddModule` instead.

If you have used a previous version of Apache and are reading this book as a refresher, you should be aware of the differences. We will discuss this and DSOs in more depth in the "Installing Apache Web Server 1.3" section later in this chapter. Reliable piped logs were also added, enabling Apache to respawn the logging process if it hangs, dies, or otherwise gets stuck. This of course is much better than Apache having to completely restart itself.

Apache 1.3 Features

Apache features are expressed in configuration parameters that can be specified in the `httpd.conf` file. Later in this chapter we will delve into the actual configuration of Apache after its installation. For now, let's take a look at the available and applicable options Apache has to offer in terms of customizing your server:

`AcceptFilter` `AcceptFilter on|off`

This directive is supported only by FreeBSD. `AcceptFilter` is used to control a BSD-specified filter optimization.

AcceptMutex   AcceptMutex *mode*

This controls which `accept()` `mutex` method Apache will use. For a list of methods supported by your system, type **httpd -V**.

AccessConfig   AccessConfig *file|directory|wildcard*

This directive enables you to specify a directory or file that contains additional configuration files. This directive is removed in Apache 2.0.

AccessFileName   AccessFileName *filename* [*filename*] ...

This directive enables you to specify an access control document for the purposes of password-protecting directories and files on your web server. When a request is returned to the client by the server, it will check for the file in all directories, from the root leading to the current directory, and parse the file looking for the access privileges.

AddDefaultCharset   AddDefaultCharset *On|Off|charset*

This will add a default character set to your HTML pages. Whatever is supplied to this directive will automatically be added to the header section of your HTML documents.

AddModule   AddModule *module* [*module*] ...

This directive is used to activate any modules that are compiled into Apache. You can read more on the modules available and what they do in the next section.

AllowOverride   AllowOverride *All|None|directive-type* ...

This enables you to overwrite the ability to use `.htaccess` files. These files allow anyone with permissions to overwrite the settings of Apache for the directory they are located in. With the `AllowOverride` directive, you can disallow `.htaccess` files or limit exactly what the `.htaccess` file might contain.

AuthName   AuthName *auth-domain*

This sets the authorization realm name for a directory. This directive is used to display a message such as "Restricted Area" in the login box that is displayed when a user tries to access a password protected directory.

AuthType   AuthType *Basic|Digest*

This tells the server what type of authorization is required to access the authorization realm in question. *Basic* is the most common `AuthType` used.

BindAddress   BindAddress *|IP-address|domain-name

This enables you to tell your web server to listen only on a certain IP address or fully qualified domain name. By default, the web server will listen to any IP address that is bound to its network interfaces.

CGICommandArgs   CGICommandArgs On|Off

This enables you to take a command-line parameter and pass it directly to a CGI script. This is generally an unsafe practice and is not used today. It is provided by Apache for backward compatibility only.

ClearModuleList   ClearModuleList

This command clears the list of any active modules. You will need to use the AddModule directive to rebuild the active modules you need after supplying this command.

ContentDigest   ContentDigest On|Off

This directive supplies an MD5 header for the MD5 value of the request. This value is not cached, so every request will require the server to create an MD5 value for the page to serve. This is an excellent way to check data integrity but has a high performance cost.

CoreDumpDirectory   CoreDumpDirectory directory-path

This tells Apache to switch to the provided directory as Apache is dying so that the core dump file will be placed here. By default Apache is set to dump into the ServerRoot directory to which the web server user does not have access. Therefore, the core dump file is usually not written.

DefaultType   DefaultType MIME-type

This enables you to add a header MIME type if none is provided. This MIME-type setting will be added to the header if no *MIME-type* is specified.

<Directory>   <Directory directory-path|proxy:url-path>

This directive must have a closing tag of </Directory>. Any directives for the specified directory should be contained between the opening and closing tags. We will cover this in more depth in the "Using Apache Virtual Hosts" section later in this chapter.

<DirectoryMatch>   <DirectoryMatch regex>

Instead of specifying individual directories, you can match directories by using a provided regular expression. This can save a lot of time if you have 100+ directories that might need authentication.

DocumentRoot   DocumentRoot *directory-path*

This specifies the root directory for the web server or for a specific virtual host. By default this is the htdocs/ subdirectory located in your Apache installation directory.

EnableExceptionHook   EnableExceptionHook on|off

This directive is useful when trying to diagnose problems resulting in a crash. This feature enables Apache to allow modules to continue to be called after a child process has crashed, which allows modules to log diagnostic information that may help you determine what caused the crash.

ErrorDocument   ErrorDocument *error-code document*

With this directive, you can specify what pages a client will see if the server returns an error code. For example, Error 404 is the page not found code. You can redirect all Error 404s to a page of your choice in the *document* argument.

ErrorLog   ErrorLog *file-path*|syslog[:*facility*]

This sets the log file that errors are reported to. Specifying a *file-path* that begins with a slash will log the error message to a file. If the argument begins with a | symbol, the server will assume the argument is a call to a process that will handle the logging.

FileETag   FileETag *component* ...

This controls the attributes used by the web server to create an entity tag. You can specify *INode*, *MTime*, *Size*, *All*, or *None*.

<Files>   <Files *filename*> ...

Much like the <Directory> tag, this enables you to specify additional directives that should be applied to the *filename* provided. You will also need a closing tag to end the subdirectives.

<FilesMatch>   <FilesMatch *regex*> ...

FilesMatch uses the supplied regular expression to include all files that fall into its match.

Group   Group *unix-group*

This directive enables you to specify the group level under which the web server will operate.

HostnameLookups   HostnameLookups On|Off|double

This turns on DNS lookups for the IP addresses that access your system for logging purposes. The double option will tell the server to also do a forward lookup after the reverse to ensure a match. This is referred to as *paranoid* in TCP wrappers.

IdentityCheck IdentityCheck On|Off

This directive enables RFC 1413–compliant logging. If the client machine is running identd or something similar, it will log the user information in the access log file.

<IfDefine> <IfDefine [!]*parameter-name*> ...

Any directive located in this set is processed only if the *parameter-name* is true—or false if the exclamation symbol (!) is used. The presence of the tag type structure means that it must have a closing tag as well.

<IfModule> <IfModule [!]*module-name*> ...

This makes sure any directives contained within the opening and closing tags are processed only if the module is active—or inactive if a bang (!) is used.

Include Include *file-path*|*directory-path*|*wildcard-path*

This tells Apache to include any other configuration files located at the appropriate path or directory.

KeepAlive KeepAlive *max-requests*

KeepAlive On|Off

This is used to control persistent connections in Apache. You can specify whether this should be turned on and the max number of requests this is applicable to.

KeepAliveTimeout KeepAliveTimeout *seconds*

This directive enables you to specify the number of seconds to keep a request alive. The default it 15.

<Limit> <Limit *method* [*method*] ... > ...

This is used to restrict the effect of access controls to provided HTTP methods. Any other methods will not behave according to the supplied directives contained within the <Limit>.

<LimitExcept> <LimitExcept *method* [*method*] ... > ...

This is the opposite of <Limit>; anything not meeting the supplied methods has the directives supplied within the tag applied to it.

LimitInternalRecursion LimitInternalRecursion *number* [*number*]

This keeps Apache from entering into an infinite loop if a lookup request in the module continually tries to apply a lookup command. The default is set to 20.

LimitRequestBody   LimitRequestBody *bytes*

This enables you to limit the size of a request to Apache by a client. This is generally applied to limiting information in forms.

LimitRequestFields   LimitRequestFields *number*

This enables you to limit the number of fields or variables allowed to be passed to a page. The default is set to 100.

LimitRequestFieldssize   LimitRequestFieldsize *bytes*

This directive enables you to specify a max size for a request field within a header. The Apache documentation states that this allows greater control over client request behavior and can be useful in avoiding some types of Denial of Service (DoS) attacks.

LimitRequestLine   LimitRequestLine *bytes*

This limits the number of bytes allowed on the HTTP request line. The default is 8190.

Listen   Listen [*IP-address*:]*port*

Listen can be used instead of BindAddress discussed earlier. The Listen directive can be supplied as many times as needed with as many IP addresses and/or ports.

ListenBacklog   ListenBacklog *backlog*

This by default is set to 511. ListenBacklog sets the maximum length of the queue of pending connections.

<Location>   <Location *URL-path|URL*> ...

This provides access control by URL instead of by actual path or file. Much like <Directory> or <File>, you can specify additional directives to be applied to the request.

<LocationMatch>   <LocationMatch *regex*> ...

Like all the other match tags, this enables you to use regular expressions to match a string. In this case, the string is the location provided by Apache.

LockFile   LockFile *file-path*

This directive should normally be left as is. The main reason for changing this is if the logs/ directory is NFS mounted because the lockfile must be stored on a local disk.

LogLevel   LogLevel *level*

This enables you to set the verbosity of logging. You can specify *emerg*, *alert*, *crit*, *error*, *warn*, *notice*, *info*, and *debug*. They are provided here in descending order of severity and ascending order of verbosity.

MaxClients   MaxClients *number*

This sets the limit of simultaneous requests the server can handle. This is set to 256 by default, and to increase this number you will need to modify the http.h file and recompile Apache. Look for the HARD_SERVER_LIMIT variable if you are attempting to do so.

MaxKeepAliveRequests   MaxKeepAliveRequests *number*

This limits the number of requests allowed per connection.

MaxRequestPerChild   MaxRequestsPerChild *number*

This is set to 0 by default, but a couple of key benefits can be achieved by setting this value to something greater than the default. First, it limits the amount of memory a child process can take up in case of memory leaks and, second, it helps reduce the number of processes when the server load reduces and children are left straggling behind.

MaxSpareServers   MaxSpareServers *number*

This sets the number of idle child server processes allowed. If you are running an extremely high-traffic site, you might wish to have a greater number of idle processes. This will speed up access time by the client, giving the client a better chance of accessing an idle process rather than having to wait for a child server process to spawn.

MinSpareServers   MinSpareServers *number*

This controls the minimum number of servers to spawn at startup. This feature is used with MaxSpareServers and should be set to a lower number than MaxSpareServers.

NameVirtualHost   NameVirtualHost *addr[:port]*

This is a required directive when configuring name-based virtual hosts. It is possible to supply a domain name with NameVirtualHost but it is highly recommended that you use IP addresses and wildcards.

Options   Options [+|-]*option* [+|-]*option* ...

This controls what features are available in a certain directory or for a certain file. For all the different options, refer to the Apache documentation.

PidFile   PidFile *file-path*

This sets the file where Apache will store the process IDs for each of its children servers. This is used only in standalone mode.

Port   Port *number*

Any number from *0* to *65535* can be specified in this directive. Of course, the default is port *80* for standard requests and *443* for SSL requests.

ProtocolReqCheck   `ProtocolReqCheck On|Off`

This directive is new to Apache 1.3.27 and checks the incoming `Protocol` field in the request for authenticity.

Require   `Require entity-name [entity-name] ...`

This enables you to specify the authentication required to view the appropriate directory or file. You might specify `Require user username` or you can use `group`, `valid-user`, `file-owner`, or `file-group`.

ResourceConfig   `ResourceConfig file|directory|wildcard`

This tells Apache to look for additional configuration files after processing `httpd.conf`. As the syntax indicates, you can specify a `directory`, `file`, or `wildcard`.

RLimitCPU   `RLimitCPU number|max [number|max]`

This enables you to specify the maximum CPU resource limit for processes forked off of Apache (that is, SSI or CGI commands). The first argument is the soft limit and can be expressed in seconds per process or `max` for the maximum allowed by the operating system. The second value is expressed the same way as the first and is the hard limit.

RLimitMEM   `RLimitMEM number|max [number|max]`

This operates the same way as the previous directive, by controlling the amount of memory a process forked off of Apache can use. This is expressed in bytes per process.

RLimitNPROC   `RLimitNPROC number|max [number|max]`

The directive is the same as the previous two, except that this directive does limit on processes forked off of Apache per user.

Satisfy   `Satisfy any|all`

This directive is used when both `Allow` and `Require` are used. Because these directives permit users who pass the host restrictions and username/password respectively, the `Satisfy` directive can be used to specify whether the user should meet both of these directives (`all`) or any of these directives (`any`).

ScoreBoardFile   `ScoreBoardFile file-path`

This file is required by some system architectures that require a file be placed on the server that will be used to communicate between its children and parent. If you need to use a scoreboard file, you might wish to place this file on a RAM disk for performance reasons.

ScriptInterpreterSource ScriptInterpreterSource *registry|script*

This directive is used to control how Apache finds the interpreter for CGI scripts. The registry specification tells Apache to search the Windows Registry.

SendBufferSize SendBufferSize *bytes*

This sets the TCP buffer size for Apache.

ServerAdmin ServerAdmin *email-address*

This sets the default e-mail address to be returned to a client during any error messages delivered by Apache.

ServerAlias ServerAlias *hostname [hostname]* ...

This is used to specify any alternate hostnames for the server.

ServerName ServerName *fully-qualified-domain-name*

This sets the hostname for the server. This is used when clients are being redirected by Apache.

ServerPath ServerPath *directory-path*

This sets the legacy URL pathname for a host. This directive should be used in conjunction with name-based virtual hosts.

ServerRoot ServerRoot *directory-path*

This, as the name indicates, sets the root directory path for the server. The default installation for Apache is at /usr/local/apache; however, the exercises in this book will leave Apache at /www.

ServerSignature ServerSignature *On|Off|EMail*

This directive enables you to specify a footer line at the bottom of server-generated documents. FTP, error pages, and directory listings are a few examples.

ServerTokens ServerTokens *Minimal|ProductOnly|OS|Full*

This directive might not be set for individual virtual hosts. It is a global server setting only. It controls how much information is sent back to a client in the server response header field. You can specify *Prod*, *Min*, *OS*, and *Full*.

TIP   If you really want to hide information, set ServerSignature to *Off* and change the ServerTokens setting to *Prod*.

ServerType   `ServerType inetd|standalone`

By default, this is set to *standalone*. You can also run Apache under *inetd*, which would need to be specified here.

ShmemUIDisUser   `ShmemUIDisUser On|Off`

This controls whether Apache changes the `uid` and `gid` ownership of System V shared memory–based scoreboard files to the server settings of `User` and `Group`.

StartServers   `StartServers number`

This adjusts the number of child servers started upon startup. You shouldn't need to change this directive because it and your `Min` and `Max` settings discussed earlier will automatically adjust this number.

TimeOut   `TimeOut number`

This directive defines the amount of time Apache will wait to receive a `GET` request, the amount of time between receipt of TCP packets on a `POST` or `PUT` request, and the amount of time between ACKs on transmissions of TCP packets in response.

UseCanonicalName   `UseCanonicalName On|Off|DNS`

A *canonical* name includes the fully qualified domain name and the port number. If the port is set to 80, which is the default for HTTP, then it will automatically be emitted.

User   `User unix-userid`

This sets the username at which the server will handle requests. In order to use this directive, the stand-alone server must be originally run as *root*.

<VirtualHost>   `<VirtualHost addr[:port] [addr[:port]] ...> ...`

The `VirtualHost` directive will be discussed at greater length in the "Using Apache Virtual Hosts" section later in this chapter. This directive enables you to create multiple servers all with settings of their own on one machine. There is no limit to the number of virtual hosts a server can support.

Apache 1.3 Modules

In addition to the standard directives supplied for use in Apache, there are also groups of added functionality called *modules*. Apache modules provide you with advanced and more-complicated functionality than can normally be expressed in a few short lines. These modules can be turned on and off for individual virtual hosts or for the entire server. You will read more about the actual application of these modules later in this chapter. For now, here is a list of modules that come with the default installation of Apache:

NOTE   Depreciated and Windows-only modules have been excluded from the following list.
---

mod_access   This module provides restricted access to clients from a specific hostname or IP address.

mod_actions   This module allows the execution of CGI scripts to be dependent on media type or request method.

mod_alias   This module enables you to use URL redirection to map different parts of a hostname to different locations within the document tree.

mod_asis   This module enables you to configure Apache to send files that contain their own HTTP headers.

mod_auth   This provides the user authentication via text file functionality.

mod_auth_anon   This module allows anonymous user authentication for restricted areas.

mod_auth_db   This module allows user authentication via Berkeley DB files for restricted areas.

mod_auth_dbm   This module is the same as the previous one except that it uses DBM files instead of the Berkeley format.

mod_auth_digest   This is another authentication method, but based on MD5.

mod_autoindex   This module provides automatic directory listings for directories that do not have index files.

mod_cern_meta   This module adds support for HTTP header metafiles.

mod_cgi   This module is required if you wish to run CGI scripts on your server.

mod_cookies   This module provides support for Netscape-like cookies.

mod_dir   This provides basic directory-handling functionality to Apache.

mod_env   This module allows the passing of environments to CGI scripts.

mod_example   This module demonstrates how the Apache 1.2 API handles module callbacks.

mod_expires   This module provides for the generation of Expires HTTP headers according to user-specified criteria.

mod_headers   This module provides for the customization of HTTP headers.

mod_imap   This module provides the functionality necessary for handling server-side image map processing.

mod_include   This module allows documents with Server Side Includes (SSI).

mod_info   This module provides a comprehensive overview of the server configuration, including all installed modules and directives in the configuration files.

mod_log_agent   This module allows the server to log the type of client a user is accessing the system from.

mod_log_config   This module provides for logging of the requests made to the server, using the Common Log Format or a user-specified format.

mod_log_forensic   This module provides for forensic logging of the requests made to the server.

mod_mime   This enables Apache to determine document types by using the file extension of a file.

mod_mime_magic   This module provides the functionality for Apache to determine the document type by examining a few bytes from within a file.

mod_mmap_static   This module is labeled as *experimental*. This module provides caching and mapping of a statically configured list of frequently requested files.

mod_negotiation   This module provides the ability for Apache to select the best matched type of document for a client's capabilities.

mod_proxy   This enables Apache to use an HTTP 1.1 caching proxy server.

mod_rewrite   The mod_rewrite module is probably one of the most extensive and complicated modules. It enables you to use a combination of directives and regular expressions to rewrite a request URL to another URL depending on a plethora of options. This can be especially useful for Search Engine Optimization (SEO).

mod_setenvif   This module enables you to set environment variables based on whether different aspects of a request match a regular expression.

mod_so   This module provides the ability to load executable code and modules at runtime for Apache.

mod_speling   This module attempts to rewrite a URL if the document is not found. It will search a directory for a similar file and redirect the user to the found file.

mod_status   This enables Apache to create an HTML page that will display server performance and statistics. You can even have the page automatically refresh after a given period of time.

mod_unique_id   This module enables an environment variable to be set that contains a unique identifier for each request.

mod_usedir   This enables user home directories to automatically be served. They are normally reached by using http://*www.domain.com/~username*.

mod_usertrack   This module uses cookies to create a clickstream log of user activity on a site.

mod_vhost_alias   This module provides support for dynamically configuring mass virtual hosting. This allows for easy use of massive numbers of virtual hosts on one server.

Preparing to Install Apache Web Server

Installing the Apache Web Server is fairly straightforward; on the other hand, it could be a difficult task. There are multiple methods to install Apache and its components. We will cover the most common methods to install, configure, and run the server as well as enable modules and Secure Sockets Layer (SSL) support. Let's get started with some system preparation. The preparation consists of removing any existing pre-installed HTTP server packages, downloading the files, and adding the applicable firewall rules to allow HTTP access.

Removing Pre-Installed Apache Web Server RPMs

Your Fedora system might have Apache already installed, so you are going to remove the RPM packages from your system; you want to control how Apache is built on your system and you want to be able to apply patches and updates as they come out.

The reasoning behind building your own installation is that most distributions such as Fedora, Red Hat, and others take a while to release security updates. You do not want to leave your system vulnerable while you wait for the distributions to release their upgrades, especially after announcements are made about these vulnerabilities.

Now that we have justified the importance of running a custom-built installation, you can go ahead and remove any versions of Apache that might be installed. Follow these steps:

1. Query the RPM database to see whether any Apache packages are installed:

    ```
    rpm -q httpd
    ```

    If you don't see any result, then you do not have any packages for Apache installed, and you may skip the rest of the steps. On our system, Apache was installed and this is the output:
    ```
    httpd-2.0.48-1.2
    ```

2. If you have a result, find the dependencies of the package so you can remove them first:

```
rpm -q --whatrequires httpd
```

On our system, the result returned was as follows:

```
redhat-config-httpd-1.1.0-5
```

3. Begin removing the packages from your system, starting with the dependencies:

```
rpm -e redhat-config-httpd
rpm -e httpd
```

4. Ensure that no Apache servers are still running, and if they are, kill them:

```
ps aux | grep httpd
killall httpd
```

The system appears to be clean of Apache, so let's move on to obtaining the source files and unpacking them.

Downloading and Unpacking Apache

To prepare for installation, you need to download Apache 1.3. We recommend you obtain the files from the official source, so go to `httpd.apache.org/download.cgi` and select the Unix Source under the Apache 1.3 section. The file should be named something similar to `apache_1.3.XX.tar.gz`.

NOTE We left off the exact version number because by the time you download, it might be higher than the one we are using at the time of this writing.

Use these steps to unpack Apache:

1. Create a new directory:

```
mkdir -p /usr/local/src/webserver
```

On our Fedora system, we created a new directory located at `/usr/local/src/webserver`.

2. Download the source code by using `wget`:

```
wget 'http://apache.tarchive.com/httpd/apache_1.3.29.tar.gz'
```

NOTE You should check `http://httpd.apache.org` for an updated download URL. The example URL in this step may become invalid over time.

3. Unpack the source code file:

```
tar zxpf apache_1.3.29.tar.gz
```

You should see a directory named similar to `apache_1.3.29` now.

Allowing HTTP Server Access through the Firewall

In Chapter 6, "Linux Security," you configured your firewall for the server. Now you need to expand upon your firewall installation and allow the appropriate HTTP access for your web server. Let's add HTTP and HTTPS access to your our firewall.

1. If you did not enable port 80 for normal HTTP access or port 443 for HTTPS access, you need to do so now.

    We added the following lines to our port access section of the firewall script located at `/usr/local/etc/firewall`:

    ```
    #Allow incoming HTTP requests (to Web server)
    $IPTABLES -A INPUT -p tcp --dport 80 -j ACCEPT
    $IPTABLES -A INPUT -p tcp --dport 443 -j ACCEPT
    ```

NOTE   If you do not wish to run an SSL server, simply place a comment symbol (#) in front of the third line in the previous code to comment out the port 443 access.

2. Run your firewall script to ensure the changes have taken effect.

    ```
    /usr/local/etc/firewall
    ```

3. Run `iptables -L` to check whether the HTTP and HTTPS ports are open. Here is the HTTP and HTTPS access of the `iptables` output:

    ```
    ACCEPT  tcp  --  anywhere  anywhere  tcp dpt:http
    ACCEPT  tcp  --  anywhere  anywhere  tcp dpt:https
    ```

Installing Apache Web Server 1.3

Because Apache Web Server is flexible, there are different methods of installing it. One method uses Dynamic Shared Objects as modules, whereas the traditional method of installation does not.

In addition to these installation methods, you might want to install an SSL-enabled web server. If you want to use an SSL-enabled web server, the installation procedure is slightly different. We will show you how to install an SSL-enabled server by using `mod_ssl` with the Dynamic Shared Objects method.

Let's begin by installing Apache with Dynamic Shared Objects—the *recommended* method of installation.

Using the Non-SSL Dynamic Shared Objects Installation Method

Now that you have downloaded the source code, you need to configure, build, and install it. This is where you can pick a crossroad to follow. As we have said, there are multiple methods of installing Apache. The first and simplest method is to enable Dynamic Shared Objects (DSO), which enables you to easily integrate future modules, such as PHP, without compiling the Apache Web Server all over again.

Using the DSO method might degrade performance slightly, but the degradation levels are so minimal you might not ever notice. Because this is a simple method to follow, we will cover this first.

Creating Installation Scripts

The most important advice we can give you at the moment is to create a script that will run the configure options and prepare the package for build. We create a new file named apache_install, and it contains the following contents:

```
cd /usr/local/src/webserver/apache_1.3.29
make distclean
./configure \
      --prefix=/www \
      --enable-module=so \
      --enable-module=rewrite \
      --enable-shared=rewrite \
      --enable-module=setenvif \
      --enable-shared=setenvif \
      --enable-module=mime \
      --enable-shared=mime \
      --enable-module=mime_magic \
      --enable-shared=mime_magic \
      --enable-module=dir \
      --enable-shared=dir \
      --enable-module=auth \
      --enable-shared=auth \
      --enable-module=access \
      --enable-shared=access \
      --enable-module=alias \
      --enable-shared=alias \
      --enable-module=status \
      --enable-shared=status \
      --enable-module=userdir \
      --enable-shared=userdir \
      --enable-module=vhost_alias \
      --enable-shared=vhost_alias \
      --enable-module=env \
      --enable-shared=env \
      --enable-module=log_referer \
      --enable-shared=log_referer \
      --enable-module=log_config \
      --enable-shared=log_config \
```

```
--enable-module=log_agent \
--enable-shared=log_agent \
--enable-module=headers \
--enable-shared=headers
```

NOTE   The previous script might generate an error the first time you run it. This error is associated with the `make distclean` command. Disregard this error because it is normal.

The previous script will `cd` into your Apache source directory and run the command `make distclean`, which will clean out any previous compilations you might have and rebuild the package from scratch. This script will enable many of the Apache modules that we have found uses for.

If you are curious about what each of these modules uses, please refer to the "Apache 1.3 Modules" section earlier in this chapter.

NOTE   If you decide to remove any of the modules and shared objects from the list above, do not remove `--enable-module=so` from the list, or the rest of the shared objects will not work.

The previous script will also configure the build scripts to install the web server to the path /www on your system. This is a preference only and you can alter the path as you desire.

Once again, we prefer not to run the `make` and `make install` commands within an automated script such as this. We want to review the output before we run these commands and ensure that everything is okay.

Ensure that you `chmod` your script to allow execute permissions:

```
chmod +x apache_install
```

Running the Installation Script

Now that we have explained what the installation script is for, it is time to run it for the first time, followed by the `make`, `make install` process to install your server.

1. Run your newly created installation script and watch the output:

   ```
   ./apache_install
   ```

2. If you do not have any noticeable errors, cd into your Apache source directory and run make:

   ```
   cd /usr/local/src/webserver/apache_1.3.29
   make
   ```

3. After the show is over, review as much of the output as possible for errors. If no errors are present, you are ready to run `make install` and install the server:

   ```
   make install
   ```

4. Your next step is to create a *link* to the Apache control binary to your path. This enables you to simply type apachectl from the command line regardless of where you are in the filesystem:

```
ln -s /www/bin/apachectl /usr/bin/apachectl
ln -s /www/bin/apachectl /usr/sbin/apachectl
```

5. Now start Apache!

```
apachectl start
```

6. Access your machine via the hostname or the IP address in your web browser: http://yourdomain.com. You should see an Apache web server temporary page, shown in Figure 8.1.

Using the Non-SSL Traditional Installation Method

The traditional method of installing Apache is to run the commands configure, make, and make install and then to rely on a configuration file located in the source file directory, src/Configuration, which has the common modules configured to install already. You have the ability to edit the src/Configuration file and add modules or remove modules you do not want installed before you run the configure commands to build and install Apache.

NOTE   The methods of installation we are showing you are slightly modified from the Apache documentation. The reasons for this are simple: time saving and it just makes more sense to us. The documentation will tell you to run a Configure script in the src/ directory; however, this script is not designed to install the files outside of the compilation directory. To avoid any confusion, we are using the simplest method possible.

FIGURE 8.1
Apache welcome
screen

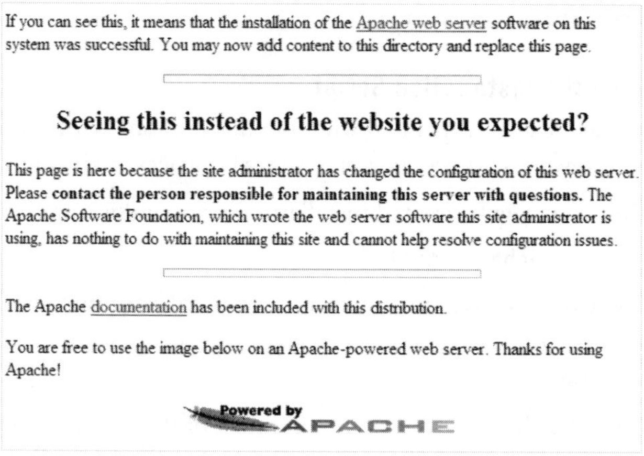

If you can see this, it means that the installation of the Apache web server software on this system was successful. You may now add content to this directory and replace this page.

Seeing this instead of the website you expected?

This page is here because the site administrator has changed the configuration of this web server. Please **contact the person responsible for maintaining this server with questions.** The Apache Software Foundation, which wrote the web server software this site administrator is using, has nothing to do with maintaining this site and cannot help resolve configuration issues.

The Apache documentation has been included with this distribution.

You are free to use the image below on an Apache-powered web server. Thanks for using Apache!

This is said to be the fastest way to get your Apache Web Server installed and running. Follow these steps:

1. Let's start out by running the configure script:

    ```
    cd /usr/local/src/webserver/apache_1.3.29
    ./configure
    ```

2. Watch for error output and then run make:

    ```
    make
    ```

3. Run the make install command to copy the files to the /usr/local/apache directory:

    ```
    make install
    ```

    Watch for error output.

    By default, your Apache will be installed to /usr/local/apache.

4. Link your apachectl files to your path:

    ```
    ln -s /usr/local/apache/bin/apachectl /usr/bin/apachectl
    ln -s /usr/local/apache/bin/apachectl /usr/sbin/apachectl
    ```

5. Start Apache!

    ```
    apachectl start
    ```

6. Access your machine via the hostname or the IP address in your web browser: http://yourdomain.com. You should see a nice Apache web server temporary page, shown in Figure 8.1 earlier.

Using the SSL Dynamic Shared Object Installation Method

The installation method includes Secure Sockets Layer (SSL) and uses Dynamic Shared Objects. Before you begin this installation method, you must do some preparation.

Downloading and Building OpenSSL

When you are going to install an SSL enabled version of Apache with mod_ssl, you must first download and build OpenSSL. You do not need to install OpenSSL because we only need the header files to be built for mod_ssl to install and there is already a default installation located on your server for certificate management. Let's get started with building OpenSSL now.

1. Download OpenSSL and mod_ssl to enable you to compile Apache with SSL:

    ```
    cd /usr/local/src/webserver
    ```

NOTE   Always check www.openssl.org/source for the version marked [Latest] before down-loading the files.

```
wget http://www.openssl.org/source/openssl-0.9.7c.tar.gz
```

NOTE   Always check www.modssl.org for the latest version before downloading the files.

```
wget http://www.modssl.org/source/mod_ssl-2.8.16-1.3.29.tar.gz
```

2. Unpack the source files:

```
tar zxpf openssl*
tar zxpf mod_ssl*
```

3. For this installation, you do not need to install OpenSSL; you simply need to build the source code headers required for mod_ssl:

```
cd /usr/local/src/webserver/openssl-0.9.7c
./config
make
```

Creating Installation Scripts

As we mentioned earlier, we always create a script that will run those long configure options instead of trying to remember what we used to compile the system. Here are the steps for creating installation scripts:

1. Create a file in /usr/local/src/webserver named apache_ssl_install and add the following contents to it:

```
cd /usr/local/src/webserver/mod_ssl-2.8.16-1.3.29
./configure \
--with-apache=/usr/local/src/webserver/apache_1.3.29 \
--with-ssl=/usr/local/src/webserver/openssl-0.9.7c \
--prefix=/www \
--enable-module=so \
--enable-module=rewrite \
--enable-shared=rewrite \
--enable-module=setenvif \
 --enable-shared=setenvif \
 --enable-module=mime \
 --enable-shared=mime \
 --enable-module=mime_magic \
 --enable-shared=mime_magic \
 --enable-module=dir \
 --enable-shared=dir \
 --enable-module=auth \
 --enable-shared=auth \
 --enable-module=access \
 --enable-shared=access \
 --enable-module=alias \
 --enable-shared=alias \
 --enable-module=status \
 --enable-shared=status \
```

```
--enable-module=userdir \
--enable-shared=userdir \
--enable-module=vhost_alias \
--enable-shared=vhost_alias \
--enable-module=env \
--enable-shared=env \
--enable-module=log_referer \
--enable-shared=log_referer \
--enable-module=log_config \
--enable-shared=log_config \
--enable-module=log_agent \
--enable-shared=log_agent \
--enable-module=headers \
--enable-shared=headers
```

You should notice there are a few differences in this script compared to our non-SSL based installations. The first noticeable difference is that you cd into the mod_ssl directory to do the initial configuration. Additionally, you must define where the Apache Web Server source files and OpenSSL source files are located. The rest of the script is very similar to the previous script shown in the "Using the Non-SSL Dynamic Shared Object Installation Method" section.

1. Add the execute permissions to your script and then run it:

```
chmod +x apache_ssl_install
./apache_ssl_install
```

2. Watch the output for errors. If no errors are present, cd into the Apache source directory and complete the installation:

```
cd /usr/local/src/webserver/apache_1.3.29
make
```

3. You need to make a fake SSL certificate required by the web server to run in SSL mode. The make certificate command will do that for you. Entering the default values (pressing the Enter key) will work fine for this test certificate. Don't spend too much time trying to enter the real values because this certificate is invalid anyway. Before you begin, see the next note.

NOTE   When prompted Encrypt this private key now? [Y/n], enter **n** for the value; otherwise you will be required to enter a password when starting your SSL-enabled server.

```
make certificate
make install
```

4. Link the apachectl executable to your path.

```
ln -s /www/bin/apachectl /usr/bin/apachectl
ln -s /www/bin/apachectl /usr/sbin/apachectl
```

5. Start Apache with SSL!

   ```
   apachectl startssl
   ```

6. Test your Apache SSL installation by accessing the server IP address or domain name: `https://yourdomain.com`. You should see a page that says `Hey, it worked! The SSL/TLS-aware Apache webserver was successfully installed on this website`. If you see this message, congratulations! You have installed an SSL-capable web server. See Figure 8.2.

Exploring Apache Directories

It is important for you to understand what directories are installed and their purposes for your Apache Web Server installation. For this chapter, we assume that you have installed Apache with the prefix of `/www`. Let's take a look at the installed directories now:

`/www`   This directory is the `ServerRoot`—the place where all of your Apache files are installed.

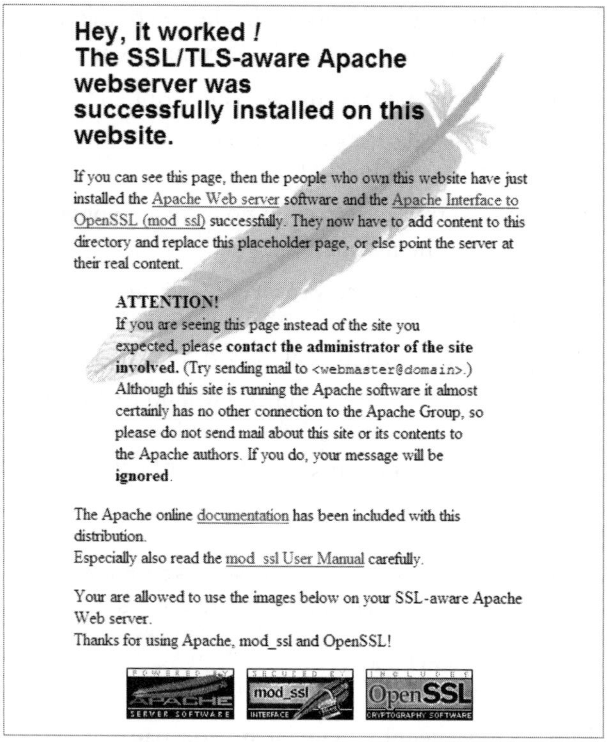

FIGURE 8.2
Apache mod_ssl
welcome screen

> ## Hey, it worked !
> ## The SSL/TLS-aware Apache webserver was successfully installed on this website.
>
> If you can see this page, then the people who own this website have just installed the Apache Web server software and the Apache Interface to OpenSSL (mod_ssl) successfully. They now have to add content to this directory and replace this placeholder page, or else point the server at their real content.
>
> **ATTENTION!**
> If you are seeing this page instead of the site you expected, please **contact the administrator of the site involved.** (Try sending mail to <webmaster@domain>.) Although this site is running the Apache software it almost certainly has no other connection to the Apache Group, so please do not send mail about this site or its contents to the Apache authors. If you do, your message will be **ignored**.
>
> The Apache online documentation has been included with this distribution.
> Especially also read the mod_ssl User Manual carefully.
>
> Your are allowed to use the images below on your SSL-aware Apache Web server.
> Thanks for using Apache, mod_ssl and OpenSSL!
>
>

/www/bin   This directory houses the Apache programs that we will discuss in the following "Becoming Familiar with Apache Programs" section.

/www/cgi-bin   This directory is a default cgi-bin used to run executable files such as PERL scripts. You will not be using this directory in this book; instead you will be creating your own cgi-bin directories for virtual hosts.

/www/conf   This directory contains all of the configuration files such as httpd.conf and others. The httpd.conf file is outlined thoroughly in the "Understanding the httpd.conf File" section later in this chapter.

/www/htdocs   By default, this is the DocumentRoot directory of the Apache Web Server. If you have not modified any settings and you access the server via your web browser, you will see the files located in this directory. You will be creating your own DocumentRoot directories in the "Using Apache virtual hosts" section later in this chapter.

/www/icons   This directory contains the icons for the Apache Web Server. These icons are used in various places such as the directory listings, which we will discuss in the "Enabling Directory Listings" section.

/www/include   This directory—which should not be modified—contains the header files used to run the Apache Web Server. It contains the core files and others that are essential to operation. Be very careful here.

/www/libexec   This directory contains the Apache modules that you compiled during installation. Once again, be very careful with this directory and its contents.

/www/logs   By default, this directory will log any web server activity to files located here.

NOTE   If you are having problems starting the server, check the error_log file located in this directory.

/www/man   This directory contains the manual files used for the system.

/www/proxy   This directory is configured to proxy the web content, a topic that is beyond the scope of this book.

Becoming Familiar with Apache Programs

Apache has a few programs that enable you to *stop*, *start*, *restart*, and *manage* various aspects of the server. Let's take a look at them now.

apachectl

The first command is apachectl (Apache Control), which you linked to your path so you will have a shortcut in your command line. The apachectl command accepts multiple arguments that enable you to perform certain actions for the server:

apachectl start   This command starts the Apache Web Server.

apachectl startssl   This command is available when you compile with mod_ssl. It starts Apache in normal mode and enables the SSL server mode as well.

apachectl stop   This command stops the Apache Web Server.

apachectl restart   This command attempts to restart the Apache Web Server if it is already running; otherwise, it will start the server.

apachectl fullstatus   This command dumps the *full* status of the server to the screen. It requires that you have the Lynx web browser installed and the mod_status Apache module enabled in the httpd.conf configuration.

apachectl status   This command dumps the *short* status of the server to the screen. It requires that you have the Lynx web browser installed and the mod_status Apache module enabled in the httpd.conf configuration.

apachectl graceful   This command is used to gracefully restart the web server by sending a SIGUSR1 to the system, or to start it if it is not already running. We have used this command for log rotation purposes.

apachectl configtest   This command performs a syntax check of your configuration files such as httpd.conf.

TIP   Always run apachectl configtest after you make changes to your configuration files and before you restart the server. It could help prevent downtime because Apache will fail to start if there are syntax errors in your configuration files.

apachectl help   This command displays a list of options for the apachectl executable.

apxs

The APache eXtenSion tool (APXS) is used for building and installing extension modules using the Dynamic Shared Object (DSO) support. It is useful for installing, enabling, or disabling modules within an already built and installed Apache Web Server.

We will not cover usage of apxs in this book; however, here is the output from the command-line options:

```
Usage: apxs -g [-S <var>=<val>] -n <modname>
       apxs -q [-S <var>=<val>] <query> ...
```

```
apxs -c [-S <var>=<val>] [-o <dsofile>] [-D
          <name>[=<value>]]
      [-I <incdir>] [-L <libdir>] [-l <libname>]
      [-Wc,<flags>]
      [-Wl,<flags>] [-p] <files> ...
apxs -i [-S <var>=<val>] [-a] [-A] [-n <modname>]
      <dsofile> ...
apxs -e [-S <var>=<val>] [-a] [-A] [-n <modname>]
      <dsofile> ...
```

htdigest

The htdigest program allows management of user files for digest authentication. Because digest authentication is not very common, this is rarely used. Usage is as follows:

```
htdigest [ -c ] passwdfile realm username
```

htpasswd

htpasswd is used to create and update the password files for basic authentication of HTTP users. This is more commonly used than htdigest. We will cover the procedure to create passwords and protect directories later in this chapter.

httpd

httpd is the server daemon for apachectl and it has a wide array of control options available for determining configuration and status of your server. Keep in mind that depending on the method you used to build Apache, some of these options might not be available.

> **NOTE**   The httpd command should not be invoked directly for start, stop, or restart commands. Instead, use the apachectl executable.

The options are as follows:

-d   Sets the initial value for the ServerRoot directive.

-f   Defines a configuration file to run the server with.

-k   Options: start, restart, graceful, and stop.

-C   Processes a directive *before* reading the configuration files.

-c   Processes a configuration directive *after* reading the configuration files.

-D   Defines a configuration parameter to be used within an <IfDefine> section.

-e   Defines the LogLevel during startup.

-E   Redirects error messages during startup to a specified file.

-R   Defines the directory for the shared object files if the server is compiled with SHARED_CORE.

-h   Displays a short summary of available command-line options. Also known as help.

-l   Displays a list of non-dynamically loaded modules compiled into the server.

-L   Outputs a list of directives with arguments.

-S   Displays the settings as they are parsed from the configuration file.

-t   Runs syntax tests for configuration files only (*with* docroot check). This will cause the program to exit after a Syntax return is detected.

-T   Runs syntax tests for configuration files only (*without* docroot check). This will cause the program to exit after a Syntax return is detected.

-v   Displays the version of the installed Apache Web Server.

-V   Displays the version and build parameters of the installed Apache Web Server.

-X   Runs Apache in debug mode.

logresolve

This application is run on old log files and will resolve IP addresses that are logged by the web server to hostnames. This is useful to reduce the load on your name server by using its own built-in hash tables and performing only one single lookup per IP address.

rotatelogs

This tool is used to rotate the Apache log files and to archive them for storage. It helps prevent excessive log file lengths and aids in reducing the load of your web server.

Understanding the *httpd.conf* File

Apache, like many other Linux applications, has configuration files in with runtime settings that can be configured and controlled by the system administrators. Apache uses the file named httpd.conf, which is located in the conf/ directory where you installed Apache. Let's take a look at the important directives of this file now:

ServerType standalone   By using the *standalone* directive, the ServerType directive enables your server to run as a daemon, as a service using *inetd*, or as a *standalone* server. For the purposes of this book, you will run the server as standalone.

ServerRoot "/www"   The ServerRoot directive defines where Apache is installed. If you are running Apache as a local server on that particular machine, this directive should not be modified. If you wish to run Apache through the network while it is installed on another machine, you would modify this path for the network path relative to the server handling the public HTTP requests.

PidFile /www/logs/httpd.pid   A PID file is the file responsible for reporting the process ID to the system. This should not be modified from the default configuration.

ScoreBoardFile /www/logs/httpd.scoreboard   The ScoreboardFile is used to store internal server process information and should not be modified. It might not be needed by your system, but just in case, leave this directive alone.

Timeout 300   The Timeout directive prevents a hung request from never ending. If the request exceeds this setting, it will die and free the process for other connections.

KeepAlive On   The KeepAlive directive enables the processes to stay alive by allowing a client to make more than one request during a network session instead of opening and closing them each time a process is handled. Leaving this setting to On will reduce the cycles required to operate your web server by allowing multiple uses per thread. This directive is used for one-to-one connections.

MaxKeepAliveRequests 100   This directive defines the maximum number of requests to allow during a persistent connection. If you want to allow unlimited requests, set this to 0; however, you could make your system vulnerable. You should modify this number only if you are having connection errors during peak hours.

KeepAliveTimeout 15   The KeepAliveTimeout directive defines the number of seconds to wait for a particular user's request before it frees the process to be used by another user. The default number is 15 and should not be modified unless you fully understand what will happen to your server by doing so.

MinSpareServers 5   This directive indicates the number of minimum spare servers to spawn as a backup to catch any traffic bursts to your server. A good starting point for a standard server is 5. You might want to evaluate this as your traffic increases.

MaxSpareServers 10   This directive indicates the *maximum* number of spare servers to spawn as a backup to catch any traffic bursts to your server. A good starting point for a standard server is 10. Once again, you might want to evaluate this as your traffic increases. Also, you should note that this number should be larger than the MinSpareServers directive.

StartServers 5   This directive indicates the number of servers to start initially. As traffic starts to utilize this number of servers, the MinSpareServers and MaxSpareservers directives will come into effect.

MaxClients 150   The MaxClients directive is one you should analyze very carefully. This directive will prevent your server from becoming too busy; however, if you have the hardware to handle more, we recommend setting this to a higher number, depending on the traffic load of your website. If more than 150 users try to connect, they will be locked out of the site until users start to time out.

> **NOTE** We have not had to modify this number, even with 30,000 visitors per day on LinuxForum.com. You might want to consider increasing this number if your server has a high traffic load.

MaxRequestsPerChild 0   This directive defines the number of requests each child process is allowed to process before it dies. The default setting is 0, which means unlimited. If you are having performance issues, you might want to consider assigning a value to this setting.

Listen 12.34.56.78:80   By default, Apache will listen on all IP addresses assigned to a machine. Therefore, this directive is commented out and not used by default. If you want to limit which IP addresses can be accessed via the Internet, you can assign them here. One IP address is allowed per line, for example:

```
Listen 12.34.56.78:80
Listen 12.34.56.79:80
```

BindAddress *   This directive is also disabled by default. It is used to support virtual hosts and addresses. If you use the Listen directive, you should also use this directive.

LoadModule *name file*   The LoadModule directive loads the module into Apache. If you performed the DSO installation method, you will see all of the modules that you entered into your configuration options here. This section should be coordinated with the following AddModule section.

AddModule *header file name*   This directive should be coordinated with the previous LoadModule section and it defines the C header files of the modules.

Port 80   By default, Apache is designed to listen on port 80, which is the standard web server port. If you do not want to listen on port 80, define your port here.

> **NOTE** If you change the port number, make sure to update your firewall settings.

> **NOTE** If you change this port number, you must define what port you are using in your URL request—for example: http://yourdomain.com:8080.

You might also notice the following code for your SSL installation:

```
<IfDefine SSL>
Listen 80
Listen 443
```

```
</IfDefine>
```

This code will be executed if you start Apache with SSL:

```
apachectl startssl
```

User nobody Apache will run as a user and group defined in the configuration file. For security purposes, Apache is set to nobody or apache because these users do not have any permission to execute commands or to write or delete files that that they do not explicitly own.

NOTE Do not be fooled by this setting. If you chmod a file or directory to 777, or chown a directory to the same user and group the server runs as, the web server will have ability to write to it and potentially cause harm to your system.

Group nobody This directive is the same as the User directive except it defines the group that the server runs as.

ServerAdmin *root@yourdomain.com* The ServerAdmin directive is simply a contact e-mail address for the administrator of the server. It is not required, and we would hesitate to put a legitimate or an important e-mail address in this setting.

ServerName *www.yourdomain.com* By default, Apache will deliver any web pages located in the default DocumentRoot directive to any name that resolves to your IP address. For example, if you have yourdomain.com and mydomain.com pointed to your IP address, a web page from the DocumentRoot will be displayed.

TIP If you get a message that says [alert] httpd: Could not determine the server's fully qualified domain name, using 127.0.0.1 for ServerName when you start your Apache Web Server, uncomment this line and enter your hostname. Additionally, you should put the fully qualified domain name in the /etc/hosts file.

DocumentRoot "/www/htdocs" This is the directory where your website files are located. Try to remember this term because you will see it in many locations, including PHP.

Directory The Directory directive enables you to specify certain options for a directory. There are many directives that might fall into these sections. If you would like to learn more about these directives, refer to the "Apache 1.3 Features" section earlier in this chapter.

A Directory directive has an opening and closing tag. The directory you are configuring is defined in the opening tag. See the following example:

```
<Directory /path/to/directory>
    Options FollowSymLinks
    AllowOverride None
```

```
</Directory>
```

UserDir   If you enabled `mod_user`, you can allow system users to have their own websites on your server. By default, these directives are allowed to be utilized only if the `mod_user` module is installed by using the `IfModule` settings:

```
<IfModule mod_userdir.c>
    UserDir public_html
</IfModule>
```

An example of a system user website is as follows:

```
http://www.yourdomain.com/~username
```

The user's website files will be located in their home directory under a subdirectory called `public_html`.

DirectoryIndex *files*   The `DirectoryIndex` directive defines which page to be displayed by default. For example, currently it is defined to load `index.html` if one exists.

This is one of the directives that we feel are commonly configured improperly by default in the Apache configuration. Every time we have set up an Apache Web Server, we have had to modify this setting. We add `index.htm`, `default.html`, `default.htm`, `default.php`, and `index.php` to each of our web server configurations.

```
<IfModule mod_dir.c>
    DirectoryIndex index.html
</IfModule>
```

AccessFileName .htaccess   The `AccessFileName` is the name of a file that is placed inside a directory and enables you to control the directives within that directory on the web server. These files can have the same directives that the `Directory` directive can have.

Worth noting are the default settings in the `httpd.conf` file that prevent web clients from accessing these file types:

```
<Files ~ "^\.ht">
    Order allow,deny
    Deny from all
    Satisfy All
</Files>
```

NOTE   It is important that the `AccessFileName` file begin with a period (.) as long as you leave the default settings listed in the preceding code for the `Files` directive. If you alter the `Files` directive listed and you use `.ht` prefixes, these sensitive files can become accessible via the web browser, and potential hackers might see what types of settings you use.

UseCanonicalName On   This setting is important to the operation of CGI- and PHP-style scripts that use SERVER_NAME environment variables. It handles the way self-referencing URLs are returned from the server. When this directive is turned on, it will display the ServerName directive and port in the form of a canonical name.

TypesConfig   The TypesConfig directive defines the file that is responsible for translating MIME types for files. This directive, by default, falls into the IfModule setting.

```
<IfModule mod_mime.c>
    TypesConfig /www/conf/mime.types
</IfModule>
```

DefaultType text/plain   DefaultType defines the MIME type to send a file as if the file is not defined in the mime.types file defined by TypesConfig.

MIMEMagicFile /www/conf/magic   MIMEMagicFile is a module that enables certain hints from a file's contents to determine which type of file it is; therefore it is known as *magic*. This directive also falls into an IfModule setting.

```
<IfModule mod_mime_magic.c>
    MIMEMagicFile /www/conf/magic
</IfModule>
```

HostnameLookups Off   This directive enables you to perform hostname lookups on each IP address that connects to your Apache Web Server. We recommend you leave this setting disabled and use the logresolve utility provided by the Apache developers to do hostname lookups after the log file has been rotated.

ErrorLog /www/logs/error_log   The ErrorLog directive defines a file to log errors for the applicable server or virtual host.

LogLevel warn   The LogLevel directive defines the minimum level of an error to log. The default setting, warn, works well.

LogFormat   LogFormat enables you to format your log files to your desire. The standard log format produces the following output:

```
127.0.0.1 - frank [17/Mar/2004:09:30:25 -0500] "GET /index.php
➥HTTP/1.0" 200 2326
```

CustomLog /www/logs/access_log common   CustomLog is an alternative to TransferLog and the other log file types. We prefer to append the combined format instead of common format to the end of the log file name. The combined log file is more verbose and has more information:

```
CustomLog /www/logs/access_log combined
```

ServerSignature On   The ServerSignature setting enables the server type, version, and possibly some of the configuration options to be displayed when requested by an error document or an outside source. We feel that displaying this information might be a security risk so we turn it off.

Alias /icons/ "/www/icons/"   An Alias directive enables you to store files and directories outside of the DocumentRoot and then alias them into a website.

ScriptAlias /cgi-bin/ "/www/cgi-bin/"   ScriptAlias is much like Alias except the directories defined here are known to be executable, for example, cgi-bin.

IndexOptions FancyIndexing   IndexOptions enables you to display a directory's contents as icons—if the files listed in the DirectoryIndex directive are not available. Having this setting enabled by default is a bad idea and using *FancyIndexing* should be explicitly defined in a Directory option.

NameVirtualHost *   NameVirtualHost is a directive for allowing name-based virtual hosts. We enable this setting with a simple * as the value. We will discuss this later in the "Configuring Apache Virtual Hosts" section.

VirtualHost   Virtual hosts enable you to run multiple websites on a single machine and a single IP address or multiple IP addresses. We will discuss this later in the "Configuring Apache Virtual Hosts" section.

Using Apache Virtual Hosts

Apache has an excellent built-in feature called virtual hosts. This feature enables you to host multiple domain names from the same server and either use a single IP address for all of the virtual hosts or assign a group of hosts to an IP address while assigning another group to a different IP address and so on. This widely flexible feature is well designed and very configurable. In fact, virtual hosts enable web-hosting companies to pack many clients onto a single machine with little overhead.

Apache's virtual hosting features are quite extensive; in fact, there are too many to list in this chapter. Here is a list of the most important features you might find uses for in this book:

- IP or name-based virtual hosts
- Each host can have their own DocumentRoot
- Separate logging facilities for each host
- Ability to share directories between virtual hosts by using ScriptAlias and Alias directives
- Ability to allow override options per directory or virtual host

When using SSL-enabled virtual hosts, you must take some things into consideration. First, you must have a separate IP address or SSL port per IP address for each unique SSL virtual host. If you decide to use different ports, the port must be specified in the URL—for example, `https://www.yoursite.com:444` if you are using port 444 for an alternate. Second, you can use a single IP address with one single SSL virtual host and multiple non-SSL virtual hosts. SSL virtual hosts are beyond the scope of this book, so if you want to learn more about them, check the `httpd.conf` examples or read the `mod_ssl` documentation.

Directives Supported by Virtual Hosts

We have already mentioned that Apache virtual hosts are widely configurable; therefore, in this section we will provide a list of directives that can be used in virtual hosts. If you are interested in learning more about these directives, read the upcoming "Configuring Apache Virtual Hosts" section, and also refer to the "Apache 1.3 Features" section earlier in this chapter.

Here is the list of documented directives available in Apache virtual hosts:

- `AccessConfig`
- `AccessFileName`
- `ContentDigest`
- `DefaultType`
- `<Directory>`
- `<DirectoryMatch>`
- `DocumentRoot`
- `EBCDICConvert`
- `EBCDICConvertByType`
- `EBCDICKludge`
- `ErrorDocument`
- `ErrorLog`
- `FileETag`
- `<Files>`
- `<FilesMatch>`
- `<Group>` (Requires suEXEC installed)
- `HostnameLookups`
- `IdentityCheck`
- `LimitInternalRecursion`

- `LimitRequestBody`
- `<Location>`
- `<LocationMatch>`
- `LogLevel`
- `Options`
- `ResourceConfig`
- `RLimitCPU`
- `RLimitMEM`
- `RLimitNPROC`
- `ServerAdmin`
- `ServerAlias`
- `ServerName`
- `ServerPath`
- `ServerSignature`
- `UseCanonicalName`
- `User` (Requires suEXEC installed)
- Let's put some of these directives to use in configuring an Apache virtual host.

Configuring Apache Virtual Hosts

It is now time to start planning and configuring your virtual hosts. By the end of this section, you will be very familiar with how well designed and flexible the Apache Web Server really is.

Got DNS?

For this example, we are going to assume you have two domain names with DNS set up to point to the IP address of your server. If you do not have DNS set up or you do not own domain names yet, you can simply edit your system's `hosts` file and trick your system into resolving a fake name for your server's IP address.

On Linux, the `HOSTS` file is located in `/etc/hosts`, and you will need to add the following lines to it, assuming your server's IP address is `123.456.789.1`.

NOTE   The IP addresses used here are fictional will not work on a real server. You *must* substitute `123.456.789.1` with your real IP addresses!

```
123.456.789.1 yourdomain.com www.yourdomain.com
123.456.789.1 yourotherdomain.com www.yourotherdomain.com
```

On Windows systems, you should search your `C:\Windows` directory for a file named `hosts`. It is usually located in `C:\Windows\System32\Drivers\etc\hosts`. In this file, you will add the following lines:

```
123.456.789.1 yourdomain.com www.yourdomain.com
123.456.789.1 yourotherdomain.com www.yourotherdomain.com
```

Now your system is tricked into resolving the domain names `yourdomain.com`, `www.yourdomain.com`, `yourotherdomain.com`, and `www.yourotherdomain.com` to the IP address of the server.

TIP   Keep this previous trick in mind the next time you register a domain name. You can set up your HOSTS files so you can start building your website while you wait for DNS to register and resolve.

Preparation

Before you start digging into the configuration files, you need to prepare the system by creating the `DocumentRoot` and `Logging` directories. A rule of thumb that usually works well is to use the domain name for the parent directory. You can store your `DocumentRoot` directories anywhere you would like. We prefer to use `/home`. Follow these steps:

1. Create the directories:

   ```
   mkdir -p /home/www.yourdomain.com/public_html/cgi-bin
   mkdir -p /home/www.yourdomain.com/logs
   mkdir -p /home/www.yourotherdomain.com/public_html/cgi-bin
   mkdir -p /home/www.yourotherdomain.com/logs
   ```

NOTE   The traditional method of using `cgi-bin` directories is to place them outside of your document root and use the `cgi-bin ScriptAlias` and `Alias` directives. However, this method works and can be used if you understand that there might be minimal risks involved.

2. Now you have your directories created, you should change the permissions of these directories because you are probably running as `root`. It is good practice to assign the files to a user other than `root`. This prevents your users from logging in to the server as `root` to edit files and manage websites. Change the permissions as follows:

   ```
   chown -R someuser.somegroup /home/www.yourdomain.com/
   chown -R someuser.somegroup /home/www.yourotherdomain.com/
   ```

3. You need to create a directory that will store your virtual host files. You have the ability to simply append the virtual host configurations directly to the `httpd.conf` file; however, you can also have Apache include a directory of configuration files when it starts up. Keeping

a separate directory of individual virtual host files seems more practical than editing a configuration file of 500+ lines each time you need to manage one of those hosts. Make the directory now:

```
mkdir /www/conf/vhosts
```

4. Modify the httpd.conf file to include this new directory of configuration files you will be creating; open the /www/conf/httpd.conf file and add the following line to the end of it:

```
include conf/vhosts
```

5. Because you are editing the httpd.conf file, you need to enable one more setting for your virtual hosts. Locate the NameVirtualHost directive line and remove the comment symbol (#); then change it to the following setting:

```
NameVirtualHost *
```

The previous setting enables virtual hosts to be configured for any IP address.

You should be all set to create your virtual host configurations now.

Virtual Host Configuration Files

In the previous section, we mentioned that creating separate files for each host makes virtual hosts much easier to manage. Let's set up the first file for www.yourdomain.com and name this file www.yourdomain.com.conf in the /www/conf/vhosts directory. The file will contain the following contents:

```
<VirtualHost *>
    ServerName www.yourdomain.com
    ServerAlias yourdomain.com
    DocumentRoot /home/www.yourdomain.com/public_html
    CustomLog /home/www.yourdomain.com/logs/access_log combined
    ErrorLog /home/www.yourdomain.com/logs/error_log
</VirtualHost>
```

NOTE   When using the backslash to continue directives, you should avoid allowing any additional spaces or characters after the backslash (\), which could cause parse errors in the configuration files.

Let's break down this configuration file for better understanding. The following line is the opening tag for the virtual host. Everything between this line and the last line, </VirtualHost>, will contain the settings for this virtual host that you are configuring. Take special notice of the setting * in the open tag. The * indicates that this virtual host will respond to the request for this domain name on any IP address it is used for:

```
<VirtualHost *>
```

The next directive is the name of your server, hence the name `ServerName`:

```
ServerName www.yourdomain.com
```

Next, you define the `ServerAlias` directive. This enables you to point `yourdomain.com` to the same virtual host. This is important because web users have a tendency to access your site without the leading `www`, and you do not want to lose any users by an improperly configured server:

```
ServerAlias yourdomain.com
```

The following `DocumentRoot` directive is the path to the directory where the website's files are located:

```
DocumentRoot /home/www.yourdomain.com/public_html
```

The following `CustomLog` directive is the path to the log file that will contain the access information about the virtual host. In the "Understanding the `httpd.conf` File" section of this chapter, we discussed the options and settings for this directive.

```
CustomLog /home/www.yourdomain.com/logs/access_log \
    combined
```

The `ErrorLog` directive was also discussed in the "Understanding the `httpd.conf` File" section in this chapter and it contains error information regarding the domain:

```
ErrorLog /home/www.yourdomain.com/logs/error_log
```

Finally, you close the Virtual Host configuration for this domain name by using the closing tag:

```
</VirtualHost>
```

Now that you have a good understanding of the virtual host configuration, let's make another virtual host for your other domain name. Create a file located at `/www/conf/www.yourotherdomain.com.conf` and enter the following information:

```
<VirtualHost *>
    ServerName www.yourotherdomain.com
    ServerAlias yourotherdomain.com
    DocumentRoot /home/www.yourotherdomain.com/public_html
    CustomLog /home/www.yourotherdomain.com/logs/access_log\
        combined
    ErrorLog /home/www.yourotherdomain.com/logs/error_log
</VirtualHost>
```

The next task you will perform is to create an `index.html` file that will display a message indicating which virtual host is being displayed when you access the domain name.

In your `/home/www.yourdomain.com/public_html` directory, create a file named `index.html` with the following contents:

```
<html>
<head><title>YourDomain.com</title></head>
<body>Welcome to YourDomain.com</body>
</html>
```

In your /home/www.yourotherdomain.com/public_html directory, create a file named index.html with the following contents:

```
<html>
<head><title>YourOtherDomain.com</title></head>
<body>Welcome to YourOtherDomain.com</body>
</html>
```

Before you go any further, read the next section, "A Lesson in Testing Configuration File Changes." After you have completed those steps, access your domain names configured in this section via your web browser and you should see the appropriate files for each virtual host.

A Lesson in Testing Configuration File Changes

Because adding your virtual hosts has been the first real editing you have done with your configuration files, you need to go through a small routine that prevents you from taking your web server offline.

Because Apache will not read configuration files on the fly, any changes you make to the configuration files will require the server to be restarted to take effect. The kind developers of Apache have taken measures to prevent you from taking your server offline in the event you "fat-fingered" your way through the configuration file.

You might have noticed in the "Becoming Familiar with Apache Programs" section of this chapter that we gave you a list of commands to run. The command for apachectl contains a special setting that enables you to test your configuration files while the server is still running and prevent you from taking your server offline.

Let's issue the apachectl configtest command now and check the output:

Good syntax output:
```
Processing config directory: /www/conf/vhosts/
 Processing config file: /www/conf/vhosts/www.yourdomain.com.conf
Syntax OK
```

In this example, everything parsed as expected by the server and you are clear to start, stop, or restart your server as needed to make the changes take effect.

Bad syntax output:
```
Processing config directory: /www/conf/vhosts/
 Processing config file: /www/conf/vhosts/www.yourdomain.com.conf
Syntax error on line 2 of /www/conf/vhosts/www.yourdomain.com.conf:
Invalid command 'Oops', perhaps mis-spelled or defined by a module not
included in the server configuration
```

In this example, you have a bad token on line 2 of your www.yourdomain.com.conf file. (We purposely entered the text *Oops* because we knew that it would cause a syntax error in Apache.)

After you get the Syntax OK output from your configuration files, you are clear to restart the server. We prefer to completely stop the server and then start it instead of using the restart command because we have had experiences in the past where the changes would not take effect by using the restart command.

```
apachectl stop
apachectl start
```

Alternatively, if you are using SSL:

```
apachectl stop
apachectl startssl
```

Now is a good time for you to check your website and ensure the changes have taken effect.

Performing Other Apache Configurations

Apache has many configurations you can use to enable directory listings, password-protect directories, enable cgi-bin directories, and more. We'll cover the most requested and popular configurations now.

Enabling Directory Listings

Apache directory listings enable you to view the contents of a directory in your DocumentRoot as icons. There are a few things you must keep in mind before you attempt to perform this configuration:

- You must ensure that there are no files in the directory that are listed in your DirectoryIndex directive of the httpd.conf file.

- You must ensure that there are no files in the directory that you want the public to find.

After you have met these criteria, you can begin.

You have an option to directly enter these configuration directives into the httpd.conf, or alternatively you can enter these directives into a virtual host configuration file. It is up to you how you wish to organize. Here are the steps:

1. Create a directory in the www.yourdomain.com DocumentRoot:

```
mkdir -p /home/www.yourdomain.com/public_html/listing
```

2. Add a few files to this directory for your listing purposes:

```
cd /home/www.yourdomain.com/public_html/listing
touch file1.txt
touch file2.jpg
touch file3.exe
touch file4.tar.gz
touch file5.zip
```

```
cd ../
chown -R someuser.somegroup listing
```

3. Add the configuration directives to the /www/conf/vhosts/www.yourdomain.com.conf file:

    ```
    <Directory /home/www.yourdomain.com/public_html/listing>
      Options +Indexes
      IndexOptions FancyIndexing IconsAreLinks
    </Directory>
    ```

4. Following the steps in the "A Lesson in Testing Configuration File Changes" section, run the configuration test and restart the server:

    ```
    apachectl configtest
    apachectl stop
    apachectl start
    ```

    Alternatively, if you are using SSL:

    ```
    apachectl configtest
    apachectl stop
    apachectl startssl
    ```

5. Access the www.yourdomain.com/listing directory in your web browser and you should see a list of icons like those in Figure 8.3.

    Let's move on to password-protecting a directory on your virtual host.

Password-Protecting Web Directories

Password-protecting directories is another popular request item. Because of the complicated documentation in Apache, many people end up finding alternate means to perform this simple operation. We will make this easier for you!

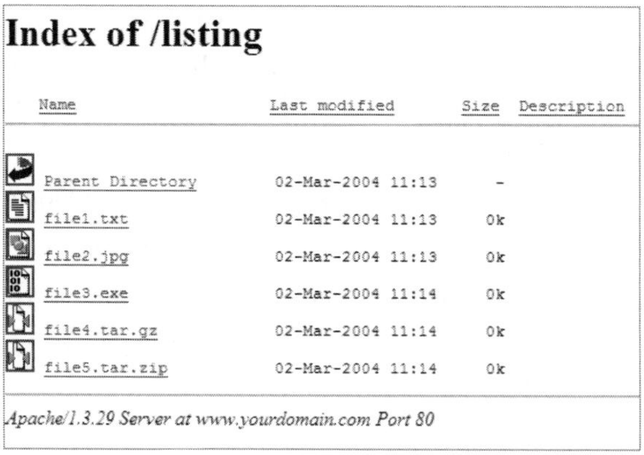

FIGURE 8.3
Apache directory
listing

Index of /listing

	Name	Last modified	Size	Description
	Parent Directory	02-Mar-2004 11:13	-	
	file1.txt	02-Mar-2004 11:13	0k	
	file2.jpg	02-Mar-2004 11:13	0k	
	file3.exe	02-Mar-2004 11:14	0k	
	file4.tar.gz	02-Mar-2004 11:14	0k	
	file5.tar.zip	02-Mar-2004 11:14	0k	

Apache/1.3.29 Server at www.yourdomain.com Port 80

The password protection directives will almost always fall into a <Directory> section of your configuration files. As we mentioned in the previous section, "Enabling Directory Listings," you are going to set up a directory on your virtual host, www.yourdomain.com. Follow these steps:

1. Prepare this directory:

```
cd /home/www.yourdomain.com/public_html
mkdir -p protected
touch protected/index.html
cd ../
chown -R someuser.somegroup protected
```

2. Edit the configuration file /www/conf/vhosts/www.yourdomain.com.conf and add the following lines to it:

```
<Directory /home/www.yourdomain.com/public_html/protected>
  AuthType Basic
  AuthName "Members Only"
  AuthUserFile /home/www.yourdomain.com/.htpasswd
  require valid-user
</Directory>
```

3. Create the password file used by Apache to authenticate the username and password. We use the htpasswd program provided by Apache to generate the file. Simply run the following:

```
cd /home/www.yourdomain.com
/www/bin/htpasswd -c .htpasswd username
```

You are prompted to enter and confirm the password for the user *username*. Additionally, a file is created at /home/www.yourdomain.com/.htpasswd.

NOTE   For more information about using .ht prefixed files, see the AccessFileName .htaccess entry in the "Understanding the httpd.conf File" section earlier in this chapter.

4. Run the commands to test your configuration and restart the server to make the changes take effect:

```
apachectl configtest
apachectl stop
apachectl start
```

Alternatively, if you are using SSL:

```
apachectl configtest
apachectl stop
apachectl startssl
```

5. Open your web browser and try to access the password-protected directory: http://www.yourdomain.com/protected. You should be prompted for a username and password. If you enter the correct username and password, you will be shown the index.html page,

which in this case is a blank page. If you do not enter the correct username or password, you might be prompted continuously until Apache displays an error page.

TIP

If you want to simplify the process of creating and configuring the password-protected directories, you might be interested in the *Apache Password Wizzard* we have created (yes, that is spelled with two *z*s intentionally). It is located at `www.apachefreaks.com/apache-password-wizzard.php`. This Web-based script will take you through the steps in configuring your password-protected directories and provide you with the password files and directives to configure the directories with ease.

Configuring *cgi-bin* Directories

Even though this book is written for PHP, we acknowledge that you might need to use CGI scripts occasionally. Therefore, we will show you how to create a `cgi-bin` directory to house your executable CGI scripts.

1. Let's start by ensuring that your `cgi-bin` directory is created and has the proper permissions.

```
mkdir -p /home/www.yourdomain.com/public_html/cgi-bin
chmod 755 /home/www.yourdomain.com/public_html/cgi-bin
chown -R someuser.somegroup /home/www.yourdomain.com/public_html/cgi-bin
```

NOTE

The traditional method of using `cgi-bin` directories is to place them outside of your document root and use the `cgi-bin ScriptAlias` and `Alias` directives. However, this method works and can be used if you understand that there might be minimal risks involved.

2. Edit the `/www/conf/vhosts/www.yourdomain.com.conf` file and add the following lines to the end of it:

```
<Directory /home/www.yourdomain.com/public_html/cgi-bin>
  Options +ExecCGI
  AddHandler cgi-script cgi pl
</Directory>
```

3. Because you are editing the `www.yourdomain.com.conf` file, you need to add one more line into the `<VirtualHost>` section. Add the following lines directly above the `</VirtualHost>` closing tag:

```
ScriptAlias /cgi-bin/ /home/www.yourdomain.com/public_html/cgi-bin/
```

4. Test your configuration file changes and restart the server.

```
apachectl configtest
apachectl stop
apachectl start
```

Alternatively, if you are using SSL:

```
apachectl configtest
apachectl stop
apachectl startssl
```

5. Create a test CGI script to ensure this directory works properly. Create a file located at /home/www.yourdomain.com/public_html/cgi-bin/index.cgi and add the following contents:

```
#!/usr/bin/perl
print "Content-type: text/html"

print "This CGI Script Works Properly.";
```

6. Change the permissions and ownership of the script:

```
cd /home/www.yourdomain.com/public_html
chmod -R 755 cgi-bin
chown -R someuser.somegroup cgi-bin
```

7. Execute this script in your web browser: www.yourdomain.com/cgi-bin/index.cgi and you should see a message that says This CGI Script Works Properly.

If you see the message, then all is well. Your cgi-bin is working properly!

Using *.htaccess* Files for Local Directory Configurations

Editing the httpd.conf file for each directory configuration can become painful over time. You can, however, include per-directory settings in a file named .htaccess located in that directory. A rule of thumb is that any directive that will work in <Directory *xxxx*></Directory> settings for the httpd.conf file will work in the .htaccess. You might need to add something like this to the httpd.conf file:

```
<Directory /path/to/directory>
AllowOverride All
</Directory>
```

The previous settings will allow the .htaccess file in the directory to change any settings. You should determine which settings to use in the AllowOverride directive so that you do not open your system to security holes, especially if you are virtual hosting for clients.

Configuration File Summary

If you have performed all of these exercises, your configuration file should appear as in Listing 8.1.

Listing 8.1   **Virtual Host Configuration File**

```
<VirtualHost *>
   ServerName www.yourdomain.com
   ServerAlias yourdomain.com
   DocumentRoot /home/www.yourdomain.com/public_html
   CustomLog /home/www.yourdomain.com/logs/access_log \
      combined
   ErrorLog /home/www.yourdomain.com/logs/error_log
   ScriptAlias /cgi-bin/ \
         /home/www.yourdomain.com/public_html/cgi-bin/
</VirtualHost>

<Directory /home/www.yourdomain.com/public_html/listing>
   Options +Indexes
   IndexOptions FancyIndexing IconsAreLinks
</Directory>

<Directory /home/www.yourdomain.com/public_html/protected>
   AuthType Basic
   AuthName "Members Only"
   AuthUserFile /home/www.yourdomain.com/.htpasswd
   require valid-user
</Directory>

<Directory /home/www.yourdomain.com/public_html/cgi-bin>
   Options +ExecCGI
   AddHandler cgi-script cgi pl
</Directory>
```

Starting Apache During Boot

Now that Apache is installed and configured correctly, it's time to add Apache Web Server to your startup files so that it will automatically start up during the boot process. To do this, you will be editing the /etc/rc.d/rc.local file. All you'll need to do is add one line to the end of this file for your command to start Apache.

Go ahead and add the following:

```
/www/bin/apachectl start
```

Alternatively, if you are using SSL:

```
/www/bin/apachectl startssl
```

That's all there is to it. Now when your server is rebooted for whatever reason, Apache will spawn at startup.

NOTE   If you want to, you can create a startup script for the /etc/init.d directory and add it by using chkconfig. The firewall script in Chapter 6 is a good example to follow and it will work with slight modifications for the relative information.

Apache Web Server Installation and Configuration Checklist

By now you should be able to plan, install, and administrate a successful Apache Web Server. We have taken years of experience and research and compiled it into this chapter to provide you with filtered information that is handy enough to get you going. After reading this chapter, you should be able to do the following:

- Understand the development of Apache Web Server.
- Know the differences between Apache 1.3 and 2.0.
- Know how to install Apache 1.3 by using multiple methods.
- Set up an SSL-enabled server.
- Understand Apache directories.
- Know the Apache programs and commands.
- Understand the Apache configuration files.
- Understand Apache Virtual Hosts.
- Understand Apache directory listings.
- Understand Apache password protection.
- Understand using the Apache cgi-bin directories.
- Get support for Apache.

Let's move on to the next chapter, where you'll learn about installing and administrating MySQL.

## CHAPTER 9

MySQL: Installation and Administration

- Understanding MySQL and Database Structure

- Downloading MySQL

- Installing MySQL

- Configuring MySQL after Installation

- Performing MySQL Administration

- Performance and Replication

MySQL is pronounced My-S-Q-L, not My-Sequel. Many people have the habit of pronouncing this wrong, so we thought we'd mention it to start this chapter properly.

The MySQL database server, as we discussed in Chapter 1, "Introducing LAMP," enables you to store data in a manner that allows the server to access it quickly and efficiently. In this chapter, we'll show you how to choose the proper installation method for your solution and then demonstrate how to perform the actual installation of MySQL. After that is complete, we will show you how to configure your server by using the proper directives and then how to administrate your server to add new password-protected user accounts, set permissions, and more.

First, we'll go over some basic information so you can gain some insight as to what you will be installing and why it is imperative to creating dynamic websites on your server.

Understanding MySQL and Database Structure

At the time of writing this book, MySQL is on development version 4.1. However, there is also a preview version available, MySQL 5.0, which contains many additional upgrades to performance and an abundance of new, useful features. Because webmasters everywhere will soon be switching to MySQL 5, we will be covering the MySQL 5 installation in this book. Although the installations are nearly the same, there are a few differences in configuration. The majority of differences, however, are transparent during the installation procedure, so you will be able to use this chapter as an excellent reference should you choose to install a version earlier than 5.0.

MySQL includes all the necessary requirements and features for enterprise-level development with additional innovations as well. The MySQL database server allows for multiple storage engines that include full transition support. This means that you can use commit, rollback, crash recovery, and low-level locking capabilities. MySQL also offers query caching, which delivers improved performance and database replication so that many slave systems can run off of a single master server. With the addition of SSL transport-layer encryption and an advanced permission system, MySQL can be locked down to an extremely reliable point. MySQL even includes full text indexing, which enables a text field to be searched faster and more efficiently.

One of the major reasons for using MySQL 5 over MySQL 4 is the use of stored procedures and functions. Stored procedures enable MySQL to manipulate data when certain conditions are met. This does put more load on the host server, but allows less data to travel between the web server and the database server. This is especially useful when the data being transferred between the two is sensitive. Financial institutions, for instance, use many stored procedures and functions to maintain tighter data security. Another major reason, as with all software, is that it contains performance upgrades and bug fixes over other previous versions.

Differences between Flat-File and Relational Databases

Flat files provide a method of storing data that uses single or multiple text files. These files are formatted by using special characters to delimit fields and records from each other. The most common type is Comma Separated Values or CSV. This type of file stores fields separated by commas, and rows separated by new lines or carriage returns. These files must be parsed each time data needs to be accessed, which can equate to a high load on the computer if the data types become complicated or advanced. That is not to say it is impossible to store complex data in a flat-file format, only that it is not nearly as efficient as using a relational database.

Imagine a filing cabinet filed with folders and files. If you wanted to search for a particular record that might be written on one of these documents, you would have to locate the appropriate drawer and then the correct folder. In that folder you would find numerous papers. Locating the correct paper would take some time, and reading down the appropriate document for the correct row containing your record would take even longer.

Another problem with flat files is that they are prone to corruption. There is no inherent locking system for flat files, so the file must be locked by the application accessing the file. This can lead to serious problems if two or more instances of an application or applications try to access the file at the same time. These instances can create a battle for the file lock and could possibly end up corrupting or even erasing the file. Not a situation you want to be in.

This is why *Database Management (DBM)* was developed for flat files. A DBM layer adds more functionality and the addition of keys. These keys are unique, and the manager can locate information faster to supply to the client. However, this does not eliminate the locking file issue inherent to flat-file storage.

This brings us to relational databases. *Relational databases* store information in a way that mimics real life. The information is separated into *tables,* or groups of records. Each record in a table can have *properties*—like a car having an engine, wheels, and so on. These properties can also have their own relational tables—hence the term *relational database.* To continue the car example, tables could be used to store types of engines and types of wheels. Each of the tables can be linked to each other by the use of keys. A *key* is a unique ID associated with each record in a table. For instance, our wheel table might have a unique integer for each wheel. This number could be used in the car table so that each car would have to store only the relationship to its wheel, not all the information about the wheel. If your car table stored all the information about a wheel, every car in the database would contain duplicate information about the wheel over and over again. The relational database solves this problem by breaking out the wheel information into its own table and storing its relation (the unique ID) in the car table.

This sort of structure would be nearly impossible to replicate by using flat files, and the performance would be severely less than optimal. Another major advantage is being able to eliminate duplication of data and thereby save on file size, which becomes important when you are storing millions of records. However, when working with databases of this size, some duplication might be necessary to make queries significantly faster. These duplications are usually created by the use of indexes. We will cover indexes in more depth later in this section.

Relational databases also have built-in functions that enable data to be manipulated and retrieved. Instead of the client program sifting through countless records, only certain records are accessed as needed when querying the database. Databases also introduce complex locking systems to counteract the problems found in flat files. In many databases, MySQL included, row locking is available. This enables only a single record to be locked while it is updated instead of having an entire table or file locked. Because the database manager is the only one allowed to access the files where data is stored, the database manager can also queue queries so that nothing will be accidentally overwritten.

Now that you have a good idea of why to choose a relational database over flat files, you're ready to take a look at the different solutions available and learn why we are using MySQL as our database server of choice.

Advantages and Limitations of MySQL

Let's take a look at some of the key advantages and features offered by MySQL.

First up, we have the American National Standards Institute (ANSI) SQL syntax support. MySQL supports a broad spectrum of the ANSI SQL 99 syntax commands. *SQL*, pronounced *sequel*, is a language with which you "talk" to the database by using commands such as SELECT, and UPDATE. While these two commands are ANSI SQL 99 commands, MySQL adds additional commands to help maximize the efficiency of your queries. REPLACE and LIMIT are two excellent examples of such commands. MySQL also adds alternate syntaxes for commands to make porting pre-built applications easier. This allows fewer modifications of existing queries for other databases, resulting in many statements not needing any changes at all.

MySQL also has excellent cross-platform support. MySQL is available for Linux, Microsoft Windows, FreeBSD, Sun Microsystems' Solaris, IBM's AIX, Apple Computer's Mac OS X, Hewlett-Packard's HP-UX, QNX Neutrino, Novell NetWare, SCO OpenUnix, SGI IRIX, DEC OSF, and a few other less common operating systems as well. MySQL also offers a standard thread-safe library and a variety of database drivers for virtually every programming language.

MySQL also provides independent storage engines that enable you to choose which type of database is suited for your particular application. If you need row-level locking and transaction support, you can choose to use the InnoDB; otherwise, you can choose the MyISAM storage engine, which will help maximize your performance.

Transactions, as we mentioned, enable you to use ROLLBACK and COMMIT commands within an application. This enables you to make multiple changes to a database and commit them all at once. The ROLLBACK command would then enable you to roll back the database to a point before those changes had been made. This, however, has its disadvantages. It requires more storage space, more memory, and greater CPU usage. If you do not need this functionality, it is recommended that you choose the MyISAM type. This allows for atomic changes, as they have been named by MySQL. An *atomic change* just means that while you are updating a specific table, no other process can interfere with it. This ensures that the data will be updated correctly, and the next user or process attempting to read the data of the updated row will receive the most up-to-date results.

Next up we have the security features. MySQL offers a flexible security package that even allows for SSL support. A built-in user system allows for individual privileges down to a table level to be assigned to a single user. Users have passwords and as of MySQL 4+ can even be limited to a predefined limit of resources. We will cover the administration of users later in this chapter.

Query caching offers massive performance increases without any additional attention or development by the user. The MySQL Server will cache the most frequently issued queries, which can result in performance gains of over 200 percent in typical usage. For additional performance in larger-scale systems requiring multiple servers, you can set up database replication. This enables you to duplicate a single master server as many times as needed for slave servers. This allows for a more robust solution than a typical single-server setup.

MySQL also offers full-text indexing and searching. When indexing a text field, MySQL will create a complex indexing system that enables you to search for specific words or phrases and even includes relevance rankings. MySQL 4 even introduced exact phrase matching and Boolean search operations—excellent for larger databases that require search functions for the user.

An interesting feature also available with MySQL is the use of an embedded database library. Although this will have no impact on your web server or on using PHP to interface with MySQL, it is important to note for many other uses. Running this feature requires only that you run the `libmysql` daemon. This would enable you to create applications for systems such as Internet appliances and kiosks with MySQL being virtually transparent. You could even create a self-contained database on a CD-ROM for distribution.

MySQL 4.1 also saw the addition of GIS, or Geographical Information System. This allows for a subset of SQL 92 standards that allow geometry types. Geometry types allow the storing and manipulating of spatial and geographic data. MySQL 4.1 also saw the introduction of subqueries. Subqueries enable you to select data into an `INSERT` statement or to select a subset of selected rows. This can greatly simplify the coding side of your work by combining multiple queries into one.

As far as limitations to MySQL, there are really none that would concern the average or even most experienced users. The only upgrade to speak of would be installing Oracle, and with a cost upward of $30,000, it shouldn't be considered as an option unless you have a system that requires multiple clusters of servers—especially when such a reliable and powerful open source solution as MySQL is available at no cost. With MySQL 4, the maximum table size was raised from the old 4GB to 64TB. This should be plenty of space for any table. Nearing this point would require an enormous amount of data, and tables of this size should be broken into multiple tables from an optimization standpoint.

NOTE   If you would like a true list of almost all the features available on any database server as well as a comparison of most of the major database servers, check out `www.mysql.com/ information/crash-me.php`. The tests offered here are extremely numerous but interesting nonetheless. MySQL says they provide this web application "so you can get the real limitations from the database server (not the information from sales managers!)."

MySQL Version Differences

When looking at the different MySQL database server versions, you will be presented with a few choices. The first choice is whether you want to pay for MySQL. If you choose not to pay, you must release all of your source code for the program that interfaces with MySQL. This does not mean that you need to release your PHP, only the connection portion that is already taken care of by PHP for you. None of the other software residing on your system will need to be taken into account unless it uses MySQL. If you are building an application that uses MySQL and you do not want to release your source code, you can purchase a license from MySQL for a marginal cost and be exempt from the rules governing the GPL.

Whatever your decision, you can download MySQL Classic, MySQL Standard, MySQL Pro, or MySQL Max:

MySQL Classic is the simplest of servers and contains only the standard MySQL storage engine.

MySQL Standard includes the standard MySQL storage engines and the InnoDB storage engine.

MySQL Pro is the licensed version of MySQL Standard.

MySQL Max contains many features not yet available in other releases. This enables you to take advantage of extras such as the Berkeley database (BDB) storage engine, splitting tables across multiple files, and so on.

NOTE   In the words of Sleepycat Software, the makers of BDB, Berkeley DB is an open source embedded database library that provides scalable, high-performance, transaction-protected data management services to applications. Berkeley DB provides a simple function-call API for data access and management.

After you have decided what type of MySQL installation you want, it's time to take a look at the different versions. You can refer back to the discussions earlier in this chapter about what has been added in 4.1 and 5.0. As we said, we will be using 5.0 for the purposes of this book because 5.0 contains additional performance enhancements and features not available in previous releases. At the time of writing this book, there is no production release of 5.0, but that's never stopped us before. If there is not yet a production release for 5.0 as you are performing installation and configuration, and you do not need to take advantage of the benefits of version 5, you can choose an older version of MySQL. However, to help ensure the greatest number of similarities between your installation and ours, you should use MySQL 4.0 or later.

Using the MySQL Documentation

The searchable documentation for MySQL is available on their site located at `mysql.com/doc/`. Here you can view a table of contents for the manual divided by section as well as access the search command available in the top-left side of the screen, just below the navigation bar. This documentation contains a plethora of information on everything from installation to optimization. The documentation contained here is always up-to-date with the latest information including, at the time of writing this book, information on MySQL 5. Although the information contained in the manual is vast, it contains only reference information. It does not provide general information on concepts or how to employ a certain practice or standard.

Reading the information contained within the manual requires that you understand the conventions they use to describe the syntax of MySQL. First, you should know the following standards:

Constant   When you see text that uses a `constant-width`, you should know that you are reading command names and options. SQL statements or column and table names are a few commonly used examples.

Single quotes   When you see single quotes used in the documentation surrounding a `constant-width` font, you know you are reading one of two things. The quotes could be signifying a filename or pathname, or could be used to indicate a specific character or character sequence. For instance, you might read something that says, "To specify a wildcard, use the '%' character."

Italics   *Italics* are used for emphasis within the MySQL documentation.

Boldface   A **boldface** font is used for an especially strong emphasis within the MySQL documentation.

`shell>`   When you see a line of text that is `constant-width` and is preceded with `shell>`, you will know that this is a command meant to be run from a command prompt.

Continued on next page

mysql>   When you see a line of text that is `constant-width` and is preceded with `mysql>`, you will know that this is a command meant to be run from the MySQL Client program.

Substitutions   The MySQL documentation also uses `db_name`, `tbl_name`, and `col_name` to represent variables that should be substituted for your database, table, and column names, respectively. You will also see these names in all lowercase, whereas the SQL syntax will be in all uppercase.

Square brackets   Brackets within the MySQL documentation are used to express a value or directive that is optional. For example, if you see an argument such as p[*password*], the password is optional here. You will be prompted later, but the password is not required for the argument.

Braces   Braces are used when something has more than one option and you must choose one of them. You will generally see each option listed in brackets and separated by a pike symbol (|). For example, the protocol flag for `mysqladmin` requires the following syntax:

```
--protocol={TCP | SOCKET | PIPE | MEMORY}
```
Here you see that an argument is required, and you can specify only one.

Ellipsis points   Ellipsis points are the three dots used to indicate an *ellipsis* (omission) in text. Similarly, in the MySQL documentation, this is used as a form of shorthand to avoid having to write an example over and over again and confusing the reader with additional syntax that is not relevant to the example. For instance, you might see a sub select expressed as INSERT ... SELECT. This simply indicates a SELECT statement following an INSERT statement. Ellipsis points can also be used to express that multiple options or values of the preceding syntax might follow but are optional.

By knowing how to read the MySQL documentation, you will be well on your way to finding near-immediate answers to any questions you might have. During the installation procedure, you might want to refer to the documentation if you are planning on performing a unique installation that is not covered by this book. After your installation and during your time developing applications that use MySQL, the documentation will become an invaluable resource. Remember or refer back to the standards listed here to make researching your answers much more efficient and painless.

Downloading MySQL

Now that you know which version of MySQL you will be installing, it's time to locate the source files for the installation procedure. For the purposes of this book, we will be installing from source; this is a more complicated procedure but might be necessary for your system. You might wish to install from binary, in which case you can skip the next "Installing SQL" section and proceed to the "Configuring MySQL after Installation" section.

First, travel to `http://www.mysql.com/downloads/index.html` in your favorite browser and take a look at your options. You will see that the first download page is divided into four main sections for files pertaining to installation. You should have MySQL Database Server & Standard Clients, MaxDB by MySQL, Graphical Clients, and Application Programming Interfaces (APIs).

For the purposes of this book, we will be using the first section, MySQL Database Server & Standard Clients. In this section you should see several versions of MySQL that we discussed earlier in this chapter as well as a link to older releases and snapshots. For now, go ahead and select which version you would like to install. We will be selecting MySQL 5.0.

You will then be brought to a new page containing all the installation types for your selected version of MySQL. First you will see Linux Downloads, which contains the non-RPM binary files for installing MySQL. The next section is Linux x86 RPM Downloads, which of course contains the binary installation files that you might want to use if you opt for the RPM installation. Following these first two sections are the rest of the files for different OSs and system architectures.

> **NOTE**   If you are installing from RPM, be sure to download both the server and the client. You will need the client to be able to access the MySQL command-line interface. This is imperative when administering your system without using any third-party software.

Go ahead and look under the very last section, Source Downloads, for your source file types. Choose the Tarball by clicking or following the Pick a Mirror link. This will take you to the next page, which displays a list of mirrors from which you can download this file. Make sure you are downloading to your `/usr/local/src/mysql` directory and you will be ready to make your mirror selection. If this directory does not already exist, you should create it. With your file or file(s) downloaded, you will be ready to continue to the next section, "Installing MySQL."

Installing MySQL

Congratulations—you are almost ready to begin installing MySQL Server and Client. You will need to do a few things first to make sure that the installation goes smoothly. Installing MySQL is relatively easy but can sometimes be seen as overly complicated because of the number of options available. First you will need to prepare your system.

Preparing the System

As in Chapter 8, "Apache Web Server: Installation and Configuration," you will need to make sure there are no previous versions currently installed on your server as well as unpack the `tar` file in your `/usr/local/src/mysql` directory. Let's begin by checking with RPM to see whether there are any previous installations.

Removing Pre-installed MySQL Server and Client RPMs

Your Fedora system might already have MySQL installed, so you are going to remove the RPM packages from your system. In the future, you will want to be able to control what patches are downloaded and applied, and what upgrades are made to the system and when.

As with Apache, the reasoning behind building your own installation is that most distributions such as Fedora, Red Hat, and others take a while to release security updates. You do not want to leave your system vulnerable while you wait for the distributions to release their upgrades, especially after announcements are made about those vulnerabilities.

Now that we have justified the importance of running a custom-built installation, you can remove any versions of MySQL that may be installed. Follow these steps:

1. Query the RPM database to see whether any MySQL packages are installed:

   ```
   rpm -qa | grep -i MySQL
   ```

   If you see a result similar to the following, then you have one or more MySQL applications installed:

   ```
   MySQL-client-4.0.18
   MySQL-server-4.0.18
   MySQL-devel-4.0.18
   ```

   If you have a result like this one, you have both the client and the server installed as well as the development tools.

2. Let's find the dependencies of the packages so you can remove them first. Start with the client because this should be the only one that might have a dependency:

   ```
   rpm -q --whatrequires MySQL-client
   ```

   On our system, the result returned was as follows:
   ```
   MySQL-devel-4.0.18
   ```

3. Remove this package from your system:

   ```
   rpm -e MySQL-devel
   ```

4. With that out of the way, you are almost ready to uninstall the client and server. First, you'll need to stop any MySQL process that might be running on your server. Check for and remove any processes by using the following:

   ```
   ps aux | grep mysqld
   killall mysqld
   ```

5. With your system now clean of any MySQL processes, remove the last two packages:

   ```
   rpm -e MySQL-client
   rpm -e MySQL-server
   ```

Unpacking the Installation Files

With that out of the way, you are ready to unpack the `tar` files you downloaded at the end of the preceding section. As always, you have placed them in your `/usr/local/src/mysql` directory. To decompress and extract them to the appropriate subdirectory, run the following:

```
gunzip mysql-*
tar -xvf mysql-*
```

The MySQL source installation files will then be un-archived into the `mysql-version` directory, where *version* is the version of MySQL that you downloaded.

Creating a MySQL User for *mysqld*

With your files uncompressed and un-archived, you will need to perform two final commands before you can install MySQL. The MySQL daemon `mysqld` needs a user and a group to operate under. To create these, use the following:

```
groupadd mysql
useradd -g mysql mysql
```

You are now ready to begin creating your installation script with the proper directives for your installation.

Using Common Configuration Directives

Like all configuration scripts, the MySQL configuration script allows you a great deal of control over how MySQL is built and installed. We've listed some of the more common configuration directives in this section for reference. The end of this section will cover creating your configuration script for your Fedora Core 2 installation.

`--without-server`   This option enables you to install just the client from source. This might come in handy if you do not wish to upgrade your server version but would like to update the client application.

`--with-embedded-server`   This directive enables you to install the embedded MySQL library, `libmysqld.a`.

`--prefix=/path/to/dir`   This option enables you to specify the base path to which MySQL will install.

`--localstatedir=/path/to/dir`   This option enables you to specify the location where the actual data files for MySQL will be installed.

`--with-unix-socket-path=/path/to/file/mysql.sock`   This directive enables you to change the location and name of the `mysql.sock` file. This is located in the `/tmp` directory by default.

`--with-client-ldflags=-all-static`

`--with-mysqld-ldflags=-all-static`

These two directives when used together enable you to compile MySQL Server and Client as statically linked programs. This allows greater speed and should always be used if you are creating a workaround for an RPM package.

Also, when using the GCC compiler, you will need to set a few CFLAGS and CXXFLAGS environment variables. This will tell the GCC compiler to use only GCC instead of linking to libg++ and libstdc++. MySQL reports that many users have experienced strange problems when using these compilers. You should also use the following:

```
CXXFLAGS="-03 \
    -mpentiumpro \
    -mstack-align-double \
    -felide-constructors \
    -fno-exceptions -fno-rtti"
```

WARNING This code is listed as *imperative* for newer GCC compilers that understand these directives. Failure to do so can result in random crashes of the MySQL Server.

Now that you know the most commonly used directives, you can configure your script for your MySQL configuration:

1. Create a new file to edit within the MySQL directory called **conf_mysql**.

2. Inside, place the following contents:

```
CFLAGS="-03"
CXX=gcc
CXXFLAGS="-03 \
    -mpentiumpro \
    -mstack-align-double \
    -felide-constructors \
    -fno-exceptions -fno-rtti"

./configure \
    --prefix=/usr/local/mysql \
    --with-extra-charsets=complex \
    --enable-thread-safe-client \
    --enable-local-infile \
    --enable-assembler \
    --disable-shared \
    --with-client-ldflags=-all-static \
    --with-mysqld-ldflags=-all-static
```

3. Exit and save and then chmod 775 conf_mysql.

4. If you need to specify additional directives, check Appendix B, "MySQL Configuration Directives." Otherwise, you can skip directly to the next section, "Installing MySQL Server and Client."

NOTE We could not locate the complete list of directives in the MySQL documentation. The only way we were able to locate them was by performing a `./configure --help`. Although you can also find these directives there, we thought it might be a bit easier to have a reference that is not on the same computer you are using. See Appendix B for the complete list. If you do not need any additional directives for this installation, then by all means ignore that reference and proceed with the installation. If you do need a few of these, we hope you get some use of Appendix B. Most of the directive explanations are taken directly from the `--help` listing.

Installing MySQL Server and Client

With your configuration script now complete, it's time to give it a test. Follow these steps:

1. From your MySQL directory that contains your script, run the file:

   ```
   ./conf_mysql
   ```

   If everything went according to plan, you should not receive any error messages. You will see quite a few configurations and creations of make files taking place and should then be dropped to a prompt after seeing a couple of paragraphs and the final line:

   ```
   Thank you for choosing MySQL!
   ```

2. With that out of the way it's time to:

   ```
   make
   ```

3. If you haven't received any errors, you should be ready to run the actual installation. Go ahead and run the following:

   ```
   make install
   ```

   This process should be a significantly quicker process that the `configure` and `make` processes.

4. After the installation has been completed without any errors, you will then need to create the MySQL grant tables if this is your first installation. Run the following:

   ```
   scripts/mysql_install_db
   ```

5. You should now change the ownership of the binary files for obvious security reasons:

   ```
   chown -R root  /usr/local/mysql
   chown -R mysql /usr/local/mysql/var
   chgrp -R mysql /usr/local/mysql
   ```

   Congratulations—you are now ready to configure and test your MySQL installation.

Configuring MySQL after Installation

This first thing you will want to do after your installation is complete is to test the installation. To do so, follow these steps:

1. Launch MySQL by using the following command:

   ```
   /usr/local/mysql/bin/mysqld_safe --user=mysql &
   ```

   If you do not receive any error messages, your MySQL Server should now be running.

2. To test this, you can use the mysqladmin command. This command enables you to set and test a number of different options and values within the MySQL Server. First let's use:

   ```
   /usr/local/mysql/bin/mysqladmin version
   ```

   If your MySQL Server is indeed running, you should be presented with something like the following:

   ```
   bin/mysqladmin  Ver 8.40 Distrib 5.0.0-alpha, for pc-linux
   on i686 Copyright (C) 2000 MySQL AB & MySQL Finland AB &
   TCX DataKonsult AB This software comes with ABSOLUTELY NO
   WARRANTY. This is free software, and you are welcome to
   modify and redistribute it under the GPL license

   Server version          5.0.0-alpha
   Protocol version        10
   Connection              Localhost via UNIX socket
   UNIX socket             /tmp/mysql.sock
   Uptime:                 46 sec

   Threads: 1  Questions: 1  Slow queries: 0  Opens: 6  Flush
   tables: 1  Open tables: 0  Queries per second avg: 0.022
   ```

   Here you can see the version of MySQL you are running as well as other well-labeled pertinent information about your installation.

3. You can also run the following:

   ```
   /usr/local/mysql/bin/mysqladmin variables
   ```

   This presents you with a list of MySQL variables that control different aspects of your server. If both of these commands have run without a hitch, then you are now ready to create a password for your root user. This will prevent anyone from being able to access your database after your initial installation.

4. To create your password, run the following:

   ```
   /usr/local/mysql/bin/mysqladmin -u root password 'new-password'
   /usr/local/mysql/bin/mysqladmin -u root -h fullyQualifiedDomain password
   'new-password'
   ```

Here, the first command will set the root password for localhost and the second command will set the root password for the domain name. Make sure both of these are set correctly. It is typical to set both of these passwords to be the same.

WARNING If you are using special characters in your password, make sure you enclose your password in single quotes. You can also leave the password blank, and MySQL will prompt you to enter your password on the next line.

5. You can also perform these password changes by accessing the MySQL Client and logging in as root to use the mysql database:

```
/usr/local/mysql/bin/mysql -u root mysql -p
```

The -p on the end tells MySQL you will be using a password. Because none is specified as the next argument, you will be prompted on the following line before you are allowed to gain access. This is the preferred method so that your password is not saved in your history. If you have not yet set the root password, you can leave off the -p and you will be allowed to access the database.

6. From here you can perform these commands:

```
SET PASSWORD FOR 'root'@'localhost' = PASSWORD('newpwd');
SET PASSWORD FOR 'root'@'host_name' = PASSWORD('newpwd');
```

7. After these commands have been run, you will then need to:

```
FLUSH PRIVILEGES;
```

Performing these actions will give you the same result as the mysqladmin commands we discussed earlier.

With your root password now set, you can turn your attention to configuring your server for general usage and preparing for the future.

Editing the Configuration Files

MySQL allows options for MySQL Server to be specified in three ways. You can specify options by using option files, by setting environment variables, and through the command line when running the application. In this section, you'll review all three.

Using Option Files

Option files can be located in a number of locations on the filesystem and are read in order, with later files taking precedence over preceding files. In order these files are as follows:

```
/etc/my.cnf
/usr/local/mysql/var/my.cnf
defaults-extra-file (specified with a directive)
~/my.cnf
```

These files can contain any options that can also be specified on the command line. For a full list, refer to Appendix B. For now, let's take a look at the proper format of a configuration file. To do so you will look at two typical configuration files. The first is considered a global configuration file:

```
[client]
port=3306
socket=/tmp/mysql.sock

[mysqld]
port=3306
socket=/tmp/mysql.sock
key_buffer_size=16M
max_allowed_packet=1M

[mysqldump]
quick
```

Here you will see that the directives listed are divided into three groups, the first of which is called client. Each group is specified by the use of brackets enclosing the name. The following two groups are the names of programs that MySQL recognizes. The client group enables you to specify options for using the MySQL Client application you installed. The two simple directives here specify 3306 as the port to connect to when using the client as well as the location of the socket file.

The mysqld portion specifies the same directives with the addition of two new variables as well: key_buffer_size and max_allowed_packet. You can find the exact meaning of these two directives in Appendix B. For now you should just be aware of the format they are specified in. They appear much as a command-line directive but without the preceding two dashes (--). The last group, mysqldump, sets the type of dump to be quick. This can be overwritten by specifying a new option on the command line.

Now that you have seen an example of a global configuration file, let's take a look at a few options that would be set in a typical user configuration file:

```
[client]
password="my_password"

[mysql]
no-auto-rehash
set-variable = connect_timeout=2

[mysqlhotcopy]
interactive-timeout
```

Here you can see that you can specify a password for this particular user. This would enable the user not to have to specify the password each time they connect to the database when using the MySQL Client. The other two groups set variables and directives that are applicable to a specific user rather than to all users on the system.

Using Environment Variables

As we mentioned, it is also possible to specify MySQL options by using environment variables. To do so on your Fedora server, you can simply use the variable name followed by your value:

```
MYSQL_TCP_PORT=3306
```

This of course will last only as long as you don't log out. To have these settings permanently take effect, you would need to add them to your `.bash_profile` file located in your home directory. In addition, you should use the `export` command to export this variable so that it is available to the parent process and its children or scripts. On the line following your declaration, use the following:

```
export MYSQL_TCP_PORT
```

Using Command-Line Directives

Now that we have covered two of the three ways to specify directives and variables for MySQL, let's take a look at the final method of specifying a directive: as an option from the command line. This is done by using the standard method of flags or options as in most command-line programs. Simply use double dashes in front of your directive and specify the option. For the complete list, see Appendix B or run the `mysqld --help` command.

Configuring MySQL to Start During Boot

Like all of the services you have installed and will be installing, you want MySQL to start up during the boot process. Follow these steps:

1. Copy the `mysql.server` file into the `/etc/init.d` directory:

```
cp /usr/local/mysql/share/mysql/mysql.server /etc/init.d/
```

2. Use the `chkconfig` command to add your new service:

```
chkconfig --add mysql.server
```

That's it; during your next reboot, MySQL will start up automatically with any of the options you have specified in your configuration files. You can try it now if you wish. After you are finished, you will be ready to move on to security.

Enhancing Security

As with all of your applications, you want to make sure that MySQL is secure from any types of attacks. In most cases, for smaller web applications it is not necessary for a client or user to access MySQL from outside the network or even from a remote computer. If you will be using PHP installed on the same machine to access your data, you can make sure your firewall does not allow outside access to port 3036. This port is the default port for MySQL. You might have changed this during your installation or with your configuration files, but for the purposes of this book we will be assuming you are connecting through port 3036.

Follow these steps to ensure that your firewall is setup correctly for your particular installation:

1. Take a look at your firewall rules and make sure that this port is closed. Issue the following command:

   ```
   iptables -L
   ```

   If you followed along with our chapters on firewall rules and security, this port should already be closed and you should be returned something similar to the following:

   ```
   Chain INPUT (policy ACCEPT)
   target prot opt source      destination
   ACCEPT icmp --  anywhere    anywhere      state ESTABLISHED
   ACCEPT tcp  --  anywhere    anywhere      state ESTABLISHED
   ACCEPT udp  --  anywhere    anywhere      state ESTABLISHED
   ACCEPT tcp  --  anywhere    anywhere      tcp dpt:ssh
   ACCEPT tcp  --  anywhere    anywhere      tcp dpt:smtp
   ACCEPT tcp  --  anywhere    anywhere      tcp dpt:pop3
   ACCEPT tcp  --  anywhere    anywhere      tcp dpt:imap
   ACCEPT udp  --  anywhere    anywhere      udp dpt:domain
   ACCEPT tcp  --  anywhere    anywhere      tcp dpt:domain
   ACCEPT tcp  --  anywhere    anywhere      tcp dpt:http
   ACCEPT tcp  --  anywhere    anywhere      tcp dpt:https
   ACCEPT icmp --  anywhere    anywhere
   DROP   all  --  anywhere    anywhere
   ```

   As you might notice from this `iptables -L` output, there is nothing mentioned about MySQL, so therefore the ports are closed from outside traffic.

2. From this point, you have two choices depending on your needs and configuration. If you need to be able to access MySQL from outside your network, open the appropriate port (3306 by default) by adding one of the following to your firewall script.

WARNING   We *strongly* recommend that if you will be opening a port, you configure your server for SSL. Otherwise, all the information in your database will be transferred as plain text between your servers.

To allow anyone to access MySQL, add this:

```
$IPTABLES -A INPUT -p tcp --dport 3306 -j ACCEPT
```

Or, to allow only one IP address to access MySQL:

```
$IPTABLES -A INPUT -p tcp --dport 3306 -s [IP ADDRESS] \
-j ACCEPT
```

NOTE   You can have multiple rules for different IP addresses to access MySQL. If you want to allow an entire subnet, use an IP range such as 192.168.0.1/24.

3. Remember to restart your firewall by either running the firewall script directly or by using the service you created:

```
/usr/local/etc/firewall
```

Optionally:

```
service firewall restart
```

If you do not need to access MySQL Server from outside your network, you can simply leave your firewall rules alone.

You should then turn your attention to a few other things. In our previous examples of starting MySQL Server, you used the command --user=mysql. This ensured that MySQL was run as the user mysql, which you created before your installation procedure. The reason for this change is due largely to the file command within MySQL. The file command enables a user of MySQL Server to read any file that can be accessed by the user running the server. If MySQL Server was running as root, any user would be able to access and read any file within your system. This presents an obvious security hole.

To correct the problem:

1. Create an /etc/my.cnf file if you have not already done so. Then add the following lines to your file:

```
[mysqld]
user=mysql
```

This directive will tell the MySQL daemon to run as the user mysql each time it starts. This is the easiest and most secure way to specify this.

2. Another directive that you might want to add is --skip-simlink. This prevents users from using symbolic links to any of your MySQL tables and potentially deleting them at will if they have access. To prevent this, add a line under your mysqld group within the file you just created (or modified), /etc/my.cnf. The line should read as follows:

```
--skip-symbolic-links
```

In addition to adding both of these directives, there are also a few other concerns when administering your MySQL Server:

- Never grant the *super* privilege to any users who will not be trusted administrators. This would allow the user to terminate client connections, alter server operation by changing system variables, and control replication servers—not advised for your average user.

- Take care when granting the file privilege to nonadministrative users. Although you are not running your MySQL Server as root, you are running it as mysql, and mysql has access to all of the databases within your system. Having this privilege also allows a user to write a file to any areas of the filesystem where mysql has access.

- If your DNS is not a trusted source, do not use hostnames when granting privileges. Instead, use IP addresses to specify where a user is allowed access from. This of course does not apply if all of your users will be accessing your system from only the local server.

Let's take a closer look at some additional startup directives that can be used to tighten security in your system. Remember that any of these can be added to your /etc/my.cnf files to automatically be taken into account when MySQL Server is run, or any other MySQL service as well.

local-infile=0   Specifying this directive prevents the usage of local when using a load data statement. This will stop users from reading files on your system that the mysql user has access to.

safe-user-create   If this option is enabled, a user cannot create new users with the grant statement unless the user has privileges to the mysql.user table. We will cover user creation and privilege granting in more depth later in this chapter.

skip-grant-tables   This option gives every user *full access* to every database and table on your system. This is not recommended unless only one user will be using the database.

skip-name-resolve   This will tighten down your privileges system by allowing only IP addresses to be specified in your grant tables.

skip-networking   This tells the MySQL Server to allow connections only through the mysql.sock file. This can be useful if only local users will be accessing the MySQL Server.

After you have followed all the instructions within this section, you should have a secure database server. You should still take care, however, when assigning privileges to MySQL users. You should never give more access than is needed to any single user. We will be covering this in greater detail in the next section, "Performing MySQL Administration."

Performing MySQL Administration

This section will cover the basics of administering your MySQL Server. There are a variety of methods to accomplish any given task for your MySQL Server. In this section we will show you how to use the command-line tools that MySQL provides with its installation as well as some basic MySQL Client work to create and administer databases and users. We will also cover how to correctly back up and restore your databases to minimize data loss during a disaster recovery or if a user has accidentally deleted or corrupted their data.

Using Command-Line Tools

MySQL offers a variety of commands to accomplish administrative tasks for your MySQL Server. When used properly, these commands will enable you to perform more advanced tasks with ease and efficiency. All of the commands that we will cover are located in the /usr/local/ mysql/bin directory. If you need to access these commands frequently, you might wish to create symbolic links to them within your /usr/local/bin directory. This will, of course, prevent having to type the full pathname before each command. You could also opt to add the directory to your path configuration.

Because each one of these commands offers a wide variety of options, we will cover only the basic usage of each. If you need more information for any given command, you should consult the MySQL documentation, Section 8. You can also use the --help flag or man command for additional information about any command as well.

myisampack

This is the MySQL Compressed Read-Only Table Generator. This utility is used to compress MyISAM tables. Each column is compressed separately and will usually result in the file size being reduced by about 40 percent to 70 percent. When the table is read later, the required information will then be uncompressed and read into memory. You should note that when a table becomes compressed, it also becomes read-only. This is useful for databases that will be placed onto a read-only media such as a CD-ROM.

To invoke the command, you should use the following syntax:

```
myisampack [options] filename ...
```

Each filename in this instance should be the name of an index file denoted in MySQL by the .myi extension. There are about 13 options that you can specify to myisampack and that can be found by using the --help flag.

After you have compressed a table, it is generally a good rule of thumb to use the following:

```
myisamchk -rq --sort-index --analyze table_name.MYI
```

This will re-create and sort your indexes. This will serve as an excellent optimization to your database by enabling MySQL to locate rows quicker. If you ever need to uncompress a database to make modifications, you can use the `myisamchk` command with the `--unpack` command.

mysql

The `mysql` command is your *client*. This command provides a simple SQL shell so that you can administer your server or any given database. To invoke the MySQL shell, you use this command:

```
mysql db_name
```

This will tell MySQL Client to start and automatically begin using the database specified. This will not work, however, if user/password access is required. Instead you should use this:

```
mysql db_name -u username -p
```

MySQL will then prompt you to enter your password on the following line. Entering the correct password will take you to a MySQL prompt. If you attempt to access a database that you do not have access to, or if your password is incorrect, you will receive an error message similar to the following:

```
ERROR 1045 (28000): Access denied for user: 'username'@'hostname' (Using
password: YES)
```

As with all the other MySQL command-line operations, a plethora of options are available. Each of these options can also be specified in a `my.cnf` file under the `[client]` grouping and can be found by using the `--help` flag.

After you have successfully logged in to the client, there are a variety of commands you can use that are specific to the MySQL Client. Here is the output you should receive when you use the `help` command:

```
MySQL commands:
?          (\h)    Synonym for 'help'.
clear      (\c)    Clear command.
connect    (\r)    Reconnect to the server.
                   Optional arguments are db and host.
delimiter  (\d)    Set query delimiter.
edit       (\e)    Edit command with $EDITOR.
ego        (\G)    Send command to mysql server,
                   display result vertically.
exit       (\q)    Exit mysql. Same as quit.
go         (\g)    Send command to mysql server.
help       (\h)    Display this help.
nopager    (\n)    Disable pager, print to stdout.
notee      (\t)    Don't write into outfile.
```

```
pager      (\P)    Set PAGER [to_pager].
                   Print the query results via PAGER.
print      (\p)    Print current command.
prompt     (\R)    Change your mysql prompt.
quit       (\q)    Quit mysql.
rehash     (\#)    Rebuild completion hash.
source     (\.)    Execute an SQL script file.
                   Takes a file name as an argument.
status     (\s)    Get status information from the server.
system     (\!)    Execute a system shell command.
tee        (\T)    Set outfile [to_outfile].
                   Append everything into given outfile.
use        (\u)    Use another database.
                   Takes database name as argument.
```

For a more detailed description, refer to the MySQL documentation. For now you should be aware of the options and know that you exit from the SQL shell by using the quit command. MySQL will tell you "bye," and you will be dropped back into your Linux shell.

mysqladmin

Earlier in this chapter, we covered one of the many usages of the mysqladmin command by showing you how to change a password for a user. In this section, we've put together a list of commands you can specify with mysqladmin that will enable you to perform administrative tasks on the server as well as check the current status. The proper usage of the command is as follows:

```
mysqladmin [options] command [command-option] command ...
```

You can find a full list of options by using the --help flag as always. For now, familiarize yourself with the capabilities of this command-line program so that you can return to this section later as a reference when you need to administer your server. It can often be easier to use these commands than to log in by using a client and perform much more complicated commands to accomplish the same results:

create databasename   Create a new database.

drop databasename   Delete a database and all its tables.

extended-status   Display the server status variables and their values.

flush-hosts   Flush all information in the host cache.

flush-logs   Flush all logs.

flush-privileges   Reload the grant tables (same as reload).

flush-status   Clear status variables.

flush-tables   Flush all tables.

flush-threads   Flush the thread cache. (Added in MySQL 3.23.16.)

kill *id,id,...*   Kill server threads.

password *new-password*   Set a new password. This changes the password to *new-password* for the account that you use with mysqladmin for connecting to the server.

ping   Check whether the server is alive.

processlist   Show a list of active server threads. This is like the output of the SHOW PROCESSLIST statement. If the --verbose option is given, the output is like that of SHOW FULL PROCESSLIST.

reload   Reload the grant tables.

refresh   Flush all tables, and close and open log files.

shutdown   Stop the server.

start-slave   Start replication on a slave server. (Added in MySQL 3.23.16.)

status   Display a short server status message.

stop-slave   Stop replication on a slave server. (Added in MySQL 3.23.16.)

variables   Display the server system variables and their values.

version   Display version information from the server.

mysqlbinlog

This command enables you to examine the contents of a binary log file. A *binary log file* stores a history of commands that have modified any data. Therefore, if an update command is performed and no rows were matched and updated, it would not be located in a log file. These occurrences are then stored along with various other information such as timestamp, issuing thread, time the statement took, and so on.

The correct syntax for mysqlbinlog usage is as follows:

```
mysqlbinlog [options] log_file ...
```

It is also possible to pipe those results back into the MySQL Client for execution. This would enable you to apply all changes to a database that were made after a certain time (since the last backup). This is an excellent tool that will be covered in more depth in the section "Backing Up and Restoring Databases."

mysqlcheck

The mysqlcheck command is used to analyze, optimize, and repair MyISAM tables. This command must be used while the database server is running. This can be a huge benefit in a production environment when taking down the entire server is not an option to check or repair a single database. You can specify a single database, multiple databases, or all databases to check or repair. Here are the three methods:

```
mysqlcheck [options] db_name [tables]
mysqlcheck [options] --databases DB1 [DB2 DB3 ...]
mysqlcheck [options] --all-databases
```

The mysqlcheck command is unique in that you can rename the file or create a symbolic link under a different name that will specify a different default option. For example, if you were to rename mysqlcheck to mysqlrepair, the command would then perform an -r operation. You can also use mysqlanalyze for -a, and mysqloptimize for -o.

mysqldump

The mysqldump command is an important command that you will most likely be using quite frequently during your affair with MySQL. You can specify one or more databases by using the same syntax as mysqlcheck:

```
mysqldump [options] db_name [tables]
mysqldump [options] --databases DB1 [DB2 DB3 ...]
mysqldump [options] --all-databases
```

If you are going to be dumping a very large database, you should make sure you specify the --quick flag. This will cause MySQL to not load the entire result into memory before dumping the result. In addition to the quick option, a large number of options are available for this command. Many of them will enable you to dump the data into virtually any other text data type. You could if you wished create a flat-file database from this command. One of the simplest and most common usages for a situation like this is to create a CSV file.

mysqlhotcopy

This command is the quickest way to make a backup of a database. This command can be run only on the local machine that the MySQL Server data directory resides on, and uses a Perl script to quickly copy the database. The proper usage is as follows:

```
mysqlhotcopy db_name [/path/to/new/directory/]
mysqlhotcopy db_name_1 ... /path/to/new/directory/
mysqlhotcopy db_name./regex/
```

For more information on options for this command, refer to the manual or MySQL documentation.

NOTE   This program might require the installation of the DBI (DataBase Interface) Perl module. This is available from CPAN for installation.

mysqlimport

This command provides the same functionality as using the LOAD DATA INFILES SQL statement. From the command line you can tell MySQL to load data stored in a text file located on your system. To do so, use the following syntax:

```
mysqlimport [options] database textfile1 [textfile2 ...]
```

As with mysqldump, you can specify many options to tell MySQL what format the text-file data is in. It is recommended that you attempt this command on a new table or database and check your results before overwriting your actual data. This would afford you the opportunity to correct any mistakes ahead of time and ensure much less pain and suffering.

mysqlshow

This command can be used to quickly examine the contents of a database, table, table columns, and/or table indexes. This command provides the same functionality as the SQL command SHOW. When using the command, you should follow this syntax:

```
mysqlshow [options] [database [table [column]]]
```

If any of the parameters are left out when using this command, it is assumed you are using a wildcard. For example, if you leave off the table, all tables will be displayed. This command also supports the usage of wildcards for a parameter as well.

perror

This command enables you to obtain a more verbose version of an error code you might receive. Any time you see an error message in MySQL, it will present you with an error number in the following form:

```
message ... (errno: #)
message ... (Errcode: #)
```

You can then take these error numbers and pass them into perror to receive a better explanation of what the error means. The correct syntax is as follows:

```
perror [options] errorcode ...
```

The perror command will then return a statement that looks like the following:

```
Error code 13: Permission Denied
```

replace

The `replace` utility enables you to change strings in place in files or in standard input. For example, the following statement will replace `foo` with `bar`, and `bar` with `foo`, in files `mine` and `yours`.

```
replace 'foo' 'bar' 'bar' 'foo' -- mine yours
```

You should take note that the dashes (`--`) represent where the replacements end and the file list begins. If you wish to change strings in piped input, you can leave off the `--` and the filenames.

Creating and Administering Databases

This section will cover how to view, create, edit, and delete databases on your MySQL Server. You will be using SQL commands from the MySQL Client SQL shell. You could, however, also perform these operations by using `mysqladmin`. If you would like, you can refer to the previous section about the administration command-line tool and attempt to perform the same actions. We will be covering the SQL usage because it is applicable to almost any database.

To start, follow these steps to access the SQL shell:

1. Log in to MySQL through the client:

    ```
    /usr/local/bin/mysql -u root -p
    ```

2. Enter your password if prompted. After a welcome message is displayed, you will then be taken to a prompt similar to the following:

    ```
    Welcome to the MySQL monitor. Commands end with ; or \g.
    Your MySQL connection id is 12 to server version: 5.0.0

    Type 'help;' or '\h' for help. Type '\c' to clear the buffer.
    ```

    ```
    mysql>
    ```

Now you can begin learning a little about MySQL and its SQL commands. Note that we will be omitting the `mysql>` prompt from our commands to make room for longer SQL commands that might need to be executed.

The first thing you will want to do is learn how to view the databases currently running on your server. Use:

```
SHOW DATABASES;
```

Notice that the line ends in a semicolon (`;`). This denotes the end of a command in SQL and allows for commands that span across multiple lines. If you accidentally forget your semicolon, do not fear. You only need to enter a semicolon on the next line and press Enter to complete your SQL statement. That being said, let's take a look at the output and see what you have:

```
+----------+
| Database |
+----------+
| mysql    |
| test     |
+----------+
2 rows in set (0.05 sec)
```

Some nicely formatted ASCII for you. Here you can see that you are listing the databases, seen in the title of the column at the top of the return. You also see that you have two active databases: mysql and test.

WARNING   Don't delete the mysql database. This contains all of your system variables, users, and privileges.

The test database was created during your installation procedure and is provided here so you can see that everything is functioning normally.

Next, try deleting your test database. Use this command:

```
DROP DATABASE test;
```

Notice here that you are using uppercase (CAPS) to express SQL commands, as we discussed earlier in this chapter. You should know that the actual commands are case insensitive, meaning you can use upper, lower, or mixed case. The names of databases, tables, columns, and so on are case sensitive. We express the statements by using uppercase for syntax for readability purposes only.

With that out of the way, let's break down your statement. First you have DROP, which tells MySQL you will be dropping something, or removing it. Next you tell MySQL what type of thing you are dropping. In this case you are dropping a DATABASE. Finally, you tell MySQL which database you are dropping: test. You will be returned a single-row message, as follows:

```
Query OK, 0 rows affected (0.36 sec)
```

That's all there is to it. Now that it's gone, however, you need a new one. Use this command:

```
CREATE DATABASE test;
```

Here you have the same format as DROP but you have replaced the command with CREATE. The preceding statement will create a new, empty database named test and print out the following message letting you know everything was successful:

```
Query OK, 1 row affected (0.02 sec)
```

Now let's begin using the database and learn how to create and delete tables. To do this, you will need to specify the USE command exactly as follows:

```
USE test;
```

After the command has been executed, you will be told

```
Database Changed
```

Now you can view the tables in your test database:

```
SHOW TABLES;
Empty set (0.00 sec)
```

You should receive the preceding output after entering your command, letting you know that there are currently no tables available in your test database to show.

Adding a table is a bit more complex then adding a database. Adding a table requires that you specify types and sizes for each column within the table. We will show only one example of a table addition because this book is focused on setting up and administering your server. There are many good books dedicated to teaching you MySQL and SQL statements should you need further instruction. For now, let's assume you need to create a simple table called food. The food table will have three columns: food_id, food_name, and expiration_date. To create this table, you will use the following syntax:

```
CREATE TABLE food (
food_id INT(11),
food_name VARCHAR(30),
expiration_date DATE
);
```

As a result, you should see a Query OK statement and be returned to a SQL prompt.

Let's break down the statement and see what happened. First, you told MySQL that you would be creating a new table with the name food. Then you used parentheses to house each column separated by commas. Each column is specified by using the column name followed by its type. There are many types of columns supported by MySQL, many of which require additional parameters to be set up correctly. The INT specification, which stands for Integer, needs to know the maximum length allowed for the Integer value for each row. The VARCHAR specification needs to know the maximum length of the VARiable CHARacter it is allowed to store. The DATE specification does not require any additional parameters. Now let's check the results of your handy work by using the SHOW TABLES command again. This time you should see the following:

```
+---------------+
| Tables_in_test |
+---------------+
| food          |
+---------------+
1 row in set (0.01 sec)
```

Here you can see your first table had been correctly inserted into the database.

Now take a look at the details of the table by using a new command, DESCRIBE:

```
DESCRIBE food;
```

You should then be given a result as follows:

```
+-----------------+-------------+------+-----+---------+-------+
| Field           | Type        | Null | Key | Default | Extra |
+-----------------+-------------+------+-----+---------+-------+
| food_id         | int(11)     | YES  |     | NULL    |       |
| food_name       | varchar(30) | YES  |     | NULL    |       |
| expiration_date | date        | YES  |     | NULL    |       |
+-----------------+-------------+------+-----+---------+-------+
3 rows in set (0.01 sec)
```

Here, formatted nicely with ASCII characters, you can see each column name listed along with its type, null, key, default, and extra values. These values call all be changed through other commands and during the table creation. Because of the complex nature of the many possibilities of MySQL, we will not be covering this in depth.

Now that you have your table, drop the table:

```
DROP TABLE food;
```

You can follow it up with this command:

```
DROP DATABASE test;
```

You will once again have a clean installation with only your mysql database installed. With these exercises completed, you will be ready to move on to administering users within MySQL.

Creating and Administering Users

If you are logged in to the MySQL Client, go ahead and quit so you can reenter by using a database from the command line. Because all privileges and user accounts are modified through the mysql database, use the following command to launch the client:

```
/usr/local/mysql/bin/mysql -u root mysql -p
```

After you have entered your password, you will once again be brought into the database, but this time you will receive a slightly different message letting you know that MySQL has read the table information into memory for quicker queries.

In this section, we will show you several GRANT statements that allow for varying levels of access to be assigned to a user. The first one we will show you is the way to create a *super user*, someone who has access to all commands for all databases and tables as well as the ability to create new users.

The following is the correct syntax for a user named `eric` with a password of `inst1234` who is allowed to access the system from `localhost` only:

```
GRANT ALL PRIVILEGES ON *.* TO 'eric'@'localhost'
 IDENTIFIED BY 'inst1234' WITH GRANT OPTION;
```

Using the `GRANT` command does not require that you use that `PASSWORD()` function because it is already taken care of for you. You will not need to use the `FLUSH PRIVILEGES` command either, as you would normally need to if you were to use a direct `INSERT` statement.

The syntax of the preceding `GRANT` statement is to use `GRANT` and then pass in the privileges. Next you specify `ON`, followed by which databases and tables you are granting privileges to. Then you use `TO`, followed by the *username @ hostname*. You can choose to leave off this option because most users will not need to grant privileges to other users.

Here is another example of creating a new user. This is much like the previous example but instead provides access only to all tables on one specific database and does not enable the user to grant privileges:

```
GRANT ALL PRIVILEGES ON test.* TO 'eric'@'localhost' IDENTIFIED BY 'inst1234';
```

This example is easy enough to follow; we simply changed the wildcard where the database name was to an actual database and left off the `WITH` statement. You could further narrow their restrictions by replacing the wildcard located after the database name with a table name. This would only allow the given user access to that single table.

Now let's take a look at another way to create an account. This example creates an account with no access but to use the MySQL Server, and this user doesn't require a password to connect:

```
GRANT USAGE ON *.* TO 'eric'@'localhost';
```

That's all there is to it—very simple.

Next you'll be looking into a more practical application. You do not want all users to have all privileges or no privileges for your database server. More than likely you will want them to be able to administer the databases they have access to, but no more. To do so, you can replace the `ALL PRIVILEGES` or `USAGE` portion with a comma-separated list of the privileges you wish grant.

The following is a typical setup for the `eric` user identified by a password of `inst1234` who can use the server from any subdomain of `mydomain.com`. Notice you will need to use a wildcard here, and in MySQL the wildcard symbol for this instance is a percent symbol (%). The `eric` user will have access only to the `freak` database:

```
GRANT SELECT,INSERT,UPDATE,DELETE,CREATE,DROP ON freak.* TO 'eric'@'localhost'
 IDENTIFIED BY 'inst1234';
```

Easy enough.

You are now ready to create new users at will for your MySQL Server. After creating a few test users, though, you might wish to delete them. To do so, you use the REVOKE command in addition to the DROP USER statement. These need to be performed in order to ensure that the user is completely eradicated. First you will need to REVOKE all privileges associated with a user:

```
REVOKE ALL PRIVILEGES ON *.* FROM 'eric'@'localhost';
REVOKE GRANT OPTION ON *.* FROM 'eric'@'localhost';
```

This user will no longer have any privileges on the system including the GRANT ability. After this is complete, you will need to use the following:

```
DELETE FROM mysql.user WHERE User='eric';
FLUSH PRIVILEGES;
```

This removes all users named eric from any host. After you have completed the deletion, flush the privileges to force MySQL to reload all privileges. With that done, you are now ready to begin administering the users of your MySQL Server.

Backing Up and Restoring Databases

The easiest and most efficient way to perform a backup of a database or all databases is by using the mysqldump command we covered earlier in this chapter. We talked about how you can specify --all-databases or any number of databases and tables. For the purpose of this chapter, we will be running a backup of all databases. You might wish to perform a backup of some databases more often then others. It is now up to you, the system administrator, to judge how important your data is and determine how often you should back up that data. You can choose to have a script run by the cron daemon if you wish or you can choose to back up the server manually. We of course recommend using an automated script because the human memory is anything but infallible.

The command you should be using within your script to back up all databases should read like the following:

```
mysqldump -uuser -ppassword --all-databases > /path/to/backup/dir/filename.sql
```

This will ensure that all of your databases are then backed up to the location you specify. Additionally, the backup script you have already created, if following along with the book, will backup these backup files to your remote server for safe keeping. You might wish, however, to dump each database individually rather than all together. This makes it easier to rebuild your database(s) should anything go wrong. You can use a command similar to the following:

```
mysqldump --flush-logs --quick --add-drop-table --extended-insert  --add-locks
-uusername -ppassword database > /path/to/backup/dir/filename.sql
```

NOTE   You might also wish to create a separate user who has only the SELECT and LOCK TABLES privileges just for the purposes of backing up your databases.

Restoring your database is nearly as simple, and you will be happy to know that you can recover to an even more recent state then your last backup. However you must have the `--log-bin` option enabled when running the server. To do so, simply place the directive in your /etc/ `my.cnf` file. All changes made to the database will then be saved in `hostname-bin.xxx` files.

To perform a full recovery, if you have dumped each database individually, first locate your most recent `mysqldump` files and perform the following command for each database that needs to be recovered:

```
mysql -uuser -p database < filename.sql
```

This will then return your database to the state it was during the last backup. To bring your database, further up-to-date you can then use the following command to execute all binary (bin), logs on your database:

```
mysqlbinlog hostname-bin.[0-9]* | mysql -uuser -p
```

Enter your password when prompted, and all queries will then be run on your database.

NOTE The preceding statement will execute *all* bin logs on your database. For practical application, you will want to locate the file that has the closest date to your backup and use the
bin logs starting from that point.

Performance and Replication

Performance and replication can be a complicated issue. With thousands, if not millions, of possible setups, each installation is unique. Truly tuning a server to reach maximum performance requires an understanding of the entire system. This type of understanding reaches a level that is beyond the scope of this book. (See Appendix C, "Getting Support," for a list of books and other resources.) For now, we are going to cover some of the more simple procedures and methods of using multiple database servers through replication via a master/slave approach.

Replication enables you to run multiple database servers that share the same information. For large-scale projects, this becomes necessary in order to keep queries down to acceptable speeds. If your single database server is being backlogged with requests, and you have made every effort to optimize your queries by adding additional indexes and perhaps additional reference tables for quicker lookups, it is time to consider using replication to enhance your application.

Replication is accomplished by MySQL by having the master server keep track of all changes. Therefore, it is necessary to have binary logging enabled for your master server. Each slave server then receives these logging statements from the master server so that it can process the same commands on itself. Remember that the binary log stores only queries and statements that have actually modified data. This prevents a slave server from running needless queries taking up valuable resources.

When setting up your slave servers, you must have an exact copy of each database to be replicated in place on each slave server. This way, when the binary log makes a change, each database on each slave server will be an exact duplicate. To do this, you can use the LOAD DATA FROM MASTER command. This command uses a global lock on the master server to ensure that all data is replicated at that point in time. This works only for MyISAM tables, however, and you will need to specify additional privileges your slave account on the master. After you use this command, the slave transfers all data from the master. Then, after the slave is started, it establishes a connection and waits for any additional data that is written to the binary log file. If the server for some reason loses its connection, it will attempt to reestablish that connection every 60 seconds. You can change this by using the --master-connect-retry directive.

NOTE   The master is never aware of how many slave servers are present.

Understanding How Replication Threads Work

Before you begin issuing commands to set up your master and slave servers, let's take a closer look at how replication works in regard to threads. On the master server, there will be one thread for each slave. Each of these threads is referred to as the *BinLog Dump thread* and it is in charge of sending each new statement that updates data to a slave. Each slave server will run two additional threads: I/O and SQL. The *I/O thread* is the thread that connects to the master server and receives the commands from the BinLog Dump thread. These commands are then copied to local files for processing by the *SQL thread*. These files are called *relay logs*.

Using these two separate slave threads enables the slave server to separate the reading and execution of the statements. Therefore, the reading of the statements from the master is not slowed down by SQL's ability to process these statements. This allows for a type of queue. To view these threads later, after your installation is complete, you can use the SHOW PROCESSLIST command. To make this a bit easier to read, try substituting the semicolon normally used to end a command with \G. This will give you a vertical print for better human readability. Performing this command on a slave server will give you an output similar to the following:

```
*************************** 1. row ***************************
     Id: 10
   User: system user
   Host:
     db: NULL
Command: Connect
   Time: 11
  State: Waiting for master to send event
   Info: NULL
*************************** 2. row ***************************
     Id: 11
   User: system user
```

```
      Host:
        db: NULL
   Command: Connect
      Time: 11
     State: Has read all relay log; waiting for the slave I/O
            thread to update it
      Info: NULL
```

In this example, thread 10 is your I/O thread, and thread 11 is your SQL thread. These states, however, can change depending on what action they are performing. Your master server's BinLog Dump thread can have the following states:

Sending binlog event to slave   This means that the master has received a statement that has updated its binlog and it is currently sending this information to the slave.

Finished reading one binlog; switching to the next binlog   This means that the master server has finished reading a binlog and is opening the next to send to the slave.

Has sent all binlog to slave; waiting for binlog to be updated   Quite verbose, this means that the slave I/O thread has read all the statements sent by the master.

Waiting to finalize termination   You will most likely not see this state appear because it occurs for only the brief moment the thread is stopping.

Each thread has its own thread states that will be given. The slave I/O thread can have the following states:

Connecting to master   The thread is attempting to connect to the master.

Checking master version   This status is displayed for a brief moment after a connection with the master has been established.

Registering slave on master   This status is displayed for a brief moment after a connection with the master has been established.

Requesting binlog dump   This status is displayed for a brief moment after a connection with the master has been established. This is the request to the master for the contents of its bin log.

Waiting to reconnect after a failed binlog dump request   This state is displayed during the time the thread is "asleep," while it is waiting for the timeout to connect again.

Reconnecting after a failed binlog dump request   The slave I/O thread is attempting to reconnect to the master.

Waiting for master to send event   This is the idle status of the thread. When the I/O thread has read all the changes to the database and the master is not currently updating and sending new events, the I/O thread will read this state.

Queuing master event to the relay log   The I/O thread has received a new event and is currently writing it to the relay log.

Waiting to reconnect after a failed master event read   An error has occurred in the connection, and the thread is waiting for the appropriate timeout to occur so that it can attempt to reconnect to the master.

Reconnecting after a failed master event read   The thread is currently attempting to reconnect.

Waiting for the slave SQL thread to free enough relay log space   This means that the SQL thread is currently backed up with work and that the relay log size has reached its maximum. This shows only if you have specifically set the relay log space limit.

Waiting for slave mutex on exit   This is a brief state denoting the thread is stopping.

The last thread, the SQL thread, has the least amount of states because of its single purpose of processing events from the relay log. Listed here are its states:

Reading an event from the relay log   The thread is reading an event from the relay log for processing.

Has read all relay log; waiting for the slave I/O thread to update it   All events from the relay log have been processed. This is the SQL thread's idle state.

Waiting for slave mutex on exit   This is a brief state denoting the thread is stopping.

Introduction to Replication Application

With an understanding of how MySQL database replication works and an insight into the responsibilities of each applicable thread, you can now take a look at the process for creating a replication setup. This is not the only way to set up replication; there are many techniques. It will, however, give you a straightforward method that works.

1. First, you must have valid installations of MySQL on each server for your replication process. We will be using two servers, but you can use as many as you wish, performing the actions on each slave server when we perform them on our single slave server.

2. Next you will need to make a few changes to your my.cnf files if they do not already exist. On your master server you should have /etc/my.cnf, including the following two lines:

   ```
   [mysqld]
   log-bin
   server_id=1
   ```

   This will enable the bin logs as we discussed earlier as well as provide this server with a unique ID. Remember that each server must have a unique ID and be an integer from 1 to 2^{32}. On each slave server you will need to add a `server_id` value to the `/etc/my.cnf` files as well. After you have made these changes, restart each of the servers so that the changes will take effect.

3. Next, you will need to set up an account on the master server that the slave will be using to connect. A special privilege is required for this user, called `REPLICATION SLAVE`. Because you will be using this account for replication only, you do not need to assign any additional privileges. If you are using more than one slave server, you do not need to create multiple users. In this example, you will be creating a user named `slave_account` with a password of `yes_master`. You should make sure that this slave server can access the master only from the domain it resides in, which will be `mydomain.com`. To create the account, you will be using the MySQL Client. Log in as the `root` user and issue the following `GRANT` command:

```
GRANT REPLICATION SLAVE ON *.*
TO 'slave_account'@'mydomain.com'
IDENTIFIED BY 'yes_master';
```

NOTE   Remember that if you are planning on using the LOAD DATA FROM MASTER command on your slave, you will need to add additional privileges to the account. You should grant the SUPER and RELOAD privileges to this account in addition to SELECT privileges for each table that will be replicated. For the purposes of this book, we will be using the `tar` command to copy our database so we will not be assigning these privileges.

4. Now, with your user created, you will need to lock the current state of your database. Perform the following:

```
FLUSH TABLES WITH READ LOCK;
```

This prevents any changes from taking effect while you `tar` the database and transfer it to your slave server(s).

WARNING   If you exit the MySQL Client in this terminal (or terminal window) it may cause MySQL to remove the read lock. It is recommended that you open a new terminal and stay connected the MySQL Client.

5. With the database locked, open a new terminal window or switch to a different terminal and move into the `/usr/local/mysql/var` directory.

6. Perform the following:

```
tar -cvf /tmp/mysql.snapshot.1.tar .
```

This backs up your database to the `tmp` directory. If you wish to use only a specific database, then use the `tar` command to `tar` only that database. You might also wish to exclude the `mysql` database from your `tar` so that the user accounts and privileges will not be transferred over.

7. Return to MySQL Client and use this command:

   ```
   SHOW MASTER STATUS;
   ```

   This presents you with the bin log file and offset where the newest record is currently located for your snapshot.

8. Write this information down! You will need it later. The printed results should look similar to the following:

   ```
   +---------------+----------+--------------+------------------+
   | File          | Position | Binlog_Do_DB | Binlog_Ignore_DB |
   +---------------+----------+--------------+------------------+
   | mysql-bin.003 | 73       | test,bar     | foo,manual,mysql |
   +---------------+----------+--------------+------------------+
   ```

   Here you see the current file is mysql-bin.003, and the offset is 73.

1. Now you can unlock the tables by using this command:

   ```
   UNLOCK TABLES;
   ```

2. Transfer the /tmp/mysql.snapshot.1.tar file to each of your slave servers' /tmp directories. You can choose any manner you wish to do this.

3. Move into your slave servers' data directories and untar the file and restart the servers.

4. Log in to the MySQL Client for each slave and perform the following command:

   ```
   CHANGE MASTER TO
   MASTER_HOST='masterHostName',
   MASTER_USER='slave_account',
   MASTER_PASSWORD='yes_master',
   MASTER_LOG_FILE='recorded binlog name',
   MASTER_LOG_POS=recordedOffset;
   ```

   The recorded binlog name is the name of the bin log file from the master server you received from performing the SHOW MASTER STATUS command. The recorded offset is the offset you received from the same print statement.

5. Run the following to place your slave server in action:

   ```
   START SLAVE;
   ```

   After you have completed this for each slave server, you will have a robust solution scalable to almost any size. If you would like to further customize your replication setup, you should look into the startup directives in Appendix B.

6. You should add the following lines to your my.cnf file to ensure that if your server has to be rebooted or MySQL restarted, everything will come back online properly:

```
[mysqld]
server-id=serverID
master-host=masterHost
master-port=3306
master-user=slaveUser
master-password=slavePassword
master-connect-retry=60
```

MySQL Installation and Administration Checklist

Congratulations on completing this chapter. We have covered a myriad of administrative tasks for your new MySQL Server as well as the entire installation process. As always, you should review the bullet points below and make sure you have a firm understanding of each of them. If you feel weak in any areas, don't be afraid to go back and experiment with creating and removing users, databases, and so on. A little practice goes a long way, and it is better to change things now before pushing your server into live usage.

You should now be familiar with the following:

- Know the differences between a database and flat files.
- Understand the limitations and advantages of MySQL.
- Know how to read the MySQL documentation.
- Download, install, and configure MySQL from source.
- Use the various command-line operations provided by the MySQL installation.
- Administer databases and users.
- Back up and restore databases.
- Set up database replication.

In the next chapter, we will cover the final piece of required software to bring your LAMP server together: PHP. You've almost made it through your entire LAMP installation so there's no need to slow down now. Take a deep breath, relax, and you'll be ready to head into Chapter 10, "PHP: Installation and Configuration."

PHP: Installation and Configuration

- Why Use PHP?

- PHP Versions

- Installing PHP

- The PHP INI File

At this point, your LAMP setup is almost complete if you have been following along in the book. You have nearly all of the elements in place to complete your LAMP acronym. Now all you have to do is install and configure PHP and you will be on your way to running a full-blown LAMP server.

PHP has been around for many years and has become a fully featured and mature programming language. If you are curious about PHP's development, please refer to Chapter 1, "Introducing LAMP"; otherwise, let's get moving along so you can learn why you should use PHP and the important features it has to offer.

Why Use PHP?

Simply stated, PHP is the fastest parsing server-side scripting language available. ASP and Java both require separate objects to be instantiated to accomplish almost any task. For instance, in ASP when a programmer uses VBScript, he is running a COM (Component Object Model) object. When he writes to the client, he's calling the `Response` COM object's `Write` method. When he accesses a database, he uses another COM object. Then when he accesses the filesystem, yet another COM object is called. Because of this, more and more resources are required to perform tasks. When hundreds or even thousands of users are accessing these pages and functionality, all this overhead adds up fast and significantly reduces system performance and speed. PHP, however, accomplishes all the preceding tasks entirely in PHP's own memory space. This of course uses drastically less resources.

Features, features, features: PHP comes installed with *tons* of support for features such as FTP, data compression, file uploads, XML (eXtensible Markup Language), MD5, e-mail, and so on. To enable these features in ASP, you would need to purchase expensive third-party packages. These hidden costs, in our opinion, are simply unacceptable—and those are just the basic options. PHP also offers complex functionality such as dynamic images, IMAP, SNMP, dynamic Flash, PDF (Portable Document Format), native access to Oracle and other DBs, LDAP (Lightweight Directory Access Protocol), and sockets. Not only that, PHP is actually more mature than ASP. ASP has been around only since 1996, whereas PHP has been in development since 1994.

Last is the cost factor. If you want to run ASP efficiently, you'll want to run Windows, probably access Microsoft SQL, most likely want Visual Studio, and probably run IIS—money, money, money, and poor performance when compared to Linux, Apache, MySQL, and PHP.

PHP, in a general sense and at its base level, is capable of creating dynamic web pages that incorporate data from databases or other sources not found directly on those web pages. PHP can also be run from the command line and can be used from `cron` jobs or even for client-side GUI applications, although these last two abilities are rarely seen.

The most likely reason for your PHP installation, however, is the ability to create client-side scripts for websites. PHP makes it easy to integrate with virtually every database available, in our case MySQL. PHP also makes efficient use of POST and GET variables sent through Apache for easy integration and manipulation. This is handy for processing HTML forms for storage into a database or sending an e-mail, and so on.

PHP Versions

PHP currently has two versions available: PHP 4.3.*x* and PHP 5.0. For this book we will be using 5.0 because it introduces an abundance of optimizations and additional functionality not seen in 4.3.*x*. PHP 5.0 also introduces Zend Engine 2. The new Zend engine has been completely rewritten to include an entirely new object model. The use of objects now includes a wide variety of new functionality not previously seen, such as private and protected methods, abstract classes and methods, interfaces, class type hints, object cloning, unified constructors, destructors, exceptions, and more. This alone, for the object-oriented coder, is more than enough reason to switch to PHP 5.0 from earlier versions.

For the procedural developers out there or for those who have less experience with PHP, there are also a myriad of new functions and additions that apply to any coding methods and standards. The XML system has been completely overhauled and will now support SimpleXML and the DOM and Extensible Stylesheet Language (XSL) extensions. New php.ini options have also been added, stream support has been improved, the GD Graphics Library extension has been improved—too many functions to list have been added, and countless bugs have been fixed.

Overall it's a good idea to install PHP 5.0 over 4.3.*x*. If you would like a full list of all the changes that have been made, you can visit the PHP site for more information and look for the change log. We just wanted to give you some insight into why we chose 5.0 for this book.

Installing PHP

PHP is your final installation before your server is complete with its core functionality. Quite a few directives can be specified both during compilation and in its configuration files. This chapter will cover all of the more common options enabling PHP to run as needed. You will probably need to go back and recompile PHP later, when you discover that you, or someone else using your server, needs to add a new library for usage within a script. Do not worry, however—after a couple of installations you'll have it down to a science.

Determining Configuration Options and Extensions

PHP itself comes with a large list of features for you to utilize. However, there are additional features you can enable by using PHP extensions. An *extension* is a group of functions and routines that are considered *extra* in that you have to manually enable them during installation. Usually, extensions require additional software installed before you can enable them.

Compiling extensions for PHP can be tricky. We recommend that if you do not need it, do not install it. A common problem with most pre-built packages for PHP is that they come with every extension installed; this reduces performance and, more important, could lead to a vulnerable system. If you can relate enabling extensions in PHP to opening ports on your system firewall that are not needed, you will have a better picture of what we mean.

Now that we have those concerns out of the way, let's take a look at *some* of the common configuration directives and extensions available for PHP. Keep in mind that because of the extremely long list of directives, we are covering only the most commonly used ones.

Common Configuration Directives

--prefix=*PREFIX*   This tells PHP to install all architecture-independent files into the supplied directory location. By default this directory is /usr/local.

--help   This prints a list of configuration directives.

--no-create   This does not create output files.

--quiet, --silent   This tells the compiler not to print checking… messages.

--version   This prints the version of autoconf that created the configure file.

Features and Packages

The following list details the flags used to enable, disable, and include or not include features and packages in your PHP compilation.

--disable-*FEATURE*   Do not include *FEATURE* (same as --enable-*FEATURE*=no).

--enable-*FEATURE*[=*ARG*]   Include *FEATURE* [ARG=yes].

--with-*PACKAGE*[=*ARG*]   Use *PACKAGE* [ARG=yes].

--without-*PACKAGE*   Do not use *PACKAGE* (same as --with-*PACKAGE*=no).

Server Application Programming Interface (SAPI)

SAPI extensions handle interaction with the web server. Because this book is written for the Apache web server, we will cover only the applicable extensions.

--with-apxs[=FILE] | --with-axps2[=FILE] The first of these tells PHP to compile as a shared object for Apache 1.3; the second is used for Apache 2.0+.

--with-apache[=DIR] This tells PHP to compile as a built-in Apache module.

--disable-cli *CLI* is the Command Line Interface. If you disable this, you will also disable the PHP Extension Application Repository (PEAR).

--disable-cgi This disables building the CGI version of PHP.

--enable-force-cgi-redirect If you will be running the CGI version of PHP, you will want to enable this feature. This tells Apache to perform a security check when using an internal redirect.

General Settings

The below list provides you with settings and options that do not directly fit into any of the other groupings we have provided:

--enable-safe-mode We will discuss this in more detail later in this chapter. In a nutshell, PHP safe mode attempts to solve shared-server security problems.

--enable-sigchild This directive is needed only when you are connecting to Oracle 8.1.0+ via the Bequeeze interface. It enables PHP's own SIGCHLD handler.

--enable-magic-quotes This enables magic quotes by default. The magic quotes feature automatically adds backslashes to POST and GET variables on your site.

--disable-ipv6 IPv6 is the new version of IP. It contains new functionality for future expansions to IP architecture and is optimized for high-performance networks such as gigabit and ATM (Asynchronous Transfer Mode) technology.

--with-mysql-sock[=DIR] This tells PHP to use the mysql.sock file located at the supplied directory.

--disable-session This disables sessions in PHP.

Extensions

As we said earlier, extensions are the add-ons for PHP. Keep in mind that most of these will require additional software installed, depending on your system configuration.

--disable-all As it says, this disables all PHP extensions.

--with-inifile This is new to 5.0 and enables you to specify Microsoft-style INI files.

Database-Specific Directives

Each directive listed here compiles PHP with support for a different database server, or for a set of functions or a library applicable to a certain database server. Each list item below will list the long name for the database type.

--enable-dba   Build PHP with built-in modules.

--with-qdbm[=DIR]   Quick Database Manager.

--with-gdbm[=DIR]   GNU's interpretation of Database Manager.

--with-ndbm[=DIR]   Neuros Database Manipulator.

--with-db4[=DIR]   Berkeley DB4.

--with-db3[=DIR]   Berkeley DB3.

--with-db2[=DIR]   Berkeley DB2.

--with-dbm[=DIR]   Berkeley Database Manager.

--with-cdb[=DIR]   Common database.

--enable-dbase   dBASE.

--enable-dbx   A database abstraction layer implemented in C.

--with-flatfile   Flat-file database.

--with-msql[=DIR]   mSQL.

--with-mysql[=DIR]   MySQL.

--with-mysqli[=FILE]   Available as of PHP 5.0, this directive and adds support for functions found in MySQL 4.1 and later that are not covered by the standard --with-mysql.

--enable-embedded-mysql   This should be enabled if you are using the embedded MySQL Server.

--with-unixODBC[=DIR]   This adds support for the standard ODBC library on a non-Microsoft system.

--with-dbmaker[=DIR]   This provides support for DBMaker.

--with-oracle[=DIR]   This provides support for Oracle.

--with-ovrimos[=DIR]   This adds support for Oracle Ovrimos SQL functions.

--without-sqlite   This tells PHP to compile without SQLite, which comes prepackaged as of PHP 5.0.

--with-pgsql[=DIR]   This provides support for PostgreSQL.

--enable-sqlite-utf8   This enables SQLite with the UTF-8 character set.

--with-sybase[=DIR]   Sybase database server.

--with-sybase-ct[=DIR]   This indicates the location of the Sybase CT (ClienT) library.

--with-custom-odbc[=DIR]   This tells PHP to look in the specified directory for a custom ODBC library.

--with-iodbc[=DIR]   iODBC (Independent Open DataBase Connectivity) is another database server available.

--with-fbsql[=DIR]   This provides FrontBase support.

--enable-filepro   This provides FilePro database support.

--with-hwapi[=DIR]   This provides support for Hyperwave, which is not free software. Hyperwave is an information system similar to a database.

--with-informix[=DIR]   This provides support for the IBM Informix database.

--with-ingres[=DIR]   This adds Ingres II database support.

--with-interbase[=DIR]   This adds Borland InterBase database support.

--with-oci8[=DIR]   Oracle 8 Call Interface support.

--with-adabas[=DIR]   AG's Adabas is a high-performance database that processes online transactions.

--with-sapdb[=DIR]   SAP DB is a free, enterprise-class, open source database.

--with-solid[=DIR]   This includes Solid DB support.

--with-ibm-db2[=DIR]   Support for IBM's DB2 database.

--with-empress[=DIR]   Support for Empress Software's Empress Embedded Database.

--with-birdstep[=DIR]   Support for Birdstep Technology's databases.

--with-esoob[=DIR]   This adds support for Easysoft OOB (ODBC-ODBC Bridge) software, which is an ODBC gateway.

File-Handling and General Directives

This list will detail flags used to enable support for different types of file handling as well as some of the more general directives:

--with-bz2[=DIR]   This provides support for the bzip2 compression library.

--with-zlib[=DIR] and --with-zlib-dir[=DIR]   zlib is a compression library which uses the same compression algorithm as gzip.

--with-openssl[=DIR]   This compiles PHP with OpenSSL support.

--enable-calendar   This enables calendar support for PHP through the implementation of date math.

--disable-ctype   This disables the standard C-library for PHP.

--enable-bcmath   This supplies number theory math functions to PHP.

XML
The flags in the below list allow for varying levels and functionality packages for XML to be disabled or enabled:

--disable-libxml   This turns off support for XML.

--with-libxml-dir[=DIR]   This enables you to specify a custom directory for a PHP XML library.

--disable-dom   This turns off Document Object Model support used by XML.

--disable-simplexml   This turns off simple XML support for PHP.

--enable-soap   SOAP (Simple Object Access Protocol) is much like XML Remote Procedural Calls (XML-RPC) and is an XML-based remote procedure call.

--disable-xml   This completely disables all XML extensions.

--with-libexpat-dir=DIR   This enables a specific set of XML parser functions.

--with-xmlrpc[=DIR]   This enables XML-RPC.

--with-ircg   This provides support for XML real-time streaming.

Graphics, Fonts, and PDF
These options allow for graphics, font, and PDF functionality to be added to PHP:

--enable-exif   This enables Exchangeable Image File Format (EXIF) support.

--with-cpdflib[=DIR]   This adds the ClibPDF library.

--with-jpeg-dir[=DIR]   This enables functions used to manipulate JPEG files.

--with-tiff-dir[=DIR]   This enables functions used to manipulate TIFF files.

--with-pdflib[=DIR]   This enables basic functions used to manipulate PDF files.

--with-png-dir[=DIR]   This enables basic functions used to manipulate PNG files.

--with-ttf[=DIR]   This provides TrueType font support.

--with-gd[=DIR]   This enables all graphics file formats covered in the GD library: GIF, JPEG, PNG, SWF, TIFF, and JPEG2000.

--with-freetype-dir[=DIR]   This adds support for a popular free font engine called FreeType.

--with-t1lib[=DIR]   This library enables you to generate bitmaps from Type-1 fonts.

--enable-gd-native-ttf   This gives the GD library support for TrueType fonts.

--enable-gd-jis-conv   This allows the GD library, if enabled, to convert between Unicode and JIS (Japanese Industry Standards) character encodings.

--with-xpm-dir[=DIR]   XPixMap consists of an ASCII image format and C library.

Other Protocols
Other miscellaneous protocols which do not fall into other categories:

--with-curl[=DIR]   cURL is a command-line tool used for transferring files with URL syntax, which supports FTP, FTPS, HTTP, HTTPS, and so on. This is a common extension needed for many online payment gateways.

--with-curlwrappers   This is a set of wrappers used for cURL.

--enable-dio   This provides support for Direct I/O functions.

--with-fam   This is the Posadis monitor module.

--enable-ftp   This enables a set of client functions that can be used to interface with FTP servers.

--with-gettext[=DIR]   This provides functionality for GNU's gettext. It contains commands to translate strings.

--with-gmp[=DIR]   This provides support for the GNU Multiple Precision Bignum library.

--with-iconv[=DIR]   This is another Unicode conversion library from GNU.

--with-imap[=DIR]   The IMAP library is used for mail procedures in PHP.

--with-kerberos[=DIR]   This compiles in Kerberos Network Authentication Protocol support.

--with-imap-ssl=[DIR]   This provides support for IMAP with SSL.

--with-ldap[=DIR]   This provides support for the Lightweight Directory Access Protocol.

--enable-mbstring   This adds support for multi-byte strings and characters used in some foreign languages.

--disable-mbregex   This disables support for Multi-Byte Regex (JRegex and others).

--with-libmbfl[=DIR]   This provides more multibyte language support.

--with-mcrypt[=DIR]   This is a replacement for the old crypt() package, which is an old Unix file-encryption method.

--with-mcve[=DIR]   This provides support for Main Street Softworks' solution to direct credit-card processing for Linux.

--with-mhash[=DIR]   Another GNU library, this provides functionality for large-number hashing algorithms.

--with-mime-magic[=FILE]   Mime magic will try to determine a file type based on characters contained within the first part of a file.

--with-ming[=DIR]   This is a SWF (Small Web File) output library.

--with-mnogosearch[=DIR]   Lavtech.Com's mnoGoSearch is a free search engine package.

--with-mono   This enables PHP to access .NET assemblies via the Mono library.

--with-msession[=DIR]   This enables PHP to communicate and control the msession daemon if msession is running on your machine.

--with-ncurses[=DIR]   Ncurses displays and updates text on text-only machines.

--enable-pcntl   This enables process-control support in PHP.

--without-pcre-regex   Do not include built-in support for Perl-type Regex.

--with-pfpro[=DIR]   This directive enables the ability to use VeriSign Payflow Pro functions.

--disable-posix   This directive disables POSIX support.

--with-pspell[=DIR]   Provides spell-checking functionality for PHP.

--with-libedit[=DIR]   This non-GPL replacement for the Readline library is a spin-off from NetBSD code.

--with-readline[=DIR]   This provides support for the GNU Readline library.

--with-recode[=DIR]   This library provides functionality for converting files between character types.

--enable-shmop   This provides support for shared memory operations.

--with-snmp[=DIR]   This adds Simple Network Management Protocol support into PHP.

--enable-sockets   This enables PHP socketing control.

--with-xsl[=DIR] This adds support for the Extensible Stylesheet Language format.

--with-yaz[=DIR] By using this extension, you can easily implement a Z39.50 origin (client) that searches or scans Z39.50 targets (servers) in parallel.

--enable-yp This enables network management of important administrative files; Yellow-Pages (YP) is also known as NIS.

Downloading and Preparation

Now that we have explained the important configuration directives and extensions, it is up to you to determine which ones you want to use with your installation. Because we want to ensure that you will be able to get up and running as smoothly as possible, we are going to show you how to do a basic PHP installation that will work. Let's get started by downloading the packages:

1. In the previous chapters of this book, you created a directory for downloading and installing your source files. Move to that directory now:

    ```
    cd /usr/local/src/webserver
    ```

2. Go to www.php.net/downloads.php and select the PHP 5 tarball under the Complete Source Code section. PHP.net uses a mirroring system, so you will have to choose the mirror that is closest to you for downloading your file. After you find a mirror (the closest is usually highlighted for you), copy the URL to the files and use the single-quotes in wget to follow the redirect:

    ```
    wget 'http://us3.php.net/get/php 5.0.0.tar.gz/from/this/mirror'
    ```

3. Unpack the tarball:

    ```
    tar zxpf php-5.0.0.tar.gz
    ```

    A new directory will be created for you with the contents of the tarball.

Compiling and Installing PHP

The next step is to create your installation script. As we mentioned in previous chapters, it is always a good idea to create a script that has the configure options for your compilation in case you need to install again later.

Your script is named php_install and contains the following:

```
cd php-5.0.0
./configure \
--with-apxs=/www/bin/apxs \
--with-mysql=/usr/local/mysql \
--enable-ftp \
--enable-trans-sid
```

This `configure` script utilizes the Apache SAPI extension for Dynamic Shared Object (DSO) and the system MySQL installation. The script also enables FTP support and transparent session ID support for PHP.

TIP   If you Linux distribution uses RPM packages and you are having problems getting a feature compiled, you may go to rpm.pbone.net and download the development package for the feature you are trying to install. Example: if you are enabling the *foo* package with PHP (`--with-foo`) and you get a complaint from PHP during compile, simply go do the RPM website and download RPMs for your platform for *foo* and *foo-devel*. Install these RPMs and try to compile again.

This is a basic set of options that do not require anything but Apache and MySQL installed on your system, so at this point your system should be configured to run this installation without any problems.

NOTE   Depending on which MySQL installation type you performed, you might need to modify the `--with-mysql` directive to the correct path of `libmysqlclient` located on your machine. In Chapter 9, "MySQL: Installation and Administration," you performed a manual installation; the path is `/usr/local/mysql`. With a pre-built package such as RPM, it might be `/usr/mysql`.

If you want to enable additional extensions or features, you can do so by adding the directives for them in this script. Make sure that the last line of the script does not have a trailing backslash but that all lines before the last do contain the trailing backslash.

1. Change the permissions on this script to enable you to execute and run it:

    ```
    chmod 755 php_install
    ```

2. Run the installation script and watch for errors:

    ```
    ./php_install
    ```

3. At this point, you should see the message `Thank you for using PHP` in the last portion of output in your console. If this is the case, you are ready to move on to the `make` process:

    ```
    cd php-5.0.0
    make
    ```

4. Now you wait a little while and enjoy the show during the `make` process. If you do not see any error messages on the last few lines of output, you are clear to proceed with the `make install`:

    ```
    make install
    ```

5. Your next small task is to copy the `php.ini` example file to the correct location:

    ```
    cp php.ini-dist /usr/local/lib/php.ini
    ```

Configuring Apache to Handle PHP

Now that PHP is installed, you need to configure Apache to handle PHP files by passing them to the PHP engine for processing. You do this by adding some information into your Apache configuration file, `httpd.conf`. Here are the steps:

1. At the very end of your `httpd.conf` file, add the following line:

   ```
   AddType application/x-httpd-php .php .php3
   ```

2. If you wish to enable the source code highlight extension (`.phps`) for your files, add the following below the previous line:

   ```
   AddType application/x-httpd-php-source .phps
   ```

> **NOTE**
>
> If you are using `mod_ssl` with your Apache installation, you might want to find the line that says `AddModule mod_php5.c` and move it below the regular `AddModule` list instead of allowing it to remain in the `<IfDefine SSL>` section. Depending on which version of PHP you are installing, this might have already been done for you.

3. Next, there is a directive in Apache called `DirectoryIndex` and it should be modified to add PHP index files. Locate the following line:

   ```
   DirectoryIndex  index.html
   ```

   And change it to the following:
   ```
   DirectoryIndex index.php default.php index.html index.htm
   ```

4. Now you are all set to test PHP. First, you need to completely stop and then start Apache to ensure that the PHP module was successfully loaded:

   ```
   apachectl stop
   apachectl start
   ```

5. If you are using Apache with `mod_ssl`, you need to start Apache as follows:

   ```
   apachectl startssl
   ```

   Now your PHP installation should be complete, and all you have to do is test it.

Testing the PHP Installation

To test your PHP installation, you are going to create a simple script that will display the PHP information. If the script is executed and parsed properly, it will display a nice HTML page that is generated by PHP. If it is not executed and parsed properly, it will display the code that you typed into the script.

Depending on how much of Chapter 8, "Apache Web Server: Installation and Configuration," you followed, you might have a virtual host configured. If this is the case, you will need to place the test script into your virtual host's document root; otherwise you will place it into the default document root.

We're going to assume that you did not configure any virtual hosts and so will place the test script into /www/htdocs for the default document root. Follow these steps:

1. Make a file located at /www/htdocs/info.php and add the following contents to it:

```
<?php
phpinfo();
?>
```

2. Additionally, you can follow the trend of creating a Hello World script such as /www/htdocs/hello.php with the following contents:

```
<?php
echo "Hello World, PHP Rocks!";
?>
```

3. Access these scripts in your web browser by going to the web address of the script and check the output. The output of our phpinfo() function is depicted in Figure 10.1. The output for the Hello World script would simply be the text Hello World, PHP Rocks!

FIGURE 10.1
phpinfo() function
output

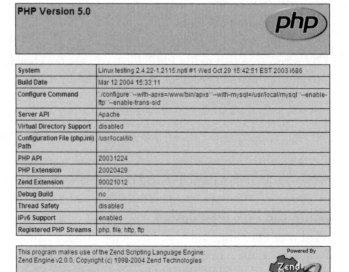

PHP Version 5.0

System	Linux testing 2.4.22-1.2115.nptl #1 Wed Oct 29 15:42:51 EST 2003 i686
Build Date	Mar 12 2004 15:33:11
Configure Command	'./configure' '--with-apxs=/www/bin/apxs' '--with-mysql=/usr/local/mysql' '--enable-ftp' '--enable-trans-sid'
Server API	Apache
Virtual Directory Support	disabled
Configuration File (php.ini) Path	/usr/local/lib
PHP API	20031224
PHP Extension	20020429
Zend Extension	90021012
Debug Build	no
Thread Safety	disabled
IPv6 Support	enabled
Registered PHP Streams	php, file, http, ftp

This program makes use of the Zend Scripting Language Engine:
Zend Engine v2.0.0, Copyright (c) 1998-2004 Zend Technologies

Powered By

PHP Credits

The PHP INI File

During the installation process, you copied an INI file to the /usr/local/lib directory of your server. This file, although optional, handles the default server-wide configuration directives for PHP. Let's break down the important elements of this INI file for better understanding. If we do not cover a section it is because that section is rarely modified and more than likely commented in detail of the php.ini file.

engine

Default: On

Allowed: On, Off

This setting enables or disables the PHP engine under Apache. This configuration directive can be useful for disabling PHP on certain Apache virtual hosts by using the Off setting.

short_open_tag

Default: On

Allowed: On, Off

The *short open tag* enables you to abbreviate the open tag that starts the PHP engine. The open tag normally consists of <?php; however, with this directive enabled, you can use only <?.

WARNING   You should avoid developing scripts with the short open tag if they are to be redistributed. There is a remote chance that your scripts or libraries might not execute if this setting is disabled on a remote server.

asp_tags

Default: Off

Allowed: On, Off

This setting enables those developers who have not fully moved on from using ASP to develop with ASP-style tags: <% and %>. Why you would use these with PHP is beyond us and the PHP developers, so this setting is turned off by default.

precision

Default: 12

Allowed: Any integer

The precision setting displays the number of significant digits in floating-point numbers. The default setting is sufficient for everyday use; however, if you want your floating-point numbers to be less precise, you can lower this setting—and vice versa for more precise numbers.

y2k_compliance = On

Default: On

Allowed: On, Off

This setting enforces the Year 2000 compliance, which can cause problems on non-Y2K-compliant web browsers.

output_buffering

Default: Off

Allowed: On, Off, size limit in bytes (for example, 1024), max bytes: 4096

Output buffering enables you to send header lines even after you send body content—with a trade-off in system performance. Using output buffering causes PHP to run slower. It is recommended to leave this setting off and to instead call the output buffering functions within your PHP scripts only when you need them.

output_handler

Default: Disabled by a comment mark (;)

Allowed: mb_output_handler *or* ob_iconv_handler

WARNING   You cannot use both ob_gzhandler (this setting) and the zlib.output_compression setting together.

The output_handler setting enables you to redirect the output of your PHP scripts to a function for handling. You might have the option to change the encoding of the output by using this setting. You can use only the mb_output_handler *or* the ob_iconv_handler, not both at the same time.

NOTE   We do not recommend that you utilize the output_handler setting; instead use the *output buffering* functions within your script and then pass them through the handler function.

zlib.output_compression

Default: Off

Allowed: On, Off, specific buffer size in bytes (default: 4)

The zlib.output_compression setting enables transparent compression by using the zlib library.

zlib.output_handler

Default: Disabled by a comment mark (;)

Allowed: Any zlib output handler function

This setting enables you to enable additional zlib output handler functions if available. By default, this setting is disabled.

implicit_flush

Default: Off

Allowed: On, Off

This setting tells PHP to flush itself after every output block instead of waiting until the engine is done parsing the code before the flush. Enabling this will dramatically reduce system performance.

TIP   If you want to display a script's output as it is generated, enable this setting for that script. An example is running the ping command and showing the output as it would display in the console instead of waiting for the command to complete and then displaying all output at one time.

unserialize_callback_func

Default: Empty—not defined

Allowed: Function name

This setting is used to call a function when PHP unserializes an object it does not recognize. *Unserialization* is the unpacking of an object that you have serialized. This enables you to store arrays and pass them through other objects.

serialize_precision

Default: 100

Allowed: Integer

This setting is similar to the precision setting except it is used to define the number of precision digits after the floating point to store a serialized float or double.

allow_call_time_pass_reference

Default: On

Allowed: On, Off

This setting allows forcing of values to be passed by reference at function call time. This setting is deprecated and might not be supported by future versions of the Zend engine.

Security and Safe Mode

The PHP INI file enables you to crack down on the security settings if you would like. You can hide PHP, limit memory usage and execution times, and enable safe-mode operation.

Safe mode is ideal for virtual hosting environments. It enables you to lock down the way PHP operates for the system. This prevents users from doing many malicious things such as opening system core files, reading other client's files, tampering with system information, or executing certain functions.

safe_mode

Default: Off

Allowed: On, Off

This is the master safe mode setting. If enabled, the rest of the safe mode settings will be enforced with their default values. If you are not running a virtual hosting client system, you can opt to leave this setting disabled and disregard the rest of the safe mode settings.

WARNING   If you are a security-conscious server administrator and make these settings effective in a virtual hosting environment, be prepared for a barrage of complaints from your PHP users, especially when using third-party PHP scripts. Most third-party PHP scripts are not developed with these settings in mind and might fail when they are executed.

safe_mode_gid

Default: Off

Allowed: Group ID/User ID

This setting allows access to files owned by the user running the script.

NOTE   You should define this setting in an Apache virtual host configuration and use the User ID for that virtual host file to this setting.

safe_mode_include_dir

Default: Empty—not defined

Allowed: Path to directory (/directory/path)

This setting defines a specific path of files to be included, and the security checks (safe_mode_gid) are bypassed.

safe_mode_exec_dir

Default: Empty—not defined

Allowed: Path to directory (*/directory/path*)

This setting defines a specific path of files that are allowed to be executed by exec family functions: exec, shell_exec, and so on.

safe_mode_allowed_env_vars

Default: PHP_

Allowed: Colon-delimited list of prefixes

This setting allows only the listed environment variables to be modified.

WARNING Using the default PHP_ setting allows *any* environment variable to be modified, which can induce a security risk.

safe_mode_protected_env_vars

Default: LD_LIBRARY_PATH

Allowed: Path or environment variable path

A colon-delimited list of environment variables that the user will not be able to modify by using the putenv function. These variables will be protected even if the safe_mode_allowed_env_vars setting is set to allow changes to them.

open_basedir

Default: Empty—not defined

Allowed: Path to directory (*/directory/path*)

This setting limits all file changes to the defined directory. This setting should really be used in a virtual hosting or directory configuration.

NOTE The open_basedir setting is independent of the safe_mode directive, which means that it does not matter whether safe_mode is on or off.

disable_functions

Default: Empty—not defined

Allowed: Comma-delimited list of function names

This setting enables you to disable specified functions.

> **NOTE**   The disable_functions setting is independent of the safe_mode directive, which means that it does not matter whether safe_mode is on or off.

disable_classes

Default: Empty—not defined

Allowed: Comma-delimited list of class names

This setting enables you to disable specified classes.

> **NOTE**   The disable_classes setting is independent of the safe_mode directive, which means that it does not matter whether safe_mode is on or off.

expose_php

Default: On

Allowed: On, Off

This setting enables you to hide PHP from the header output and web server signature. If you do not want anyone to know that you are running PHP (other than by seeing the .php in your filenames), you can do so by disabling this directive. This feature will at least allow you to hide which version of PHP you are running in case you are on vacation when a major security exploit is found.

max_execution_time

Default: 30

Allowed: Number of seconds

This is the number of seconds you will allow a PHP script to run before it dies.

> **WARNING**   If you set max_execution_time to zero (0), your scripts might run forever and potentially take all of your server resources, and your server might become inaccessible. Be careful.

max_input_time

Default: 60

Allowed: Number of seconds

This is the number of seconds a script can take to parse requested data.

> **WARNING**   If you set max_input_time to zero (0), your scripts might run forever and potentially take all of your server resources, and your server might become inaccessible. Be careful.

memory_limit

Default: 8M

Allowed: Bytes (no suffix), kilobytes (k suffix), megabytes (M suffix)

This is the memory limit for PHP to utilize before halting. Be careful with this setting.

Error Handling and Reporting

error_reporting

Default: E_ALL & ~E_NOTICE & ~E_STRICT

Allowed: Level or integer. See php.ini for levels and descriptions.

This setting is the level of error reporting displayed in the output of PHP. You have multiple error-reporting levels to choose from, and these are defined in detail inside the php.ini file.

NOTE   To utilize the error_reporting in the output, display_errors must be enabled.

display_errors

Default: On

Allowed: On, Off

This setting is enabled by default and allows errors to be printed to the screen. It is highly recommended for production-level servers that you disable this setting!

display_startup_errors

Default: Off

Allowed: On, Off

Primarily used for debugging, this setting displays startup errors. It is recommended to leave this setting off by default.

log_errors

Default: Off

Allowed: On, Off

This directive enables PHP to log all errors to a file. This is the preferred method for managing errors on a production-level site. Define the path of the actual file to log errors to with the error_log directive.

log_errors_max_len

Default: 1024

Allowed: Integer

The maximum length for error messages written to a log file. For no limit, use zero (0).

ignore_repeated_errors

Default: Off

Allowed: On, Off

This enables PHP to ignore duplicate errors in a file. If you are debugging, this directive should be set to Off.

ignore_repeated_source

Default: Off

Allowed: On, Off

This directive is used only when ignore_repeated_errors is enabled; it forces PHP to ignore any error that matches the previous error message.

report_memleaks

Default: Off

Allowed: On, Off

If you have compiled PHP with debugging mode, this directive can allow PHP to report memory leaks.

track_errors

Default: Off

Allowed: On, Off

This enables PHP to store the last error in the global variable php_errormsg.

html_errors

Default: Off

Allowed: On, Off

This enables PHP to include HTML tags in error messages. It is recommended to leave this off on production-level servers.

docref_root

Default: Disabled by a comment mark (;)

Allowed: Path to local PHP manual

This directive enables you to store a local copy of the PHP manual for reference. Generated errors will link to the appropriate fields in the PHP manual to assist you in troubleshooting practices.

docref_ext

Default: Disabled by a comment mark (;)

Allowed: File extension (.html, .php)

This is the extension of the files for your PHP manual and it is used in conjunction with docref_root.

error_prepend_string

Default: Disabled by a comment mark (;)

Allowed: HTML element open tags

This setting is used with error_append_string. It enables you to change the HTML attributes of the error messages. For example, you can add the style tags to change font size, color, style, and so on.

error_append_string

Default: Disabled by a comment mark (;)

Allowed: HTML element close tags

This setting is used with error_prepend_string and is used to close the HTML elements defined there.

error_log

Default: Disabled by a comment mark (;)

Allowed: Path to log file (/path/to/log_file) *or* syslog

This indicates the actual path and filename of the file that will contain the error logs. You can also use the system's log to log errors by using the syslog directive.

Data Handling

arg_separator.output

Default: &

Allowed: Any characters

This directive is the separator value for URL-parsed values. The most common is the ampersand symbol (&), which is used to distinguish between variable and value sets. Example: `index.php?var1=val1&var2=val3`.

NOTE   By default, to follow HTML compliance standards, the & symbol is converted to &.

NOTE   We recommend that you do not alter the `arg_separator.output` setting because it conforms with coding standards.

variables_order

Default: EGPCS

Allowed: G, P, C, E, S

This is the order of precedence for variable scopes. These scopes are Environment, Get, Post, Cookie, and Sessions. If you understand what you are doing with these values, you can change them; otherwise, it is a good idea to leave them the way they are.

register_globals

Default: Off

Allowed: On, Off

`register_globals` is the largest security hole in PHP; therefore, it is disabled by default for a very good reason. This setting turns every form field and cookie value into a global variable.

WARNING   If you are attempting to run a third-party PHP script that will not work with `register_globals` disabled, do not run it. Instead, contact the author and ask them to update it or to refund your money because the script causes a security risk to your system.

register_long_arrays

Default: On

Allowed: On, Off

This setting allows you to enable the *old* HTTP_*_VARS such as POST, GET, COOKIE, and so on. If you are running a script that still relies on these types of arrays, you should reevaluate the script as something that needs to be updated to use the $_* style arrays.

register_argc_argv

Default: On

Allowed: On, Off

This setting enables PHP to define argc & argv variables. If you are not using these types of variables, you can disable this setting to get a performance increase.

post_max_size

Default: 8M

Allowed: Bytes (no suffix), kilobytes (k suffix), megabytes (M suffix)

This indicates the maximum size of data allowed from a form through the POST method.

magic_quotes_gpc

Default: On

Allowed: On, Off

Sets the state for the magic quotes Get/Post/Cookie (GPC). This is useful for automatically adding and removing backslashes from escape sequences in data such as MySQL, forms, and so on.

magic_quotes_runtime

Default: Off

Allowed: On, Off

Enabling this directive tells PHP to use magic quotes.

magic_quotes_sybase

Default: Off

Allowed: On, Off

This enables a different type of magic quotes for Sybase databases.

auto_prepend_file

Default: Empty—not defined

Allowed: Path to filename (*/path/to/filename*)

This section allows you to specify a file that will automatically be added before every page is accessed. If you ran only one site from this server, you could include a header file this way.

`auto_append_file`

Default: Empty—not defined

Allowed: Path to filename (*/path/to/filename*)

This section allows you to specify a file that will automatically be added before every page accessed. If you ran only one site from this server, you could include a footer file this way.

`default_mimetype`

Default: `"text/html"`

Allowed: Valid MIME type

This is the default MIME type for files that do not contain a valid extension.

`default_charset`

Default: Disabled by comment mark (;)

Allowed: Any valid charset

This indicates the default character set to be used by PHP.

Paths and Directories

`include_path`

Default: `PHP_INCLUDE_PATH`

Allowed: Path to directory (*/path/to/directory*)

This allows you to set the path to the includes directory for PHP.

`doc_root`

Default: Empty—not defined

Allowed: Path to directory (*/path/to/directory*)

This directive is used to specify the root directory for your web server documents.

`user_dir`

Default: Empty—not defined

Allowed: Path to directory (*/path/to/directory*)

This specifies the directory under which PHP opens the script using /~username. This is used only if not empty.

File Handling

enable_dl

Default: On

Allowed: On, Off

This enables the dl(), or dynamic library, function. The dl() function does not work correctly on multithreaded servers such as IIS or Zeus and is automatically disabled in those cases.

file_uploads

Default: On

Allowed: On, Off

This turns the ability to upload files on or off.

upload_tmp_dir

Default: Commented out

Allowed: Path to directory (/path/to/directory)

Here you can specify where PHP should store uploaded files temporarily before actions are performed on them.

upload_max_filesize

Default: 2M

Allowed: Valid byte number

This allows you to set the maximum file size anyone can upload through PHP.

allow_url_fopen

Default: On

Allowed: On, Off

This tells PHP to allow the treatment of URLs as files.

user_agent

Default: Commented out

Allowed: String

This allows you to set the user agent of PHP. This can be useful if connecting to remote websites.

E-mail

SMTP

Default: Localhost

Allowed: Host address or domain name

This is for Win32 only and defines the SMTP server address.

sendmail_from

Default: Commented out

Allowed: E-mail address

This is for Win32 only and defines the "from" e-mail address e-mail that the e-mail will be sent with through PHP.

sendmail_path

Default: Commented out

Allowed: Path to file (/path/to/file)

Used on Unix/Linux systems only, this directive sets the path to the sendmail function. You can also specify flags for the command, for example, sendmail -t -i.

mail.force_extra_paramaters

Default: Commented out

Allowed: Valid Sendmail parameters

This allows you to automatically pass e-mail parameters to override any that might be set in the fifth parameter of the mail() function. This will even override the values during safe mode.

SQL

sql.safe_mode

Default: Off

Allowed: On, Off

This turns on and off the safe mode for SQL.

ODBC

odbc.allow_persistent

Default: On

Allowed: On, Off

This allows or prevents persistent connections for ODBC.

odbc.check_persistant

Default: On

Allowed: On, Off

This tells PHP to make sure a connection to the database is present before sending a command.

odbc.max_persistent

Default: -1

Allowed: -1, positive integer

This tells PHP to allow only a maximum number or persistent connections; -1 tells PHP to disable this option.

odbc.max_links

Default: -1

Allowed: -1, 0, or positive integer

-1 for this option means no limit as well. Setting a value here defines the maximum number of links allowed to the database for both persistent and nonpersistent connections.

odbc.defaultlrl

Default: 4096

Allowed: 0, positive integer

This is used for handling LONG fields. This value returns the number of bytes to variables.

MySQL

mysql.allow_persistent

Default: On

Allowed: On, Off

This allows or prevents persistent links to MySQL.

mysql.max_persistent

Default: -1

Allowed: -1, positive integer

This sets the maximum number of persistent connections; -1 is no limit.

mysql.max_links

Default: -1

Allowed: -1, 0, or positive integer

This is the maximum number of links allowed to MySQL for both persistent and nonpersistent connections.

mysql.default_port

Default: Empty—not defined

Allowed: Any valid port number

This is the default port to use when connecting to the MySQL Server.

mysql.default_socket

Default: Empty—not defined

Allowed: Location of any valid socket file

This is the default socket to connect to a MySQL Server.

mysql.default_host

Default: Empty—not defined

Allowed: Any valid domain name or IP address

This is the default hostname or IP address for your MySQL Server.

mysql.default_user

Default: Empty—not defined

Allowed: MySQL username

This indicates the default username for connecting to MySQL.

mysql.default_password

Default: Empty—not defined

Allowed: MySQL password

This indicates the default password for connecting to MySQL.

mysql.connect_timeout

Default: 60

Allowed: -1, positive integer

This is the default timeout limit when attempting to connect to a MySQL Server; -1 means no limit.

mysql.trace_mode

Default: `Off`

Allowed: `On`, `Off`

When trace mode is enabled, MySQL will print out all error messages relating to table index/scans.

Sessions

session.save_handler

Default: `Files`

Allowed: Handler names

This sets the handler type used to store and retrieve data.

session.save_path

Default: `/tmp`

Allowed: Any valid path to which Apache has access

You should use the format `N;MODE;/path` when using this directive, where `N` is an integer defining the number of levels that deep session information should be saved, and `MODE` defines the permissions mode the files should be saved as (for example, 600). PHP will not make this directory structure for you, however. You should use the `ext/session` script for this purpose.

session.use_cookies

Default: `1`

Allowed: `0`, `1`

This turns on and off the use of cookies in PHP.

session.name

Default: `PHPSESSID`

Allowed: All CAPS variable name that is not reserved

This indicates the name of the cookie variable the session ID should be stored as.

session.auto_start

Default: `0`

Allowed: `0`, `1`

This, if set, will initialize a session on request startup.

`session.cookie_lifetime`

Default: 0

Allowed: 0, integer

The default is 0, which tells the cookie to expire after the browser is closed. An integer used here will tell the cookie to expire in the number of seconds provided.

`session.cookie_domain`

Default: Empty—not defined

Allowed: Any valid domain name

This is the domain name for which the cookie is valid.

`session.serialize_handler`

Default: php

Allowed: Valid handler

This allows you to specify a custom handler to serialize data.

`session.gc_probability :: session.gc_divisor`

Default: 1 :: 100

Allowed: Integer :: Integer

This allows you to specify the probability that the garbage collection process is initialized. Using 1 and 100 would be a 1 percent change.

`session.gc_maxlifetime`

Default: 1440

Allowed: Positive integer

After this number of seconds, stored data will be seen as "garbage" and cleaned up by the garbage collection process.

`session.referer_check`

Default: Empty—not defined

Allowed: String

Check `HTTP_REFERER` to invalidate externally stored URLs containing IDs. `HTTP_REFERER` has to contain this substring for the session to be considered valid.

session.entropy_length

Default: 0

Allowed: 0, 1

This indicates the number of bytes to read from the entropy file.

session.entropy_file

Default: Empty—not defined

Allowed: The file used to create the session ID.

This is used to specify an external file that can be used to generate the session ID.

session.cache_limiter

Default: nocache

Allowed: nocache, private, public, NULL

This is used to determine caching aspects of your server. You can leave this blank to avoid setting anti-caching headers.

session.cache_expire

Default: 180

Allowed: Positive integer

This requested document will expire after this number of minutes.

session.use_trans_sid

Default: 0

Allowed: 0, 1

This allows the session ID to be passed through the URL. This can allow users to exploit the system by potentially copying the session ID and reusing it later.

session.hash_function

Default: 0

Allowed: 0, 1

The 0 specifies using MD5, whereas 1 uses SHA-1 (160-bits).

session.hash_bits_per_character

Default: 4

Allowed: 4, 5, 6

This defines the number of bits stored in each character when converting the binary hash data to something readable.

> 4 bits: 0–9, a–f
>
> 5 bits: 0–9, a–v
>
> 6 bits: 0–9, a–z, A–Z, "-", ","

Sockets

sockets.use_system_read

Default: On

Allowed: On, Off

This tells PHP to use the system read() function instead of the php_read() wrapper.

default_socket_timeout

Default: 60

Allowed: Positive integer

This indicates the default timeout (in seconds) for socket-based streams.

Miscellaneous

bcmath.scale

Default: 0

Allowed: Integer

This indicates the number of decimal digits for all bcmath functions.

browscap

Default: Commented out

Allowed: Path to file (/path/to/file)

The browscap (browser capability) defines the capabilities of certain browsers. This setting points to the browscap.ini file.

tidy.clean_output

Default: Off

Allowed: On, Off

This option tells PHP's tidy to clean and repair HTML content automatically. You should not use this option if you are generating images because tidy will attempt to clean the binary data as well.

define_syslog_variables

Default: Off

Allowed: On, Off

This directive is used to turn PHP's syslog variables off and on. For performance reasons, it is disabled by default. If you need access to the variables, it is recommended to turn them on for specific pages by using the define_syslog_variables() function.

PHP Installation and Configuration Checklist

In this chapter, we have presented a lot of information as well as shown you how to install and configure PHP. You should now have a strong understanding of how to do the following:

- Understand what PHP can do for you.
- Download and unpack PHP.
- Build and install PHP.
- Use configuration directives.
- Display PHP information via the web browser.

In the next chapter, you are going to perform some exercises that will enable you to test your Apache, MySQL, and PHP installation by using them together.

## CHAPTER 11

Testing Your LAMP Installation

- Setting Up the Apache Virtual Host

- Preparing the MySQL Database and User

- Testing Apache, PHP, and MySQL

- Troubleshooting

Now that you have everything installed, it is time to perform a few tests that will ensure the elements are working properly. In this chapter, we are going to cover how to ensure that Apache, MySQL, and PHP are working together on your Linux system. You will create an Apache virtual host, a MySQL database, and a MySQL user; you will also grant permissions to the database and then create a set of PHP scripts that will enter data into the database and extract it into formatted HTML.

Keep in mind that this book is not written to teach you development with PHP; therefore, we are going to give you enough information in this chapter to test the core elements of your installation. If you wish to learn more about PHP development, you should check out the resources we have listed in Appendix C, "Getting Support."

NOTE   This chapter assumes that you already have DNS set up for your domain name. DNS configuration is beyond the scope of this book and therefore is not covered here.

Setting Up the Apache Virtual Host

If you did not set up an Apache virtual host in Chapter 8, "Apache Web Server: Installation and Configuration," you should do so now in order to test your skills at editing the Apache configuration file. You'll create a virtual host for a domain name called *yourtest.com*, which will reside in the /home/*yourtest.com*/public_html directory. Follow these steps:

1. If you followed our examples in Chapter 8 on creating a separate vhosts directory for configuration files, add a new file there now; otherwise, edit your httpd.conf file and append the following code to it (remembering to substitute a domain name you have access to for *yourtest.com*):

```
<VirtualHost *>
    ServerName yourtest.com
    ServerAlias www.yourtest.com
    DocumentRoot /home/yourtest.com/public_html
</VirtualHost>
```

NOTE   If you have not already configured the NameVirtualHost directive, you will need to do so now. Find the NameVirtualHost directive and alter the line to the following: NameVirtualHost *

2. Create the directories for *yourtest.com*:

```
mkdir -p /home/yourtest.com/public_html
```

3. Restart Apache, and your new virtual host should take effect.

Preparing the MySQL Database and User

To retrieve information from the database for your PHP script, you'll first need to create a database with a table as well as a user for that database. You will begin with creating the database. Follow these steps:

1. Log in to MySQL as the root user (or another user who has access to create new databases, tables, and users). You should use something similar to the following:

   ```
   mysql -uuser -p
   ```

2. After you have logged in, create your database:

   ```
   CREATE DATABASE my_test;
   ```

   If the database has successfully been created you will see this:
   ```
   Query OK, 1 row affected (0.02 sec)
   ```

3. Switch to using the database by typing the following:

   ```
   USE my_test;
   ```

   After the command has been executed, you will be told
   ```
   Database Changed
   ```

4. With our database selected perform:

   ```
   CREATE TABLE my_table (
       my_table_id INT(11) NOT NULL AUTO_INCREMENT,
       my_value VARCHAR(30),
       my_date DATE,
       PRIMARY KEY(`my_table_id`)
   );
   ```

   As a result you should see a Query OK statement and be returned to a SQL prompt. You now have a database and table created.

5. Now you'll create a unique user just for this database with full privileges so that you can connect using PHP. This prevents anyone who might gain access to your PHP script from tampering with your entire MySQL Server. Run this query:

   ```
   GRANT ALL PRIVILEGES ON my_test.* TO 'test_user'@'localhost'
       IDENTIFIED BY 'test_pass';
   ```

   That's it; now you have a database, table, and test user ready for your PHP script.

Testing Apache, PHP, and MySQL

In this section you are going to run a few quick tests to ensure that Apache is parsing your PHP files properly, and that PHP and MySQL are connecting and working together. You'll know if Apache and PHP are working correctly because you will see the output from PHP as we discuss it throughout the rest of this chapter.

Database Connection Script

To start, you will create your PHP script that is responsible for performing the database connection. This script is named `database-connection.php` and will be located in your virtual hosts' document root directory (`/home/mytest/public_html`). This script will contain information such as the MySQL host, username, password, and database you will be using for this script. The script will contain the information in Listing 11.1, assuming you followed our example in the preceding section, "Preparing the MySQL Database and User."

Listing 11.1   `database-connection.php` **Script**

```php
<?php
// Database Connection Script

$dbUser = 'test_user';
$dbPass = 'test_pass';
$dbName = 'my_test';
$dbHost = 'localhost';

$sql = mysql_connect($dbHost, $dbUser, $dbPass)
       or die (mysql_error());

mysql_select_db($dbName, $sql) or die (mysql_error());
?>
```

Data Insertion Script

Now that your database connection script is ready to use, let's create a script that will insert some information into your database. This script will include the database connection file (`database-connection.php`) created in Listing 11.1, which in turn makes your database connection available for the `$sql` resource identifier. Next, this script will run a `foreach` loop that will create 50 entries of data into your database. Take a look at Listing 11.2 for the `database-insert.php` script.

Listing 11.2   `database-insert.php` **Script**

```php
<?php
// Data insertion script
include('database-connection.php');
for($i = 0; $i <= 50; $i++){
    if($i % 2) {
        $data = $i.' - Odd Result';
    } else {
```

```
        $data = $i.'- Even Result';
    }
    mysql_query("INSERT INTO my_table (my_value, my_date)
        VALUES ('$data', now())") or die (mysql_error());
        echo "Inserting: $data<br />";
}
echo "Done<br />";
?>
```

At this point, you should run the `database-insert.php` script from your web browser by using: `http://yourtest.com/database-insert.php` as the URL.

If your MySQL is working properly, you will see some results echoed to your web browser that will appear similar to the following:

```
Inserting: 0- Even Result
Inserting: 1 - Odd Result
Inserting: 2- Even Result
Inserting: 3 - Odd Result
Inserting: 4- Even Result
Inserting: 5 - Odd Result
Inserting: 6- Even Result
Inserting: 7 - Odd Result
Inserting: 8- Even Result
Inserting: 9 - Odd Result
Inserting: 10- Even Result
```

NOTE   We have truncated the output of this script for this book.

Data Extraction and Formatting Script

Now that your data is inserted into the database, you will perform your final test, which will extract the data and format it for HTML output with PHP. Take a look at the script in Listing 11.3.

Listing 11.3   `database-test.php` **Script**

```
<?php
// Data test script
include('database-connection.php');

$sql = mysql_query("SELECT * FROM my_table");

while($row = mysql_fetch_array($sql)){
    echo "Database Entry: ".$row['my_table_id']." | Value: ~CA".$row['my_
value']." | Date: ".$row['my_date']."<br />

}
?>
```

Now that you have your `database-test.php` script created, run it from your web browser by using `http://yourtest.com/database-test.php` as your URL and you should see some output such as the following:

```
Database Entry: 1 | Value: 0- Even Result | Date: 2004-04-01
Database Entry: 2 | Value: 1 - Odd Result | Date: 2004-04-01
Database Entry: 3 | Value: 2- Even Result | Date: 2004-04-01
Database Entry: 4 | Value: 3 - Odd Result | Date: 2004-04-01
Database Entry: 5 | Value: 4- Even Result | Date: 2004-04-01
Database Entry: 6 | Value: 5 - Odd Result | Date: 2004-04-01
Database Entry: 7 | Value: 6- Even Result | Date: 2004-04-01
Database Entry: 8 | Value: 7 - Odd Result | Date: 2004-04-01
Database Entry: 9 | Value: 8- Even Result | Date: 2004-04-01
Database Entry: 10 | Value: 9 - Odd Result | Date: 2004-04-01
```

NOTE   We have truncated the output of this script for this book.

If your output is the same as ours, then congratulations again! Your Linux, Apache, MySQL, and PHP are working together in harmony, and you have concluded the installation, testing, and implementation of these excellent technologies together. If you are having difficulties, take a look at the next section for problems and causes.

Troubleshooting

It is important for you to understand some of the common problems and why they occur. This section covers only the problems that might occur for the code and configuration we have given you, and their potential causes.

- *My scripts are displayed in my web browser exactly as I have coded them.* This problem occurs when Apache is not parsing your scripts through the PHP engine. You will need to ensure that the proper configuration directives such as `AddModule`, `LoadModule`, and `AddType` have been entered into your `httpd.conf` file as described in Chapter 10, "PHP: Installation and Configuration."

- *PHP says,* `Fatal error: undefined function mysql_connect() in line x of filename.php`. This means that you have somehow disabled or not configured MySQL support in PHP. You should refer to Chapter 10 to learn how to enable MySQL with PHP. By default, we have shown you how to enable it.

- *PHP says,* `Warning: mysql_connect(): Access denied for user: 'test_user@localhost' (Using password: YES) in /home/yourdomain.com/public_html/database-connection.php on line x`. This occurs when your username or password do not match the database username and password. Follow the steps correctly in the "Preparing the MySQL Database and User" section earlier in this chapter and ensure you have used the correct username and password in your `database-connection.php` script.

- *PHP says*, `Access denied for user: 'test_user@localhost' to database 'database'`. This indicates that either you do not have the database and user privileges set properly or you have not defined them correctly in your `database-connection.php` script.

- *The output from the database is empty*. This indicates that either you did not run the `database-insert.php` script or you have an error in one of your other scripts. Check your code against the code in this chapter and try again.

If you have any additional problems, check the chapter related to your problem type, or seek help in one of the resources listed in Appendix C.

Testing Your LAMP Installation Checklist

In this brief chapter, you have taken the steps necessary to perform a quick test on the core elements of your new system. We have shown you how to accomplish the following:

- Create an Apache virtual host.
- Create a MySQL database from the command line.
- Create a MySQL database table from the command line.
- Grant MySQL privileges to a user from the command line.
- Create a database connection PHP script.
- Insert data into MySQL from PHP.
- Extract and format data from MySQL with PHP.
- Troubleshoot the most likely problems to find their solutions.

At this point you should be very familiar with Linux, Apache, MySQL, and PHP. We have included appendices in this book that provide a quick reference checklist for setting up LAMP, additional MySQL configuration options, and information about getting support and finding additional resources.

APPENDIX A

LAMP Quick Installation

Over the course of the years that we have worked in the web development field, we have performed many LAMP installations. During this time, we have always wanted a quick reference for setting up LAMP. After you know the *why* of installing everything and you have a firm grasp of the requirements needed to install certain libraries and the effects that specific configuration directives will have on your system, you don't want to go back and search through pages of text to reference a single command. This appendix will walk you through the process of installing everything you need based on the default installation from this book.

We are sure that in the years ahead this appendix will serve as a useful reference during your installations. Everything you need in one place—you can't ask for more than that.

Because you are now familiar with all the particulars, we will assume in some parts of this appendix that you remember how to change permissions, continue to the next section, and so on. If you have trouble with a particular command or area, refer to the appropriate chapter and take time to review the discussions and explanations for that command or area.

> **WARNING** This appendix is not a substitute for the expanded information found in the chapters of this book. It is also not a substitute for updated documentation that might be found in the source files or official online documentation. Please ensure that you are familiar with *all* aspects of what you are doing *before* you proceed with the quick instructions outlined here.

Linux

This section outlines information covered in Chapter 2, "Installing Linux." Follow these steps to install Linux:

1. After obtaining your Linux distribution, place the first disc in the CD-ROM or DVD drive and reboot the computer. Make sure that the CD-ROM is in front of the hard disk for boot order.

2. Enter the installation procedure in graphic or text mode, and if this is the first time you are using these discs you might want to verify the integrity of the discs.

3. Continue on, selecting Server as your installation type, and set up your hard disk partitions.

4. Use the GRUB boot loader and set up your network accordingly.

5. Enable the default firewall for now and fill out your miscellaneous settings.

6. Now it's time to select your packages. For this installation we will choose the following:
   - X Window System
   - GNOME or KDE (or both) Desktop System
   - Text-Based Internet

- Server Configuration Tools
- Development Tools

7. Breeze through the other screens and use the defaults. Begin your installation, changing discs when prompted.

8. Create a boot disc if you wish and reboot.

9. After the first reboot, you will need to fill out some basic forms before you are brought to the X Window interface. Log in as root and open a terminal window. After that window is open, vi the /etc/inittab file and change your run level from 5 to 3. Reboot and make sure everything is working properly.

10. Use this command to download the latest version of pine with pico:

```
wget http://www.linuxforum.com/lfiles/pine.i386.rpm
```

You will need to install it by using the following:
```
rpm -Uvh pine.i386.rpm
```

Security

This section covers information in Chapter 6, "Linux Security." Follow these steps to tighten up your security:

1. First, edit your sshd_config file:

```
pico /etc/ssh/sshd_config
```

2. Change

```
# PermitRootLogin yes
```

to
```
PermitRootLogin no
```

3. Change

```
#Protocol 2,1
```

to
```
Protocol 2
```

4. Restart the daemon:

```
/etc/init.d/sshd restart
```

5. Create your custom firewall script:

```
pico /usr/local/etc/firewall
```

6. Add the following:

```
#!/bin/sh
# Change the part after the = to where your
# IPTABLES is on your system

IPTABLES=/sbin/iptables

# Flush existing rules

$IPTABLES -F INPUT

# Allow connections going outbound
# from this machine to reply back

$IPTABLES -A INPUT -j ACCEPT -m state --state \
    ESTABLISHED -i eth0 -p icmp

$IPTABLES -A INPUT -j ACCEPT -m state --state \
    ESTABLISHED -i eth0 -p tcp

$IPTABLES -A INPUT -j ACCEPT -m state --state \
    ESTABLISHED -i eth0 -p udp

#Allow incoming SSH requests

$IPTABLES -A INPUT -p tcp --dport 22 -j ACCEPT

#Allow incoming DNS

$IPTABLES -A INPUT -p udp --dport 53 -j ACCEPT
$IPTABLES -A INPUT -p tcp --dport 53 -j ACCEPT

#Allow incoming HTTP requests (to Web server)

$IPTABLES -A INPUT -p tcp --dport 80 -j ACCEPT
$IPTABLES -A INPUT -p tcp --dport 443 -j ACCEPT


#Allow Ping echo

$IPTABLES -A INPUT -p icmp -j ACCEPT

# Load Modules
        insmod ip_conntrack_ftp
        insmod ipt_LOG
```

```
        insmod ipt_REJECT
        insmod ipt_limit
        insmod ipt_state

# The logging is set so if more than 5 packets are dropped
# in three seconds they will be ignored. This
# helps to prevent a DOS attack
# Crashing the computer the firewall is running on

$IPTABLES -A INPUT -m limit --limit 3/second \
--limit-burst 5 -i ! lo -j LOG

# Drop and log all other data

$IPTABLES -A INPUT -i ! lo -j DROP
```

7. Change the file permissions:

```
chmod 700 /usr/local/etc/firewall
```

8. Activate the firewall:

```
/usr/local/etc/firewall
```

9. Create your service file:

```
/etc/init.d/firewall
```

10. Add the following lines of code:

```
#!/bin/sh
#
# This script is responsible for loading the custom
# IPTables Firewall settings.
#
# chkconfig: 345 96 96
#
# processname: /usr/local/etc/firewall
#
# description: Controls the custom built firewall rules
#
# Source function library:
. /etc/init.d/functions

RETVAL=0
start () {
   echo "Loading Firewall Rules: "
   /usr/local/etc/firewall > /dev/null
   touch /var/lock/subsys/firewall
   RETVAL=$?
   [ $RETVAL -eq 0 ] && success || failure
```

```
      echo -n "Status:"
      echo
      return $RETVAL
}

flush () {
    echo -n "Turning Firewall Off"
    iptables -F
    rm -rf /var/lock/subsys/firewall
    RETVAL=$?
    [ $RETVAL -eq 0 ] && success || failure
    echo
    return $RETVAL
}

status () {
      echo "Current Firewall Configuration:"
      RETVAL=$?
      iptables -L
      return $RETVAL
}

panic () {
      echo "Enabling Panic Mode. Only SSH access allowed!!"
      echo -n "You must run '$0 start' to allow other ports "
      echo " through the firewall again."
      echo -n "Panic Mode Status:"
      /sbin/iptables -F
      /sbin/iptables -A INPUT -p tcp --dport 22 -j ACCEPT
      /sbin/iptables -A INPUT -j DROP
      [ $RETVAL -eq 0 ] && success || failure
      echo
      return $RETVAL

}

case "$1" in
  start)
    start
    ;;
  restart)
   start
    ;;
  flush)
    flush
    ;;
  stop)
```

```
    flush
    ;;
status)
    status
    ;;
list)
    status
    ;;
panic)
    panic
    ;;
*)

    echo "Usage:$0 {start|stop|restart|flush|status|list|panic}"
    exit 1
esac

exit $RETVAL
```

11. Change the permissions, add the firewall to the list of enabled services, and test it to make sure it works:

```
chmod 700 /etc/init.d/firewall
chkconfig --add firewall
service firewall restart
```

Congratulations—you are now finished with your Linux installation procedure. You might wish to further customize your installation at this point or you can continue to the next section.

NOTE   You might want to run up2date now to make sure your default packages are up-to-date.

NOTE   You might want to create your backup script now, or you can wait until you have installed everything to make sure all of your wanted directories are included in your backup.

E-Mail

This section covers the information in Chapter 7, "Electronic Mail."

Now that you have your Linux installation up and running, it's time to install your mail servers:

1. Begin by creating your temporary storage for all the packages and source files you are about to download, and move into it:

```
mkdir -p /usr/local/src/mailserver
cd /usr/local/src/mailserver
```

2. Download all those packages:

```
wget http://www.qmail.org/netqmail-1.05.tar.gz
wget ftp://cr.yp.to/ucspi-tcp/ucspi-tcp-0.88.tar.gz
wget ftp://cr.yp.to/daemontools/daemontools-0.76.tar.gz
wget http://www.inter7.com/vpopmail/vpopmail-5.2.2.tar.gz
wget http://www.courier-mta.org/beta/imap/courier-imap-
➥2.2.2.20040207.tar.bz2
wget http://osdn.dl.sourceforge.net/sourceforge/clamav/clamav-0.67-1.tar.gz
wget http://eu.spamassassin.org/released/Mail-SpamAssassin-.63.tar.gz
wget http://unc.dl.sourceforge.net/sourceforge/qmail-scanner/qmail-scanner-
➥1.20.tgz
wget http://unc.dl.sourceforge.net/sourceforge/tnef/tnef-1.2.3.1.tar.gz
wget
http://unc.dl.sourceforge.net/sourceforge/courier/maildrop-1.6.3.tar.bz2
```

3. Rip those files open with the following:

```
tar zxpf clamav*.tar.gz
tar jxpf courier-imap*.tar.bz2
tar zxpf daemontools*.tar.gz
tar jxpf maildrop*.tar.bz2
tar zxpf Mail-SpamAssassin*.tar.gz
tar zxpf netqmail*.tar.gz
tar zxpf qmail-scanner*.tgz
tar zxpf tnef*.tar.gz
tar zxpf ucspi-tcp*.tar.gz
tar zxpf vpopmail*.tar.gz
```

4. Whew—now that you have your files right where you want them, install your Perl modules including SpamAssassin:

```
perl -MCPAN -e shell

cpan> install Bundle::CPAN
cpan> install ExUtils::MakeMaker
cpan> install Time::HiRes
cpan> install DB_File
cpan> install HTML::Parser
cpan> install Net::DNS
cpan> install Mail::SpamAssassin
cpan> quit
```

5. Begin the qmail installation by creating your directories:

```
cd /usr/local/src/mailserver
mkdir /package
mv admin /package
mkdir /var/qmail
mkdir /var/log/qmail
mkdir -p /var/qmail/supervise/qmail-send/log
```

```
mkdir -p /var/qmail/supervise/qmail-smtpd/log
mkdir -p /var/log/qmail/smtpd
```

6. Create all of the needed users and groups:

```
groupadd nofiles
useradd -g nofiles -d /var/qmail/alias alias
useradd -g nofiles -d /var/qmail qmaild
useradd -g nofiles -d /var/qmail qmaill
useradd -g nofiles -d /var/qmail qmailp
groupadd qmail
useradd -g qmail -d /var/qmail qmailq
useradd -g qmail -d /var/qmail qmailr
useradd -g qmail -d /var/qmail -s /nonexistent qmails
```

7. Prepare and build qmail; then configure it with your *fully qualified domain name:*

```
cd /usr/local/src/mailserver/netqmail*
./collate.sh
cd netqmail-1.05
make setup check
./config-fast fully_qualified_domain_name
```

8. Build and install uscpi-tcp:

```
cd /usr/local/src/mailserver/ucspi-tcp*
patch < /usr/local/src/mailserver/netqmail-1.05/other-patches/ucspi-tcp-
0.88.errno.patch
make
make setup check
```

9. Do the same for daemontools:

```
cd /package/admin/daemontools*/src
patch < /usr/local/src/mailserver/netqmail-1.05/other-patches/daemontools-
➥0.76.errno.patch
cd ..
package/install
```

10. Create your qmail startup scripts:

```
pico /var/qmail/rc
```

11. Add the following text:

```
#!/bin/sh

exec env - PATH="/var/qmail/bin:$PATH" \
qmail-start "`cat /var/qmail/control/defaultdelivery`"
```

12. Change the permissions:

```
chmod 755 /var/qmail/rc
```

13. Configure your mailbox type:

    ```
    echo ./Maildir >/var/qmail/control/defaultdelivery
    ```

14. Download your qmail startup script:

    ```
    cd /var/qmail/bin
    wget http://www.lifewithqmail.org/qmailctl-script-dt70
    mv qmailctl-script-dt70 qmailctl
    ```

15. Change the permissions and link the file:

    ```
    chmod 755 /var/qmail/bin/qmailctl
    ln -s /var/qmail/bin/qmailctl /usr/bin
    ```

16. Create each of the supervise scripts:

    ```
    pico /var/qmail/supervise/qmail-send/run
    ```

    and add the following to it:
    ```
    #!/bin/sh
    exec /var/qmail/rc
    ```

17. Make this script executable:

    ```
    chmod 755 /var/qmail/supervise/qmail-send/run
    ```

18. Create another script:

    ```
    pico /var/qmail/supervise/qmail-send/log/run
    ```

    Add the following to this script:
    ```
    #!/bin/sh
    exec /usr/local/bin/setuidgid \
    qmaill /usr/local/bin/multilog t /var/log/qmail
    ```

    Make this script executable:
    ```
    chmod 755 /var/qmail/supervise/qmail-send/log/run
    ```

19. Create the next script:

    ```
    pico /var/qmail/supervise/qmail-smtpd/run
    ```

    Add the following to this script:
    ```
    #!/bin/sh

    QMAILDUID='id -u qmaild'
    NOFILESGID='id -g qmaild'
    MAXSMTPD='cat /var/qmail/control/concurrencyincoming'
    LOCAL='head -1 /var/qmail/control/me'

    if [ -z "$QMAILDUID" -o -z "$NOFILESGID" -o -z "$MAXSMTPD" -o -z "$LOCAL"
    ➥]; then
        echo QMAILDUID, NOFILESGID, MAXSMTPD, or LOCAL is unset in
        echo /var/qmail/supervise/qmail-smtpd/run
    ```

```
        exit 1
fi

if [ ! -f /var/qmail/control/rcpthosts ]; then
    echo "No /var/qmail/control/rcpthosts!"
    echo "Refusing to start SMTP listener because it'll create an open
➥relay"
    exit 1
fi

exec /usr/local/bin/softlimit -m 20000000 \
    /usr/local/bin/tcpserver -v -R -l "$LOCAL" -x /etc/tcp.smtp.cdb -c
➥"$MAXSMTPD" \
        -u "$QMAILDUID" -g "$NOFILESGID" 0 smtp /var/qmail/bin/qmail-smtpd
➥2>&1
```

Make this script executable:

```
chmod 755 /var/qmail/supervise/qmail-smtpd/run
```

20. Now for yet another script:

```
pico /var/qmail/supervise/qmail-smtpd/log/run
```

Add the following to this script:

```
#!/bin/sh
exec /usr/local/bin/setuidgid \
    qmaill /usr/local/bin/multilog t /var/log/qmail/smtpd
```

Make this script executable:

```
chmod 755 /var/qmail/supervise/qmail-smtpd/log/run
```

21. Link the supervise directories to /service, which is where daemontools will be installed:

```
ln -s /var/qmail/supervise/qmail-send /var/qmail/supervise/qmail-smtpd
➥/service
```

22. Stop qmail from running while you perform the next few steps:

```
qmailctl stop
```

23. Set the concurrencyincoming script:

```
echo 20 > /var/qmail/control/concurrencyincoming
chmod 644 /var/qmail/control/concurrencyincoming
```

24. Control SMTP access:

```
echo '127.:allow,RELAYCLIENT=""' >>/etc/tcp.smtp
qmailctl cdb
```

25. Set all permissions:

```
chmod 755 /var/qmail/rc
chmod 755 /var/qmail/bin/qmailctl
```

```
chmod 755 /var/qmail/supervise/qmail-send/run
chmod 755 /var/qmail/supervise/qmail-send/log/run
chmod 755 /var/qmail/supervise/qmail-smtpd/run
chmod 755 /var/qmail/supervise/qmail-smtpd/log/run
chown qmaill /var/log/qmail /var/log/qmail/smtpd
chmod 644 /var/qmail/control/concurrencyincoming
chmod 644 /etc/tcp.smtp*
```

26. Use the following to remove all old mail servers and replace sendmail with qmail:

```
/etc/init.d/sendmail stop
/etc/init.d/postfix stop
rpm -q sendmail
rpm -q exim
rpm -q postfix
```

The previous rpm -q commands perform a query to see whether the packages are installed. If they are installed, select the following steps applicable for the packages you have on your system:

```
rpm -e mutt
rpm -e fetchmail
rpm -e squirrelmail
rpm -e --nodeps sendmail
rpm -e postfix
mv /usr/lib/sendmail /usr/lib/sendmail.old
chmod 0 /usr/lib/sendmail.old
ln -s /var/qmail/bin/sendmail /usr/lib
mv /usr/sbin/sendmail /usr/sbin/sendmail.old
chmod 0 /usr/sbin/sendmail.old
ln -s /var/qmail/bin/sendmail /usr/sbin
```

27. Create the qmail alias files:

```
echo root > /var/qmail/alias/.qmail-root
echo root > /var/qmail/alias/.qmail-postmaster
ln -s .qmail-postmaster /var/qmail/alias/.qmail-mailer-daemon
chmod 644 /var/qmail/alias/.qmail-root /var/qmail/alias/.qmail-postmaster
```

28. Test the installation to make sure it's running:

```
qmailctl stop
qmailctl start
qmailctl stat
cd /var/qmail
wget http://lifewithqmail.org/inst_check
chmod 755 inst_check
./inst_check
```

Make sure everything looks okay and get ready for the add-ons.

Vpopmail

Now we will install vpopmail onto our server:

1. First add our user and group for vpopmail:

```
cd /usr/local/src/mailserver/vpopmail*
groupadd -g 109 vchkpw
useradd -g vchkpw -u 109 -d /home/vpopmail vpopmail
./configure --enable-roaming-users=y
make
make install
crontab -e
```

2. Add the following to the crontab:

```
40 * * * * /home/vpopmail/bin/clearopensmtp 2>&1 > /dev/null
```

3. Create an admin account and make sure to substitute the correct information for the user and domain names:

```
cd /home/vpopmail/bin
./vadddomain yourdomain.com
./vadduser admin@yourdomain.com
```

Courier-IMAP

Next we will install Courier-IMAP:

1. First, compile and install the binaries:

```
cd /usr/local/src/mailserver/
chown -R someuser.someuser courier-imap*
su someuser
cd /usr/local/src/mailserver/courier-imap*
./configure --with-redhat
```

NOTE   You might get an error when the make command tries to compile the authvchkpw. Disregard this error and continue.

```
exit
cd /usr/local/src/mailserver/courier-imap*
make
make install
make install-configure
```

2. Once again, disregard any errors you might receive. Then add IMAP as a service:

```
cp courier-imap.sysvinit /etc/init.d/imapd
```

3. Add and start the service:

```
chkconfig --add imapd
/etc/init.d/imapd start
```

POP3

Now we will install POP3 support for your server:

1. First, make the appropriate directories and begin editing the run file:

```
mkdir -p /var/qmail/supervise/qmail-pop3d
mkdir -p /var/qmail/supervise/qmail-pop3d/log/
mkdir -p /var/log/qmail/pop3d
pico /var/qmail/supervise/qmail-pop3d/run
```

2. Add the following:

```
#!/bin/sh
exec /usr/local/bin/softlimit -m 20000000 \
    /usr/local/bin/tcpserver -v -R -H -l 0 0 110 \
    /var/qmail/bin/qmail-popup \
    your.domain.com  /home/vpopmail/bin/vchkpw \
    /var/qmail/bin/qmail-pop3d Maildir 2>&1
```

NOTE   Substitute *your.domain.com* with your hostname in the previous script.

3. Now edit the next run file:

```
pico /var/qmail/supervise/qmail-pop3d/log/run
```

4. Add the following:

```
#!/bin/sh
exec /usr/local/bin/setuidgid qmaill \
    /usr/local/bin/multilog t \
    /var/log/qmail/pop3d
```

5. Set your permissions and link the file:

```
chown qmaill /var/log/qmail/pop3d
chmod 755 /var/qmail/supervise/qmail-pop3d/run
chmod 755 /var/qmail/supervise/qmail-pop3d/log/run
ln -s /var/qmail/supervise/qmail-pop3d /service
```

6. You are almost there! Next, you need to edit the /var/qmail/bin/qmailctl script and add the qmail-pop3d information:

```
pico /var/qmail/bin/qmailctl
```

In the start section, add the following directly above the two semicolons:

```
if svok /service/qmail-pop3d ; then
    svc -u /service/qmail-pop3d /service/qmail-pop3d/log
else
    echo qmail-pop3d supervise not running
fi
```

In the stop section, add the following directly above the two semicolons:

```
echo "  qmail-pop3d"
svc -d /service/qmail-pop3d /service/qmail-pop3d/log
```

In the stat section, add the following directly above the qmail-qstat section:

```
svstat /service/qmail-pop3d
svstat /service/qmail-pop3d/log
```

In the pause section, add the following directly above the two semicolons:

```
echo "Pausing qmail-pop3d"
svc -p /service/qmail-pop3d
```

In the cont section, add the following directly above the two semicolons:

```
echo "Continuing qmail-pop3d"
svc -c /service/qmail-pop3d
```

In the restart section, add the following directly above the two semicolons:

```
echo "* Restarting qmail-pop3d."
svc -t /service/qmail-pop3d /service/qmail-pop3d/log
```

7. Save this file and then restart qmail:

```
qmailctl stop
qmailctl start
```

Clam AntiVirus

Now we are ready to install Clam AntiVirus:

1. Begin by creating that appropriate group and user, compiling and installing the binaries and start editing the crontab once again:

```
cd /usr/local/src/mailserver/clamav*
groupadd clamav
useradd -g clamav -s /bin/false -c "Clam AntiVirus" clamav
./configure
make
make install
touch /var/log/clam-update.log
```

```
chmod 600 /var/log/clam-update.log
chown clamav /var/log/clam-update.log
freshclam -d -c 2 -l /var/log/clam-update.log
crontab - e
```

2. Add the following:

```
0 8 * * * /usr/local/bin/freshclam --quiet -l /var/log/clam-update.log
```

3. Now link the log file:

```
/usr/local/bin/freshclam -l /var/log/clam-update.log
```

qmail-Scanner

It's qmail-Scanner installation time:

1. Make and install the proper files:

```
cd /usr/local/src/mailserver/tnef*
./configure
make
make install

cd /usr/local/src/mailserver/maildrop*
./configure
make
make install
```

> **NOTE** Before you begin, you will need to make sure you have `perl-suidperl` installed. You can find an RPM version of this by querying your RPM database first with `rpm -q perl-suidperl`. If the package is installed, you can continue. If not, check `rpm.pbone.net` for a Fedora Core 2 package.

> **NOTE** If you install a version of `perl-suid` that requires you to update Perl, ensure that all of your other modules work correctly before you proceed any further. You might need to reinstall modules in some cases.

2. Continue on by performing the following:

```
cd /usr/local/src/mailserver/qmail-scanner*
groupadd qscand
useradd -c "qmail-Scanner Account" -g qscand -s /bin/false qscand
./configure --scanners "clamscan,verbose_spamassassin"
➥--admin "you" --domain "yourdomain.com" --install
setuidgid qmaild /var/qmail/bin/qmail-scanner-queue.pl -g
pico /var/qmail/supervise/qmail-smtpd/run
```

3. Add the following line directly below LOCAL=`'head -1 /var/qmail/control/me'`:

```
QMAILQUEUE="/var/qmail/bin/qmail-scanner-queue
export QMAILQUEUE
```

4. Edit another file and change the first line:

```
pico /etc/tcp.smtp
```

```
127.:allow,RELAYCLIENT="",QMAILQUEUE="/var/qmail/bin/qmail-scanner-
➥queue.pl"
```

5. Restart qmail and open the ports in your firewall script:

```
pico /usr/local/etc/firewall
```

6. Add the following to the script:

```
$IPTABLES -A INPUT -p tcp --dport 25 -j ACCEPT
$IPTABLES -A INPUT -p tcp --dport 110 -j ACCEPT
$IPTABLES -A INPUT -p tcp --dport 143 -j ACCEPT
```

7. Restart:

```
service firewall restart
```

Now it's time for Apache!

Apache Web Server

This section covers the information found in Chapter 8, "Apache Web Server: Installation and Configuration."

This section shows the installation without SSL support and compiles Apache using Dynamic Shared Objects:

1. Remove any old packages if they exist and kill the processes:

```
rpm -e redhat-config-httpd
rpm -e httpd
ps aux | grep httpd
killall httpd
```

2. Create a new directory for your source, move to that directory, and download your files:

```
mkdir -p /usr/local/src/webserver
cd /usr/local/src/webserver
wget
➥ 'http://apache.tarchive.com/httpd/apache_1.3.29.tar.gz'
tar zxpf apache_1.3*.tar.gz
```

3. Create your configure script:

```
pico apache_install
```

4. Add the following to the script:

```
cd /usr/local/src/webserver/apache_1.3.29
make distclean
./configure \
    --prefix=/www \
    --enable-module=so \
    --enable-module=rewrite \
    --enable-shared=rewrite \
    --enable-module=setenvif \
    --enable-shared=setenvif \
    --enable-module=mime \
    --enable-shared=mime \
    --enable-module=mime_magic \
    --enable-shared=mime_magic \
    --enable-module=dir \
    --enable-shared=dir \
    --enable-module=auth \
    --enable-shared=auth \
    --enable-module=access \
    --enable-shared=access \
    --enable-module=alias \
    --enable-shared=alias \
    --enable-module=status \
    --enable-shared=status \
    --enable-module=userdir \
    --enable-shared=userdir \
    --enable-module=vhost_alias \
    --enable-shared=vhost_alias \
    --enable-module=env \
    --enable-shared=env \
    --enable-module=log_referer \
    --enable-shared=log_referer \
    --enable-module=log_config \
    --enable-shared=log_config \
    --enable-module=log_agent \
    --enable-shared=log_agent \
    --enable-module=headers \
    --enable-shared=headers
```

5. Make the script executable:

```
chmod +x apache_install
```

6. Build and install Apache:

```
./apache_install
cd /usr/local/src/webserver/apache_1.3*
make
make install
```

7. Link your control files:

```
ln -s /www/bin/apachectl /usr/bin/apachectl
ln -s /www/bin/apachectl /usr/sbin/apachectl
```

8. Start it up:

```
apachectl start
```

NOTE   Now it's time to configure your web server. Modify your `httpd.conf` file appropriately and continue to the "MySQL" section.

MySQL

This section covers the information found in Chapter 9, "MySQL: Installation and Configuration" and will perform a clean install of MySQL.

1. Remove all the old packages if they're installed and kill the processes if they exist:

```
rpm -e MySQL-devel
rpm -e MySQL-client
rpm -e MySQL-server
killall mysqld
```

2. Create your source file directory:

```
mkdir /usr/local/src/mysql
cd /usr/local/src/mysql
```

3. Download your source files into this directory. You can find the source files at www.mysql .com/downloads/index.html.

4. After that is complete, let's get the installation rolling by adding the mysql user and begin editing the conf_mysql file:

```
tar -zxvf mysql-*
cd /usr/local/src/mysql/mysql-5.0.0-alpha
groupadd mysql
useradd -g mysql mysql
pico conf_mysql
```

5. Now add the following to the conf_mysql file:

```
CFLAGS="-O3"
CXX=gcc
CXXFLAGS="-O3 \
  -felide-constructors \
  -fno-exceptions -fno-rtti"

./configure \
  --prefix=/usr/local/mysql \
```

```
--with-extra-charsets=complex \
--enable-thread-safe-client \
--enable-local-infile \
--enable-assembler \
--disable-shared \
--with-client-ldflags=-all-static \
--with-mysqld-ldflags=-all-static
```

6. Change the permissions, run the file, and complete the installation. Then create the first test database, change the permissions, and test the installation:

```
chmod 755 conf_mysql
./conf_mysql
make
make install
scripts/mysql_install_db
chown -R root  /usr/local/mysql
chown -R mysql /usr/local/mysql/var
chgrp -R mysql /usr/local/mysql
/usr/local/mysql/bin/mysqld_safe --user=mysql &
```

7. Don't forget to set the root passwords, substituting the required password and domain with yours:

```
/usr/local/mysql/bin/mysqladmin -u root password
➡ 'new-password'
/usr/local/mysql/bin/mysqladmin -u root -h domain password
➡ 'new-password'
```

PHP

This section covers the information found in Chapter 10, "PHP: Installation and Configuration" and will perform an installation of PHP 5.

1. Start by downloading and untaring PHP:

```
cd /usr/local/src/webserver
wget 'http://us3.php.net/get/php-5.0.0.tar.gz/from/this/mirror'
tar zxpf php-5*.tar.gz
```

2. Create your configuration file:

```
pico php_install
```

3. Add the following:

```
cd php-5.0.0
./configure \
--with-apxs=/www/bin/apxs \
```

```
--with-mysql=/usr/local/mysql \
--enable-ftp \
--enable-trans-sid
```

4. Change the permissions, configure, make, and install then copy your INI file over:

```
chmod 755 php_install
./php_install
cd php-5.0.0
make
make install
cp php.ini-dist /usr/local/lib/php.ini
```

5. To finish it off, you will need to add PHP support into Apache by editing the `httpd.conf` file. Go ahead and add the following to the bottom of the file:

```
AddType application/x-httpd-php .php .php3
AddType application/x-httpd-php-source .phps
```

6. Change your `DirectoryIndex` setting from

```
DirectoryIndex  index.html
```

to

```
DirectoryIndex index.php default.php index.html index.htm
```

Congratulations—after you restart Apache, you will have a server ready to run. We hope the appendix has been of value to you and we're sure you'll be using it again. Good luck!

Appendix B

MySQL Configuration Directives

MySQL Configuration Directives

--abort-slave-event-count=#   Option used by mysql-test for debugging and testing of replication.

--ansi   Use ANSI SQL syntax instead of MySQL syntax.

--back_log=#   The number of outstanding connection requests MySQL can have. This comes into play when the main MySQL thread receives many connection requests in a very short time.

--basedir=*name*   The path to the installation directory. All paths are usually resolved relative to this.

--bdb   Enable Berkeley DB (if this version of MySQL supports it). Disable with --skip-bdb (this will save memory).

--big-tables   Allow big result sets by saving all temporary sets on file (solves most table full errors).

--bind-address=*name*   The IP address to bind to.

--binlog_cache_size=#   The size of the cache to hold the SQL statements for the binary log during a transaction. If you often use big, multi-statement transactions, you can increase this to get more performance.

--binlog-do-db=*name*   Tells the master it should log updates for the specified database and should exclude all others not explicitly mentioned.

--binlog-ignore-db=*name*   Tells the master that updates to the given database should not be logged to the binary log.

--bootstrap   Used by MySQL installation scripts.

--bulk_insert_buffer_size=#   The size of the tree cache used in bulk insert optimization. Note that this is a limit per thread!

--character-sets-dir=*name*   The directory where character sets are located.

--chroot=*name*   Chroot the mysqld daemon during startup.

--concurrent-insert   Use concurrent insert with MyISAM. Disable with --skip-concurrent-insert.

--connect_timeout=#   The number of seconds the mysqld server is waiting for a connect packet before responding with Bad handshake.

--console   Write error output on screen; don't remove the console window on Windows.

--core-file   Write core on errors.

--datadir=*name*   The path to the database root.

--date-format=*name*   The date format (for future).

--datetime-format=*name*   The DateTime/Timestamp format (for future).

--default-character-set=*name*   Set the default character set.

--default-collation=*name*   Set the default collation.

--default-storage-engine=*name*   Set the default storage engine (table type) for tables.

--default-table-type=*name*   Deprecated option—use `default-storage-engine` instead.

--default-week-format=#   The default week format used by `WEEK()` functions.

--delay-key-write-for-all-tables   Don't flush key buffers between writes for any MyISAM table. Deprecated option—use `--delay-key-write=all` instead.

--delay-key-write[=*name*]   Type of `DELAY_KEY_WRITE`.

--delayed_insert_limit=#   After inserting the number of rows indicated by this option, the `INSERT DELAYED` handler will check whether there are any `SELECT` statements pending. If so, the handler allows these to execute before continuing.

--delayed_insert_timeout=#   The length of time an `INSERT DELAYED` thread should wait for `INSERT` statements before terminating.

--delayed_queue_size=#   The queue size (in rows) that should be allocated for handling `INSERT DELAYED`. If the queue becomes full, any client that performs `INSERT DELAYED` will wait until there is room in the queue again.

--disconnect-slave-event-count=#   Option used by `mysql-test` for debugging and testing of replication.

--enable-locking   Deprecated option—use `--external-locking` instead.

--enable-pstack   Print a symbolic stack trace on failure.

--exit-info=#   Used for debugging. Use at your own risk!

--expire_logs_days=#   Logs will be rotated after the number of days indicated by this option.

--external-locking   Use system (external) locking. With this option enabled, you can run `myisamchk` to test (not repair) tables while the MySQL server is running.

--flush   Flush tables to disk between SQL commands.

--flush_time=#   A dedicated thread is created to flush all tables at the given interval.

--ft_max_word_len=#   The maximum length of the word to be included in a FULLTEXT index. Note: FULLTEXT indexes must be rebuilt after changing this variable.

--ft_min_word_len=#   The minimum length of the word to be included in a FULLTEXT index. Note: FULLTEXT indexes must be rebuilt after changing this variable.

--ft_query_expansion_limit=#   The number of best matches to use for query expansion.

--ft_stopword_file=*name*   Use stopwords from this file instead of from a built-in list.

--gdb   Set up signals usable for debugging.

--group_concat_max_len=#   The maximum length of the result of the function group_concat.

--help   Display this help and exit.

--init-connect=*name*   Command(s) that are executed for each new connection.

--init-file=*name*   Read SQL commands from this file at startup.

--init-rpl-role=*name*   Set the replication role.

--init-slave=*name*   Command(s) that are executed when a slave connects to this master.

--innodb   Enable InnoDB (if this version of MySQL supports it). Disable with **--skip-innodb** (this will save memory).

--innodb_additional_mem_pool_size=#   The size of a memory pool InnoDB uses to store data dictionary information and other internal data structures.

--innodb_buffer_pool_awe_mem_mb=#   If Windows AWE (Advanced Windowing Extensions) is used, this option indicates the size of the InnoDB buffer pool allocated from the AWE memory.

--innodb_buffer_pool_size=#   The size of the memory buffer that InnoDB uses to cache data and indexes of its tables.

--innodb_data_file_path=*name*   The path to individual files and their sizes.

--innodb_data_home_dir=*name*   The common part for InnoDB tablespaces.

--innodb_fast_shutdown   Speeds up the server shutdown process.

--innodb_file_io_threads=#   The number of file I/O threads in InnoDB.

--innodb_file_per_table   Stores each InnoDB table to an .ibd file in the database directory.

--innodb_flush_log_at_trx_commit=#   Set to 0 (write and flush once per second), 1 (write and flush at each commit), or 2 (write at commit, flush once per second).

--innodb_flush_method=*name*   Set which method to use for flushing data.

--innodb_force_recovery=#   Helps to save your data in case the disk image of the database becomes corrupt.

--innodb_lock_wait_timeout=#   The timeout (in seconds) an InnoDB transaction can wait for a lock before being rolled back.

--innodb_log_arch_dir=*name*   The directory where full logs should be archived.

--innodb_log_archive=#   Set to 1 if you want to have logs archived.

--innodb_log_buffer_size=#   The size of the buffer that InnoDB uses to write logs to the log files on disk.

--innodb_log_file_size=#   The size, in megabytes, of each log file in a log group.

--innodb_log_files_in_group=#   The number of log files in the log group. InnoDB writes to the files in a circular fashion. Value 3 is recommended here.

--innodb_log_group_home_dir=*name*   The path to InnoDB log files.

--innodb_max_dirty_pages_pct=#   The percentage of dirty pages allowed in the buffer pool.

--innodb_mirrored_log_groups=#   The number of identical copies of log groups you keep for the database. Currently this should be set to 1.

--innodb_open_files=#   The maximum number of files that InnoDB keeps open at the same time.

--innodb_thread_concurrency=#   Helps in performance tuning in heavily concurrent environments.

--interactive_timeout=#   The number of seconds the server waits for activity on an interactive connection before closing it.

--isam   Enable ISAM (if this version of MySQL supports it). Disable with --skip-isam.

--join_buffer_size=#   The size of the buffer that is used for full joins.

--key_buffer_size=#   The size of the buffer used for index blocks for MyISAM tables. Increase this number to as much as you can afford to get better index handling (for all reads and multiple writes); 64MB on a 256MB machine that mainly runs MySQL is quite common.

--key_cache_block_size=#   The default size of key cache blocks.

--key_cache_division_age_threshold=#   This characterizes the number of hits a hot block has to be untouched until it is considered aged enough to be downgraded to a warm block. This specifies the percentage ratio of that number of hits to the total number of blocks in key cache.

--key_cache_division_limit=#   The minimum percentage of warm blocks in the key cache.

--language=*name*   Client error messages in a given language. Can be given as a full path.

--local-infile   Enable/disable LOAD DATA LOCAL INFILE (takes values 1|0).

--log-bin=*name*   Log update queries in binary format.

--log-bin-index=*name*   The file holding the names for the last binary log files.

--log-error=*name*   The log error file.

--log-isam=*name*   Log all MyISAM changes to file.

--log-long-format   Log some extra information to the update log. This option is deprecated; see the --log-short-format option.

--log=*name*   Log connections and queries to file.

--log-queries-not-using-indexes   Log queries that are executed without benefit of any index.

--log-short-format   Don't log extra information to update and slow-query logs.

--log-slave-updates   Tells the slave to log the updates from the slave thread to the binary log. You will need to turn it on if you plan to daisy-chain the slaves.

--log-slow-queries=*name*   Log slow queries to this log file. Defaults logging to *hostname*-slow.log file.

--log-update=*name*   The update log is deprecated since version 5.0 and is replaced by the binary log. This option turns on --log-bin instead.

--log-warnings   Log some noncritical warnings to the log file.

--long_query_time=#   Log all queries that have taken more than long_query_time seconds to execute to file.

--low-priority-updates   INSERT/DELETE/UPDATE has lower priority than SELECTs.

--lower_case_table_names   If this option is set to 1, table names are stored in lowercase on disk and are case insensitive.

--master-connect-retry=#   The number of seconds the slave thread will sleep before retrying to connect to the master in case the master goes down or the connection is lost.

--master-host=*name*   The master hostname or IP address for replication. If this option is not set, the slave thread will not be started. Note that the setting of master-host will be ignored if a valid master.info file exists.

--master-info-file=*name*   The location and name of the file that remembers the master and where the I/O replication thread is in the master's bin logs.

--master-password=*name*   The password the slave thread will authenticate with when connecting to the master. If this option is not set, an empty password is assumed. The value in master.info will take precedence if it can be read.

--master-port=#   The port the master is listening on. If this option is not set, the compiled setting of MYSQL_PORT is assumed. If you have not tinkered with the configuration options, this should be 3306. The value in master.info will take precedence if it can be read.

--master-retry-count=#   The number of tries the slave will make to connect to the master before giving up.

--master-ssl   Enable the slave to connect to the master by using SSL.

--master-ssl-ca=*name*   The master SSL CA file. Applies only if you have enabled master-ssl.

--master-ssl-capath=*name*   The master SSL CA path. Applies only if you have enabled master-ssl.

--master-ssl-cert=*name*   The master SSL certificate filename. Applies only if you have enabled master-ssl.

--master-ssl-cipher=*name*   The master SSL cipher. Applies only if you have enabled master-ssl.

--master-ssl-key=*name*   The master SSL keyfile name. Applies only if you have enabled master-ssl.

--master-user=*name*   The username the slave thread will use for authentication when connecting to the master. The user must have FILE privilege. If the master user is not set, user test is assumed. The value in master.info will take precedence if it can be read.

--max_allowed_packet=#   The maximum packet length to send to or receive from the server.

--max_binlog_cache_size=#   Can be used to restrict the total size for caching a multi-transaction query.

--max-binlog-dump-events=#   Option used by `mysql-test` for debugging and testing of replication.

--max_binlog_size=#   Binary log will be rotated automatically when the size exceeds this value. Will also apply to relay logs if `max_relay_log_size` is 0. The minimum value for this variable is 4096.

--max_connect_errors=#   If there is more than this number of interrupted connections from a host, this host will be blocked from further connections.

--max_connections=#   The number of simultaneous clients allowed.

--max_delayed_threads=#   Don't start more than this number of threads to handle INSERT DELAYED statements. If set to zero, this means INSERT DELAYED is not used.

--max_error_count=#   The maximum number of errors/warnings to store for a statement.

--max_heap_table_size=#   Don't allow creation of heap tables bigger than this.

--max_join_size=#   Joins that are probably going to read more than `max_join_size` records return an error.

--max_length_for_sort_data=#   The maximum number of bytes in sorted records.

--max_relay_log_size=#   If this is a nonzero value, the relay log will be rotated automatically when the size exceeds this value. If this value is zero (the default), when the size exceeds `max_binlog_size` it will be rotated. The minimum value for this variable is 4096.

--max_seeks_for_key=#   Limit assumed maximum number of seeks when looking up rows based on a key.

--max_sort_length=#   The number of bytes to use when sorting BLOB or TEXT values. (Only the first `max_sort_length` bytes of each value are used; the rest are ignored.)

--max_tmp_tables=#   The maximum number of temporary tables a client can keep open at a time.

--max_user_connections=#   The maximum number of active connections for a single user (0 = no limit).

--max_write_lock_count=#   After this many write locks, allow some read locks to run in between.

--memlock   Lock `mysqld` in memory.

--myisam_block_size=#   The block size to be used for MyISAM index pages.

--myisam_max_extra_sort_file_size=#   Used to help MySQL decide when to use the slow but safe key cache index creation method.

--myisam_max_sort_file_size=#   Don't use the fast sort index method to create an index if the temporary file would get bigger than this.

--myisam-recover=*name*   Syntax: `myisam-recover[=`*option*`[,`*option*`...]]`, where *option* can be `DEFAULT`, `BACKUP`, `FORCE`, or `QUICK`.

--myisam_repair_threads=#   The number of threads to use when repairing MyISAM tables. The value of 1 disables parallel repair.

--myisam_sort_buffer_size=#   The buffer that is allocated during index sorting when performing a `REPAIR` or when creating indexes with `CREATE INDEX` or `ALTER TABLE`.

--net_buffer_length=#   The buffer length for TCP/IP and socket communication.

--net_read_timeout=#   The number of seconds to wait for more data from a connection before aborting the read.

--net_retry_count=#   If a read on a communication port is interrupted, retry this many times before giving up.

--net_write_timeout=#   The number of seconds to wait for a block to be written to a vconnection before aborting the write.

--new   Use very new, possibly unsafe functions.

--old-passwords   Use old password encryption method (needed for 4.0 and older clients).

--old-rpl-compat   Use old `LOAD DATA` format in the binary log (don't save data in file).

--open_files_limit=#   If this is not 0, `mysqld` will use this value to reserve file descriptors to use with `setrlimit()`. If this value is 0, `mysqld` will reserve the `max_connections*5` or `max_connections + table_cache*2` number of files (whichever is larger).

--pid-file=*name*   The PID file used by `safe_mysqld`.

--port=#   The port number to use for the connection.

--preload_buffer_size=#   The size of the buffer that is allocated when preloading indexes.

--query_alloc_block_size=#   The allocation block size for query parsing and execution.

--query_cache_limit=#   Don't cache results that are bigger than this.

--query_cache_min_res_unit=#   The minimal size of unit in which space for results is allocated (the last unit will be trimmed after writing all result data).

--query_cache_size=#   The memory allocated to store results from old queries.

--query_cache_type=#   0 = OFF = Don't cache or retrieve results.

1 = ON = Cache all results except SELECT SQL_NO_CACHE … queries.

2 = DEMAND = Cache only SELECT SQL_CACHE … queries.

--query_prealloc_size=#   The persistent buffer for query parsing and execution.

--range_alloc_block_size=#   The allocation block size for storing ranges during optimization.

--read_buffer_size=#   Each thread that does a sequential scan allocates a buffer of this size for each table it scans. If you perform many sequential scans, you might want to increase this value.

--read-only   Make all tables read-only, with the exception of replication (slave) threads and users with the SUPER privilege.

--read_rnd_buffer_size=#   When reading rows in sorted order after a sort, the rows are read through this buffer to avoid a disk seek. If this value is not set, then it defaults to the value of record_buffer.

--record_buffer=#   The alias for read_buffer_size.

--relay-log-index=*name*   The location and name to use for the file that keeps a list of the last relay logs.

--relay-log-info-file=*name*   The location and name of the file that remembers where the SQL replication thread is in the relay logs.

--relay-log=*name*   The location and name to use for relay logs.

--relay_log_purge   0 = Do not purge relay logs. 1 = Purge them as soon as they are no longer needed.

--relay_log_space_limit=#   The maximum space to use for all relay logs.

--replicate-do-db=*name*   Tells the slave thread to restrict replication to the specified database. To specify more than one database, use the directive multiple times, once for each database. Note that this will work only if you do not use cross-database queries such as UPDATE *some_db.some_table* SET *foo*='*bar*' while having selected a different or no database. If you need cross-database updates to work, make sure you have 3.23.28 or later, and use replicate-wild-do-table=db_name.%.

`--replicate-do-table=`*name*   Tells the slave thread to restrict replication to the specified table. To specify more than one table, use the directive multiple times, once for each table. This will work for cross-database updates, in contrast to `replicate-do-db`.

`--replicate-ignore-db=`*name*   Tells the slave thread to not replicate to the specified database. To specify more than one database to ignore, use the directive multiple times, once for each database. This option will not work if you use cross-database updates. If you need cross-database updates to work, make sure you have 3.23.28 or later, and use `replicate-wild-ignore-table=db_name.%`.

`--replicate-ignore-table=`*name*   Tells the slave thread to not replicate to the specified table. To specify more than one table to ignore, use the directive multiple times, once for each table. This will work for cross-database updates, in contrast to `replicate-ignore-db`.

`--replicate-rewrite-db=`*name*   Updates to a database with a different name than the original. Example: `replicate-rewrite-db=master_db_name->slave_db_name`.

`--replicate-wild-do-table=`*name*   Tells the slave thread to restrict replication to the tables that match the specified wildcard pattern. To specify more than one table, use the directive multiple times, once for each table. This will work for cross-database updates. Example: `replicate-wild-do-table=foo%.bar%` will replicate only updates to tables in all databases that start with *foo* and whose table names start with *bar*.

`--replicate-wild-ignore-table=`*name*   Tells the slave thread to not replicate to the tables that match the given wildcard pattern. To specify more than one table to ignore, use the directive multiple times, once for each table. This will work for cross-database updates. Example: `replicate-wild-ignore-table=foo%.bar%` will not update tables in databases that start with *foo* and whose table names start with *bar*.

`--report-host=`*name*   The hostname or IP of the slave to be reported to the master during slave registration. This will appear in the output of SHOW SLAVE HOSTS. Leave unset if you do not want the slave to register itself with the master. Note that it is not sufficient for the master to simply read the IP of the slave off the socket after the slave connects. Because of Network Address Translation (NAT) and other routing issues, that IP might not be valid for connecting to the slave from the master or other hosts.

`--report-password=`*name*   Undocumented.

`--report-port=#`   The port for connecting to the slave, reported to the master during slave registration. Set it only if the slave is listening on a nondefault port or if you have a special tunnel from the master or other clients to the slave. If you are not sure, leave this option unset.

--report-user=*name*   Undocumented.

--rpl-recovery-rank=#   Undocumented.

--safemalloc-mem-limit=#   Simulate memory shortage when compiled with the --with-debug=full option.

--safe-mode   Skip some optimize stages (for testing).

--safe-show-database   Deprecated option—use GRANT SHOW DATABASES instead.

--safe-user-create   Don't allow new user creation by the user who has no write privileges to the mysql.user table.

--secure-auth   Disallow authentication for accounts that have old (pre-4.1) passwords.

--server-id=#   Uniquely identifies the server instance in the community of replication partners.

--set-variable=*name*   Change the value of a variable. This option is deprecated; you can set variables directly with --variable-name=*value*.

--show-slave-auth-info   Show user and password in SHOW SLAVE HOSTS.

--skip-grant-tables   Start without grant tables. This gives all users *full access* to all tables!

--skip-host-cache   Don't cache hostnames.

--skip-locking   Deprecated option—use --skip-external-locking instead.

--skip-name-resolve   Don't resolve hostnames. All hostnames are IPs or localhost.

--skip-networking   Don't allow connection with TCP/IP.

--skip-new   Don't use new, possibly wrong routines.

--skip-show-database   Don't allow SHOW DATABASE commands.

--skip-slave-start   If this option is set, the slave is not autostarted.

--skip-stack-trace   Don't print a stack trace on failure.

--skip-symlink   Don't allow symlinking of tables. Deprecated option—use --skip-symbolic-links instead.

--skip-thread-priority   Don't give threads different priorities.

--slave_compressed_protocol   Use compression on master/slave protocol.

--slave-load-tmpdir=*name* The location where the slave should put its temporary files when replicating a LOAD DATA INFILE command.

--slave_net_timeout=# The number of seconds to wait for more data from a master/slave connection before aborting the read.

--slave-skip-errors=*name* Tells the slave thread to continue replication when a query returns an error from the provided list.

--slow_launch_time=# If creating the thread takes longer than this value (in seconds), the slow_launch_threads counter will be incremented.

--socket=*name* The socket file to use for the connection.

--sort_buffer_size=# Each thread that needs to do a sort allocates a buffer of this size.

--sporadic-binlog-dump-fail Option used by mysql-test for debugging and testing of replication.

--sql-bin-update-same The update log is deprecated since version 5.0 and is replaced by the binary log. This option no longer does anything.

--sql-mode=*name* Syntax: sql-mode=*option*[,*option*[,*option*...]], where *option* can be one of the following: REAL_AS_FLOAT, PIPES_AS_CONCAT, ANSI_QUOTES, IGNORE_SPACE, ONLY_FULL_GROUP_BY, NO_UNSIGNED_SUBTRACTION.

--symbolic-links Enable symbolic link support.

--table_cache=# The number of open tables for all threads.

--temp-pool Using this option will cause most temporary files created to use a small set of names, rather than a unique name for each new file.

--thread_cache_size=# The number of threads you should keep in a cache for reuse.

--thread_concurrency=# Permits the application to give the threads system a hint for the desired number of threads that should be run at the same time.

--thread_stack=# The stack size for each thread.

--time-format=*name* The time format (for future).

--tmp_table_size=# If an in-memory temporary table exceeds this size, MySQL will automatically convert it to an on-disk MyISAM table.

--tmpdir=*name* The path for temporary files. Several paths can be specified, separated by a colon (:); in this case, they are used in a round-robin fashion.

--transaction_alloc_block_size=# The allocation block size for transactions to be stored in the binary log.

--transaction-isolation=*name* The default transaction isolation level.

--transaction_prealloc_size=# The persistent buffer for transactions to be stored in binary log.

--use-symbolic-links Enable symbolic link support. Deprecated option—use --symbolic-links instead.

--user=*name* Run the mysqld daemon as the specified user.

--verbose Used with the --help option for detailed help.

--version Output the version information and exit.

--wait_timeout=# The number of seconds the server waits for activity on a connection before closing it.

--warnings Deprecated option—use --log-warnings instead.

Installation Configuration Directives

--bindir=*DIR* This will specify the location of the user executables.

--build=*BUILD* Configure for building on *BUILD* [guessed].

--datadir=*DIR* Read-only, architecture-independent data.

--disable-dependency-tracking Speeds up one-time builds.

--disable-*FEATURE* Do not include *FEATURE*.

--disable-largefile Omit support for large files.

--disable-libtool-lock Avoid locking (might break parallel builds).

--enable-assembler Use assembler versions of some string functions if available.

--enable-dependency-tracking Do not reject slow dependency extractors.

--enable-fast-install=*PKGS* Optimize for fast installation; the default is yes.

--enable-*FEATURE*[=*ARG*] Include *FEATURE* if *ARG* is yes.

--enable-local-infile Enable LOAD DATA LOCAL INFILE (default: disabled).

--enable-maintainer-mode   Enable make rules and dependencies not useful (and sometimes confusing) to the casual installer.

--enable-shared=*PKGS*   Build shared libraries; the default is yes.

--enable-static=*PKGS*   Build static libraries; the default is yes.

--enable-thread-safe-client   Compile the client with threads.

--host=*HOST*   Cross-compile to build programs to run on *HOST* [*BUILD*].

--includedir=*DIR*   C header files.

--infodir=*DIR*   Specify the directory where the information documentation should be placed.

--libdir=*DIR*   Object code libraries.

--libexecdir=*DIR*   Program executables.

--localstatedir=*DIR*   Modifiable, single-machine data.

--mandir=*DIR*   The manual directory location.

--oldincludedir=*DIR*   C header files for non-GCC.

--program-prefix=*PREFIX*   Prepend *PREFIX* to installed program names.

--program-suffix=*SUFFIX*   Append *SUFFIX* to installed program names.

--program-transform-name=*PROGRAM*   Run specified *PROGRAM* on installed program names.

--sbindir=*DIR*   This will tell MySQL where to install the System administrator binaries.

--sharedstatedir=*DIR*   Modifiable, architecture-independent data.

--sysconfdir=*DIR*   Read-only, single-machine data.

--target=*TARGET*   Configure for building compilers for *TARGET* [*HOST*].

--with-berkeley-db=*DIR*   Use BerkeleyDB located in *DIR*.

--with-berkeley-db-includes=*DIR*   Find Berkeley DB headers in *DIR*.

--with-berkeley-db-libs=*DIR*   Find Berkeley DB libraries in *DIR*.

--with-charset=*CHARSET*   The default character set. Use one of the following: ascii, armscii8, big5, cp1250, cp1251, cp1256, cp1257, cp850, cp852, cp866, dec8, euckr, gb2312, gbk, greek, hebrew, hp8, keybcs2, koi8r, koi8u, latin1, latin2, latin5, latin7, macce, macroman, sjis, swe7, tis620, ucs2, ujis, or utf8.

--with-client-ldflags   Extra linking arguments for clients.

--with-collation=*COLLATION*   This is defined with a charset, as seen in the --with-charset directive. You can specify a collation of a charset such as latin1_swedish_ci for latin1.

--with-comment   Add a comment about compilation environment.

--with-embedded-server   Build the embedded server (libmysqld).

--with-extra-charsets=*CHARSET,CHARSET,*   Use charsets in addition to the default (none, complex, all, or a list selected from the --with-charset directive).

--with-gnu-ld   Assume the C compiler uses GNU ld; the default is no.

--with-isam   Enable the ISAM table type.

--with-lib-ccflags   Extra CC options for libraries.

--with-libwrap=*DIR*   Compile in libwrap (tcp_wrappers) support.

--with-low-memory   To avoid memory limitations, try to use less memory for compiling.

--with-mit-threads   Always use included thread library.

--with-mysqld-ldflags   Extra linking arguments for mysqld.

--with-mysqld-user=*username*   Indicate the user the mysqld daemon shall be run as.

--with-mysqlfs   Include the CORBA-based MySQL filesystem (Common Object Request Broker Architecture).

--with-named-curses-libs=*ARG*   Use specified curses libraries instead of those automatically found by configure.

--with-named-thread-libs=*ARG*   Use specified thread libraries instead of those automatically found by configure.

--with-named-z-libs=*ARG*   Use specified zlib libraries instead of those automatically found by configure.

--with-openssl   Include the OpenSSL support.

--with-openssl-includes=*DIR*   Find OpenSSL headers in *DIR*.

--with-openssl-libs=*DIR*   Find OpenSSL libraries in *DIR*.

--with-other-libc=*DIR*   Link against libc and other standard libraries installed in the specified nonstandard location overriding the default. Originally added to be able to link against glibc 2.2 without making the user upgrade the standard libc installation.

--with-PACKAGE=*ARG*   Use *PACKAGE* [*ARG*=yes].

--with-pic   Try to use only PIC/non-PIC objects; the default is to use both.

--with-pstack   Compile in libwrap (tcp_wrappers) support.

--with-pthread   Force use of pthread library.

--with-raid   Enable MySQL internal RAID support for systems that have large file support.

--with-server-suffix   Append value to the version string.

--with-tcp-port=*port-number*   Indicate which port to use for MySQL services (the default is 3306).

--with-unix-socket-path=*SOCKET*   Indicate where to put the Unix-domain socket. *SOCKET* must be an absolute filename.

--with-vio   Include the virtual IO support.

--without-bench   Skip building of the benchmark suite.

--without-debug   Build a production version without debugging code.

--without-docs   Skip building of the documentation.

--without-extra-tools   Skip building utilities in the tools directory.

--without-innodb   Do not include the InnoDB table handler.

--without-libedit   Use system libedit instead of bundled copy.

--without-*PACKAGE*   Do not use *PACKAGE* (same as --with-*PACKAGE*=no).

--without-query-cache   Do not build query cache.

--without-readline   Use system readline instead of bundled copy.

--without-server   Build only the client.

Appendix C

Getting Support

You've learned quite a bit over the course of this book, and we're sure you will have a few questions on the many options available throughout all the installations. Every installation is different because of its unique purpose, and your future with LAMP depends upon your being able to gain further knowledge outside the scope of this book.

There are many options available when you are looking for answers to questions or researching installation types. In this appendix, we'll cover various methods of finding information and keeping up-to-date with the latest software and patches.

Books on Open Source Technologies

The following selection of books is organized by technology.

Linux

Hunt, Craig. *Linux Network Servers*. **Alameda, Calif.: Sybex, 2002.**   This book is an excellent source of information for running and managing Linux network services on a server.

Hontañón, Ramón J. *Linux Security*. **Alameda, Calif.: Sybex, 2001.**   This book goes far in depth on many aspects of Linux security.

Jang, Michael. *Mastering Red Hat Linux 9*. **Alameda, Calif.: Sybex, 2003.**   This book is written by a Red Hat Certified Engineer (RHCE) and covers everything from installation to networking.

Smith, Roderick W. *Linux Power Tools*. **Alameda, Calif.: Sybex, 2003.**   This book shows step-by-step instructions on how to enhance and optimize your Linux system.

Stanfield, Vicki, and Roderick W. Smith. *Linux System Administration*. **Alameda, Calif.: Sybex, 2003.**   This book provides an excellent set of instructions on how to install and maintain your Linux system.

Apache

Aulds, Charles. *Linux Apache Web Server Administration*. **Alameda, Calif.: Sybex, 2002.** This book is a complete and advanced guide to the Apache web server. It teaches all of the standard and advanced techniques needed to administer Apache on a Linux server.

Coar, Ken, and Rich Bowen. *Apache Cookbook*. **Sebastopol, Calif., 2003.**   This book is a collection of problems, solutions, and practical examples for anyone who deals with Apache. Sticking to its name, it includes recipes for many aspects of your server.

MySQL

DuBois, Paul. *MySQL.* **2d ed. Indianapolis, Ind., 2003.**   This book is another excellent resource of MySQL information.

Gilfillan, Ian. *Mastering MySQL 4.* **Alameda, Calif.: Sybex, 2002.**   This book covers MySQL 4; however, it is still an excellent reference even for MySQL 5.

Reese, George, Randy Jay Yarger, and Tim King. *Managing and Using MySQL.* **2d ed. Sebastopol, Calif., 2002.**   This book covers installation and configuration as well as programming interfaces and administration.

Zawodny, Jeremy D., and Derek J. Balling. *High Performance MySQL: Optimization, Backups, Replication and Load Balancing.* **Sebastopol, Calif., 2004.**   As the title says, this book teaches you how to optimize, back up, replicate, and load-balance your MySQL server.

PHP

Atkinson, Leon, and Zeev Suraski. *Core PHP Programming.* **3d ed. Upper Saddle River, N.J., 2003.**   This book is written by one of the founders of the Zend engine and it covers PHP 5 in depth.

Lerdorf, Rasmus, and Kevin Tatroe. *Programming PHP.* **Sebastopol, Calif., 2002.**   This book is written by the founder of PHP, Rasmus Lerdorf. It covers a wide array of information about PHP, including history, installation, usage, and more.

Rosebrock, Eric. *Creating Interactive Websites with PHP and Web Services.* **Alameda, Calif.: Sybex, 2003.**   This book provides hands-on experience for practical uses of PHP. Included in this book is an introduction to PHP, MySQL, and web services.

Additional Software

There are also two pieces of additional software you might wish to install on your server depending upon the usage of the system:

FTP server   An FTP server handles the file uploading and downloading to your server from a remote computer such as your workstation. It is the Internet standard protocol used for handling such transactions. There are two servers that we recommend:

- Pure-FTPd (www.pureftpd.org)
- ProFTPD (www.proftpd.org)

These installations are relatively painless and both can be found in the tutorials section for servers on the `linuxforum.com` site. To install them, visit the site and look in the left column for the Servers link in the Tutorial submenu.

BIND   BIND is a DNS server (called *named*) which stands for Berkeley Internet Name Domain. DNS servers are used to translate domain names to IP addresses, which in turn tells the client computer where to find the web server, e-mail server, name servers, and so on.

If you are going to be using virtual hosts on your system, you might want to look into installing and configuring a name server. This can be a complicated process, however, so you might wish to pick up one of the books we referenced in the preceding section covering network servers. You can find information and the download to the latest version of BIND on the Internet Systems Consortium (ISC) site located at `www.isc.org`.

Local Resources

In addition to published books, you should also make use of your local resources. By this we mean the actual operating system you are working on. Get to know the man command and make frequent use of the `--help` flag for most command-line programs on your system. These can provide quick answers after you get used to reading their format. Remember, you can pipe the results of your `--help` flag to more or `less` for easier reading if they present you with hundreds of lines of options.

Although the manuals can often leave you looking for more answers, they are an excellent place to begin. If you are still confused or need more information, it is time to turn to one of your books or the Internet.

Internet Resources

Internet resources come in many flavors: websites, mailing lists, newsgroups, and Internet Relay Chat services (IRC). Each provides crucial information in its own way. Search engines will return a staggering number of resources, and you can spend days sifting through them. The following selections will get you started and might provide all you need.

Websites

We have taken the time to create support communities for Linux, Apache, MySQL, and PHP, which are available for free with no membership needed and no money to pay (the first site listed in each of the following categories). In addition to our sites, there are many other communities available through the Web that feature information pertaining to LAMP. Listed here are websites that we feel are making a significant impact in the open source community by offering quality content for free:

Linux

- www.linuxforum.com
- linux.tucows.com
- www.linuxsecurity.com
- www.learninglinux.com
- www.linuxtoday.com
- www.linuxhelp.net
- www.linuxquestions.org

Apache

- www.apachefreaks.com
- www.apache.org
- www.apache-ssl.org

MySQL

- www.mysqlfreaks.com
- www.mysql.com
- www.phpmyadmin.net
- www.sql.org
- www.mysqldeveloper.com

PHP

- www.phpfreaks.com
- www.php.net
- www.zend.com
- www.devshed.com
- www.hotscripts.com
- www.php-editors.com
- www.phpkitchen.com
- www.scriptz.com

Mailing Lists

Mailing lists are a great way to stay up-to-date on the latest patches, fixes, bugs, and updates. There are official and unofficial mailing lists for almost every technology that will enable you to automatically receive e-mails on the latest happenings. Many of these mailing lists also have their own newsgroups. Some of these mailing lists are moderated, and some are not. Many of the lists will provide you with too many e-mails to reasonably go through if you subscribed to them all. Here are a few links to the official mailing lists for the technologies used in this book:

- www.tux.org/lkml/
- www.apache.org/foundation/mailinglists.html
- lists.mysql.com
- www.php.net/mailing-lists.php

NOTE These are just the links to the official mailing lists, which will pertain to everyone reading this book. You can find additional mailing lists by performing a search on the Web or by visiting the links we provided in the "Websites" section.

Newsgroups

Newsgroups can be an excellent source of information. Finding good newsgroups can be tricky, so here's a helpful selection:

NOTE Some of these newsgroups might not be available to your news service provider. If you wish to find a high-power news service provider with high retention rates, check out www.giganews.com.

Linux

- alt.os.linux
- alt.comp.linux
- alt.linux.redhat
- comp.os.linux
- comp.os.linux.hardware

Apache

- alt.apache.configuration

MySQL

- `mailing.database.mysql`
- `mysql.users`

PHP

- `alt.comp.lang.php`
- `alt.php`
- `alt.php.sql`
- `php.qa`

To use newsgroups, you must have access to a news server. If you are a residential user, most ISPs will have one or more servers dedicated to this purpose and available to you as part of your service. If not, you will need to locate a paid service that will provide access to newsgroups.

To view newsgroups, you will also need to have a client installed to handle the communications and to format your data. It might be easier to install a client for X11 that will provide you with a more graphical layout and greater usability. Listed here are a few of the more popular news clients for Linux:

- Netscape
- Knews
- News Peruser
- GFetchnews

You could choose to install your own news server, although this can take an enormous amount of server process and bandwidth so it is not recommended. If you have access to both of these and would like to give it a shot, here are a few available news servers to take a look at:

- DNews
- InterNetNews (INN)
- Leafnode
- Ozway

Internet Relay Chat

Internet Relay Chat (IRC) is an excellent source for near-instant help for free. IRC enables you to connect to a server that provides you with chat rooms and the ability to send files through a Data Communications Channel (DCC). Each room might have one or more operators to keep messages organized and many times free from spam. Here are a few IRC channels for you to visit in your search for help:

Linux

- `#linux`
- `#redhat`
- `#linuxforum`

Apache

- `#apache`

MySQL

- `#mysql`

PHP

- `#phpfreaks`
- `#php`

An excellent IRC server that is dedicated to providing an interactive environment for coordination and support of peer-directed projects such as open source is `irc.freenode.net`. You can find more information on freenode by going to `www.freenode.net` as well. This server originally started in 1998 and had only about 200 users in 20 channels. Now there are over 13,000 channels with as many as 16,000 simultaneous users. Most likely someone there can help you find the answers you need. They might even be able to provide you with scripts and files to make administration life easier.

To connect to the freenode network, you will need to acquire an IRC client for your computer. This is required as `irc.freenode.net` is not a web server. You might wish to use a command client such as ircII, XChat, or BitchX if you will be accessing IRC from your Linux computer. Otherwise, you can choose any of the available clients you can find on the Web. There are plenty of free applications that will get the job done. Often, there are multiple clients based on an original program, such as ircII or mIRC (for Windows). You should refer to each program's documentation for more information on setting up and configuring your client. Just make sure you are connecting to one of the `irc.freenode.net` servers if you wish to access their channels.

Index

Note to the reader: Throughout this index **boldfaced** page numbers indicate primary discussions of a topic. *Italicized* page numbers indicate illustrations.

N

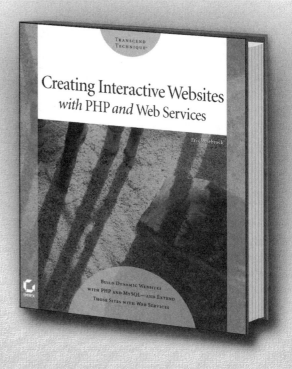